AWS®
Certified Data

Study Guide

Specialty (DBS-C01) Exam

Matheus Arrais

Rene Martinez Bravet

Leonardo Ciccone

Angie Nobre Cocharero

Érika Kurauchi

Hugo Rozestraten

SYBEX®
A Wiley Brand

I dedicate this book to my two funny and witty daughters and my lovely husband, who were always supportive throughout the journey.
—Angie Nobre

I dedicate this book to my family and friends who supported and inspired me in this fantastic journey.
—Érika Kurauchi

I dedicate this book to my wife and son, who support me in all adventures.
—Hugo Rozestraten

To my family: Erika, Antonio, Clelia, and Leandro, your love and support made this book a reality.
—Leonardo Ciccone

I dedicate this book to my wife, my daughter Helena, my parents, and my sister, who are the foundation of my life, for supporting me since I started to be curious about technology.
—Matheus Arrais

To my wife, my son, my daughters, and my parents. Specially to my dad who also wrote a database book but couldn't get it published.
—Rene Martinez

Acknowledgments

First, we would like to thank our wonderful families for supporting us and encouraging us to start this amazing journey. We needed to focus hours on writing and reviewing, and their understanding was key for the team to work together and to succeed on finishing this study guide.

Also, we would like to show our appreciation for Amazon Web Services (AWS) for providing cloud-computing platforms, APIs, and the Specialty (DBS-C01) exam to a worldwide audience.

We'd also like to thank acquisitions editor Ken Brown for entrusting us to create this study guide for Wiley. We also appreciate the assistance of John Sleeva, the project editor, and the entire team at Wiley for their guidance in creating this book.

A special thanks to Murilo Nascimento for the detailed reviews and guidance, who agreed to work with our team as the technical editor, after having been a product manager of the AWS Database Blog for years.

Our sincere thanks to Gus Santana, who wrote the *AWS Certified Security Study Guide* years ago, for bringing the team together and showing us by example that the challenge could be met.

Finally, thanks to our readers for trusting us to guide and prepare you for this incredible learning journey.

—The Authors

About the Authors

Matheus Arrais is a senior partner solutions architect at Amazon Web Services. Prior to his tenure with AWS, he worked for a consulting company as a cloud engineer and networking administrator, accumulating more than 14 years of experience. He started as an infrastructure, experienced networking, databases, and migrations processes. Matheus holds many AWS certifications and is a frequent speaker at summits, webinars, and re:Invent. He is focused on cloud operation services on AWS.

Rene Martinez Bravet is principal solutions architect at AWS, focused on enterprise and financial services customers. Before AWS, he worked as an Authorized Google Cloud Platform trainer and as a solutions architect at Ericsson. Rene has more than 15 years of experience in IT and has worked in different roles, including as a software architect, DevOps engineer, and database administrator.

Leonardo Ciccone is a senior database migration specialist at Amazon Web Services, with a focus on database migration and modernization. Leonardo started his career working with embedded hardware, networks, and Linux administration. In 2006, he switched his focus to databases and has never stopped since. He is a certified professional with eight AWS certifications, Google Cloud Architect, Oracle Database, and Oracle Exadata. Leonardo's technical interests include databases, data engineering, cloud, and security.

Angie Nobre Cocharero has been a database specialist solution architect at Amazon Web Services for Latin America since 2020. She has worked for more than 20 years in database implementations, supporting multiple customers in architecting database environments. She has experience with high availability and disaster recovery and has supported migrations and provided best practices for deploying databases.

Érika Kurauchi is the specialist solution architecture manager at Amazon Web Services Latin America, has 20 years of experience in the IT industry. Prior to her tenure at AWS, she worked for Itaú bank for almost 12 years. She has extensive experience in migrations and mergers of large institutions in the financial market and Itaú. She collaborated with Itaú's data-driven journey, leading the enterprise Data Governance Foundation, and became an SME in data management, quality, and protection. Érika holds a degree in data processing, an MBA in business management from FVG with an advanced certificate from UC Irvine international extension, certification in negotiation and leadership from Harvard Law School, and two AWS certifications.

Hugo Rozestraten is a principal data strategy solutions architect and author of several AWS blog posts. Hugo has worked for Google, IBM, Oracle, and ZUP as a data expert. Starting as a developer in 2001, Hugo quickly moved his career toward databases, becoming a certified DBA (Oracle 8i OCP) in 2003 and diving deep into databases ever since. Hugo has a set of content creation and is a frequent presenter in summits and webinars.

About the Technical Editor

Murilo Cerone Nascimento   has experience with a variety of relational and nonrelational databases. He has been working with databases for the past 13 years, most of the time as a consultant in private companies. Murilo holds a bachelor's degree in engineering with a specialization in computer engineering from Escola Politécnica de São Paulo. He currently works as a product manager at Amazon Web Services Brazil.

Contents at a Glance

Contents

Table of Exercises

Introduction

In 2022, 97 zettabytes of data were created, copied, captured, and consumed, and 181 zettabytes are projected by 2025. Databases play a crucial role in this data world. Over the last decade, database technologies matured: from tiime series to graph, from ledger to key-value, from relational to nonrelational. It's undeniable: the database field is flourishing. Understanding and applying the concepts covered in this book will improve your contributions and impact as a DBA, developer, architect, or analyst.

The purpose of this book is to help you pass the AWS Certified Database – Specialty exam. As of the writing of this book, the exam is composed of 65 questions, either multiple response or multiple choice, with a total length of 180 minutes.

Don't just study the questions and answers! The questions on the actual exam will be different from the practice questions included in this book. The exam is designed to test your knowledge of a concept or objective, so use this book to learn the objectives behind the questions.

Non-native English speakers can request a 30-minute exam extension when taking the exam in English. For more information, check https://aws.amazon.com/certification/policies/before-testing.

When reading exam questions, try to outline the key requirements, and work backwards from the responses. This will help you eliminate wrong responses from the start, saving time.

What Does This Book Cover?

This book covers the topics outlined in the AWS Certified Database – Specialty (DBS-C01) exam guide available here:

```
https://d1.awsstatic.com/training-and-certification/docs-database-
specialty/AWS-Certified-Database-Specialty_Exam-Guide.pdf
```

Chapters follow a logical evolution of the workload-specific types of databases and their use cases, and they cover monitoring, troubleshooting and security features.

Chapter 1: Databases—From Your Server to AWS Cloud This chapter presents an evolution of databases and the differences of managing databases on premises and in the

AWS cloud. It presents important concepts and features of a self-managed database in AWS, configuring a database using Amazon EC2, and understanding the limitations. It also introduces database options in AWS.

Chapter 2: Basic AWS Concepts   This chapter introduces the basics of AWS infrastructure, networking, security, storage, and operations, which are important to understand when designing database solutions in AWS. If you are very experienced with AWS components, you may want to skip this chapter; otherwise, take your time to learn more about AWS regions, availability zones, edge locations, VPC, VPN, direct connect, network connectivity, network security, security model, identity and access management, data encryption, block storage, file storage, object storage, monitoring, logging, and auditing.

Chapter 3: Purpose-Built Databases   This chapter discusses workload-specific database design. It introduces how to evaluate application requirements and datastore characteristics, taking into consideration several important aspects: data access patterns, latency, scaling, transaction support, consistency, volume, durability, availability, security and compliance, business logic, and cost. It concludes by presenting a comprehensive way to compare the requirements with AWS managed services for databases.

Chapter 4: Relational Databases on AWS   This chapter presents transactional databases in AWS with a focus on relational databases, which are mostly used to support transactional environments using concepts of ACID transactions. It presents options for managing and installing relational databases on Amazon EC2, storage requirements and options on AWS, and monitoring, updating, and scale options for this type of installation. A large part of this chapter is dedicated to Amazon RDS, including the engine options and a deep dive into Amazon Aurora, covering all the topics related to RDS: deployment, migration options, management, operations, monitoring, troubleshooting, and database security.

Chapter 5: Low-Latency Response Time for Your Apps and APIs   This chapter introduces the concepts of low-latency and NoSQL databases, presenting two low-latency database services on AWS: Amazon DynamoDB and Amazon Keyspaces (for Apache Cassandra). It details Amazon DynamoDB table design tenets as well as partition and sort key definitions, indexing options, queries, scans, transactions, caching, and global options. For Amazon Keyspaces (for Apache Cassandra) it presents partitions, clustering keys, and static columns concepts. It also covers all the topics related to DynamoDB and Keyspaces: capacity, deployment, scalability, migration options, management, operations, monitoring, troubleshooting, and database security.

Chapter 6: Document Databases in the Cloud   This chapter discusses document database concepts and options in AWS. It presents Amazon DocumentDB (with MongoDB compatibility) with its resilient storage layer and the key architecture components such as cluster, instance, and reader endpoints. The chapter covers details of the topics related to Amazon DocumentDB: capacity, deployment, scalability, migration options, management, operations, monitoring, troubleshooting, and database security.

Chapter 7: Better Places Than Databases to Store Large Objects   This chapter presents the concept of large objects and how they were handled before AWS and how they are handled with the availability of AWS options. It introduces Amazon S3, compares it to other AWS storage options, and goes into the details of S3 storage classes, data load and retrieval, life-cycle management, operations, monitoring, access control, and security.

Chapter 8: Deliver Valuable Information at the Speed Your Business Needs   This chapter describes how to store and use analytics and time series and operational data, with purpose-built databases in AWS to extract value for business. It introduces the information latency concept, presents Amazon Redshift and Amazon Timestream in detail, and also mentions Amazon OpenSearch, a topic that is not covered on the exam. For Amazon Redshift, the chapter goes into the details of table design, loading data, cluster architecture, and cluster options. For Amazon Timestream, it also covers the architecture and loading data options. For Amazon Redshift and Amazon Timestream, it goes into detail on deployment, scalability, migration options, management, operations, monitoring, troubleshooting, and database security.

Chapter 9: Discovering Relationships Using Graph Databases   This chapter discusses the concepts of graph databases and their usage to handle relationships between data items. It presents the basic concepts of graph databases and then goes deep into Amazon Neptune data loading and query options, cluster architecture, scalability, migration options, management, operations, monitoring, troubleshooting, and database security.

Chapter 10: Immutable Database and Traceable Transactions   This chapter introduces the concept of immutable databases and the AWS service Amazon Quantum Ledger Database (QLDB). It goes into the details of Amazon QLDB and how it ensures no data can be modified or deleted after it is inserted, using an immutable transaction log. It discusses the Amazon QLDB components: ledger, table, document, journal, query engine, and cryptographic verification. It also presents how to load data to and query data from Amazon QLDB, as well as service scalability, management, operations, monitoring, troubleshooting, and database security.

Chapter 11: Caching Data with In-Memory Databases   This chapter presents caching strategies and how AWS services can help to implement them. It introduces Amazon ElastiCache service for Redis and Memcached and also Amazon MemoryDB, discussing their features and how they can handle caching requirements and strategies. It also discusses in detail how to distribute data in each engine and how to address deployment, scalability, migration options, management, operations, monitoring, troubleshooting, and database security.

Chapter 12: Migrating Your Data to AWS   This chapter presents the options to migrate data to AWS database services. It discusses network communication and specialized database migration services like AWS SCT and AWS DMS, which are native database tools that help in data migration for each engine, including AWS DataSync, AWS Snow Family, and AWS Storage Gateway. It also details database migration strategy and downtime minimization along with security and resilience options and requirements.

Chapter 13: Disaster Recovery   This chapter discusses disaster recovery requirements and strategies for database applications in AWS. It presents the concepts of RTO and RPO and how they are affected by the deployment and replication strategies. It also explores how AWS managed services for databases handle data resilience and replication using Multi-AZ and global database options.

Chapter 14: Save Time and Reduce Errors Automating Your Infrastructure   This chapter introduces the concept of infrastructure as code (IaC) and how this relates to database deployment and management. It presents AWS CloudFormation and goes into the details of how to simplify infrastructure management using templates, stacks, and change sets. It also discusses best practices related to database security and access management, using AWS System Manager Parameter and AWS Secrets Manager.

Interactive Online Learning Environment and Test Bank

Studying the material in the *AWS® Certified Database Study Guide: Specialty (DBS-C01) Exam* is an important part of preparing for the AWS Certified Database Specialty (DBS-C01) certification exam, but we provide additional tools to help you prepare. The online test bank helps you understand the types of questions that appear on the certification exam. The online test bank runs on multiple devices.

- **Sample tests:** The sample tests in the test bank include all the questions at the end of each chapter as well as the questions from the assessment test. In addition, there are two practice exams with 50 questions each. You can use these tests to evaluate your understanding and identify areas that may require additional study.

- **Flashcards:** The flashcards in the test bank will push the limits of what you should know for the certification exam. There are 100 questions that are provided in digital format. Each flashcard has one question and one correct answer.

- **Glossary:** The online glossary is a searchable list of key terms introduced in this exam guide that you should know for the AWS Certified Database Specialty (DBS-C01) certification exam.

Visit www.wiley.com/go/sybextestprep to register and gain access to this interactive online learning environment and test bank with study tools. To start using these tools to study for the AWS Certified Database Specialty (DBS-C01) exam, go to www.wiley.com/go/sybextestprep, register your book to receive your unique PIN, and once you have the

PIN, return to www.wiley.com/go/sybextestprep, find your book, and click register or log in and follow the link to register a new account or add this book to an existing account.

 Like all exams, the Certified Database – Specialty certification from AWS is updated periodically and may eventually be retired or replaced. At some point after AWS is no longer offering this exam, the old editions of our books and online tools will be retired. If you have purchased this book after the exam was retired, or are attempting to register in the Sybex online learning environment after the exam was retired, please know that we make no guarantees that this exam's online Sybex tools will be available once the exam is no longer available.

AWS Certified Database Study Guide – Specialty (DBS-C01) Exam Objectives

This study guide has been written to cover every AWS Certified Database – Specialty (DBS-C01) exam objective at a level appropriate to its exam weighting. The domains, subdomains, and objectives are taken from the AWS guide that's available here:

> https://d1.awsstatic.com/training-and-certification/docs-database-specialty/AWS-Certified-Database-Specialty_Exam-Guide.pdf

The following table provides a breakdown of this book's exam coverage, showing you the weighting of each section and the chapter where each objective or subobjective is covered:

Subject Area	% of Examination
Domain 1: Workload-Specific Database Design	26%
Domain 2: Deployment and Migration	20%
Domain 3: Management and Operations	18%
Domain 4: Monitoring and Troubleshooting	18%
Domain 5: Database Security	18%
Total	100%

Objective Map

Objective	Chapter
Domain 1: Workload-Specific Database Design	
1.1: Select appropriate database services for specific types of data and workloads.	
Differentiate between ACID and BASE workloads	3, 4, 5, 6, and 10
Explain appropriate uses of types of databases (e.g., relational, key-value, document, in-memory, graph, time series, ledger)	3
Identify use cases for persisted data vs. ephemeral data	3 and 14
1.2: Determine strategies for disaster recovery and high availability.	
Select Region and Availability Zone placement to optimize database performance	2
Determine implications of Regions and Availability Zones on disaster recovery/high availability strategies	2 and 13
Differentiate use cases for read replicas and Multi-AZ deployments	4 and 6
1.3: Design database solutions for performance, compliance, and scalability.	
Recommend serverless vs. instance-based database architecture	2, 4, 5, and 10
Evaluate requirements for scaling read replicas	4 and 6
Define database caching solutions	14
Evaluate the implications of partitioning, sharding, and indexing	4, 5, 6, 8, and 14

Objective	Chapter
Determine appropriate instance types and storage options	4, 6, and 8
Determine auto-scaling capabilities for relational and NoSQL databases	5
Determine the implications of Amazon DynamoDB adaptive capacity	5
Determine data locality based on compliance requirements	2 and 13
1.4: Compare the costs of database solutions.	
Determine cost implications of Amazon DynamoDB capacity units, including on-demand vs. provisioned capacity	5
Determine costs associated with instance types and automatic scaling	4, 6, 8, 9, 13, and 14
Design for costs including high availability, backups, multiregion, Multi-AZ, and storage type options	4, 5, 6, 7, 8, 9, 13, and 14
Compare data access costs	4, 5, 6, 7, 8, and 14
Domain 2: Deployment and Migration	
2.1: Automate database solution deployments.	
Evaluate application requirements to determine components to deploy	3
Choose appropriate deployment tools and services (e.g., AWS CloudFormation, AWS CLI)	4, 5, 6, 7, 8, 9, 10, 11, and 14
2.2: Determine data preparation and migration strategies.	
Determine the data migration method (e.g., snapshots, replication, restore)	12
Evaluate database migration tools and services (e.g., AWS DMS, native database tools)	12
Prepare data sources and targets	12
Determine schema conversion methods (e.g., AWS Schema Conversion Tool)	12
Determine heterogeneous vs. homogeneous migration strategies	12
2.3: Execute and validate data migration.	

Objective	Chapter
Design and script data migration	12
Run data extraction and migration scripts	12
Verify the successful load of data	12
Domain 3: Management and Operations	
3.1: Determine maintenance tasks and processes.	
Account for the AWS shared responsibility model for database services	2
Determine appropriate maintenance window strategies	4 and 13
Differentiate between major and minor engine upgrades	4
3.2: Determine backup and restore strategies.	
Identify the need for automatic and manual backups/ snapshots	4, 5, 6, 7, 8, 9, 10, 13, and 14
Differentiate backup and restore strategies (e.g., full backup, point-in-time, encrypting backups cross-region)	4, 5, 6, 7, 8, 9, 10, 13, and 14
Define retention policies	4, 5, 6, 7, 8, 9, 10, 11, 13, and 14
Correlate the backup and restore to recovery point objective (RPO) and recovery time objective (RTO) requirements	4, 5, 6, 7, 8, 9, 10, 13, and 14
3.3: Manage the operational environment of a database solution.	
Orchestrate the refresh of lower environments	4
Implement configuration changes (e.g., in Amazon RDS option/parameter groups or Amazon DynamoDB indexing changes)	4, 5, 6, 8, 9, and 14
Automate operational tasks	4, 5, 6, 8, and 11
Take action based on AWS Trusted Advisor reports (topic addressed on monitoring, cost, performance, resilience, and security configurations of each chapter)	4, 5, 6, 8, 10, 11, 13, and 14
Domain 4: Monitoring and Troubleshooting	
4.1: Determine monitoring and alerting strategies.	

Objective	Chapter
Evaluate monitoring tools (e.g., Amazon CloudWatch, Amazon RDS Performance Insights, database native)	4, 5, 6, 8, 9, 10, and 14
Determine appropriate parameters and thresholds for alert conditions	4, 5, 6, 8, 9, 10, and 14
Use tools to notify users when thresholds are breached (e.g., Amazon SNS, Amazon SQS, Amazon CloudWatch dashboards)	2, 4, 6, 8, and 14
4.2: Troubleshoot and resolve common database issues.	
Identify, evaluate, and respond to categories of failures (e.g., troubleshoot connectivity; instance, storage, and partitioning issues)	4, 5, 6, 8, 10, 11, and 14
Automate responses when possible	2, 4, 6, 8, and 14
4.3: Optimize database performance.	
Troubleshoot database performance issues	4, 5, 6, 8, 9, 10, and 14
Identify appropriate AWS tools and services for database optimization	4, 5, 6, 8, 9, 10, and 14
Evaluate the configuration, schema design, queries, and infrastructure to improve performance	4, 5, 6, 8, 9, 10, and 14
Domain 5: Database Security	
5.1: Encrypt data at rest and in transit.	
Encrypt data in relational and NoSQL databases	4, 5, 6, 7, 8, 9, 10, and 14
Apply SSL/TLS connectivity to databases	4, 5, 6, 7, 8, 9, 10, and 12
Implement key management (e.g., AWS KMS, AWS CloudHSM)	4, 5, 6, 7, 8, 9, 10, 11, 12, and 14
5.2: Evaluate auditing solutions.	
Determine auditing strategies for structural/schema changes (e.g., DDL)	4, 6, 8, and 10
Determine auditing strategies for data changes (e.g., DML)	4, 6, 8, and 10
Determine auditing strategies for data access (e.g., queries)	4, 6, 8, and 10
Determine auditing strategies for infrastructure changes (e.g., AWS CloudTrail)	2, 5, 6, 8, 10, and 11

Objective	Chapter
Enable the export of database logs to Amazon CloudWatch Logs	2, 4, 6, 8, and 10
5.3: Determine access control and authentication mechanisms.	
Recommend authentication controls for users and roles (e.g., IAM, native credentials, Active Directory)	2, 4, 5, 6, 7, 8, 10, and 14
Recommend authorization controls for users (e.g., policies)	2, 4, 5, 6, 7, 8, and 10
5.4: Recognize potential security vulnerabilities within database solutions.	
Determine security group rules and NACLs for database access	2, 4, 6, 8, 9, and 14
Identify relevant VPC configurations (e.g., VPC endpoints, public vs. private subnets, demilitarized zone)	2, 4, 5, 6, 8, 9, and 14
Determine appropriate storage methods for sensitive data	2, 5, 7, and 11

How to Contact the Publisher

If you believe you've found a mistake in this book, please bring it to our attention. At John Wiley & Sons, we understand how important it is to provide our customers with accurate content, but even with our best efforts an error may occur.

To submit your possible errata, please email it to our Customer Service Team at wileysupport@wiley.com with the subject line "Possible Book Errata Submission."

Assessment Test

1. Understanding an application's data access patterns is important to define the best database for each workload.

    A. True

    B. False

2. Nonrelational databases don't offer transactions with ACID compliance.

    A. True

    B. False

3. AWS offers a fully managed graph database.

    A. True

    B. False

4. You are the database specialist for a financial company, and the database is hosted on Amazon RDS for PostgreSQL. You receive complaints from the app team that at some specific moments, the application is unable to respond to any requests. They have asked for your support to investigate what is going on. What action can you take to support this tuning process with minimal effort and minimal cost? (Choose two.)

    A. Enable database encryption.

    B. Enable Performance Insights for seven days.

    C. Enable Performance Insights for two years.

    D. Enable enhanced monitoring, setting an appropriate granularity.

5. You are in charge of developing an application for an online store, with RDS for PostgreSQL database for data persistence. For security reasons, the application development team does not want to use a password to connect to the database. Which authentication method available in RDS PostgreSQL will best meet the described requirement?

    A. Require that passwords are needed to authenticate logins to all relational databases.

    B. IAM database authentication.

    C. Kerberos authentication.

    D. Store the password in an S3 file with encryption enabled and write the app code to check the file for the information that's required to connect to the database.

6. You work for a utility company and have been informed that to meet regulatory requirements, backups generated at the end of each month must be kept secure for one year. The database must be able to be restored on the same engine that originated this backup. How can you best meet this requirement with minimal effort?

    A. Modify the RDS database's automated backup to retain backups for one year.

    B. Use manual snapshots so you can handle the retention period differently than the automated backup.

    C. Export the database snapshot to Amazon S3.

    D. Use `mysqldump` for RDS for MySQL and `pg_dump` for RDS for PostgreSQL, and store the dump in Amazon S3.

7. Which of the following AWS database services implements a NoSQL database engine?

   A. Amazon DynamoDB

   B. Amazon Aurora

   C. Amazon Quantum Ledger Database (QLDB)

   D. Amazon Keyspaces

8. You can design a DynamoDB table with a multi-attribute partition key.

   A. True

   B. False

9. How can you handle Amazon DynamoDB scalability?

   A. You can leverage the Application Auto Scaling service to automatically adjust the provisioned capacity units.

   B. You need to configure the minimum and maximum DynamoDB data processing units (DPUs) so the service will automatically scale accordingly.

   C. You can enable the DynamoDB on-demand capacity mode so the service will automatically scale to support the demands of your application.

   D. You can scale up and down the DynamoDB instance compute capacity, and you can also scale out by adding read replicas.

10. What are the access options available in DynamoDB?

    A. You can connect to DynamoDB via TCP with the JDBC driver for DynamoDB.

    B. You can access Amazon DynamoDB using the AWS Management Console, the AWS Command Line Interface (AWS CLI), or the DynamoDB API.

    C. You can download and use the NoSQL Workbench for data plane and data visualization operations.

    D. DynamoDB is accessible only via Amazon Virtual Private Cloud by using the DynamoDB API.

11. A company is looking for a centralized blockchain solution for a digital car passport application. What AWS service can fulfill the customer requirement?

    A. LedgerDB running on Amazon EC2

    B. Amazon Managed Blockchain with Ethereum

    C. Amazon Managed Blockchain with Hyperledger Fabric

    D. Amazon Quantum Ledger Database (QLDB)

12. How can you handle Amazon QLDB scalability?

    A. You can leverage the Application Auto Scaling service.

    B. You need to configure the QLDB read and write capacity units so the service will automatically scale accordingly.

    C. QLDB automatically scales to support the demands of your application.

    D. You can scale up and down the Amazon QLDB instance compute capacity, and you can also scale out by adding read replicas.

13. In AWS you can use multiple managed database services, but when you have large objects like videos, pictures, and binary files to store, you should consider using Amazon S3 to store them and use a database only to index the files with their metadata.

   A. True

   B. False

14. For storage options for large objects in AWS, verify which of the following statements is correct:

   A. Amazon S3 and Amazon EBS have the same cost per gigabyte, so it makes no difference which one you use to store large objects.

   B. Amazon S3 and Amazon EBS have APIs to put and retrieve objects directly.

15. To protect the data for security reasons, you should always consider encryption for database services, in transit and at rest. This also applies to storage services like Amazon S3.

   A. True

   B. False

16. Amazon Redshift is a managed database service that can handle analytics queries of any complexity for historical data analysis, with an information latency from minutes to hours.

   A. True

   B. False

17. When considering a time-series dataset from sensor measurements and storing the data and making comparisons between different periods of time, you should use Amazon DocumentDB, which has time-series built-in functions using real-time and historical data.

   A. True

   B. False

18. When considering databases with analytics capabilities in AWS, evaluate which of the following options is true.

   A. Amazon Redshift offers a full data warehouse, plus a flexible way to join internal data with data lake data.

   B. Amazon Timestream doesn't provide a fast, near real-time ingestion and analysis of time-series data.

19. You are the solution architect responsible for the deployment of a fraud detection solution on Amazon Neptune. You have been informed that all audit information, including information such as the timestamp, IP address, and payload, must be available to enterprise security auditors. How can you best meet this requirement with minimal effort?

   A. Modify the Amazon Neptune cluster to export the audit log, so the logs will be published on Amazon CloudWatch Logs.

   B. Write a Lambda function that will store the required information in Amazon S3 in CSV files, so the auditors will be able to query the information using Amazon Athena.

   C. Use Amazon CloudWatch to monitor database activity.

   D. Use AWS CloudTrail to track database activity.

20. Which graph model represents graph elements by vertices and edges?

    A. Resource Description Framework (RDF)

    B. Relational database model

    C. Property graph

    D. openCypher

21. Which statement uses the Gremlin language to perform a lookup for John's friends?

    A.

```
select name from friendship_table

where friend_of = 'john';
```

    B.

```
select ?names where {
?howard :name "john" .
?howard :friend/:friend/:name ?names .
}
```

    C.

```
MATCH (user:User {name: 'john'})- [r1:FRIEND]- ()- [r2:FRIEND]
- (friend_of_a_friend)
RETURN friend_of_a_friend.name AS fofName
```

    D.

```
g.V().has('name', john).out('friend').out('friend').values('name')
```

22. You are the solution architect responsible for recommending an engine solution deployment. The team is concerned about storage scalability. Which statement is true? (Choose two.)

    A. Amazon Neptune Storage grows automatically up to 128 TiB.

    B. Issuing drop commands like `g.V().drop()` will reduce the allocated storage.

    C. Amazon Neptune Storage grows automatically up to 64 TiB.

    D. Neptune automatically extends the cluster volume by adding new segments of 10 GB.

23. For large database migration from on-premises databases to AWS, check which of the following options is true:

    A. Use an AWS Site-to-Site VPN, as it supports up to 100 Gbps.

    B. Use an AWS Direct Connect connection that can support up to 100 Gbps.

24. AWS DMS and AWS SCT can't be used together for a database migration where the source and target databases are from different database engines.

    A. True

    B. False

25. AWS provides tools to minimize downtime when migrating from on-premises MySQL databases to Amazon RDS for MySQL, using AWS DMS for existing data migration and ongoing replication.

A. True

B. False

26. You are the database specialist at ABC Bank and are tasked with architecting a cross-region database replication with the following requirements:

- High throughput rates

- Low replica lag

- Fast recovery

- Replicate the database to three remote regions

Which database deployment will be most appropriate?

A. Deploy an Amazon Aurora cluster with three replicas.

B. Deploy an RDS for PostgreSQL with Multi-AZ enabled.

C. Deploy an RDS for PostgreSQL with cross-region read replica in a remote region.

D. Deploy an Aurora global database, with the primary cluster in the main region and three secondary clusters in three remote regions.

27. Your company has deployed the database on RDS for Oracle and requires replicating the database to a second region for disaster recovery. It must be available for read operations, and some replication lag is acceptable. Which replication alternative will allow the replication with the least effort?

A. Launch an Aurora global database in a second region and replicate using AWS DMS.

B. Deploy a cross-region read replica of RDS for Oracle in a second region.

C. Launch a new RDS for Oracle in a second region and replicate using AWS DMS.

D. Enable backup replication for a second region.

28. You are the solution architect responsible for developing an application that will be available in two AWS regions. The tables must be available for reading and writing in the primary region and available for reading in the second region. The database must allow graph model deployment and can be promoted in the second region for both planned and unplanned failover. Which solution will best meet these requirements?

A. Amazon Aurora global database with write forwarding

B. Amazon DynamoDB

C. Amazon Neptune global database

D. Amazon RDS PostgreSQL with cross-region read replica

29. If you need to provide an extremely low-latency response time query, caching data in AWS, you will have to install and manage software for cache, like Redis and Memcached, as AWS doesn't have managed services for this purpose.

   A. True

   B. False

30. The Memcached option for Amazon ElastiCache distributes the data across cluster nodes to scale your environment, so you can control how data is distributed using a hash algorithm.

   A. True

   B. False

31. Amazon ElastiCache for Redis can be set in cluster mode disabled only, which limits it to one node group (a single shard) per cluster.

   A. True

   B. False

Answers to Assessment Test

1. **A.** Knowing which types of queries will be performed on the database is crucial to find the right tool for the job, such as if the application needs simple key-value queries or aggregation and multiple joins. For more information, please see Chapter 3.

2. **B.** Nonrelational databases have evolved through the past decade, and some engines offer ACID-compatible transactions. For more information, please see Chapter 3 and Chapter 5.

3. **A.** Amazon Neptune is a fully managed graph database that supports graph queries using SPARQL, Apache Gremlin, and openCypher. For more information, see Chapter 3 and Chapter 9.

4. **B, D.** Enabling Performance Insights will allow you to see the database load and top queries you want to start investigating; you can enable this feature for seven days at no additional cost. By enabling enhanced monitoring, you can define the granularity to be collected for easier analysis. Encryption will enable protection, but it will not be useful for tuning. You cannot modify the database to enable it; you can enable encryption only at creation time. Enabling Performance Insights for two years will incur an additional cost. For more information, see Chapter 4.

5. **B.** By using IAM database authentication, the user will connect using an authentication token; it won't require a password. The password authentication method is wrong, as it is not the only one available in the RDS for PostgreSQL. Depending on the method chosen to connect to the database, it is subject to exposing the password. The Kerberos authentication method is wrong, because it is more appropriate when you need to integrate with Active Directory. Storing the password in an S3 file is wrong, as RDS for PostgreSQL already has a more secure native alternative. Please see Chapter 4.

6. **B.** Manual snapshot backups never expire, and they are recommended for long-term backups. The RDS database automated backup allows retention for 1 to 35 days but will not meet the one-year retention requirement. Exporting a database snapshot to Amazon S3 is available for RDS for MySQL and RDS for PostgreSQL and will store the data in Apache Parquet format. You will be able to read the data using Amazon Athena or Redshift, but you will not be able to natively restore to the same database engine. RDS for MySQL supports the `mysqldump` utility, and RDS for PostgreSQL supports the `pg_dump` utility. While it is possible, it will take a lot more effort to set up and automate the process. Please see Chapter 4.

7. **A, C, D.** Amazon DynamoDB is a fully managed, serverless, key-value NoSQL database designed to run high-performance applications at any scale. Amazon QLDB is a fully managed NoSQL ledger database that provides a transparent, immutable, and cryptographically verifiable transaction log. Amazon Keyspaces (for Apache Cassandra) is a scalable, highly available, and managed NoSQL wide-column database. Amazon Aurora is a relational database management system (RDBMS) built for the cloud with full MySQL and PostgreSQL compatibility. For more information, please see Chapter 5.

8. B. DynamoDB supports two kinds of primary keys:

1. Partition key is a simple primary key, composed of one attribute known as the partition key.

2. A partition key and sort key, also known as a composite primary key, is a type of key that is composed of two attributes. The first attribute is the partition key, and the second attribute is the sort key.

9. A, C. DynamoDB has two capacity modes: on-demand and provisioned. When you choose on-demand mode, DynamoDB instantly accommodates your workloads traffic. With provisioned mode, you specify the number of reads and writes per second that you require for your application and use auto scaling to adjust your table's provisioned capacity automatically in response to traffic changes. Data processing units are used in AWS Glue. DynamoDB is serverless; you don't need to configure compute capacity or read replicas.

10. B, C. You can access Amazon DynamoDB using the AWS Management Console, the AWS Command Line Interface (AWS CLI), or the DynamoDB API. You can also use the NoSQL Workbench for Amazon DynamoDB. The NoSQL Workbench is a multiplatform GUI application that you can use for modern database development and operations. There is no JDBC driver for DynamoDB, and the access via VPC is optional; the DynamoDB API is publicly accessible by default.

11. D. Hyperledger Fabric and Ethereum are centralized blockchains. Amazon (QLDB) is a fully managed ledger database that provides a transparent, immutable, and cryptographically verifiable transaction log.

12. C. Application Auto Scaling doesn't support Amazon QLDB. With Amazon QLDB, you don't have to worry about provisioning capacity or configuring read and write limits. Amazon QLDB is serverless; you don't need to configure compute capacity or read replicas.

13. A. Amazon S3 is a fully managed object store service that is easy to integrate with the command line and SDK. It also has life-cycle policies and encryption features that make it easy and secure to use. For more information, please see Chapter 7.

14. A = False; B = False. Amazon S3 costs from 5 to 20 times less than Amazon EBS, depending on the S3 storage class in use. Also, only Amazon S3 has API commands through the command line and the SDK to put and retrieve objects, while Amazon EBS needs to be mounted as a filesystem in an operating system to receive and serve files. For more information, please see Chapter 7.

15. A. When you need to protect sensitive data, you should consider encryption in transit, usually provided with TLS encryption for most AWS database services, and encryption at rest, which can be easy to set up using AWS KMS. Both are supported by Amazon S3. For more information, please see Chapter 7.

16. A. Amazon Redshift is a managed data warehouse system that uses columnar format and is optimized to handle a large amount of data and aggregated queries. Redshift is not optimized for near real time, as you should load the data in groups of records instead of performing single records inserts, loading batches or records every 5 to 60 minutes, for example. It can handle complex queries and deliver their results in milliseconds using a massive parallel processing architecture. For more information, please see Chapter 8.

17. B. Amazon DocumentDB is a fully managed JSON document database, and although it can store time-series data, it is not optimized for this use case and queries. Amazon Timestream is a managed database service specialized in handling time-series datasets. It has built-in times series functionality using views and functions that make it easier and faster to handle complex queries for measurements or metrics data over time, compared to relational databases. It can handle near real-time data, as it supports optimized inserts operation. For more information, please see Chapter 8.

18. A = True; B = False. Amazon Redshift is a managed data warehouse system and can use Redshift Spectrum to work with external tables in a data lake on Amazon S3, joining them with Redshift internal tables and extending its functionality. Amazon Timestream provides a fast, near real-time ingestion and analysis of time-series data as a fully managed service with built-in functions and views specialized in time-series analysis. For more information, please see Chapter 8.

19. A. You can enable the audit logs, which have the necessary information, and export them to Amazon CloudWatch Logs. Writing code will take a lot more effort to implement. Amazon CloudWatch demonstrates performance information such as CPU utilization and average number of I/O writes, but not audit logs. AWS CloudTrail exclusively logs events for the Neptune Management API, such as creating an instance or a cluster. Please see Chapter 9.

20. C. The property graph model represents elements by vertices and edges. The Resource Description Framework (RDF) encodes the resource descriptions in subject-predicate-object triples format. The relational database model represents tables with columns and rows. openCypher is a property-graph query language, not a graph model. Please see Chapter 9.

21. D. Option D is the correct option because it represents the use of the Gremlin language. Option A is wrong because it is using the SQL language. Option B is wrong because it is using SPARQL. Option C is wrong because it is using openCypher. See Chapter 9.

22. A, D. Option A is correct because Amazon Neptune Storage grows up to 128 TiB. Option D is correct because the storage extends in 10 GB blocks. Option B is wrong because when data is removed using the drop command, the overall allocated space remains the same. Unused allocated space is then reused automatically when the amount of data increases in the future. Option C is wrong because Amazon Neptune Storage grows up to 128 TiB, which has been true since February 2022. Please see Chapter 9.

23. A = False; B = True. AWS Site-to-Site has a limit of 1.25 Gbps per channel, so it doesn't support 100 Gbps connection throughput, while an AWS Direct Connect connection can be established from 50 Mbps to 100 Gbps, which provides a faster way to migrate large databases to AWS. You should also consider AWS Snow Family devices for very large database migrations. For more information, please see Chapter 12.

24. B. AWS SCT facilitates heterogenous database migration, where the source and target databases are from different database engines, converting the schemas from source to target engine AWS DMS migrates the data from source database tables to target database tables and can be used with AWS SCT. For more information, please see Chapter 12.

25. A. AWS DMS has a migrate existing data and ongoing replication option that migrates existing data for tables, captures and applies changes that occur during and after the existing data migration time, and synchronizes data from source to target until the time you decide to complete the migration. MySQL and Amazon RDS for MySQL are supported as the target and source for AWS DMS. For more information, please see Chapter 12.

26. D. The Aurora global database is capable of meeting all the described requirements. It supports up to 200,000 writes/sec, the replica lag is less than one second, it allows you to recover in less than one minute of downtime after a region's unavailability, and it allows up to five remote regions. Options A and B are wrong, because they don't replicate to a remote region; it is highly available in only one region. Option C is wrong because the cross-region read replicas are subject to replication lag. Please see Chapter 13.

27. B. RDS allows you to create read replicas in a different AWS region for Amazon RDS MariaDB, MySQL, Oracle, and PostgreSQL. Using a cross-region read replica, the database is available for read operations, and you can promote the replicated instance to primary in a failure situation. Option A is wrong, because it will take significant effort to set up. Option C is wrong because it will also require significant effort to set up. Option D is wrong because the backup replication will not keep the database available for read operations. Please see Chapter 13.

28. C. Option C is correct because Amazon Neptune is a graph database and allows cross-region replication via an Amazon Neptune global database. You can perform managed planned failover for planned operational activities or promote the secondary region to recover from an unplanned outage in the primary region. Option A is wrong because Amazon Aurora is a relational database, which is not suitable for a graph model. Option B is wrong because Amazon DynamoDB is suitable for a key value, but not a graph model. Option D is wrong because Amazon RDS PostgreSQL is a relational database and not suitable for a graph model. Please see Chapter 13.

29. B. Amazon ElastiCache is an AWS managed service for caching data, compatible with Redis and Memcached. It can deliver submillisecond-range response time, is easy for API integration, can distribute data within nodes, and has many other features specific to each version. For more information, please see Chapter 11.

30. A. Amazon ElastiCache for a Memcached cluster can scale from 1 to 40 nodes to distribute and serve the data, which you control with a data partition strategy. You can use *autodiscovery* to automatically tell your client application when you add and remove nodes from the cluster. For more information, please see Chapter 11.

31. B. Amazon ElastiCache for Redis can be set in cluster mode *disabled* or cluster mode *enabled*, which allows the cluster to have up to 500 node groups (one per shard), providing large horizontal scalability and online resharding. For more information, please see Chapter 11.

Workload-Specific Database Design

Chapter

1

Databases—from Your Server to AWS Cloud

The year 1960 was a year full of great historic events. NASA launched the Pioneer 5 space probe to gather information about the deep space between Earth and Venus, making it the first space probe to venture 20 million miles away from Earth. Charles W. Backman introduced the design of the first database system, starting a trajectory that probably brought you here to read this book decades later.

This chapter won't cover any particular domain of the AWS Certified Database – Specialty exam, but it will help you set up a baseline knowledge of core database concepts. Feel free to skip this chapter if you are comfortable with this subject.

Databases from the Beginning

Every story must begin somewhere. Databases are no different. The grouping of data into logical constructs first appeared in technical articles in 1960 written by Backman. As he explained, a *database management system (DBMS)* describes how data can be gathered, guided, and protected. Before that, persistence layers for applications usually were represented by flat-file databases on mainframes. Back then, the most popular flat-file types were the Indexed Sequential Access Method (ISAM) and Virtual Storage Access Method (VSAM). Flat-file databases, however, have several disadvantages. They cannot link data from one file into another, so this task is the responsibility of the software developer. This task includes opening each file, accessing the data in each file by coding data access paths, and loading the dataset of interest in volatile memory.

Flat-file databases are fixed-form files, so any change to their structure creates a huge effort for the developers because of the absence of an abstraction layer between the software and its data. All programs consuming the modified flat file need to be updated to avoid the wrong data being pulled into memory and the corruption of the data residing in the flat file. Data redundancy was achieved by replicating it in multiple flat files, but the problem was maintaining consistency between the copies.

DBMSs were developed to address this need and improve the overall functionality of all sorts of applications. DBMSs were more expensive than flat files, they demanded more specialized professionals, and, at that time, most companies needed to invest in the professional development of their workforce. The costs of licensing, infrastructure, and personnel imposed a barrier on the initial adoption of DBMSs.

But, as with any new and improved technology, the benefits of database systems outweighed older flat-file solutions, increasing adoption drastically.

1960s

Bachman's job paved the way for the creation of the CODASYL Data Model, created by a consortium of companies to develop data processing capabilities for COBOL. This data model introduced the concept of DDL (Data Definition Language) and DML (Data Manipulation Language). File management systems flourished, enabling easier ways to access data at rest. IBM developed the database management system ICS (later renamed IMS). IMS was responsible for the persistence layer of the Apollo project and was directly involved in the Apollo 11 mission's computerized systems.

The SABRE system, developed by IBM and American Airlines, allowed user access to data over the network, enabling American Airlines to automate reservation booking. It was first in the industry to achieve such automation.

1970s

Database technologies experienced rapid growth. E. F. Codd's relational database model introduced the core concepts of database theory, including the entity-relation model in 1976. Codd presented key definitions still in use until today, such as tables, columns, primary keys (PKs), and foreign keys (FKs).

According to Codd, a table is a representation of a relation—for example, products, users, offices, and departments—and each relation is composed of several data domains, as columns. For example, a relation of "offices" consists of the following data domains: address, available space, available facilities, and number of employees. Each data domain in this example has its own numeric relation—for example, available space should be a number representing the area in a specific metric system. All these domains should be previously defined in order to avoid, for example, multiple metric systems generating data discrepancies. The allowed values for a specific domain are fixed in type, size, and expected data allowed to be stored in that particular column. One or more columns that could uniquely identify a tuple (row) define a primary key, which also enforces that no duplicate or NULL values exist in primary key columns. Each relation can have only one primary key.

A common requirement for relational databases is the ability of elements in a table to reference elements of other tables. For example, columns, or a composition of columns from relation R, that are the values of a primary key of relation S form a foreign key in table R. Foreign keys enforce referential integrity by ensuring that the data present in the domains of a foreign key exists in the primary key domains of the referring relation.

Codd also defined *indexes* as performance-oriented components of a relation, composed of one or multiple domains. When well defined, indexes improve the response time of selects and updates, but they cause additional overhead for inserts and updates due to the redundant nature of the data represented in the index.

Another crucial concept introduced by Codd is what later was named *schema-on-write*. Before writing data into a relational database, you should first prepare the schema, including the table definition and column types. An error will be raised if you try to insert data in a column not defined in a table definition. This fixed schema behavior also enforces the rule that only data formatted as designed should be stored in a relational database. For instance, suppose you have a table called `Customers` and one column of this table is `CustomerName` with a maximum length of 40 characters. If you try to insert a name that is more than 40 characters, an error will be raised.

Other DBMSs were developed in the 1970s. Ingres was developed at the University of California, Berkeley, and Adabas was developed by the University of Darmstadt. Query languages were also developed, including Square, QBE, QUEL, and the well-known Structured Query Language (SQL).

1980s

In the 1980s, databases like dBASE and Paradox were developed to run on personal computers, enabling smaller companies and industry verticals to adopt database technologies.

Commercial relational databases, such as Db2, Oracle, Sybase, and Informix, were also released. The SQL standard was published by ANSI. The era of the commercial relational databases began.

The ACID transaction concept was introduced in 1983 by Andreas Reuter and Theo Härder as an evolution based on the work of Jim Gray. ACID transactions must guarantee four basic principles: atomicity, consistency, isolation, and durability. These core principles define the basic function of a relational database and its structures.

- *Atomicity* means that there is no partially modified data. A transaction is either successful, with all the data of interest modified, or unsuccessful, with no data modified at all, rolling back to the immediate prior state. A transaction can be a single statement or a conjunction of statements. Atomicity means that all statements must be successful. An example scenario for atomicity is a financial transaction: money needs to flow from one account into another, and if anything fails, it should not move at all.

- *Consistency* means that every transaction is bound to constraints on a table and across tables. Any violations in consistency—such as duplicated values on a unique column, inserting data on a missing column, or inserting values not allowed by the column definition—should be reported immediately so the operator can resolve the inconsistency and submit the transaction again.

- *Isolation* is implemented by a queuing system. To ensure isolation, database systems developed over the years have complex locking mechanisms at the row, block, page, and memory levels. By ensuring isolation, we create a discrete transaction order mechanism that makes sure transactions can read data being manipulated by other transactions. Deadlocks, locks, mutexes, and latches are all queuing mechanisms to ensure isolation.

- *Durability* is the ability to persist changes committed successfully to the database, even during failure scenarios, outages, and corruptions. Data will remain saved and persisted until another transaction, with the right privileges, manipulates it.

Relational databases deliver ACID transactions, referential integrity, and schema-on-write. In AWS, these capabilities are delivered by Amazon Relational Database Service (Amazon RDS), including engines like Oracle, SQL Server, PostgreSQL, MySQL, MariaDB, and Amazon Aurora.

Amazon RDS will be covered in depth in Chapter 4, "Transactional Databases on AWS."

1990s

Relational databases evolved from new application types and programming languages, like spatial and multimedia data, to deliver new and needed capabilities. Data is read by multiple sources and applications. The performance of relational databases was drastically improved, and the concept of massively parallel processing (MPP) was born to address the increasing size of datasets, improving performance by spreading parallel operations in several units composed by CPU, memory, and storage slices. With MPP architectures, scalability and performance could be improved by simply adding units (slices).

The Internet boom of the late 1990s demanded evolutions in database theory and functionality, especially in web connectors for modern programming languages. Open-source database solutions started to flourish, including MySQL and Postgres95 (which later became PostgreSQL).

Databases became a critical piece in online and offline stores, powering point-of-sales (POS) transactions, transaction processing systems, and online analytics platforms.

2000–2010

The first decade of the 20th century was the golden decade for commercial relational databases, consolidating three main players in the market as leading database technologies: Microsoft, Oracle, and IBM.

The CAP theorem, introduced by Eric Brewer of the University of California, Berkeley, in 2000 during the Symposium on Principles of Distributed Computing (PODC), stated that a distributed database system could guarantee only two of three characteristics: consistency, availability, and partition tolerance. This concept was developed over the following years and helps developers choose a particular database engine and philosophy to use.

The definition of consistency in the CAP theorem is that data should be the same, no matter which node clients are connecting to. This implies that a synchronous commit should be executed on all remote nodes prior to releasing the commit on the primary node. Data should be consistent across the distributed database persistence.

Availability implies that data should be available to satisfy client requests even with the failure of multiple nodes. Modern database systems achieve that by horizontally scaling database persistence across multiple nodes.

Partition tolerance states that the distributed database system must be resilient even if nodes are not reachable over the network.

Amazon Elastic Block Store (EBS) is a block-storage service designed for Amazon Elastic Compute Cloud (Amazon EC2). Amazon EBS volumes can be added on demand in EC2 instances, thus providing storage for application and database filesystems. With technological advancements like Multi-Attach Amazon EBS volumes, which enable a single EBS volume to be added in multiple EC2 instances, the CAP theorem tends not to be a definitive rule, enabling further evolutions of distributed data persistence layers.

Amazon EBS volumes will be covered in depth in Chapter 2, "Basic Concepts of AWS."

2010–Today

New database paradigms have appeared, being rapidly leveraged in modern applications.

Not Only SQL (NoSQL) databases have gained traction and evolved, being used in countless production deployments by Internet giants such as Twitter, Facebook, and Google. NoSQL databases are a great choice for semistructured and unstructured data, having scalability and distributed processing as main features, thus leading to higher resiliency and delivering schema-on-write, meaning that the table structure can be changed and columns (attributes) can be added during insert-like operations. As opposed to relational databases, NoSQL databases in general do not require uniform table definition among rows.

Over the years, several types of NoSQL databases have arisen to solve specific challenges, with different vendors and solutions for each database type. NoSQL databases will be covered in depth in this book, including key-value databases like Amazon DynamoDB (Chapter 5, "Low Latency Response Time for Your Apps and APIs"), wide-column databases like Amazon Keyspaces for Apache Cassandra (Chapter 5), document databases like Amazon DocumentDB with MongoDB Compatibility (Chapter 6, "Document Databases in the Cloud"), graph databases like Amazon Neptune (Chapter 9, "Discover Relationships Between Objects or People Faster Than a Traditional RDBMS"), and ledger databases like Amazon QLDB (Chapter 10, "Immutable Database and Traceable Transactions").

It is always important to understand where databases came from, because this makes it easier to understand where they are going. The thinking about organized data structures in the form of stacks, lists, arrays, and databases has evolved rapidly over the years. Certainly, for the makers of SQL, it would have been impossible to achieve data volumes that for us today are trivial, such as petabytes of data. Query optimization systems, in various formats, have been created to execute queries with the best performance possible, touching the smallest number of blocks on disk as possible.

For decades, relational databases were able to satisfy the new types of applications that emerged, being positioned as the technology for the persistence layer. However, with multiple dataset types and different needs now, the relational database isn't the only response available anymore.

The history of databases is closely linked to the evolution of computational structures. With the advancement in the areas of processors, volatile memory, and persistent memory, new optimization and query execution strategies have been created to enable modern applications and to satisfy new requirements.

Databases on Premises

Databases historically are components hungry for compute resources such as CPU, memory, and disk. Over the years, several vendors have optimized their hardware to answer the need for performant databases. With solid-state drives (SSD) and nonvolatile memory express (NVME) disks, InfiniBand networks, RDMA over converged Ethernet (RoCE) protocol, and high-density processors with multiple cores and threads, the hardware evolution is evident.

Basic Infrastructure

The building blocks of a database architecture have changed drastically over the years. In the early 2000s, clustered deployments were rare, and single-instance databases running on top of a single machine with directly attached SCSI disks built in RAID were common. With exponential dataset growth comes the need to use external storage systems with dedicated storage area networks (SANs), thus decoupling compute and storage capacity. By adopting external storage systems, it was possible to develop the ability to build clustered filesystems like GPFS (General Parallel File System) from IBM, CSV (Cluster Shared Volumes) from Microsoft, and Cluster File System from Veritas. By using these clustered filesystems, database architects could span their databases across multiple nodes in an active-passive or active-active fashion.

Networks have always played a main part in database architectures. By adopting faster transport layers, database fetches could become bigger and bigger following the dataset growth observed. Without faster and reliable networks, databases would be a beautiful albeit isolated island.

Several types of virtualizations have been created to address an increasing need for faster and software-defined deployments. Virtualized compute became the new normal for database deployments, in various flavors, from IBM AIX Logical Partitions to VMware and Hyper-V virtual machines. Virtualization systems enabled faster deployments, standardization, and less dependency on physical hardware and the lengthy process of procurement.

Complex Infrastructure and Resiliency

Now that you understand the basic building blocks of database systems, let's dive a little deeper into the complex infrastructure and architectures. Over the years databases have become a critical component of every company architecture. If the database system is down, it doesn't matter how many application servers, load balancers, network links, and datacenters you have. So, the development of more resilient database architectures was needed. For each RDBMS, there are several solutions, such as Oracle Real Application Clusters (Oracle RAC), Oracle Clusterware, MS SQL Failover Cluster, MS SQL Always On, PostgreSQL, and MySQL Clustered Solutions, ranging from shared-disk to shared-nothing architectures. The ability to span multiple servers drastically reduced the recovery time objective (RTO) and improved resiliency by introducing bulkhead architectures and multiple copies of the dataset.

All these clustering solutions are highly dependent on reliable storage and reliable networks. To increase the resiliency even more, all the clustering solutions developed mechanisms to avoid split-brain and cascade failover scenarios. Today all these clustering techniques are mature and adopted in several database architectures across all industries.

RDBMS vendors have best practices and reference architectures such as the Oracle Maximum Availability Architecture (MAA). In these reference architectures, vendors have adopted several solutions and techniques to improve RTO and recovery point objective (RPO) metrics.

Management

Database management comprehends all facets of database operations, ranging from monitoring, patching, and backup to performance-related issues, data load and extraction, scheduled jobs, upgrades, and migrations.

For each of these operational tasks, several vendors have dedicated time and effort to build products to address in full or partially these operational needs. In an on-premises environment, it was normal to have multiple tools from distinct vendors, each tool with its own application stack, architecture, and responsible team.

Additionally, for each database system vendor it was normal to have specific tools, so an Oracle database administrator (DBA), for example, would use Oracle Grid Control to check the database load and execute administrative tasks at scale; a Microsoft SQL DBA, on the other hand, would use SQL Server Management Studio; and a MySQL DBA would use MySQL Workbench. All these tools, in most advanced setups, could be centralized in one tool with dashboards to monitor critical database key performance indicators (KPIs).

Backups performed with specific tools also demand specific setups to perform restore operations. An on-premises DBA should be familiar with several different tools and their operational details to manage the company's database ecosystem.

Databases in the Cloud

Amazon Elastic Compute Cloud (EC2), a service crafted to deliver compute capacity in the form of resizable virtual machines (instances), was launched in August 2006. With the advent of cloud computing, the following question arises: can I leverage the cloud as the infrastructure basis for my database deployments?

Data Remains Data

Humans tend to replicate actions and paradigms and opt always for the safer, already traveled road. Data is changing the world, but data itself isn't changing—the way we use data is. In the past, a database was a data repository for several applications, rapidly becoming a critical and intricate piece of the applications architecture. Datasets were tied to a specific application, and when needed, integrations via database links and linked servers were the norm. These integrations aren't feasible or reliable enough for modern application demands, so new technologies emerged from this need, enabling data pipelines, more complex extract transform load (ETL) and extract load transform (ELT), real-time data messaging and queueing, and distributed data patterns.

But data remains data. We are storing larger and larger datasets, using these datasets to train machine learning models, better understand customer needs, and better position our products. At the end of the day, however, the ability to satisfy data requests in a secure and performant way is more important than ever.

DBAs Are the Initial DevOps

DBAs work exactly in the middle of software and hardware, between developers and operators and between applications and infrastructure. This position provides DBAs with all sorts of challenges, from a badly written SQL statement from developers to storage bottlenecks, from network latency problems to metadata definition, and from coding database procedures to defining hardware requirements for a new database.

The connection between developers and operational teams, such as system administrators, network administrators and storage administrators, is usually done through DBAs. When developers claim that the database is slow, the cause could reside in code itself, but also in the infrastructure, like an underperformant storage, a bug in the Operational System or packets being dropped on the network due a bad cable.

With the ever-increasing number of databases and larger datasets, automated administrative tasks are the new norm. DBAs have developed scripts, procedures, functions, packages, and even graphical interfaces to facilitate daily activities, thus reducing the need for manual intervention on the database and enabling rapid database deployments through automated code. By leveraging response files and configuration management tools like Ansible, Puppet, and Chef, DBAs have reduced drastically the time needed to deploy a new solution, keeping security and best practices standardized.

DBA Career—Now What?

Some say DBA careers are almost over. We disagree. The DBA career is changing to keep up with technological advancements and new paradigms, but the demand for reliable, fast, secure, and cost-effective databases has never been higher.

The DBA career is evolving. Skills, tools, and processes are being improved, enabling lower time to market but keeping systems stable. DBAs are lifelong learners, always learning new database features and ways to make day-to-day activities easier and faster.

Keeping this learning curve rising is essential. For example, you should learn new database types, such as when to use graph databases and when not to use them, and how to leverage new services and features. Be a protagonist of your career!

Summary

This chapter provided an overview of the history of DBMSs and how this disruptive technology affects our lives today.

We covered how database architectures were built on premises, presenting core concepts such as disks, networks, database clustering, and database management. We also talked about careers in database administration.

Chapter

2

Basic AWS Concepts

IN THIS CHAPTER, YOU WILL LEARN THE BASIC CONCEPTS RELATED TO THE CLOUD, ESPECIALLY AWS. THIS CONTENT WILL HELP YOU PASS NOT ONLY THE DATABASE SPECIALTY CERTIFICATION EXAM, BUT ALL OTHER AWS CERTIFICATIONS AS WELL.

THE CHAPTER WILL FAMILIARIZE YOU WITH THE FOLLOWING IT TOPICS AND HOW THEY TRANSLATE TO CLOUD SERVICES AND COMPONENTS:

✓ **Global infrastructure:** Regions, availability zones, edge locations, and points of presence.

✓ **Networking:** Virtual private clouds, virtual private networks, AWS Direct Connect, and networking connectivity.

✓ **Security:** Network security, security model, identity and access management, and data encryption.

✓ **Storage:** Block storage, file storage, and object storage and its relation to database services.

✓ **Operations:** Monitoring, logging, and auditing.

 This chapter won't cover any particular domain of the AWS Certified Database – Specialty certification, but it will provide you with a baseline knowledge of cloud computing and AWS.

AWS Global Infrastructure

The AWS global infrastructure is composed of regions, availability zones, data centers, points of presence, local zones, and wavelength zones.

AWS Regions

An *AWS region* consists of multiple availability zones—typically three but up to six, as in the case of us-east-1, also known as N. Virginia. At the time of writing, there are 25 launched regions, and 5 have been announced. Visit the official AWS Global Infrastructure landing page (aws.amazon.com/about-aws/global-infrastructure) for the updated information.

AWS Availability Zones

An *availability zone (AZ)* is a data center with redundant power and networking connectivity at full scale; it can include hundreds of thousands of servers. Each AZ is separated from the others by the necessary distance to be isolated from natural disasters or local outages but close enough to keep high network throughput and single-digit latency (<10 milliseconds). This data center distribution within the AWS infrastructure gives customers the ability to deploy production applications that are more scalable, highly available, and fault tolerant than would be possible from a single data center on premises.

Figure 2.1 shows an example AWS region comprising three availability zones with four data centers each.

FIGURE 2.1 An AWS region

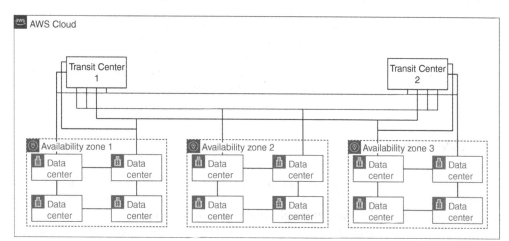

Besides the traditional AWS regions and availability zones, there is a new player in AWS infrastructure: local zones.

AWS Local Zones

AWS local zones are an extension of AWS regions where customers can run latency-sensitive applications closer to their end users using AWS services. AWS local zones provide a secure high-bandwidth connection between the workloads running on them and those running in the region. These zones offer a subset of the same services, APIs, and tools available in the parent AWS region, allowing customers to easily build, deploy, and operate their applications and providing them with a consistent AWS experience. The AWS local zones are completely managed by AWS, giving customers the same benefits regarding elasticity, scalability, and security of the cloud.

AWS Wavelength Zones

If the workload is mainly mobile or edge computing, there is another infrastructure deployment to consider: the AWS wavelength zone. A *wavelength zone* is an AWS infrastructure that integrates AWS compute and storage services with the data centers of a given telecommunication company (telco) at the edge of the 5G network. The traffic originating from applications on 5G devices can reach application servers running in wavelength zones without leaving the communication services provider network. By using an AWS wavelength, customer applications running on end-user devices can take full advantages of 5G latency and bandwidth by not having to traverse multiple hops across the Internet to reach their destination.

Points of Presence

The last concept of the global infrastructure is the AWS point of presence. *AWS points of presence* are also data centers but are not directly related to an availability zone. They are located in most of the major cities around the world and are used by Amazon CloudFront as a content delivery network (CDN) to cache and distribute content to end users at low latencies regardless of where the content is originally stored.

Networking

This is an extensive topic that requires an entire book itself. In this section, we cover only the basic concepts that you will find on the database certification exam and that are also required to understand the rest of the topics and chapters in this book.

To use AWS services, customers need an AWS account that acts as a container for their resources. Some of the AWS services are public and can be accessed directly from the Internet; the others are private and need to be deployed on Amazon Virtual Private Cloud (VPC). *Amazon VPC* is a special service that acts as a network container and is the main component of all cloud-related networking features. As shown in Figure 2.2, virtual private clouds are composed of subnets in a similar way that a region is composed of availability zones.

FIGURE 2.2   Amazon VPC

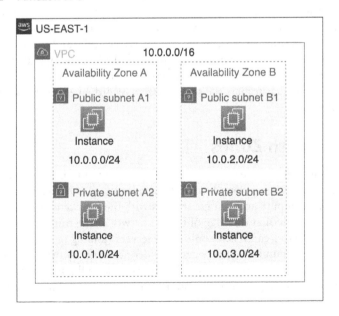

IP Addressing

The Amazon VPC service supports two types of IP addresses, private and public.

- **The internal IP address:** As the name suggests, these IP addresses are only internal to that virtual private cloud, and the addressing is from the private or shared IP spaces. (See RFC 1918 and RFC 6598 for more information.) An important point about virtual private clouds is that their CIDR cannot be modified once created and must go from /16 (up to 65,536 IP addresses) to /28 (up to 16 IP addresses).

- **The external IP address:** These are the ones that can be accessed from the public Internet. These IP addresses support bring-your-own IP (BYOIP), IPv4, and IPv6. An elastic IP address is a static, special type of external IP address that supports only IPv4. An elastic IP is dynamically assigned to your AWS account and can be remapped to another instance within the same. These IP addresses are free as long as they are attached to some network interface of a running instance.

Subnets

A *subnet* is a range of IP addresses within the Amazon VPC CIDR and is where the actual private AWS resource, such as the EC2 instance or the RDS DB instance, is deployed. While a virtual private cloud spans an entire AWS region, a subnet belongs to a single availability zone. The subnets can be private or public, and you can create multiple subnets per virtual private cloud and per availability zone. The subnets' IP addresses are allocated from the parent virtual private cloud CIDR and cannot overlap each other.

AWS reserves the first four and the last IP addresses, for each subnet, in a way that they cannot be assigned to a network interface. For example, in a subnet with a CIDR like 10.1.1.0/24, the following five IP addresses are not available:

10.1.1.0—The network address

10.1.1.1—Reserved by AWS for the VPC router

10.1.1.2—Reserved by AWS for the DNS server

10.1.0.3—Reserved by AWS for other future uses

10.1.0.255—Network broadcast address

VPC Routing

Each subnet has an associated routing table that can be exclusive to it or be inherited from the main VPC routing table. Each routing table can be associated with multiple subnets. The same thing happens on premises: the route tables direct traffic from one host to another. In AWS, this traffic can point toward many destinations (as shown in Figure 2.3), the more important of which are the following:

- Internet gateway
- NAT gateway

- VPC peering
- AWS Transit Gateway attachment
- Virtual private network
- AWS Direct Connect interface
- Network interface

FIGURE 2.3 Route table destinations

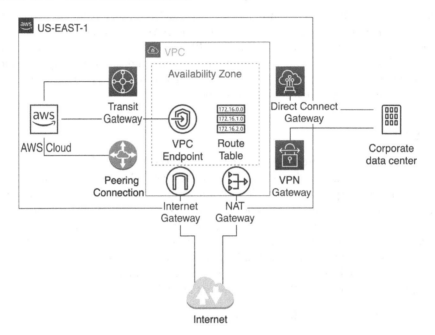

The subnets are referred to as *public* when there is a route to an Internet gateway. This route will allow not just outbound traffic but also inbound.

Gateways and Connectivity Options

There are several types of gateways and route targets available with Amazon VPC.

Internet Gateway   An *Internet gateway* is a horizontally scaled, redundant, and highly available VPC component used to connect each VPC subnet to the Internet and perform a one-to-one network address translation (NAT) between the public and private IP addresses. This kind of gateway is free, but there is a fee for the outbound traffic going through it.

NAT Gateway   A *NAT gateway* allows Internet traffic to the subnet, but only with outbound traffic; it does not allow incoming connections. This is useful to keep your environment isolated from the public Internet without losing the ability to get operating system and software packages and consume public web services. In contrast with an Internet gateway, a NAT gateway supports 5 Gbps of bandwidth and automatically scales up to 45 Gbps. If you require more bandwidth, you can split your resources into multiple subnets and create a NAT gateway in each subnet.

VPC Peering   *VPC peering* is a scalable and highly available solution used to connect two virtual private clouds. The connection can be done across AWS accounts and AWS regions at the same time and allows bidirectional traffic. There are two caveats of this kind of connectivity: there can't be IP address overlapping between the two VPCs, and transitive routing to a third VPC is not allowed.

Transit Gateway   *AWS Transit Gateway* is a highly available fully managed service that provides a hub-and-spoke connecting pattern for virtual private networks and on-premises networks without requiring you to provision virtual appliances. AWS Transit Gateway (see Figure 2.4) manages how traffic is routed among all the connected network components using route tables. This hub-and-spoke design simplifies operations and reduces management costs. AWS manages the availability and scalability of the solution up to 50 Gbps per attachment.

FIGURE 2.4   AWS Transit Gateway service

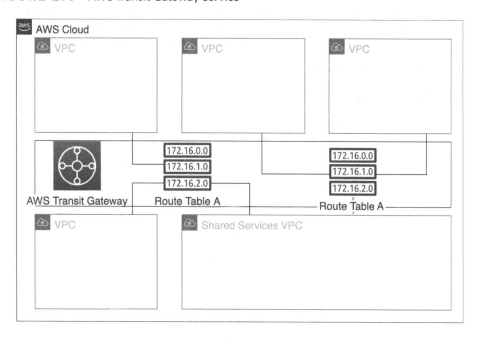

Virtual private network   The site-to-site VPN (see Figure 2.5) on AWS is an IPSec connection compatible with AES 256-bit and SHA-2 algorithms between the customer firewall (customer gateway) and a fully managed endpoint device on the AWS side (virtual private gateway). Each virtual private gateway can be associated with only one VPC. If connectivity with more than one virtual private cloud is necessary, the connection can be established with a transit gateway instead. The VPN connections can be configured in high availability with two tunnels and support dynamic (BGP) and static routing.

Direct Connect   *AWS Direct Connect* is the other choice of private connectivity with the customer on-premises data centers. The direct connection can be one of the following:

> **Dedicated:** Directly with AWS with bandwidth ranging from 1 to 10 Gbps and supports multiple virtual interfaces (VIF)
>
> **Hosted:** Through an AWS partner from 50 Mbps to 10 Gbps and a single VIF

There are three kinds of virtual interfaces:

> **Private VIF:** A private connection between the customer data center and the resources within a VPC.
>
> **Public VIF:** A private connection between the customer data center and the AWS public IP address space.
>
> **Transit VIF:** A private connection between the customer data center and a transit gateway. This simplifies the network architecture and enables a hub-and-spoke mode that spans multiple VPC, AWS accounts, and regions.

Figure 2.6 shows a Direct Connect location linked to two different AWS transit gateways.

FIGURE 2.5   Site-to-site VPN

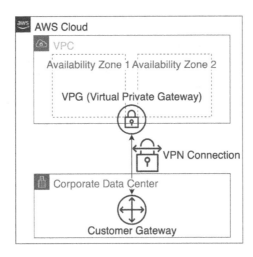

VPC endpoints   *VPC endpoints* (see Figure 2.7) are used to privately connect an Amazon VPC with the supported services that lie outside a VPC, such as Amazon S3, AWS KMS, or even a load balancer that is deployed on a different VPC. When using PrivateLink, VPC endpoints can access publicly available AWS services without needing a public IP address or Internet connection, so the traffic going through that link never leaves the AWS network. These endpoints scale horizontally and are redundant and highly available.

FIGURE 2.6   AWS Direct Connect location

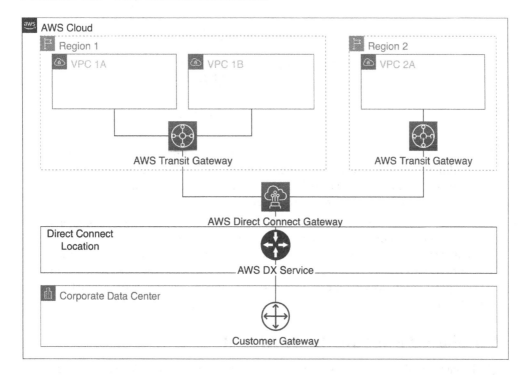

Security

Like networking, security is a broad and important topic. This chapter will cover only basic concepts.

Network Security

The network security on AWS mostly relies on the security of the VPCs. AWS provides two types of firewall for the virtual private clouds:

FIGURE 2.7 VPC endpoints

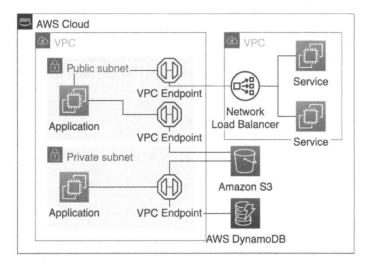

- **Network access control list (NACL):** This is a stateless IP firewall that allows inbound and outbound rules and operates at a subnet level. By default, it allows all traffic, so it's an optional level of security. The NACL rules can be written using IP addresses and TCP and UDP ports and support deny rules as well.

- **Security group (SG):** This is a stateful resource firewall that also allows inbound and outbound rules and operates at an interface level. By default, it denies all traffic, so it's a mandatory resource. All VPC-related services must have an SG associated with them. SG supports cross-references among each other, which enables the customer to perform network segmentation (as shown in Figure 2.8) by using different security groups for each application layer.

AWS Shared Responsibility Model

All AWS security white papers, presentations, and documents mention the AWS Shared Responsibility Model. As the name suggests, the compliance objectives in the AWS cloud are accomplished by both AWS and the customers. AWS takes care of the security *of* the cloud, and the customer takes care of the security *in* the cloud. Table 2.1 illustrates how this works.

If the customer chooses to use more abstract and managed services up or serverless ones, the responsibility bar moves up, restricting customers' responsibilities to the access management and the source code itself.

FIGURE 2.8   Security group network segmentation

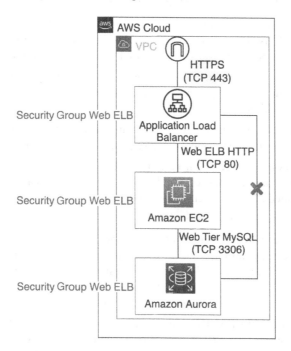

TABLE 2.1   Security Responsibility Distribution

AWS	Customer
Facilities	Network configuration
Physical security	Security groups
Compute infrastructure	OS firewalls
Storage infrastructure	Operating system
Network infrastructure	Applications
Virtualization layer	Proper service configuration
Hardened service endpoints	AuthN and account management
Rich IAM capabilities	Authorization policies

Identity and Access Management

Identity and access management allows AWS customers to implement a comprehensive access control on each AWS resource. It provides the ability to authenticate, authorize, and audit all access to AWS no matter the interface used to interact with AWS.

- **Authentication:** To authenticate a user in the console or API by using regular credentials or strong authentication options; also, to authenticate other AWS accounts or even trust other identity providers.

- **Authorize:** To specify, with high granularity, which user can do what action. Therefore, you can implement the least privilege and segregation of duties patterns.

- **Audit:** Every action executed against any IAM resources is recorded on CloudTrail, for troubleshooting or audit purposes. The IAM Access Analyzer feature lets customers identify unintended access to their resources and data.

There are three kinds of principals on AWS:

- **The account owner ID or root account:** This principal has unlimited access to all AWS subscribed services, the billing console, and customer support. Because of the importance of this user and the access level it has, it is strongly recommended to delete its programmatic access keys and enable multifactor authentication at once. AWS recommends not using this account for administration tasks unless strictly necessary.

- **IAM users, groups, and roles:** These are entities that you create in AWS. They represent persons or services that use their access to perform actions in AWS. The main purpose of an IAM user is to give people the ability to sign in to the AWS Management Console for interactive tasks via GUI or to make programmatic requests to AWS services using the API or CLI.

- **Temporary security credentials:** *Temporary security credentials* are used together with IAM roles. Customers can request temporary credentials with a more restricted set of permissions than the standard IAM user. This prevents customers from accidentally performing actions that are not permitted. A benefit of temporary credentials is that, as the name suggests, they expire automatically after a configurable period of time.

AWS uses policies and permissions to accomplish every principal's authorization. There are six kinds of policy in total, but we will cover the two main ones:

- **Identity-based policies:** *Identity-based policies* are represented by JSON documents that control what actions a principal can perform, on which resources, and under what conditions. They can be categorized in two groups:
  - **Inline policies:** Can be added directly to a single user, group, or role. This policy type maintains a strict one-to-one relationship between the policy and the identity.
  - **Managed policies:** Stand-alone identity-based policies managed by AWS or the customer, which can be attached to multiple users, groups, and roles in the AWS account.
- **Resource-based policies:** Resource-based policies are also represented by JSON documents but, in this case, can be attached to a resource like Amazon S3 instead of an IAM

principal. These policies grant the principal specified in the policy permission to perform a specific action on the resource that it was attached to under a given condition. Resource-based policies are only the inline policy type.

Other services related to IAM are the AWS single sign-on (SSO) and AWS Directory Service.

AWS SSO, as the name suggests, allows users to use a single set of credentials to access all the AWS accounts within an AWS organization. The AWS Organization service helps you manage multi-account environments by enabling centralized governance and seamless resources sharing. You can keep the user identities and groups in AWS SSO or within their current identity providers, such as Microsoft Active Directory Domain Services, Okta Universal Directory, Azure AD, or another. Users can access AWS with their existing corporate credentials, and the administrators can continue to manage users and groups in the existing identity source.

There are three flavors of the Active Directory service on AWS:

- **AWS Managed Microsoft Active Directory:** Based on Microsoft Active Directory in Windows Server 2012 R2. This supports adding trust relationships with on-premises domains.

- **Simple AD:** A Microsoft Active Directory–compatible directory powered by Samba 4.

- **AD Connector:** Connects to your on-premises Active Directory. This integrates with existing RADIUS MFA solutions.

Data Encryption

AWS provides customers with the ability to encrypt their data as it sits and flows in/out of their environment, but it also provides many services and features that make it easier.

At-Rest Encryption   Customers can encrypt data at rest by following one of these approaches:

> **Volume encryption:** Amazon EBS volume, filesystem tools, AWS Marketplace, or third-party partner vendors.

> **Object encryption:** Amazon S3 server-side encryption with AWS managed keys or customer-managed keys and client-side encryption.

> **Database encryption:** Besides the database volume encryption, Amazon RDS also supports encrypting an Oracle or SQL Server DB instance with Transparent Data Encryption (TDE).

> Besides those ways, there are several other layers of security to the data at rest in the cloud, each of which provides scalable and efficient encryption capabilities like key management features with AWS Key Management Service (AWS KMS). AWS KMS enables customers to choose whether to have AWS manage the encryption keys or do it on their own. Customers can also use a dedicated hardware-based cryptographic key storage service with AWS CloudHSM, allowing compliance with stricter regulatory requirements.

In-Transit Encryption In-transit encryption on AWS can be done using a multilevel approach. All the traffic between AWS data centers is encrypted at the physical layer by default. All traffic across AWS regions between peered VPCs is encrypted at the network layer when using AWS Nitro–based Amazon EC2 instance types. At the application layer, customers are able to use their defined encryption protocol, such as Transport Layer Security (TLS). All AWS service endpoints support TLS to make API requests.

AWS has three key services to help customers to encrypt their data and secure their credentials:

AWS Certificate Manager *AWS Certificate Manager (ACM)* allows customers to easily provision, manage, deploy, and renew SSL/TLS certificates and use them with their applications endpoints on AWS or download its private certificate to use on premises or on another provider with the private certificate authority (CA) feature.

AWS Key Management Service *AWS Key Management Service (AWS KMS)* is a managed service that makes it easy to create, rotate, delete, and manage access to the keys used to encrypt the data. AWS KMS uses Hardware Security Modules (HSMs) to protect the security of those keys. This service is integrated with most AWS data–related services to help protect the customer data within each one of them. AWS Key Management Service is also integrated with AWS CloudTrail to provide customers with audit capabilities for all key usage in order to help them meet any regulatory and compliance requirements.

AWS Secrets Manager *AWS Secrets Manager* helps customers to meet their security and compliance requirements by protecting the secrets needed to access their databases, applications, services, and other IT resources. AWS Secrets Manager enables customers to easily rotate, manage, and retrieve database credentials, API keys, and other secrets throughout their life cycles. Those secrets can be retrieved with a request to the Secrets Manager APIs, eliminating the need to hard-code sensitive information in plain text. Secrets Manager offers secret rotation with built-in integration for Amazon RDS, Amazon Redshift, and Amazon DocumentDB.

In addition, AWS provides APIs to integrate encryption and data protection with any of the AWS services the customer might use.

Storage at AWS

This section discusses the three storage types on AWS and how they relate to databases.

File storage *File storage* consists of unrelated data blocks managed by a file (serving) system like NFS, FXs, or Lustre. Examples of this storage type can be the network-attached storage (NAS) appliances or Windows File Servers. This storage type is represented in AWS by the services Amazon Elastic File System (EFS) and Amazon FSx.

Object storage   *Object storage* consists of virtual containers that encapsulate the data, data attributes, metadata, and object IDs. It's a metadata-driven storage system that uses policies to grant access and provides API access to the objects. The service related to this storage type is Amazon Simple Storage Service (Amazon S3).

Block storage   *Block storage* is a raw storage type that organizes data as an array of unrelated blocks. This storage is used to host filesystem-related data on disk, for example, like the hard drives and storage area network (SAN) appliances. The block storage type is represented by Amazon Elastic Block Storage (EBS), and it's mostly used as virtual machine data and operating system volumes.

Each storage option has a unique combination of performance, durability, cost, and interface:

- **Durability:** Measure of expected data loss
- **Availability:** Measure of expected downtime
- **Security:** Security measures for at-rest and in-transit data
- **Cost:** Amount per storage unit, e.g., money per gigabyte
- **Scalability:** Upward flexibility, storage size, number of users
- **Performance:** Performance metrics (bandwidth)

Durability and availability percentages are often confusing. Table 2.2 illustrates how those values translate to real-life examples.

TABLE 2.2   Storage Durability and Availability in Data Loss in Downtime

Percentage	Availability	Durability
99.999	5 minutes 15 seconds	1 in 100,000
99.9999	31 seconds	1 in 1,000,000
99.99999	3 seconds	1 in 10,000,000
99.999999999	300 uSeconds	1 in 100,000,000,000

Amazon Elastic Block Storage

EBS volumes are network-attached storage volumes that are dynamically resized, can be detached and attached to different instances, and can also dynamically change their type without the need to restart the instances that are using them. Amazon EBS provides the following volume types: General Purpose SSD, Provisioned IOPS SSD, Throughput Optimized HDD, and Cold HDD.

The Throughput Optimized HDD volumes are good candidates for Big Data and analytics workloads (such as Apache Kafka, Splunk, and Hadoop) and data warehousing in general. They are also useful for file sharing and media applications such as transcoding, encoding, and rendering. The common factor is high-throughput applications.

The Cold HDD storage is better suited for block-based data archiving and infrequently accessed data.

The General Purpose SSD storage balances price and performance in a way that can handle most transactional use cases such as application servers, boot disks, and medium-size single-instance databases.

The IOPS SSD volumes are best suited for high IOPS workloads, such as relational databases like PostgreSQL, MySQL, SQL Server, Oracle, and SAP HANA. They are even better for NoSQL databases like Cassandra, MongoDB, and CouchDB.

Table 2.3 shows the storage dimensions of the two EBS volume types.

TABLE 2.3   EBS Volume Storage Dimensions

Volume Type	Base IOPS	Burst IOPS	Throughput	Latency	Capacity
HDD sc1	N/A	N/A	12 MB/s per TB; up to 250 MB/s	N/A	500 GB to 16 TB
HDD st1	N/A	N/A	40 MB/s per TB; up to 500 MB/s	N/A	500 GB to 16 TB
SSD gp2	100–16.000	3000	Up to 250 MB/s	Single-digit ms	1 GB to 16 TB
SSD io1	100–64.000	N/A	Up to 1.000 MB/s	Single-digit ms	4 GB to 16 TB

Amazon Elastic File System

Amazon Elastic File System (Amazon EFS) provides a simple, petabyte-scale, fully managed elastic NFS filesystem to be used by other AWS services or on-premises resources. Amazon EFS is considered a serverless service because customers don't need to provision storage or performance capacity; it's capable of shrinking and growing automatically as the users add or remove files from it. The pricing model also complies with serverless, and the customers pay only for the amount of storage used without minimum fees.

Amazon EFS enables applications running on AWS to leverage a massively parallel shared filesystem as the storage layer. Amazon EFS provides high levels of aggregate throughput and IOPS with consistent low latencies at any scale. Those features make it perfect for workloads such as the following:

- Content management
- Web serving
- Big Data analytics
- Home directories
- Media workflow processing

That being said, there is a scenario when Amazon EFS can be useful for database workloads. Amazon EFS can be easily mounted using NFSv4 protocol in a database server and then be used as storage layer for the database backups. Customers running their databases on EC2 could take advantage of the flexibility of storing database backups in the cloud either for temporary protection during updates or for development and testing purposes.

Amazon Simple Storage Service

Object storage is the last but not least storage type we are going to cover, and it's represented by Amazon Simple Storage Service (Amazon S3). Amazon S3 was the second AWS service released after Amazon SQS in March 2006 and today is one of the most used and important services of the cloud in general. Why? Basically because of its unmatched features.

- Web accessible object store (through API or HTTPS)
- Highly durable (99.999999999 percent design)
- Highly available (99.99 percent design)
- Limitless capacity
- Limitless performance (3,500 puts and 5,500 gets per prefix)
- Multiple tiers to match your workload
- Data life-cycle rules
- Static website hosting
- Security, compliance, and audit capabilities
- Strong read-after-write and list consistency
- Standard Storage Pricing (us-east-1): $0.023 per GB

Table 2.4 shows the main characteristics of each Amazon S3 available tier. Prices may be different in each region.

TABLE 2.4   Amazon S3 Storage Classes

Class	Characteristics
S3 Standard	Active, frequently accessed data
	Millisecond access
	≥ 3 AZ replication
	$0.0210 to 0.0230/GB
	Data with changing access patterns
	Millisecond access
S3 Intelligent Tiering	≥ 3 AZ replication
	$0.0210 to $0.0125/GB
	Monitoring fee per object
	Infrequently accessed data
	Millisecond access
	≥ 3 AZ replication
S3 Standard Infrequent Access	$0.0125/GB
	Retrieval fee per gigabyte
	Minimum storage duration
	Minimum object size
	Reproducible, less accessed data
	Millisecond access
	Only one AZ copy
S3 One Zone Infrequent Access	$0.0100/GB
	Retrieval fee per gigabyte
	Minimum storage duration
	Minimum object size
	Archive data
	Select minutes or hours
	≥ 3 AZ replication
S3 Glacier	$0.0040/GB
	Retrieval fee per gigabyte
	Minimum storage duration
	Minimum object size

Class	Characteristics
	Archive data Select 12 or 48 hours $\geq$ 3 AZ replication
S3 Deep Archive	$0.00099/GB Retrieval fee per GB Minimum storage duration Minimum object size

There are several ways in which databases can take advantage of Amazon S3, but the two most important are data loading/migration and backups/archiving.

Data loading and migration   Most AWS database and analytics–related services can use S3 as a source for data loading. Some services can use these features directly via AWS CLI, and others depend on data movement services like AWS Data Pipeline and AWS Glue.

Backups and archive   Amazon S3 is the perfect place to store database backups and snapshots for short and long periods of time due to its durability, low cost, and data life-cycle features. AWS customers can use the S3 Intelligent Tiering class to monitor data access patterns and identify objects that should be moved to a more cost-effective storage class.

This is why Amazon RDS, Amazon DynamoDB, and Amazon DocumentDB, to name three database services, store their automated incremental snapshots on S3. If the customer wants to see and manage the snapshots on their own, they can choose to copy these snapshots to the desired S3 buckets. Amazon S3 is also the place where AWS Backup stores the backups for each service it controls, including, of course, the database backups.

Operations

Monitoring and logging can be challenging in many on-premise environments due to the manual configuration of physical and logical resources. Monitoring data, if even available, may span multiple systems and processes, which further complicates things. In AWS, resources are software defined, and changes to them are tracked as API calls. The current and past states of your environment can be monitored and acted on in real time. In this final topic of the chapter, we will introduce the core monitoring and logging capabilities you should be aware of as you begin operating database workloads on AWS.

There are two core services to cover this requirement: Amazon CloudWatch, which handles monitoring and logging activities, and AWS CloudTrail, which handles traces and auditing.

Monitoring and Logging

Why is monitoring important? There are five main reasons:

- **Customer experience:** Are the database users (people, applications, or services) getting a good experience?
- **Performance and cost:** How do changes in the database impact the overall performance and cost?
- **Trends:** When and how should the database scale?
- **Troubleshooting:** Where and why do the errors occur?
- **Learning and improvement:** How can the problem be avoided in the future?

It is not possible to talk about monitoring in AWS without mentioning Amazon Cloud-Watch. It is the one service to monitor them all.

Amazon CloudWatch

Customers can use Amazon CloudWatch to gain visibility into each AWS resource utilization, deployed application performance, and system-wide operational health. The customers can use these insights to react and keep their application running smoothly. CloudWatch also monitors every AWS cloud database along with every cloud-powered application. It tracks all the necessary metrics so that customers can visualize and review them in a timely manner. Customers can also set alarms that will fire when given metrics go beyond a specified threshold. CloudWatch gives you visibility into resource utilization, application performance, and operational health.

Amazon CloudWatch comprises the following main components:

Metrics A *metric* is a fundamental concept in CloudWatch. It represents a set of data points that are published to CloudWatch in a time-ordered manner. These data points can be either AWS defaults or custom metrics created by the customers. Customers can retrieve statistics about those metrics as time-series data. These are the most common CloudWatch metrics available for databases in AWS today:

- The amount of memory and CPU being used for a database
- The number of connections to a database

- The amount of storage that a database is currently using
- The amount of network traffic to and from a database
- The number of read and write operations to a database

Alarms   *CloudWatch alarms* are triggered automatically on the customers' behalf, based on specified thresholds. An alarm watches a single metric over a given period of time and performs one or more actions based on the value of the metric relative to defined parameters.

Events   Because of the importance of this feature, a new service was created just to cover the Amazon CloudWatch event features: Amazon EventBridge. It delivers a near real-time stream of system events that describe changes in AWS resources. Events are delivered through resource state changes, CloudTrail API calls, or custom publications, or they are scheduled using cron expressions. The Event Bridge rules match incoming events and route them to one or more targets for processing. Targets include AWS Lambda functions, Amazon SNS topics, Amazon SQS queues, streams in Amazon Kinesis Streams, or built-in targets.

Logs   Amazon CloudWatch Logs collects infrastructure, services, and host-based log information from all of the systems, applications, and AWS services in a single centralized location. CloudWatch Logs enables you to search all the logs, regardless of their source, as a single and consistent flow of events ordered by time. Customers can use CloudWatch Logs to watch the logs for specific phrases, values, or patterns and execute an action if any are found. For example, customers could set up an alarm on the number of errors that occur in the system logs. Then, customers can view the original log data and attempt to identify the source of the problem if needed. Log data can be stored and accessed for as long as the customers need using highly durable, low-cost storage.

Dashboards   Amazon CloudWatch Dashboards creates a single consolidated view of all your resources across AWS regions and accounts. It is a highly customizable service that lets you put together in one place all the desired metrics from the default available for each service of custom metrics created by you. It provides a common view of critical resource and application measurements that can be shared by team members for faster communication flow during operational events.

AWS CloudTrail

The same way Amazon CloudWatch is meant to monitor and log everything in the cloud, AWS CloudTrail is for auditing and recording. It records AWS API usage in the AWS account, and by recording the APIs, it also includes actions taken through command-line tools, the SDKs, the AWS Management Console, or other AWS services. The event history simplifies audit analysis, troubleshooting, and resource change tracking. In addition, customers can use AWS CloudTrail to detect anomalous activity in all the AWS accounts. These features make AWS CloudTrail the perfect tool for governance, compliance, and auditing.

A CloudTrail event enables you to answer the following questions:

- Who made the API call?
- When was the API call made?
- What was the API call?
- Which resources were acted upon in the API call?
- Where was the API call made from?

For a native AWS database service like Amazon DynamoDB, AWS CloudTrail itself is enough for auditing purposes because every action happens through an API call. But this might not be the case for relational databases on Amazon RDS. By using just AWS Cloud-Trail, you won't be able to know who accessed or modified the data or when the data was accessed or modified, or how a specific user gained access to the data. In those cases, you need to leverage the native database engine auditing capabilities, like the MySQL Audit Plugin, Oracle Audit log, or SQL Server Audit option. For each one of those cases, you will be able to see the audit logs either directly on Amazon RDS console, in CloudWatch Logs, or in Amazon S3, respectively.

CloudTrail is a useful tool for auditing but is not the only one; there is another key player in the cloud auditing landscape: AWS Config.

AWS Config provides customers with a detailed inventory of each AWS resource and its current configuration on each AWS account. It continuously listens for configuration changes to these resources (e.g., DynamoDB-provisioned capacities, RDS instance status, DocumentDB scaling events, etc.). It also identifies how a resource was configured at any point in time and sends a notification via Amazon SNS whenever a resource becomes noncompliant. Customers can also trigger automatic remediations via AWS System Manager automation documents or AWS Lambda functions.

You can define your ideal configuration of AWS by applying AWS Config rules. AWS Config provides customizable, predefined rules to help you get started, but you can also create rules of your own. If a resource violates a rule, AWS Config flags the resource and the rule as noncompliant and notifies you through Amazon SNS. You can use dashboards for visualizing compliance and identifying offending changes.

Summary

This chapter covered the basic concepts of the AWS cloud, such as its global footprint, networking, security, storage, and operations related to database services. This foundation will help you understand the following chapters and let you stitch together your current IT knowledge and the cloud world.

Chapter

3

Purpose-Built Databases

THE AWS CERTIFIED DATABASE – SPECIALTY EXAM OBJECTIVES COVERED IN THIS CHAPTER MAY INCLUDE, BUT ARE NOT LIMITED TO, THE FOLLOWING:

✓ **Domain 1.0: Workload-Specific Database Design**

- 1.1 Select appropriate database services for specific types of data and workloads.

- 1.3 Design database solutions for performance, compliance, and scalability.

- 1.4 Compare the costs of database solutions.

In this chapter, we will cover data store characteristics: access patterns, latency, scaling, transaction support, consistency, volume, durability, availability, security/compliance, business logic, and cost. We will also cover how these characteristics correlate with each other to help identify the best purpose-built database for specific uses. Then, we will present the fully managed database services available today in AWS, comparing their characteristics.

Data store Concepts

The history of databases is closely linked to the evolution of computational structures. With advances in the areas of processors, volatile memory, and persistent memory, new optimization and query execution strategies were created.

You can think about the evolution of database systems as being similar to the evolution of animal species. In the mammal family, to which we all belong, there are beings that fly, beings that swim, and beings that walk—vast is the myriad of data types. It would not be interesting, nor even practical, to subject a mammal that has evolved to fly—with lighter bone structures—to swim and dive in the deepest parts of the ocean. This flying mammal did not evolve to possess the respiratory structures necessary to withstand long dives, and it does not have the thermal protection to withstand the low temperatures of the oceans.

In the same way that animal species have evolved and become specialized to have a more harmonious and efficient relationship with their habitat, applications have evolved over the decades, demanding specialization to achieve greater efficiency. As systems and applications have evolved, whether in the adoption of new programming paradoxes or in the creation of new design patterns, it has created a need for specialized data structures.

Before you can understand what purpose-built databases are, you must first understand the main characteristics of a data store. We say *data store* instead of *database* purposely so that we can analyze the data without any particular bias.

This section details the data store characteristics that drive purpose-built database decisions. We selected these characteristics and have applied them in the field successfully over time—but this isn't a definitive list. As database engines evolve, new functionalities and limits arise, requiring revision of these characteristics to ensure effectiveness. By analyzing these characteristics together, it's possible to work backward to the purpose-built database that fits your requirements.

Data Access Patterns

Understanding an application's data access patterns is crucial to determining whether the data store is a best fit for relational or nonrelational engines. *Data access patterns* are the conjunction of requests that will be executed in the database by users or applications. This concept is defined by the PIE theorem—the iron triangle of purpose.

- *P* stands for pattern flexibility. Pattern flexibility enables random access patterns and ad hoc queries, leveraging the database optimizer mechanism to find the best access path possible. *Ad hoc queries* are requests executed on demand by users or independent processes, not mapped to defined data access patterns.

- *I* stands for infinite scale. A data store can increase throughput without practical limits.

- *E* stands for efficiency. A data store will predictably deliver required latency at all times.

Like the CAP theorem (consistency, availability, partition—explained in detail in Chapter 1, "Databases—from Your Server to AWS Cloud"), data store characteristics are defined in pairs. PE (pattern flexibility and efficiency) represents relational databases, IE (infinite scale and efficiency) represents nonrelational databases, and PI (pattern flexibility and infinite scale) represents relational analytical data warehouse databases. If the data access patterns are known, it's possible to create an efficient nonrelational data model by preparing the access path—for example, picking the right indexes and preparing the dataset to be queried. If the application design needs to give users pattern flexibility and the ability to perform any query, even inefficient ones, most likely you will have a relational data store in front of you. On the other hand, if you have a well-defined set of queries being performed by the application, the data store could be either relational or nonrelational. Analyzing data access patterns in conjunction with the characteristics of the following sections will help you identify the right data store based on the workload requirements.

Latency

Ask yourself these questions: What are the latency requirements for this data store? Should queries be satisfied in microseconds, milliseconds, seconds, or even minutes? Can the latency requirements be relaxed as the data store grows, or must we provide predictable latency levels despite data store growth? What is the expected latency for reads and writes?

Scaling

If the data store request rate is not evenly distributed through the day, the data store must be able to scale—either on compute or on storage capacity (reads per second, writes per second). We have two subdimensions of scaling: throughput and concurrency.

- **Throughput:** What are the expected queries per second (QPS) or transactions per second (TPS) for this data store over a period of time? Does the data store need to withstand abrupt variations in throughput, from low (few queries per second) to very high (thousands or even millions of queries per second) in a matter of milliseconds? Is the throughput evenly distributed through the day?

■ **Concurrency:** Does the data store need to provide concurrency mechanisms for the application? What happens when different database calls request to update the same item or row or document at the same time? To address this requirement, relational data stores implement a combination of concurrency mechanisms such as two-phase locking (2PL) and timestamp ordering (TO), which derives multiversion concurrency control (MVCC) and optimistic concurrency control (OCC). It is important to understand the concurrency requirements of the data store versus what mechanisms are provided by each purpose-built database. Amazon DynamoDB, for example, uses the OCC method.

Transaction Support

Should the data store be able to deliver ACID-compliant transactions? (We defined ACID in Chapter 1.) Over time, more and more nonrelational databases have started offering ACID transaction support as an alternative to BASE transactions (basically available, soft state, eventual consistency), which were available in the first implementations of nonrelational databases. It's crucial also to understand the isolation-level requirements for the data store, meaning the levels defined as read committed, read uncommitted, repeatable reads, and serializable—with the last two related to MVCC and 2PL, respectively, as explained previously with concurrency.

Consistency

Eventual consistency does not guarantee 100 percent effective availability. Amazon DynamoDB, for instance, offers a 99.99 percent SLA for standard tables, using consistent reads or eventual consistent reads and thus not improving availability. Eventual consistency tends to be less complex to achieve, which leads to more cost-effective designs. If a data store can accommodate eventual consistency, consider adopting it. For example, caching data can become stale, serving a previous version of data manipulated until the change propagates to the cache. Caching strategies deliver, in the majority of scenarios, eventual consistency.

Volume

What is the expected volume to be stored on the data store, per item or row or document? By understanding volume requirements, you can identify possible target engines. For example, as of the writing of this book, Amazon DynamoDB has a limit per item size of 400 KB, and Amazon Keyspaces has a maximum item size of 1 MB. After denormalizing the data, if each item is bigger than 400 KB, Amazon Keyspaces becomes a better candidate to host this data store. What are the column data type requirements? Each engine has its set of supported data types. Validating this data store requirement against the available options is crucial to identify the best suited purpose-built database. Dimensions of volume include the following:

- **Item:** What is the size of each individual item, document, or row?
- **Pagination:** What is the maximum amount of data fetched from the database to the application on each application call?
- **Data store:** What is the designed size of the entire data store?

Durability

Does the data store hold ephemeral data? Ephemeral data could be reinstated with minimal effort, like application parameters applied on the data store as an artifact of a development pipeline or data that will exist only during the lifespan of a session or business process, like the "move to cart" function on an e-commerce website. By understanding this data store characteristic, you can leverage specific purpose-built database features, such as Amazon DynamoDB time-to-live (TTL) or caching services like Amazon ElastiCache. If durability is crucial for the application, does the data store support storage multiplexing, sustaining reliability in the case of hard-drive failure, node failure, or even availability zone failures? For example, Amazon Aurora delivers high durability, replicating data six times in three availability zones.

Availability

What are the recovery point objective (RPO) and recovery time objective (RTO) requirements for this data store? Does the data store need to be available in different AWS regions supporting reads or reads and writes?

Security/Compliance

Does the data store need to comply with specific regulations or standards like PCI DSS, HIPAA, SOC, or FedRAMP? Does the data store need to integrate with external authorization, authentication, or protocols like Kerberos? As an example, as of the writing of this book, ElastiCache for Memcached is not compliant with PCI standards. If a caching strategy must be adopted, ElastiCache for Redis must be used instead.

Business Logic

Does the data store need to store or run application code such as functions, procedures, and packages? Can this business logic be decoupled from the data store, leveraging external compute environments such as AWS Lambda, Amazon ECS, Amazon Elastic Kubernetes Service, or even AWS Step Functions?

Cost

Cost is an important part of any real architecture. However, it should be considered after reviewing the other characteristics, introducing the possibility to relax a previous data store requirement in favor of cost. For example, if low throughput (few accesses per day), high availability, and very low latency (microseconds) are required from the data store, Amazon ElastiCache for Redis is an interesting choice. If this latency requirement could be relaxed in favor of cost, Amazon DynamoDB could be a better solution, leveraging its serverless architecture and consumption models.

Purpose-Built Databases on AWS

Now that you understand the main characteristics of data stores and the diverse requirements they have to address, thinking about database specialization becomes natural as a means to create more efficient data stores, enabling support to ever-evolving application requirements.

This section presents a nonexhaustive list of these main purpose-built database characteristics, and its details and use cases will be given through the next chapters of this book. Note that some characteristics will change over time as a result of product innovations and improvements, so always check the latest documentation for each database service.

In the field, reassessing the best data store for application requirements usually happens in the following scenarios:

- A compelling event or recurrent issue demanding application revision
- A new product or service being built from scratch
- A refactoring of legacy applications
- Benefits of the data store outweighing required application changes and operational learning curve

Relational Databases

In the relational database category, the following database services are presented (see Table 3.1):

- **Amazon Relational Database Service (RDS):** This offers a choice of popular relational database engines: PostgreSQL, MySQL, Oracle, SQL Server, and MariaDB.
- **Amazon Aurora:** Available in PostgreSQL-compatible and MySQL-compatible versions, Aurora offers scalability, elasticity, durability, high availability, and disaster recovery features.
- **Amazon Redshift:** This is a columnar relational database built for analytical and data warehousing workloads.

TABLE 3.1   AWS Relational Database Services

	Amazon RDS	Amazon Aurora	Amazon Redshift
Access Patterns	Flexible, using SQL queries.		
Latency	Milliseconds to minutes.	Milliseconds to minutes.	Seconds to hours.
Scaling	Scale writes vertically; reads horizontally in minutes (up to 5 replicas). Throughput very low to high Strong concurrency mechanisms.	Scale writes vertically; reads horizontally in seconds using Aurora Auto Scaling (up to 15 replicas). Throughput very low to high. Strong concurrency mechanisms.	Scale writes and reads; elastic resize with concurrency scaling in minutes. Throughput very low to high. Strong concurrency mechanisms.
Transaction Support	Fully ACID compatible.		
Consistency	Strong consistency.		
Volume	GB to TB (64 TB max).	GB to TB (128 TB max).	GB to PB.
Durability	High.	Very high (six copies).	Very high (three copies).
Availability	Multi-AZ for one additional AZ + read replicas.	Could span multiple AZs in a region with Aurora replicas; could span multiple regions with the Aurora global database.	Redshift Cluster could be relocated to another AZ in case of AZ failure.
Security and Compliance	Support for encryption in transit and at rest; compliant with PCI, HIPAA, and SOC, among others (details at aws.amazon.com/compliance/services-in-scope).		
Business Logic	The application logic could be hosted at the database level.		

(continues)

TABLE 3.1   AWS Relational Database Services *(continued)*

	Amazon RDS	Amazon Aurora	Amazon Redshift
Cost	Cost based on the following: • Number and type of nodes • Amount and type of storage • Licensing for commercial engines • High-availability options (multi-AZ and read replicas) • Storage consumed by backups	Cost based on the following: • Number and type of nodes • Amount of storage • Amount of I/O operations • Storage consumed by backups • Aurora capacity units (ACUs) consumed for Aurora Serverless	Cost based on the following: • Number and type of nodes • Amount of storage • Storage consumed by backups • Data scanned by Redshift Spectrum

Nonrelational Databases

In the nonrelational database category, the following database services are available (see Table 3.2):

- **Amazon DynamoDB:** Serverless key-value database; ideal for mission-critical, low-latency workloads at any scale

- **Amazon DocumentDB (with MongoDB compatibility):** JSON document database with scalability, elasticity, and high availability

- **Amazon Keyspaces (for Apache Cassandra):** Serverless wide-column database, which delivers low latency at any scale

- **Amazon Neptune:** Reliable graph database compatible with Gremlin and SPARQL queries

- **Amazon Timestream:** Serverless time-series database; ideal for massive ingestion workloads ordered by time

- **Amazon QLDB:** Serverless ledger database, which delivers immutability and cryptographically verifiable data manipulations

- **Amazon ElastiCache:** In-memory key-value database; available in Memcached and Redis versions

- **Amazon MemoryDB:** In-memory key-value database; based on Redis, with persistence layer embedded

TABLE 3.2   AWS Nonrelational Database Services

	Amazon DynamoDB	Amazon DocumentDB (with MongoDB Compatibility)	Amazon Keyspaces (for Apache Cassandra)
Access Patterns	Known and predefined during application design, programmatically access through API calls.	Known and predefined during application design, flexible access patterns enabled by database optimizer, access through libraries and drivers connecting to the database endpoint.	Known and pre-defined during application design, programmatically access through API calls and Cassandra Query Language (CQL).
Latency	Milliseconds.	Milliseconds to minutes.	Milliseconds.
Scaling	Scale writes and reads in milliseconds without practical limits. Throughput very low to very high. Light concurrency mechanisms using ordered timestamps.	Scale writes vertically and reads horizontally in minutes using DocumentDB replica instances (up to 15). Throughput very low to high. Strong concurrency mechanisms.	Scale writes and reads in milliseconds without practical limits. Throughput very low to very high. Light concurrency mechanisms using ordered timestamps.
Transaction Support	ACID support in transactions.	ACID support in transactions.	Limited ACID compatibility.
Consistency	Eventual and strong consistency options, depending on used isolation levels.		
Volume	GB to TB. Maximum item size 400 KB. Maximum fetch per call 1 MB; paginated for larger than 1 MB.	GB to TB (64 TB Max). Maximum item size 16 MB.	GB to TB. Maximum item size 1 MB. Maximum fetch per call 1 MB; paginated for larger than 1 MB.
Durability	Very high.	Very high (six copies).	Very high (three copies).
Availability	Regional service—available in multiple AZs after deployment. Multi-regional service using DynamoDB global tables.	Could span multiple AZs in a region with DocumentDB replicas; could span multiple regions with DocumentDB global clusters.	Regional service—available in multiple AZs after deployment.

(continues)

TABLE 3.2 AWS Nonrelational Database Services *(continued)*

	Amazon DynamoDB	Amazon DocumentDB (with MongoDB Compatibility)	Amazon Keyspaces (for Apache Cassandra)
Security and Compliance	Support for encryption in transit and at rest. Compliant with PCI, HIPAA, and SOC, among others (details at aws.amazon.com/compliance/ services-in-scope).		
Business Logic	The application logic cannot be hosted at the database level.		
Cost	Cost based on the following: ▪ Table class (standard or infrequent access) ▪ Amount of storage ▪ Write and read capacity units ▪ DynamoDB-specific features such as global tables ▪ Storage consumed by backups	Cost based on the following: ▪ Number and type of nodes ▪ Amount of storage ▪ Amount of I/O operations ▪ Storage consumed by backups	Cost based on the following: ▪ Amount of storage ▪ Write and read request units ▪ Storage consumed by backups ▪ Time-to-live of items

	Amazon Neptune	Amazon Timestream	Amazon QLDB
Access Patterns	Known and predefined during application design, access through API calls and tools like Neptune Workbench and Languages like Gremlin and SPARQL.	Known and predefined during application design for ingestion, flexible for analytical queries using SQL Language. Access through API calls.	Known and predefined during application design, access through API calls and tools like PartiQL and Amazon QLDB Shell.
Latency	Milliseconds to minutes.	Milliseconds to minutes.	Milliseconds to seconds.
Scaling	Scale writes vertically and reads horizontally in seconds using Neptune replicas (up to 15). Throughput very low to high. Strong concurrency mechanisms.	Scale writes and reads in milliseconds without practical limits, with adaptive autoscaling. Throughput very low to very high. Light concurrency mechanisms using timestamps.	Scale writes and reads in milliseconds without practical limits. Throughput very low to very high. Very strong concurrency mechanisms.

	Amazon Neptune	Amazon Timestream	Amazon QLDB
Transaction Support	ACID compatible.	No ACID compatibility.	ACID compatible.
Consistency	Strong consistency.	Eventual consistency.	Strong consistency.
Volume	GB to TB (64–128 TB max).	GB to PB.	GB to TB. Maximum item size 128 KB, maximum transaction size of 4 MB.
Durability	Very high (six copies).	Very high.	Very high.
Availability	Could span multiple AZs in a region with Neptune replicas.	Span multiple AZs in a region.	Span multiple AZs in a region.
Security and Compliance	Support for encryption in transit and at rest. Compliant with PCI, HIPAA, and SOC, among others (details at aws.amazon.com/compliance/ services-in-scope).		
Business Logic	The application logic cannot be hosted at the database level.		
Cost	Cost based on the following: ■ Number and type of nodes ■ Amount of storage ■ Amount of I/O operations ■ Storage consumed by backups	Cost based on the following: ■ Amount of storage ■ Amount of data written ■ Amount of data scanned by queries ■ Amount of memory consumed by queries ■ Storage consumed by backups	Cost based on the following: ■ Amount of storage ■ Write and read requests ■ Storage consumed by backups

	Amazon ElastiCache	Amazon MemoryDB
Access Patterns	Known and predefined during application design; access through libraries and drivers connecting to database endpoint.	Known and predefined during application design; access through libraries and drivers connecting to database endpoint.
Latency	Microseconds to milliseconds.	Microseconds to milliseconds.
Scaling	Vertical scaling in ElastiCache for Memcached; vertical and horizontal scaling in ElastiCache for Redis. Throughput high to very high, light concurrency mechanisms.	Vertical and horizontal scaling. Throughput high to very high. Light concurrency mechanisms.
Transaction Support	No ACID compatibility.	No ACID compatibility.

(continues)

TABLE 3.2 AWS Nonrelational Database Services *(continued)*

	Amazon ElastiCache	Amazon MemoryDB
Consistency	Strong consistency on primary nodes, and eventual consistency on read nodes.	Strong consistency on primary nodes, and eventual consistency on read nodes.
Volume	GB to TB.	GB to TB.
Durability	Low (ephemeral data).	Very high.
Availability	Single node for Memcached. ElastiCache for Redis could span multiple AZs and multiple regions using global data stores.	Could span multiple AZs in a region.
Security and Compliance	Support for encryption in transit and at rest. Compliant with PCI, HIPAA, and SOC, among others—except when using Memcached (check aws.amazon.com/ compliance/services-in-scope).	Support for encryption in transit and at rest. Compliant with PCI, HIPAA, and SOC, among others (check aws.amazon.com/compliance/ services-in-scope).
Business Logic	The application logic could not be hosted at the database level.	
Cost	Cost based on the following: ■ Number and type of nodes ■ Storage consumed by backups	Cost based on the following: ■ Number and type of nodes ■ Amount of data written ■ Storage consumed by backups

Summary

This chapter discussed the main characteristics of data stores, working backward from these characteristics to AWS purpose-built database services.

In the next chapters, we will dive deep into each purpose-built database service and discuss key topics such as high availability, monitoring, backups, and best practices.

Exam Essentials

Understand the characteristics of data stores. Leverage the 11 data store characteristics presented in this chapter and gather this information with developers, stakeholders, and application architects.

Be able to identify whether a workload requires a relational database.   Leverage the PIE theorem to evaluate whether the application requirements are best suited for a relational database, with PI (Pattern Flexibility and Infinite Scale) or PE (Pattern Flexibility and Efficiency) characteristics.

Be able to identify whether a workload requires a nonrelational database.   Leverage the PIE theorem to evaluate whether the application requirements are best suited for a nonrelational database, with IE (Infinite Scale and Efficiency) characteristics.

Be able to identify whether a workload requires a specialized nonrelational database.   Leverage the PIE theorem to evaluate whether the application requirements are best suited for a nonrelational database, with IE (Infinite Scale and Efficiency) characteristics, and specialized datasets, like graph, time series, or ledger.

Identify the best purpose-built database for each application requirement.   Be able to map data store requirements to the most suited purpose-built database, taking advantage of the characteristics of each database-managed service.

Review Questions

1. A DBA is identifying the best purpose-built database for a new product. Application requirements include flexible data access patterns, millisecond latency, ability to scale out and scale in reads on demand, multiregion availability, and full ACID compliance. Which of the following should the DBA choose?

   A. None; no AWS database service fits these requirements.

   B. Amazon DocumentDB

   C. Amazon Neptune

   D. Amazon Aurora

2. A DBA is working on an application refactor project and needs to propose the best purpose-built database with these requirements: ACID transactions, global multimaster with the ability to perform reads and writes in more than one AWS region, predictable millisecond latency for reads, and ability to scale out and scale in on demand. Which of the following should the DBA choose?

   A. Amazon RDS for Oracle

   B. Amazon DynamoDB

   C. Amazon Timestream

   D. Amazon DocumentDB

3. A DBA is analyzing a problematic application with the following requirements: millisecond latency for reads, predefined access patterns, 600 KB per item, and ability to update individual attribute values for a team very proficient in the SQL language. Which purpose-built database services would address these requirements? (Choose two.)

   A. Amazon DynamoDB

   B. Amazon QLDB

   C. Amazon Keyspaces

   D. Amazon Aurora

4. A DBA is working on a project for Wall Street where data immutability and auditability are crucial. Which is the best purpose-built database for these requirements?

   A. Amazon Keyspaces

   B. Amazon Timestream

   C. Amazon QLDB

   D. Amazon DocumentDB

5. A retail company is searching for a new database for its inventory system. Inventory data is received in JSON format with a typical payload of 2 MB per item; access patterns are well defined; traffic is predictable; reads could scale horizontally; and the application will query nested JSON attributes and can't remodel the data at this time. Which is the best purpose-built database for these requirements?

   A. Amazon Neptune

   B. Amazon DynamoDB

   C. Amazon DocumentDB

   D. Amazon Keyspaces

6. A financial services company is searching for a new database for its transaction history. Transaction data is received in JSON format with a typical payload of 40 KB per item; access patterns are well defined; traffic is unpredictable and could scale from hundreds to millions of requests per second in 1 minute; applications need predictable latency; and data should be retrieved in few milliseconds. Which is the best purpose-built database for these requirements?

   A. Amazon Timestream

   B. Amazon DynamoDB

   C. Amazon DocumentDB

   D. Amazon Keyspaces

7. A financial services company is searching for a new database for the accounts API. Transaction data is received in JSON format with a typical payload of 80 KB per item; access patterns are well defined; traffic is unpredictable and could scale from hundreds to millions of requests per second in 1 minute; the application needs predictable latency; and data should be retrieved in few milliseconds. Developers are used to running CQL queries on the database, and to reduce friction, the new database should provide this functionality. Which is the best purpose-built database for these requirements?

   A. Amazon Timestream

   B. Amazon DynamoDB

   C. Amazon DocumentDB

   D. Amazon Keyspaces

8. An automotive company is searching for a new database for its order system. Order data is received in JSON format with a typical payload of 10 KB per item; a data store should enable aggregation functions directly at the database layer. Which would be the best purpose-built database for this requirement?

   A. Amazon QLDB

   B. Amazon DynamoDB

   C. Amazon Keyspaces

   D. Amazon DocumentDB

9. A company is searching for a new database to support a global-scale application. The new database should be available in multiple regions and receive reads and writes in each region, updating, deleting, and inserting in the same data store. Which is the best purpose-built database for these requirements?

    A. Amazon QLDB

    B. Amazon DynamoDB

    C. Amazon Keyspaces

    D. Amazon DocumentDB

10. What is the most cost-effective solution for a data store required to deliver millisecond latency with an unpredictable number of concurrent users through the day, ranging from zero users to thousands of users in a matter of seconds?

    A. Amazon RDS sized for the peak, with multiple nodes

    B. Amazon ElastiCache for Redis

    C. Amazon QLDB

    D. Amazon DynamoDB with on-demand capacity

Management and Operations, Database Security, Monitoring and Troubleshooting per Workload

Chapter 4: Transactional Databases on AWS

Chapter 5: Low Latency Response Time for Your Apps and APIs

Chapter 6: Document Databases in the Cloud

Chapter 7: Better Places Other Than Databases to Store Large Objects

Chapter 8: Deliver Valuable Information at the Speed Your Business Needs

Chapter 9: Discovering Relationships Using Graph Databases

Chapter 10: Immutable Database and Traceable Transactions

Chapter 11: Caching Data with In-memory Databases

Chapter

4

Relational Databases on AWS

THE AWS CERTIFIED DATABASE - SPECIALTY EXAM OBJECTIVES COVERED IN THIS CHAPTER MAY INCLUDE, BUT ARE NOT LIMITED TO, THE FOLLOWING:

✓ **Domain 1: Workload-Specific Database Design**

- 1.2 Determine strategies for disaster recovery and high availability.

- 1.3 Design database solutions for performance, compliance, and scalability.

- 1.4 Compare the costs of database solutions.

✓ **Domain 2: Deployment and Migration**

- 2.2 Determine data preparation and migration strategies.

- 2.3 Execute and validate data migration.

✓ **Domain 3: Management and Operations**

- 3.1 Determine maintenance tasks and processes.

- 3.2 Determine backup and restore strategies.

- 3.3 Manage the operational environment of a database solution.

✓ **Domain 4: Monitoring and troubleshooting**

- 4.2 Troubleshoot and resolve common database issues.

- 4.3 Optimize database performance.

✓ **Domain 5: Database security**

- 5.1 Encrypt data at rest and in transit.

- 5.2 Evaluate auditing solutions.

- 5.3 Determine access control and authentication mechanisms.

- 5.4 Recognize potential security vulnerabilities within database solutions.

Understanding transactional databases is important to pass the AWS Certified Database - Specialty exam. It also helps to improve the database skills you use in your daily job, especially when reviewing important topics such as understanding requirements and defining maintenance strategies for relational database management.

Relational Databases

Edgar Frank "Ted" Codd developed the "relational databases" concept in 1970 at IBM. After that, several companies and open-source communities implemented the relational model.

Relational databases store data in tables. The tables store data organized in columns and rows. In this model, the tables have references, using primary keys and foreign key constraints to enforce uniqueness and guarantee referential consistency.

The following are purposes of relational databases:

- **Supporting transactions:** A relational database handles a complex statement that changes data from different tables as a single unit of work and guarantees the commitment of all SQL statements within the transaction. If any statement within the transaction fails, the relational database will roll back all SQL statements inside the transaction declaration.

- **Avoiding data redundancy:** The relational database is based on normalization rules when storing data inside the tables to prevent data duplicity, inconsistencies, and integrity loss. It also relies on enforcement rules using the constraints to prevent storing inconsistent data.

Relational databases use Structured Query Language (SQL) for data manipulation.

Several commercial relational databases are widely used, including Db2, Oracle, Informix, and Microsoft SQL Server.

After some years, we saw the development of open-source relational databases. The MySQL community released the first MySQL database in 1995, the PostgreSQL community released its first database in 1997, and the MariaDB community released its database in 2009.

On AWS, you can deploy relational databases on Amazon EC2 instances, where you manage the operating system and database software by yourself. You can also choose Amazon Relational Database Service (Amazon RDS), a managed database service. We will discuss the differences and the benefits of choosing each type of solution.

Structured Query Language

The Structured Query Language (SQL) uses specific commands—such as `create`, `drop`, `select`, `insert`, `update`, and `delete`—to execute the statements. The SQL standard separates the commands into the following categories:

- **Data Definition Language (DDL):** DDLs are commands to create objects such as create table, drop table, create index, alter, and truncate. The following command creates a table called "students" with four columns, creates a primary key on the id column, alters the table "students" to add a column called "address," and executes truncate to exclude all rows in the "students" table.

```
create table students
(
        id datatype,
        name datatype,
        age datatype,
        dateofbirth datatype
);
create index pk_students_id on students (id);
alter table students add (address datatype);
truncate table students;
drop table students;
```

- **Data Query Language (DQL):** DQLs are commands to select data from tables. For example, the following statement is querying the column's id and name from the "students" table and is filtering people younger than 10 years old:

```
select id, name
from students
where age > 10;
```

- **Data Manipulation Language (DML):** DMLs are commands to insert, update, or delete data on tables. For example, the following command inserts a row into the "students" table:

```
insert into students (
id,
name,
age,
dateofbirth,
address
)
```

```
values
      (
      '001',
      'John Smith',
      38,
      '01/01/1983',
      '80 Queen Street, Auckland Central, Auckland 1010'
      );
update students set address = '123 Avenue Road, Greenmeadows, Napier 2112'
where id = '001';
delete students where id = '001';
```

- **Data Control Language (DCL):** DCL commands are used to grant access to the tables and stored procedures to users. For example, the first command will grant the user "dave" permission to execute select and update on the "students" table, and the second command will revoke the permissions:

```
grant select, update on students to dave;
revoke select, update on students from dave;
```

- **Transaction Control Language (TCL):** TCL commands control transactions in the database. For example, the following statements will control when the transaction is committed or rolled back or define savepoints inside the SQL code:

```
Commit;
Rollback;
Savepoint savepoint_name;
```

The following example demonstrates two SQL statements within a transaction:

```
begin
      insert into students
      (
      id,
      name,
      age,
      dateofbirth,
      address
      )
      values
      (
      '002',
      'Joseph Miller',
      42,
      '01/01/1980',
```

```
        'Triq Alamein Pembroke PBK, 1710, Malta'
        );
        update class_attendance set
(
date = current_date(),
        status = 'OK'
)
            where student_id = '001'
            and class_id = '1024';
            commit;
end;
```

Developers and architects choose relational databases to support transactional environments because of the capacity to commit or roll back an entire transaction of all statements if something goes wrong. All relational databases (PostgreSQL, MySQL, Oracle, SQL Server, and others) can handle it.

Amazon DynamoDB also handles a single all-or-nothing action using `TranctWriteItems` or `TransactGetItems`. We discuss this in Chapter 5, "Low Latency Response Time for Your Apps and APIs."

Amazon DocumentDB has the transactions capability, which we'll discuss in Chapter 6, "Document Databases in the Cloud."

The capacity for handling transactions' integrity is known as ACID (which stands for atomicity, consistency, isolation, and durability).

- Atomicity refers to the integrity of the entire database transaction and not just to a single SQL statement. If one transaction operation fails, the database rolls back the whole transaction.

- Consistency refers to following appropriate validation rules. It means that if the data complies with the validation rules, the data will persist.

- Isolation refers to the capacity for handling multiple concurrent transactions, and one transaction won't impact the data integrity of the others and vice versa.

- Durability refers to the capacity for saving data once a transaction has completed. Even if an unexpected failure in the system occurs (e.g., hardware failure), the committed data will be protected and consistent.

Install and Manage Databases Yourself

A typical way to deploy databases on AWS is to install and manage the database by yourself on Amazon EC2 or even in bare-metal instances.

You'll need to keep the following in mind:

- Certification matrix between database software and operating system
- The supported operating systems on Amazon EC2

- Filesystem's requirements
- Sizing elements (IOPS, CPU, and memory usage)

Whenever you choose to install database software on EC2, you must validate if the database software is supported and certified with the operating system. Keep in mind that all of that information depends on the product lifetime of the database software's versions (even proprietary or open-source/community) and that you need to keep it up to date accordingly.

I/O Requirement

An I/O requirement is an essential but basic configuration for database performance. We strongly recommend collecting usage metrics before resource allocation. The appropriate storage assignment, such as gp2, gp3, or Provisioned IOPS (PIOPS), is also critical due to costs.

Amazon Elastic Block Store (Amazon EBS) is the block-storage service for Amazon Elastic Compute Cloud (Amazon EC2). When assigning EBS volumes to the EC2, they are raw and unformatted block devices. To use the volumes, you must mount them as devices for the operating system. You can change the configuration of an EBS dynamically.

Amazon EBS has the following classes of volume types available to support different workloads:

- Solid-state drives (SSDs) are optimal for transactional workloads involving frequent read/write operations with small I/O size and the predominant high IOPS metric. SSD drives are the most commonly used for relational databases.

- Hard disk drives (HDDs) are optimal for handling large streaming workloads, and the throughput metric is dominant.

Amazon EBS also has previous generation hard disk drives. They are appropriate for workloads with small datasets and infrequent access, where performance is not a requirement. We do not recommend this category for transactional databases.

Solid-state drives have two classes:

- General-purpose SSDs deliver a balance between price and performance. Most workloads benefit from general-purpose SSD drives.

- Provisioned IOPS SSDs deliver high performance for business-critical, I/O-intensive, low-latency, or high-throughput workloads.

Table 4.1 shows each volume type configuration.

TABLE 4.1   I/O Requirements and Configurations

	General-Purpose SSD		Provisioned IOPS SSD		
Volume type	gp3	gp2	io2 Block Express ‡	io2	io1
Durability	99.8%–99.9% durability (0.1%–0.2% annual failure rate)	99.8%–99.9% durability (0.1%–0.2% annual failure rate)	99.999% durability (0.001% annual failure rate)		99.8%–99.9% durability (0.1%–0.2% annual failure rate)
Use cases	Low-latency interactive apps Development and test environments		Workloads that require submillisecond latency, and sustained IOPS performance or more than 64,000 IOPS or 1,000 MiB/s of throughput	Workloads that require sustained IOPS or more than 16,000 I/O-intensive database workloads	
Volume size	1 GiB–6 TiB		4 GiB–64 TiB	4 GiB–16 TiB	
Max IOPS per volume (16 KiB I/O)	16,000		256,000	64,000 †	
Max throughput per volume	1,000 MiB/s	Between 128 MiB/s and 250 MiB/s, according to the volume size.	4,000 MiB/s	1,000 MiB/s †	

Source: Adapted from AWS, https://docs.aws.amazon.com/AWSEC2/latest/UserGuide/ebs-volume-types.html

† Only instances built on Nitro System provisioned can guarantee maximum IOPS and throughput with more than 32,000 IOPS. Other instance classes guarantee up to 32,000 IOPS and 500 MiB/s.
‡ Only specific regions have io2 Block Express as an opt-in preview.

The following is important information to keep in mind when planning the database storage:

- Volume sizes smaller than or equal to 170 GiB provide the maximum throughput of 128 MiB/s.

- Volumes larger than 170 GiB but smaller than 334 GiB provide the maximum throughput of 250 MiB/s if burst credits are available.

- Volumes larger than 334 GiB provide 250 MiB/s regardless of burst credit.

Managing Databases on EC2

Managing the databases on EC2 is similar to managing them on premises. There are some reasons for managing databases on EC2 by yourself:

- To have access to the operating system level, libraries, and directories
- To have access to the database standard administration user (root, sys, system, sa, etc.)

When using databases deployed on EC2, it's necessary to implement the backup routines according to the RDBMS software. For example:

- Oracle over RMAN backup routines and storing the backup pieces in Amazon S3 use the expiration rules based on RMAN backup retention.
- SQL Server backup routines configured using file gateway to S3
- PostgreSQL backup routines configured using `pg_dump`
- MySQL backup routines configured using `mysqldump` or Percona XtraBackup
- MariaDB backup routines configured using `mysqldump` or `mariabackup`

Always remember that the backup solution will be the native backup tool of the given database deployed on EC2.

Even the backup retention and expiration rules must be defined according to the business needs. S3 rules will be very useful on this control.

Monitoring Databases on EC2

Monitoring databases on EC2 is similar to monitoring them on premises. It is strongly recommended to configure notifications when thresholds are reached. All database operations are essential to monitor—for example, when memory usage reaches more than 95 percent, when swap activity starts, or when the CPU reaches 70 percent of use.

Monitoring also is essential for sizing the CPU allocation and EBS performance requirements. On one hand, if the environment is constantly near the physical resource limits for CPU and memory, additional allocation probably will be necessary to change the instance class. On the other hand, if the environment is constantly in low-usage metrics, it will be better to change to lower-size instance types. Amazon EC2 allows you to change the instance class for increasing or decreasing whenever you need to, and it will cause a reboot.

For the system's health, it is essential to monitor the following:

- Operating system logs, to check if there are errors
- CPU usage
- Memory usage

For the database health, it is essential to monitor the following:

- Database logs, to check if there are errors related to the database software operations and the sessions operations
- Number of active database connections
- Slow queries
- Database buffers' efficiency (cache hit ratio)

Scaling Databases

There are some options to scale a relational database. The most common are vertical scaling (changing to bigger instance types) and horizontal scaling (adding standby read-only replicated instances using native replication).

Let's explore the vertical scaling option. For this option, we basically change the instance type using the AWS console, the AWS CLI, or even AWS SDK. This action requires downtime of the environment, and it's highly recommended to back up the database and all environments before the change. Depending on the resources, this operation may require minutes to accomplish.

To reduce the downtime during this operation, the alternative is to deploy a new instance with the required resources using an out-of-pace strategy. To accomplish this task, you can perform the following steps:

1. Install the same database software version as the source environment.
2. Restore a full backup in this environment, and keep the database updated using log shipping (for example, Oracle archives, MySQL binlog, and PostgreSQL WAL).
3. When the databases are completely in sync, stop the application on the source, switch over the database to the replica, and connect the application to the new database.

In this option, the downtime from the application perspective will be the following steps in a small maintenance window:

1. Disconnect the application.
2. Check if there's small sync difference to be replicated (Oracle archives, MySQL binlog, or PostgreSQL WAL).
3. Reconnect to the database.

Scaling the database environment horizontally using replicas based on log shipping replication is an alternative to reduce the I/O overhead generated by read-intensive applications. Some native database options include the following:

- MySQL binlog replication
- MariaDB replica using binlog
- PostgreSQL log-shipping standby servers or streaming replication
- Oracle Active Data Guard
- Microsoft SQL Server native replication

Upgrading Databases

When upgrading self-managed databases, you must be aware of the software version availability and follow the upgrade steps based on each database distribution.

You must be aware of business requirements during upgrades and any kind of maintenance. Although you need to follow each particular software distribution step, keep in mind that performing an out-of-place upgrade can be less risky.

You can upgrade the database version directly in the current environment; this is an in-place upgrade. If you need to undo this upgrade because you found some issue in the application, the only alternative is to restore a backup.

To manage risks and guarantee database availability, you should choose a safe strategy for performing maintenance like upgrades. For better management of the maintenance risk, instead of upgrading directly the current database software, you can choose to perform an out-of-place upgrade or perform logical replication if the database engine allows.

To perform an out of place upgrade, complete the following steps:

1. Back up the current database.

2. Launch a new EC2 instance with the required operating system.

3. Patch the operating system with the required OS libraries and parameters.

4. Install the database software.

5. Restore the backup from step 1.

6. Establish replication.

7. Sync the database.

8. Stop the replication.

9. Perform the upgrade operation on this cloned database. If something goes wrong with the operation, your original database will be untouched.

In step 7, to synchronize database, you can perform logical replication, based on the native engine method.

Some databases have native logical replication available, like PostgreSQL `pglogical`, or even use AWS Database Migration Service (AWS DMS), which handles different database engines and versions. In this scenario of replicating between different versions, you need to install the database on the desired final version in a new Amazon EC2 instance and then start replication from the previous database to the new one installed on the new Amazon EC2 instance.

Managed Services for Relational Databases

Amazon Relational Database Service (Amazon RDS) is a managed database service. It provides easier management and enables automatic installation and configuration. It offers faster setup and operation compared to self-managed databases and scales databases in the cloud. It automates time-consuming activities such as hardware provisioning, database setup, patching, and backups.

You can select among six database engines including Amazon Aurora, PostgreSQL, MySQL, MariaDB, Oracle, and SQL Server. You can choose the appropriate instance category for the given workload for better cost and performance. For example, there are instances optimized for memory, performance, or I/O.

Amazon RDS provides the following automated services and features that you can easily enable:

- Installation

- Monitoring

- Backup and snapshots
- Automated patching
- Version upgrade
- High availability with multi-AZ
- Read replicas

Launching an RDS Instance

To configure an RDS instance, perform the following steps:

1. Navigate to the RDS console, select Create Database, and then select the engine option and version appropriate to your environment (Figure 4.1).

FIGURE 4.1   Choosing the database engine

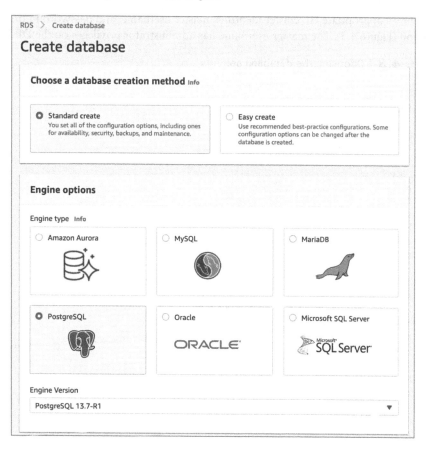

2. Select the template most appropriate to your workload: Production, Dev/Test, or Free Tier (Figure 4.2).

FIGURE 4.2   Choosing a template

3. Define an appropriate DB cluster identifier, master username, and password in the Settings section (Figure 4.3). The master username has administrator privileges on the DB instance.

FIGURE 4.3   Choosing the database settings

4. Choose the appropriate instance class in the DB Instance Class section (Figure 4.4).

FIGURE 4.4   Choosing the instance class

Instance configuration

The DB instance configuration options below are limited to those supported by the engine that you selected above.

DB instance class Info

⦿ Standard classes (includes m classes)

◯ Memory optimized classes (includes r classes)

db.m5d.xlarge
4 vCPUs   16 GiB RAM   Network: 4,750 Mbps   150 GB Instance Store   ▼

5. In the Storage section, define whether your environment requires general-purpose or provisioned IOPS, the total provisioned IOPS, the allocated storage in size (GB), the storage autoscaling enablement, and the maximum storage allowed for the autoscaling provisioning (Figure 4.5).

FIGURE 4.5   Choosing the storage configuration

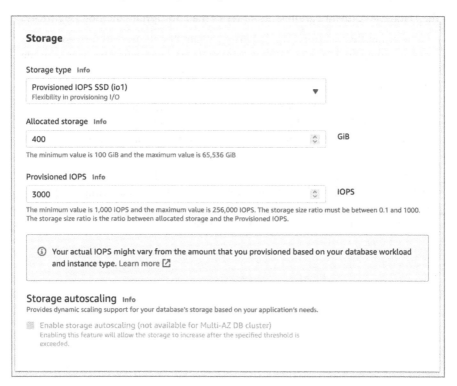

Storage

Storage type Info

Provisioned IOPS SSD (io1)
Flexibility in provisioning I/O   ▼

Allocated storage Info

400   ↕   GiB

The minimum value is 100 GiB and the maximum value is 65,536 GiB

Provisioned IOPS Info

3000   ↕   IOPS

The minimum value is 1,000 IOPS and the maximum value is 256,000 IOPS. The storage size ratio must be between 0.1 and 1000. The storage size ratio is the ratio between allocated storage and the Provisioned IOPS.

ⓘ Your actual IOPS might vary from the amount that you provisioned based on your database workload and instance type. Learn more ☑

Storage autoscaling Info
Provides dynamic scaling support for your database's storage based on your application's needs.

☐ Enable storage autoscaling (not available for Multi-AZ DB cluster)
Enabling this feature will allow the storage to increase after the specified threshold is exceeded.

6. In the Availability & Durability section, select whether your database requires the high availability provided by multi-AZ deployment (Figure 4.6).

FIGURE 4.6   Enabling multi-AZ

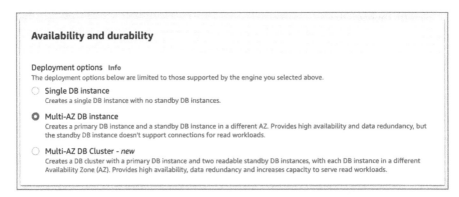

7. In the Connectivity section, select the appropriate VPC, subnet group, whether the database needs public access (it's strongly recommended *not* to assign public access for databases), and the security group (Figure 4.7). In the Additional Configuration section, you can define the database port.

8. In the Database Authentication section, select the appropriate method (Figure 4.8).

   ▪ **Password authentication:** The DB instance handles all users and passwords connected to the DB. The database maintains and authenticates user accounts. It's required to create users by the CREATE USER statement defining the username and password.

   ▪ **IAM database authentication:** This method is available for RDS for MySQL and RDS for PostgreSQL. Using IAM database authentication doesn't require the password authentication; instead, the user will connect using an authentication token.

   ▪ **Kerberos authentication:** Kerberos is a network authentication protocol based on tickets and symmetric-key cryptography to eliminate transmitting the password over the network. Kerberos has been built into Active Directory and authenticates users to network resources, such as databases.

FIGURE 4.7   Configuring the connectivity

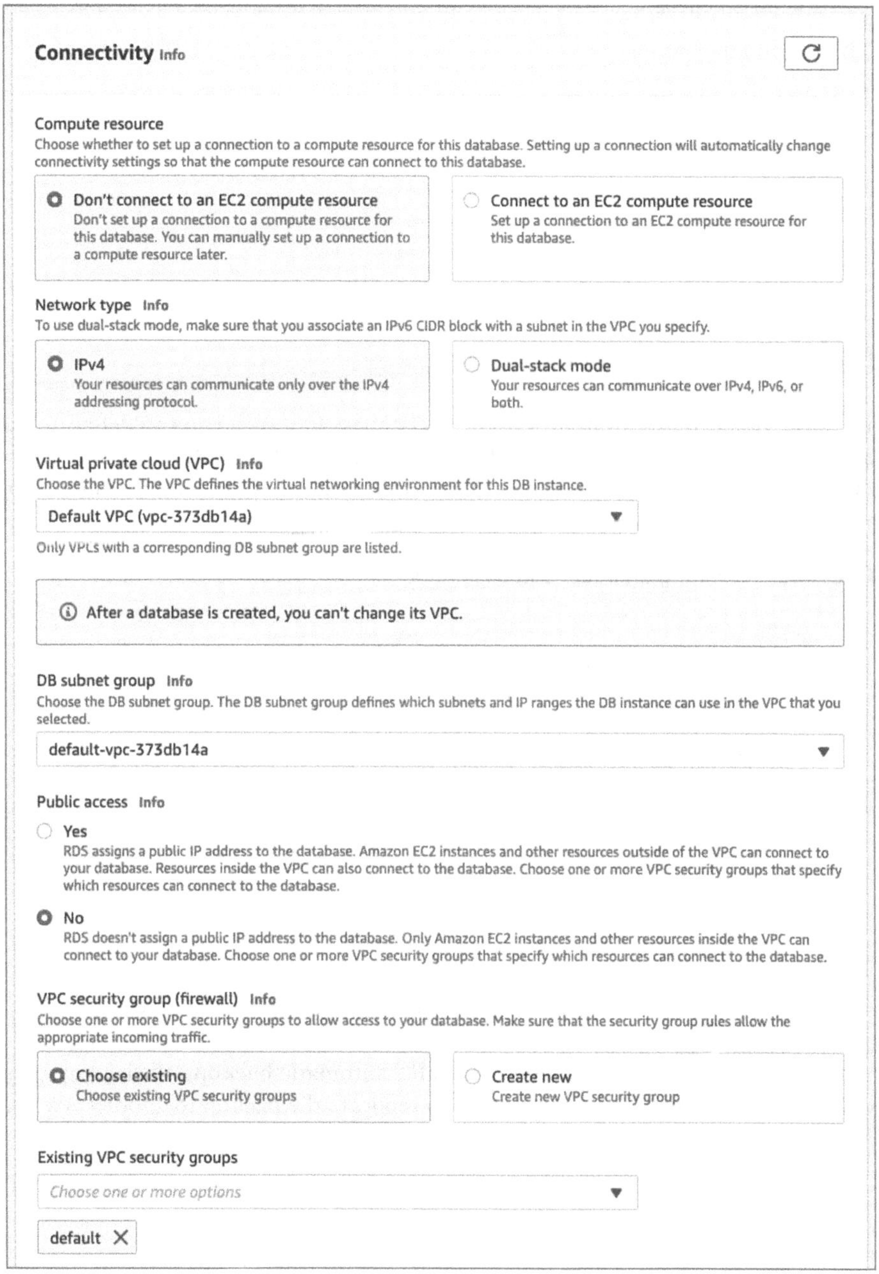

FIGURE 4.8 Choosing the authentication method

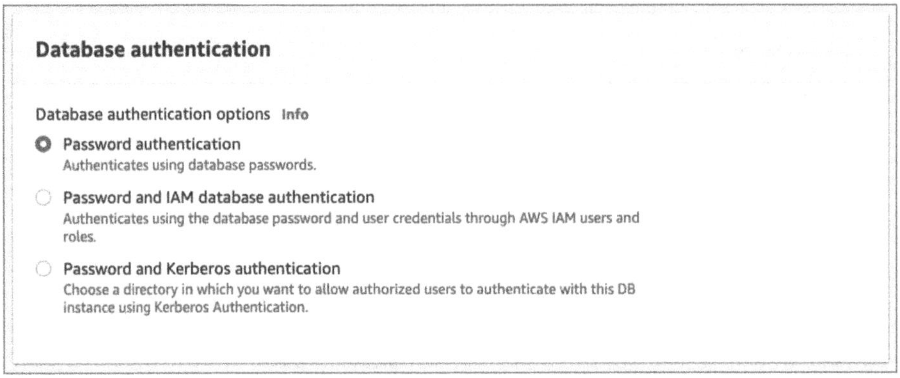

Database authentication

Database authentication options   Info

● Password authentication
Authenticates using database passwords.

○ Password and IAM database authentication
Authenticates using the database password and user credentials through AWS IAM users and roles.

○ Password and Kerberos authentication
Choose a directory in which you want to allow authorized users to authenticate with this DB instance using Kerberos Authentication.

9. In the Additional Configuration section, in Database Options, you can define an initial database name to be created and a DB parameter group (Figure 4.9). The option group is always the standard one. (You can choose a new one later defining the suitable option for parameter group and option group.)

FIGURE 4.9 Defining an initial database to be created, parameter, and option groups

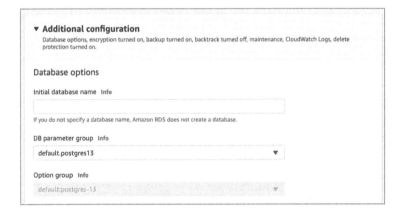

▼ **Additional configuration**
Database options, encryption turned on, backup turned on, backtrack turned off, maintenance, CloudWatch Logs, delete protection turned on.

Database options

Initial database name   Info

If you do not specify a database name, Amazon RDS does not create a database.

DB parameter group   Info

default.postgres13

Option group   Info

default:postgres-13

10. In the Backup section, select whether to enable automatic backups, the backup retention period, the backup window, and whether to replicate the backup to another AWS region (Figure 4.10).

FIGURE 4.10   Configuring backup

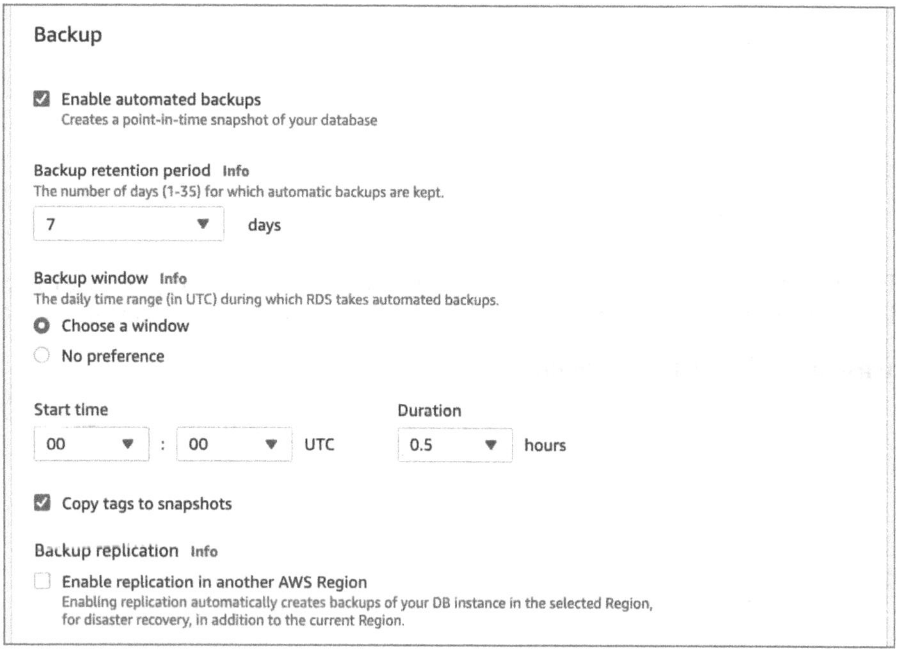

> **Backup**
>
> ☑ **Enable automated backups**
> Creates a point-in-time snapshot of your database
>
> **Backup retention period** Info
> The number of days (1-35) for which automatic backups are kept.
>
> | 7   ▼ | days
>
> **Backup window** Info
> The daily time range (in UTC) during which RDS takes automated backups.
> ◉ Choose a window
> ○ No preference
>
> Start time   Duration
> | 00 ▼ | : | 00 ▼ | UTC | 0.5 ▼ | hours
>
> ☑ Copy tags to snapshots
>
> **Backup replication** Info
> ☐ Enable replication in another AWS Region
> Enabling replication automatically creates backups of your DB instance in the selected Region,
> for disaster recovery, in addition to the current Region.

11. In the Encryption section, you can select to enable encryption and the encryption key (Figure 4.11).

FIGURE 4.11   Enabling encryption

> **Encryption**
>
> ☑ **Enable encryption**
> Choose to encrypt the given instance. Master key IDs and aliases appear in the list after they have been created using the AWS
> Key Management Service console. Info
>
> **AWS KMS key** Info
> | (default) aws/rds   ▼ |

12. In the Performance Insights section, select whether to enable Performance Insights and the retention period (Figure 4.12). For seven days, there is no additional cost for the database instance (perfect for development and test environments), and for production, you can choose to retain insights of up to two years of performance information for an extra charge (recommended for production databases).

FIGURE 4.12 Enabling Performance Insights

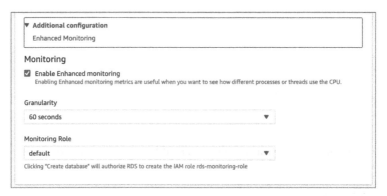

13. In the Monitoring section, you can enable enhanced monitoring, the granularity to collect, and whether you need to export database logs to CloudWatch (Figure 4.13).

FIGURE 4.13 Enabling monitoring

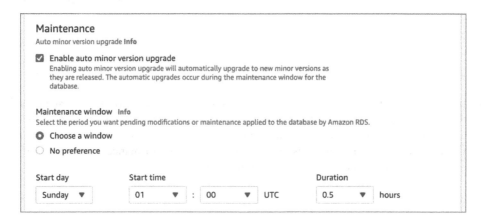

14. In the Maintenance section, you can select whether to keep auto minor version upgrades enabled and choose the maintenance window period allowed for the given database (Figure 4.14).

FIGURE 4.14 Configuring maintenance rules

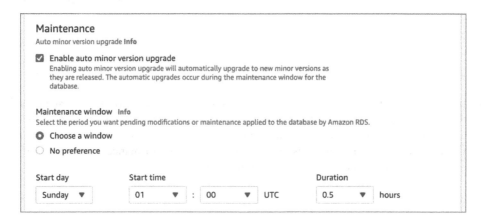

15. In the Deletion Protection section, you can choose whether the database will be protected against deletion (Figure 4.15).

FIGURE 4.15   Enabling deletion protection

Deletion protection

☑ **Enable deletion protection**
Protects the database from being deleted accidentally. While this option is enabled, you can't delete the database.

16. Select Create Database (Figure 4.16).

FIGURE 4.16   Creating the database

ⓘ You are responsible for ensuring that you have all of the necessary rights for any third-party products or services that you use with AWS services.

Cancel   **Create database**

Once the database is available, you can check the endpoint connection information by accessing the RDS Management Console, by using the AWS Command Line Interface (AWS CLI) `describe-db-instances` command, or by using the Amazon RDS API `DescribeDBInstances` operation.

This example demonstrates how to check your endpoint connectivity. As shown in Figure 4.17, there's a cluster endpoint for read-only (ro) workloads and another endpoint for read/write operations. The Type column (Reader/Writer) describes the endpoint role.

FIGURE 4.17   Checking the endpoints

Managing High Availability and Scalability

Managing high availability and scalability is a usual requirement for most production databases. For databases that require high availability, on Amazon RDS you can enable the Multi-AZ setting. For databases that require scaling read operations, you can enable read replicas.

Multi-AZ

Amazon RDS Multi-AZ provides high availability and durability for RDS instances. When enabled, Amazon RDS automatically creates a primary and a standby database using synchronous storage replication. The primary and the standby are separate instances and storages independent, in different availability zones. RDS will automatically fail over to the secondary database if the primary database fails.

RDS Multi-AZ provides the following:

- **Improved durability:** Multi-AZ deployments for the MySQL, PostgreSQL, MariaDB, and Oracle engines use synchronous physical replication based on Amazon failover technology to keep the standby database up to date. Multi-AZ deployments for Microsoft SQL Server use synchronous logical replication with SQL Server native mirroring technology called SQL Server Database Mirroring (DBM) or Always on Availability Groups (AGs).

- **Increased availability:** When a failure occurs on the primary database, the application will be impacted by the time to fail over the primary to the standby in the secondary availability zone. Typically RDS engines such as Oracle, Microsoft SQL Server, PostgreSQL, MySQL, and MariaDB take 60 to 120 seconds to complete the failover.

- **Automatic failover:** Amazon RDS changes the DNS resolution name automatically to the standby database; there's no manual activity during this operation.

- **Protection of database performance:** Backups are taken from the standby database.

Failure conditions that trigger a failover in Multi-AZ include the following:

- Failure of availability in the primary availability zone
- Network connectivity failure to the primary database
- A hardware failure on the primary database instance
- A storage failure on the primary database
- User requested; request a failover by selecting reboot with failover

The failover mechanism automatically changes the DB's instance Domain Name System (DNS) record to point to the standby database. Consequently, the application requires reconnecting to the database.

We recommend reviewing the DNS TTL on the application side. Using this configuration appropriately will guarantee that when the resource's IP address changes, the application will obtain the new IP if a failover operation has occurred.

Always test the appropriate values for the DNS TTL to assure the best configuration.

Databases configured with Multi-AZ have increased write and commit latency compared to Single-AZ databases. We strongly recommend configuring provisioned IOPS and choosing an instance class optimized for provisioned IOPS.

Scalability

To better adjust scalability in RDS, you can change your instance type to expand or reduce the compute resources assigned to the RDS instance. And to increase horizontal read scalability, you can add RDS read replicas.

Read Replicas

Amazon RDS provides horizontal read scalability using the MariaDB, Microsoft SQL Server, MySQL, Oracle, and PostgreSQL DB engines' native replication mechanisms. The origin DB instance is the primary DB instance, and the data manipulation on the original data is replicated asynchronously to the read replica. You can use the read replica to issue read operations and better scale out for read-heavy database workloads.

Figure 4.18 shows how a read replica works.

FIGURE 4.18   How to create read replicas

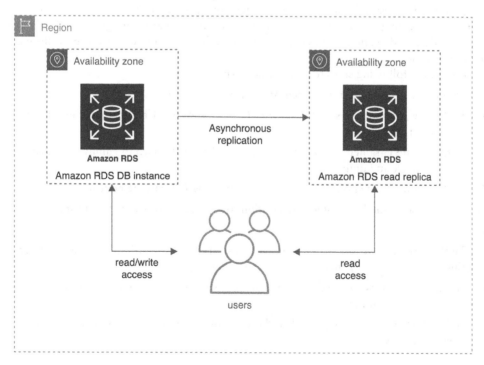

Use cases for read replica include the following:

- Scale-out compute or I/O capacity for read-intensive database workloads.

- Redirect read operations while the source instance is inaccessible. Keep in mind that the data in the read replica might be "stable" during this period.

- Provide business reporting or data warehousing read access.

You can promote a read replica to a stand-alone instance in primary DB failure for disaster recovery. Keep in mind that it becomes an independent primary database after promoting the read replica.

For multiregion high availability, you can enable cross-region read replicas for MariaDB, MySQL, Oracle, or PostgreSQL. SQL Server on Amazon RDS does not support cross-region read replicas.

Configuring RDS Parameter Groups

Parameter groups are assigned to databases to define configurations such as the instance buffer's size, `max_connections`, parameters that control queries behavior.

In RDS, to change parameters defined for `postgres.conf`, `my.cnf`, or `init.ora`, you'll customize them using the parameter groups.

Each database engine (MySQL, PostgreSQL, Oracle, MariaDB, and SQL Server) has its own standard parameter group and specific version. This engine- and version-specific parameter group has several parameters already calculated based on the database instance class.

If you need to customize a specific parameter, you must create a new parameter group based on an existing one and then assign this newly created parameter group to the database instance. This modification requires that you manually reboot the DB instance for the change to become valid.

Perform the following steps to create a new parameter group:

1. Sign in the AWS console and open Amazon RDS Console.

2. In the navigation pane, select Parameter Groups and then Create Parameter Group, as shown in Figure 4.19.

3. In the Create Parameter Group window, in the Parameter Group Family list, select a DB parameter group family.

4. In the Group Name box, enter the name of the new DB parameter group.

5. In the Description box, enter a description for the new DB parameter group.

6. Click Create.

The RDS Amazon instance may be unable to start in "incompatible-parameter" status, and this problem may be generated by the following:

- A DB instance was changed to an instance class with fewer memory resources than as defined in the parameter group.

- A database engine was upgraded, and the custom parameters are not available in the new database version.

FIGURE 4.10 Creating a parameter group

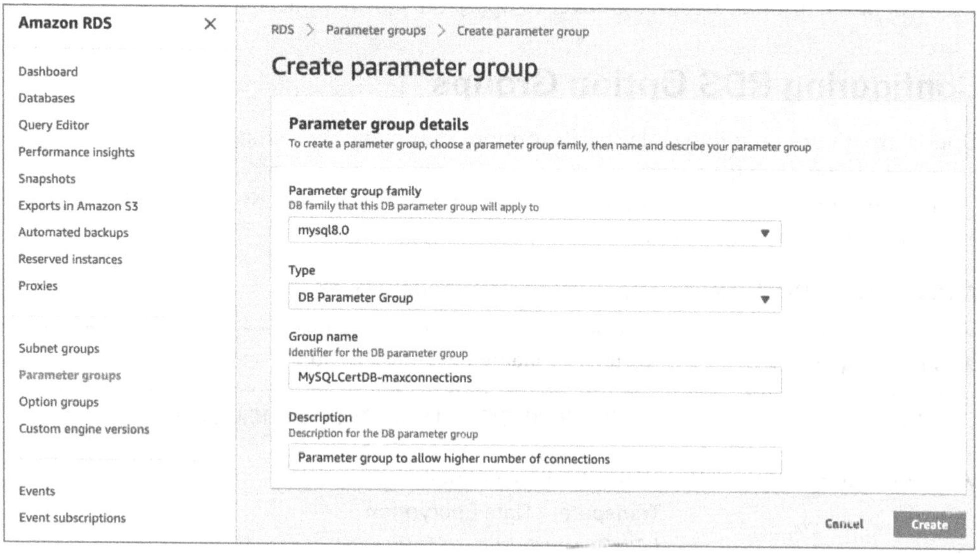

To solve this problem, you may choose the following options:

- Reset all parameters in the parameter group to the default value.
- Reset the values of the parameter that are incompatible.

If you choose to reset all parameters in a parameter group, it may affect other instances that use this parameter group. To perform this change in a better way, first create a copy of the current parameter group for which you're about to reset all values.

1. Open the RDS Console, and select parameter groups from the navigation pane.
2. Select the incompatible parameter group, and then choose Parameter Group Actions.
3. Click Copy.

Now that the values of the parameter group are safe, you can reset the values to solve the current instance unavailability.

1. Open the RDS Console, and choose parameter groups from the navigation pane.
2. Select the parameter group of the instance in trouble.
3. Select Parameter Group Actions and then Reset.
4. Click Reset.

You may also choose to change only the incompatible parameter value instead of all parameters within the parameter group. To accomplish that, follow these steps:

1. Open the RDS Console, and choose the parameter groups from the navigation pane.
2. Select the incompatible parameter group, and then choose Parameter Group Actions.
3. Select Parameter Group Actions and choose Edit.

4. Enter the correct parameter values and click Save Changes.
5. Reboot the instance without failover to apply the new parameter values.

Configuring RDS Option Groups

Option groups are used to enable specific options that make the management easier and to provide additional security.

To enable an option in the database, you need to associate an option group to the database according to the database engine, as shown in Table 4.2.

TABLE 4.2 Database Engines and Available Option Groups

Database Engine	Options Available by Option Group
MariaDB	MARIADB_AUDIT_PLUGIN (MariaDB 10.0.24 and later)
Microsoft SQL Server	Native backup and restore Transparent Data Encryption SQL Server Audit SQL Server Analysis Services SQL Server Integration Services SQL Server Reporting Services Microsoft Distributed Transaction Coordinator
MySQL	MariaDB Audit Plugin support MySQL memcached support
Oracle	Amazon S3 integration Oracle Application Express (APEX) Oracle Enterprise Manager Oracle Java virtual machine Oracle Label Security Oracle Locator Oracle Multimedia Oracle native network encryption Oracle OLAP Oracle Secure Sockets Layer Oracle Spatial Oracle SQLT Oracle Statspack Oracle time zone Oracle Transparent Data Encryption Oracle UTL_MAIL Oracle XML DB

RDS PostgreSQL does not implement options by option groups; it uses extensions and modules to provide additional features.

When you launch an RDS instance, by default the option group is empty. Perform the following steps to enable an option group for an RDS instance:

1. Create a new option group. On Amazon RDS console, select Option Group, and then select Create (Figure 4.20).

FIGURE 4.20   Amazon RDS group options

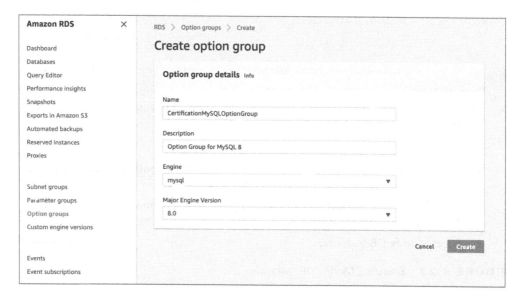

2. Add one or more options to this option group. Select the recently created option group (certificationmysqloptiongroup), as shown in Figure 4.21.

FIGURE 4.21   Adding options to the group (step 1)

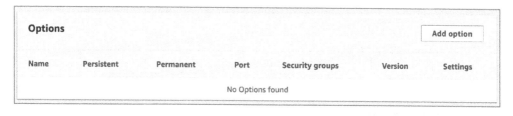

3. Select the Add option (Figure 4.22).

FIGURE 4.22   Adding options to the group (step 2)

4. Search for the available options according to the DB engine. (You can find the options in Table 4.2.)

5. To assign the option group recently created to the instance, you must perform the following steps, as shown in Figure 4.23:

   a. Select Modify the DB Instance at RDS Console.

   b. In the Additional Configuration section, search for the recently created option group—in this example *certificationmysqloptiongroup*.

   c. In the Scheduling of Modifications section, choose Apply Immediately or During The Next Maintenance Window.

   d. Select Modify DB Instance.

FIGURE 4.23   Selecting Modify DB Instance

```
▼ Additional configuration
   Database options, backup turned on, Enhanced Monitoring turned off, maintenance, CloudWatch Logs, delete protection turned
   off

Database options

DB parameter group  Info
┌─────────────────────────────────────────────────────────┬───┐
│ default.mysql8.0                                         │ ▼ │
└─────────────────────────────────────────────────────────┴───┘

Option group  Info
┌─────────────────────────────────────────────────────────┬───┐
│ certificationmysqloptiongroup                           │ ▲ │
├─────────────────────────────────────────────────────────┴───┤
│ certificationmysqloptiongroup                               │
├─────────────────────────────────────────────────────────────┤
│ default:mysql-8-0                                           │
└─────────────────────────────────────────────────────────────┘
```

Deletion Protection

RDS will only allow you to delete an instance that doesn't have the deletion protection enabled. You can configure the deletion protection at the database instance launch (creation) or when you select the modify option.

By default, the deletion protection is:

- Enabled when you create the database using the RDS Console
- Disabled when you create the database using AWS CLI or API commands

Although there are differences in the deletion protection enablement when operating the AWS Console or CLI/API, Amazon RDS enforces the deletion protection when you utilize the console, the CLI, or the API to remove a DB instance.

To delete a database instance with deletion protection enabled, you must first disable the deletion protection and then delete it.

There's no instance outage to enable or disable the deletion protection.

RDS Pricing Model

RDS allows you to choose the billing method for the database instances.

- **Pay as you go:** There's no up-front commitment. You'll pay a monthly charge for each instance launched. When you stop using the instance, you delete it and will no longer be charged.
- **Reserved instances:** In this option, you'll book the DB instance for a one-year or three-year term and, in return, receive a substantial discount compared to the on-demand price. This option is better for databases that will be up and running 24/7 and that are necessary for an extended period.

You can stop and start your databases for seven days at a time. This is an affordable option for development and quality assurance databases, which usually aren't required to be up and running 24/7.

You receive a credit of complimentary backup storage up to the total provisioned storage size within a region. If you have three instances of 1 TB of provisioned storage each, you'll have 3 TB of backup storage for free. With detailed backup billing, for each database instance in your account, the size of backup usage will be compared to the provisioned storage.

If the backup usage exceeds the provisioned storage, the exceeding part will be charged.

If the backup usage is less than the provisioned storage, the difference is counted as usage credits and discounted proportionally from charges applied to other instances.

Backup storage not associated with an RDS active instance will be charged the total price, except when you have discounts generated by other instances in the same account.

Amazon Aurora Cloud-Native Relational Database

Amazon Aurora is a fully managed relational database compatible with MySQL or PostgreSQL launched on a high-performance storage subsystem. Amazon Aurora MySQL- and

PostgreSQL-compatible database engines are optimized to take advantage of the high-performance and distributed storage.

Aurora is one of the managed database services in Amazon Relational Database Service (Amazon RDS), making it more effortless to set up, manage, and scale a relational database in the cloud. RDS automatically enables the most time-consuming activities, such as backup, monitoring, and automatic patching.

The same application code and native tools from MySQL and PostgreSQL databases can run in Aurora.

The snapshots created from Amazon RDS for MySQL and PostgreSQL are restorable on Amazon Aurora.

Another migration alternative is setting up one-way replication.

On usual benchmarks, Aurora demonstrates up to five times the throughput (usually the measure is transactions per second [TPS]) for the MySQL engine and up to three times the throughput for the PostgreSQL engine.

Amazon Aurora Storage

Aurora Storage assembles its storage in logical blocks, which are named protection groups, of 10 GB. Aurora distributes the protection groups across three availability zones (AZs) and hosts two copies of each protection group on each AZ. In total, Aurora has six copies of each protection group, as depicted in Figure 4.24. The storage continuously replicates the log data to Amazon S3 to keep up the point-in-time recovery. This architecture provides a fault tolerance of 99.999999999 percent (11 nines) of durability.

FIGURE 4.24   Full tolerance architecture

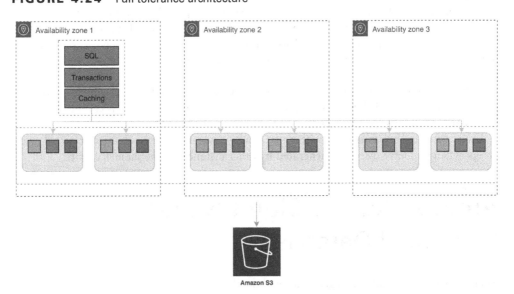

The Aurora storage grows automatically up to 128 tebibytes (TiB); there's no manual intervention during the auto-scale operation.

Amazon Aurora DB Clusters

An Amazon Aurora DB cluster contains one or more DB instances and a cluster volume that handles the data for the DB instances.

An Aurora cluster requires two kinds of instances:

- **Primary DB instance (mandatory):** Every Aurora DB cluster must have one primary DB instance to handle read and write operations for the application layer and manage all data modifications to the cluster volume.

- **Aurora replica:** Supports read-only operations and attaches to the same storage volume as the primary as depicted in Figure 4.25. To scale read operations and increase high availability, we strongly recommend adding Aurora replicas. An Aurora DB cluster can have up to 15 Aurora replicas in addition to the primary DB instance. You can launch the Aurora replicas across the availability zones that the cluster belongs to within a region.

FIGURE 4.25   Aurora replicas architecture

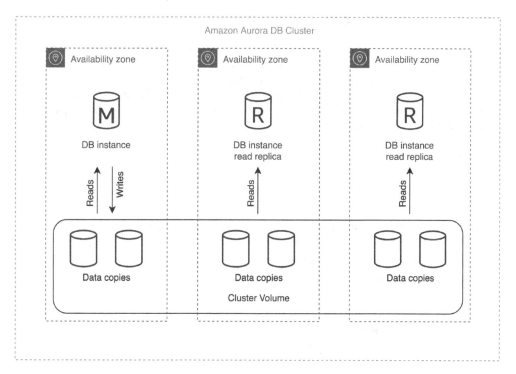

Amazon Aurora High Availability

When a primary instance fails, one of the Aurora replicas will be promoted to the primary instance to increase availability.

Aurora automatically fails over to an Aurora replica if the primary DB instance fails. The Amazon Aurora cluster allows configuring the failover priority on the read replicas. Priority values vary from 0 for the first priority to 15 for the last priority. The failover precedence sequence is as follows:

1. The failover priority defined for Aurora replicas, the instance with the lowest failover priority value, will be first chosen in a failover situation.

2. If there's no failover priority defined, the cluster will choose the highest instance's read replica node.

3. If there's no failover priority and all the instances have the same instance type, the cluster will randomly select one read replica.

> You can adjust the priority of an Aurora replica at any moment. Changing the priority value of a read replica doesn't start a failover.

Amazon Aurora Global Database

Aurora Global Database allows the replication of an Aurora Cluster to multiple regions based on storage async replication, with low replication latency (typically less than 1 second), and provides fast recovery in an entire region's outage.

The Aurora global database must have a primary DB cluster in the one region, and it allows you to add up to five secondary DB clusters in remote regions (secondary regions).

Figure 4.26 represents the Aurora global database.

FIGURE 4.26   Aurora global database architecture

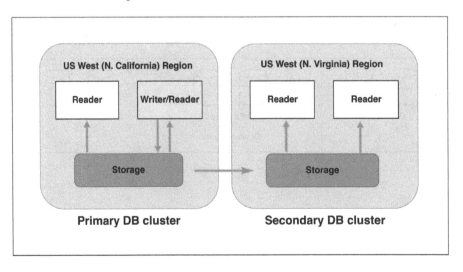

You can run distributed applications on distant regions using a database replicated with the Aurora global database. The read-only remote instances allow read operations closer to remote application users, improving data locality.

Only the primary cluster issues write operations. Using the "write forwarding" feature (available only on Aurora MySQL version 2.08.1 or later), the database cluster on the secondary region accepts the write operation; actually, it forwards the write operation to the primary database cluster, and then the primary database cluster propagates all write operations to the secondary regions.

Depending on the situation, the Aurora global database allows you to choose the following failover methods:

- **Unplanned failover process:** The Aurora global database can recover after the primary region's outage. In this rare situation, you must perform the following steps:
  1. Stop any write operations on the primary Aurora DB cluster.
  2. Choose an Aurora DB cluster to be promoted to primary. In the case of global database configurations with two or more secondary regions, you should choose the remote region with the minor replication lag.
  3. Detach the selected secondary DB cluster from the Aurora global database. This action will stop the replication and promote the selected DB cluster to a primary stand-alone. Then this newly promoted DB cluster will be available to read/write capabilities. If other secondary DB clusters are associated with the primary cluster in the outage region, they will still be open to the applications. To prevent data inconsistencies, you must re-create the Aurora global database by removing the remaining secondary regions and creating a new global database.
  4. Configure your application to connect to the newly promoted DB cluster.

- **Planned managed failover:** Relocating the primary cluster of a healthy Aurora global database to one of its remote regions with a zero recovery point objective (RPO). In this planned situation, you must perform the following steps:
  1. Select the global database, and in Actions, select Failover Global Databases.
  2. Select the remote region to be the new primary region. This action will stop the write operations in the primary region, the secondary regions that may have some replication lag will reach the same data position as the primary, and the newly selected region will become the new primary with no data loss.
  3. Configure the application to connect to the new primary DB cluster.
  Aurora global databases offer the following benefits:

- **Global reads with local latency:** For applications that need to allow the read operation in offices around the world, the remote instances will provide faster read access for local applications.

- **Scalable secondary Aurora DB clusters:** On each remote cluster you may configure up to 16 read replicas on the secondary regions, instead of only 15 allowed in the primary region.

- **Fast replication from primary to secondary Aurora DB clusters:** Data propagation performed having a minor impact on the Aurora primary cluster.

- **Recovery from region-wide outages:** For recovering from a possible primary region catastrophe, you can promote any remote clusters to primary.

Amazon Aurora Read Replica Across Regions

Aurora MySQL allows you to create read replicas across different regions. Using this feature, you can enable faster read operations in remote regions and replicate your database for disaster recovery.

You can enable up to five cross-region read replicas for each DB cluster.

Aurora MySQL read replicas require binary logging on the source Aurora MySQL cluster.

You can configure both the source DB cluster and the cross-region read replica cluster with a maximum of 15 replicas on each one of the clusters, allowing up to 90 readable instances.

A globally replicated cluster is subject to replication lag between the source DB cluster and a remote cluster in a cross-region scenario due to longer network channels between AWS regions.

The resulting data transfer from cross-region replication incurs additional fees.

Amazon Aurora Serverless

Aurora Serverless is an autoscaling configuration for Amazon Aurora. Aurora Serverless can scale up and down automatically according to resource utilization (on-demand); there's no instance class allocation. You must specify the minimum and maximum Aurora capacity units (ACUs). Aurora Serverless currently offers versions v1 and v2.

Aurora Serverless has the following characteristics:

- It is compatible with the MySQL and PostgreSQL engines.

- It reduces the complexity of managing DB instance capacity.

- It will increase and reduce computational and memory resources, if required, with no impact on client connections.

- It is a cost-efficient service due to the automatic instance resizing.

- It uses the same distributed storage as Aurora provisioned, replicating the protection groups on three availability zones and two copies on each availability zone, having a total of six copies to avoid data loss.

Aurora Serverless is good for the following uses:

- Infrequently used applications—for example, applications that access the database a few minutes per day or week.

- New applications, when you're not sure about the resources needed to size an instance type.

- Variable workloads, for example, applications where you can't predict how long it will take to complete and the resources required. Sometimes a few resources (vCPUs and memory) will be enough, and in other circumstances it will require more assigned resources. With Aurora Serverless, there's no need to allocate the resources for the maximum workload.

- Development and test databases. Usually they're required for a few hours during the day, and there's no need to be up and running during noncommercial hours.

- Environments with a high constraint on costs.

Amazon Aurora Multi-master

An *Aurora multi-master* cluster is an architecture where both instances can perform read and write operations. There's no failover when a master becomes unavailable because the remaining nodes are always ready to assume the failed node work.

Replication operates directly among writers. Every writer propagates its changes to all other writers. Multi-master clusters are attached using low-latency and low-lag Aurora replication, hosted on all peer-to-peer replication.

Amazon Aurora multi-master is exclusively available for MySQL-compatible edition v1 engines, which is MySQL 5.6. Amazon has announced an end-of-life policy for this major Aurora MySQL version (February 2023). You can have up to four DB instances in a multi-master cluster, and the instances must be in the same AWS region.

Aurora will report a write conflict to the application as a deadlock error if different instances simultaneously try to modify the same data page. This error circumstance will drive the transaction to roll back. The application must catch the error and retry the operation in this situation.

The following workloads are appropriate for Aurora multi-master:

- **Active-passive workloads:** Using this configuration, the application issues all read and write operations simultaneously; if a failure occurs on the active instance, the remaining active node will assume all workloads without performing a failover.

- **Active-active workloads:** Using this configuration, you typically segment the workload so that the different DB instances won't modify the same underlying data simultaneously. Consequently, it reduces a possible write conflict. Multi-master is a good choice for segmented workloads when dividing write operations by the instance, database, table, or table partition is applicable. For example, it's good when running multiple applications on the same cluster, each assigned for a specific node. Another option is dividing various small tables, for example, one table for each module of an app. We recommend designing the solution to avoid writing conflicts. Sharded applications are the typical use case.

Patch Management and Upgrade

Amazon RDS makes available newer versions and patches of the supported database engines, and you can keep your database up to date according to your application needs.

On Amazon RDS, you'll find two categories of upgrades:

- **Major version upgrades** introduce modifications that may not be compatible with current applications. The versioning sequence is specific to each database distribution. For illustration, RDS for MySQL 5.7 and 8.0 are major versions, and upgrading from any 5.7 version to any 8.0 is a major version upgrade.

- **Minor version upgrades** contain exclusive modifications that are backward-compatible with existing applications.

For major versions, manually select and modify the DB engine version via the AWS Management Console or issue the modify option using the AWS CLI or RDS API.

For minor version upgrades, manually choose to modify the engine version via the Amazon RDS console or enable auto minor version upgrades in the database configuration.

Monitoring and Performance Management

Monitoring is essential for database operations. Defining a monitoring plan is the foremost action.

Initially, define the monitoring goals by specifying your baselines (using metrics such as network throughput, CPU, client connections, and IO operations) and understanding which metrics are regular for your operation and which metrics will become a problem for the business. In the second step, identify the resources that require monitoring. Third, define the monitoring frequency that is most appropriate for identifying the problem and taking corrective action. Fourth, choose the monitoring tool that will be able to implement the previous requirements that you identified. Finally, identify who will receive the monitoring notification and take the appropriate action.

To fulfill the monitoring objectives, you need to specify a baseline. Then review past workloads' resource consumption to identify appropriate metrics. For databases, the following items are commonly monitored:

- Database connections
- Memory usage
- CPU usage
- Network throughput
- IOPS metrics
- Disk space consumption
- Latency lag (for replicated databases)

You can use the following to check and report issues or failure events to the database administration team when something isn't working using Amazon RDS reporting tools:

- **Amazon RDS instance status:** This allows you to check instance status using the Amazon RDS console, AWS CLI command, or RDS API.

- **Amazon RDS recommendations:** These allow you to inspect and react to "automated recommendations" for databases on RDS, like DB instances, read replicas, DB parameter groups, and patch/upgrade advice.

- **Amazon RDS Performance Insights:** Amazon RDS allows the Performance Insights enablement on the database creation or by modifying it later. Using the Performance Insights dashboard, you can visualize the database load on your Amazon RDS DB instance load and filter the load by waits, SQL statements, hosts, or users. It allows you to comprehend the events such as SQL statements causing high resource consumption and "wait for events" in the database.

- **Amazon RDS Enhanced monitoring:** Amazon RDS allows enhanced monitoring enablement at database creation or later modification. Enhanced monitoring will enable you to examine real-time operating system metrics with lower granularity. Enhanced monitoring shows a summary of operating system metrics; Amazon RDS delivers the metrics from Enhanced Monitoring to Amazon CloudWatch. For each OS metric, you can view a graph showing the metric monitored over a specific period.

- **Amazon RDS events:** Amazon RDS allows the notifications subscription to specific events that may occur to a DB instance, DB snapshot, DB parameter group, or DB security group. Some event classification examples are availability, backup, configuration change, maintenance, and failure.

- **Amazon RDS database logs:** These allow you to view, download, or watch database log files using Amazon RDS console or Amazon RDS API operations. You can also publish database logs to Amazon CloudWatch.

Amazon CloudWatch and Amazon CloudWatch Logs enable you to enhance and integrate the monitoring process.

- **Amazon CloudWatch** monitors Amazon RDS databases in near real time, and you can integrate Amazon CloudWatch metrics and Amazon CloudWatch alarms to execute one or more steps according to the value of a specific metric.

- **Amazon CloudWatch Logs** enables monitoring, storing, and accessing the database log files in CloudWatch.

To observe monitoring metrics, perform the following steps:

1. In the Amazon RDS console, choose the desired database to observe metrics and the Monitoring tab (Figure 4.27).

FIGURE 4.27   Database monitoring

2. On the Monitoring tab, you can inspect metrics such as CPU utilization, connections, memory utilization, and other metrics (Figure 4.28).

FIGURE 4.28   CPU utilization monitoring

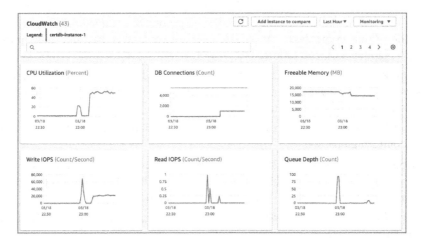

3. You can extend the Monitoring tab to access the Enhanced Monitoring, OS Process List, and Performance Insights items (Figure 4.29).

FIGURE 4.29   Monitoring expansion

4. In Enhanced Monitoring, you can verify the operating system metrics, as shown in Figure 4.30.

FIGURE 4.30   Operating system monitoring

5. In Performance Insights, you can drill down to what's going on at database perspective, and check database wait events and top SQL statements (Figure 4.31).

FIGURE 4.31   Performance insights

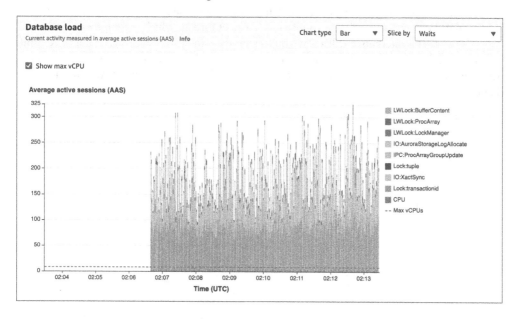

Backup and Restore

On RDS databases you can configure automated backups and you can also take manual snapshots.

- **Automated backups**
  - Automated backups are enabled by default. When launched by the Amazon RDS console, the standard is seven days of retention, and when launched by the RDS API or AWS CLI, the standard is one retention day.
  - You can configure the backup retention from 1 to 35 days.
  - Automatic backups support point-in-time recovery within any time until the maximum retention days defined for the database.
  - Automatic backups occur within the preferred backup window that you can define for the most appropriate time according to your business needs. If the backup demands more time than assigned to the backup window, the backup continues the execution after the window ends until it concludes. The backup window can't coincide with the weekly maintenance window for the DB instance.
  - By changing the retention to zero, you can disable the automatic RDS backup. If you disable automatic backups, you cannot create a read replica.
- **Manual backups (snapshots)**
  - Manual backups can be taken by choosing the Snapshot option in the Amazon RDS console, AWS CLI, and RDS API.
  - Manual backups do not support point-in-time recovery.
  - Manual backups never expire. That means they're recommended for long-term backups.
  - For backups of MariaDB, MySQL, and PostgreSQL that the business rules require storing for an extended time, we recommend exporting the snapshot data to Amazon S3. The snapshot to S3 stores the data in Apache Parquet format, which is compressed and consistent. This alternative will allow you to read the data using Amazon Athena or Redshift.

You can take a snapshot using the Amazon RDS console, RDS API, or AWS CLI. In the Amazon RDS console, select the database and select Take Snapshot on the Actions tab (Figure 4.32).

FIGURE 4.32 Taking an Amazon RDS snapshot

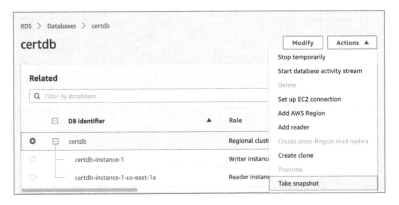

To restore from an automated backup, you can select any time within the retention period defined for the database.

Restoring from an automated backup or a snapshot will allocate a new instance and the required storage; you can't restore the database into an existing DB instance. You can choose instance classes that are different from the source database.

1. In the Amazon RDS console, select the database, and on the Actions tab, select Restore To Point In Time (Figure 4.33)

FIGURE 4.33   Selecting the database

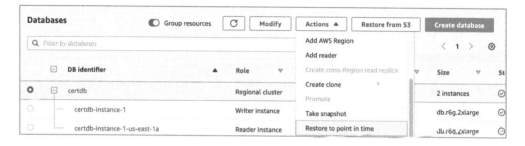

2. In the Restore Time section, choose the latest restorable time available or set the specific date and time to restore the database (Figure 4.34).

FIGURE 4.34   Choosing the restorable time

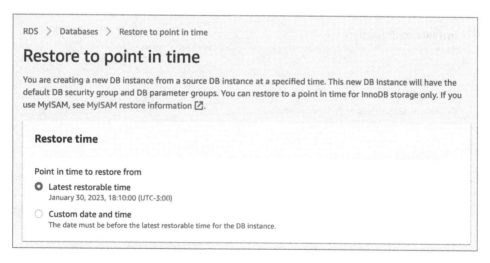

3. In the Instance Specifications section, define an identifier (Figure 4.35).

FIGURE 4.35 Defining an identifier

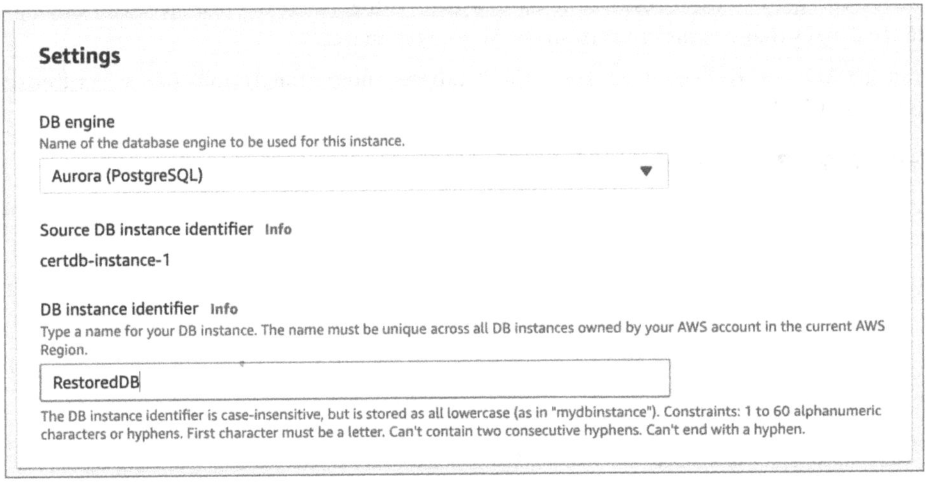

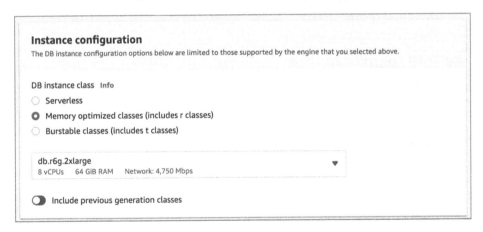

4. Define an instance class for the new database to be restored (Figure 4.36).

FIGURE 4.36 Defining an instance class

5. You can also choose a new VPC and security group for the database and then select Restore To Point In Time (Figure 4.37).

FIGURE 4.37   Choosing a new VPC and security group

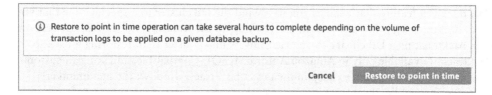

To restore from the snapshot, you can select the snapshot with the desired data. Keep in mind that there's no point-in-time recovery; the snapshot represents the image of the exact moment of its generation.

On the Amazon RDS console, select Snapshots and then the required snapshot to be restored (Figure 4.38).

FIGURE 4.38   Restoring from an Amazon RDS snapshot (step 1)

RDS > Snapshots

Snapshots

| Manual | System | Shared with me | Public | Backup service | Exports in Amazon S3 |

Manual snapshots (1)   C   Actions ▼   Take snapshot

Q *Filter by manual snapshots*   < 1 >   ⚙

| ☐ | Snapshot name | ▽ | DB instance or cluster ▽ | Snapshot creation time |
| ☐ | certificationsnap | | certdb | March 18, 2023, 23:18 (UTC-03:00) |

Then, click the Actions button and then select Restore Snapshot (Figure 4.39).

FIGURE 4.39   Restoring from an Amazon RDS snapshot (step 2)

RDS > Snapshots

Snapshots

| Manual | System | Shared with me | Public | Backup service | Exports in Amazon S3 |

Manual snapshots (1)   C   Actions ▲   Take snapshot

Q *Filter by manual snapshots*   Restore snapshot

                                                                         Copy snapshot   >   ⚙

☑	Snapshot name	▽	DB instance or cluste	Share snapshot	ime
				Migrate snapshot	
☑	certificationsnap		certdb	Export to Amazon S3	18 (UTC-03:00)

AWS Backup is a managed service for centralizing and automating backup plans of AWS services in the cloud and resources hosted on premises.

AWS Backup permits the RDS backups management using resource tagging to associate the RDS instance backup with backup plans.

Backtrack

Backtrack is a feature that enables you to rewind the DB cluster to a specific time that you need. Backtracking is not a substitute for backing up the Amazon Aurora DB cluster; however, backtracking a DB cluster to an exact time is much faster than restoring a backup. Backtrack is available only in Amazon Aurora MySQL-Compatible, and you can customize how many retention hours to keep in the target backtrack window; the maximum is 72 hours. By enabling backtracking, you can do the following:

- Revert mistaken operations, such as an update command without a where clause. In a situation like that, you can backtrack the DB cluster to a moment before the erroneous statement execution.

- Ensure that the database will be available quickly. In a similar situation without backtrack enabled, you could perform a point-in-time restore to the time before the mistaken operation, but it would take hours to complete, depending on the DB cluster size.

- Explore the DB cluster to find out when the mistake operation occurred. For example, you can backtrack the database to several different points in time to query the data from the tables; it's a nondestructive operation.

Cloning an Amazon Aurora DB Cluster Volume

Cloning is available only for Amazon Aurora. It's an instant image taken at the storage level. Cloning is quicker and more space-saving than restoring from a snapshot.

Cloning uses the *copy-on-write protocol*. Initially, a clone requires only minimal additional space, and Aurora maintains the same storage data for both clusters. The Aurora storage will allocate additional space only when data changes and generates new block images on the source or the cloned cluster.

Let's explore graphically how cloning works.

Before cloning the DB cluster, the example storage allocated shown in Figure 4.40 has four pages.

FIGURE 4.40   Before cloning the database

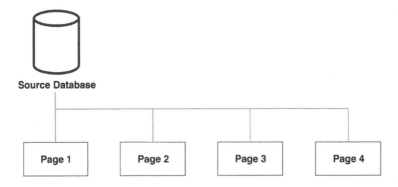

Just after cloning, both the source and the cloned DB clusters share the same storage pages (Figure 4.41).

FIGURE 4.41   Just after cloning

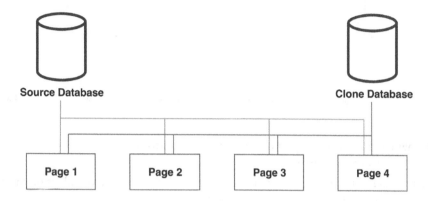

After the source database changes the data on page 1, it creates its own page 1 (Figure 4.42).

FIGURE 4.42   After some changes at source database

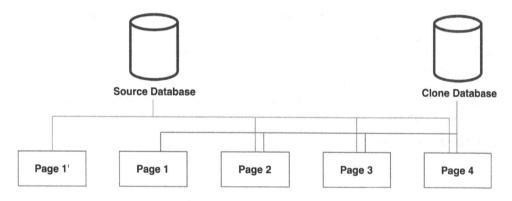

After the cloned database changes the data at page 4, now the cloned database has its own page 4 (Figure 4.43).

FIGURE 4.40   After changes at cloned database

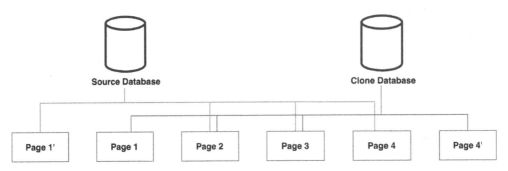

Note that cloning has no impact on Aurora cluster performance.

The following are some use cases:

- You're going to test the impact of a change in the database, even on tables or parameters. Creating a clone for testing the process and the impact is faster and more space-efficient than restoring from regular backups, enabling a safer strategy to perform the test impact in the DB cluster.

- You're going to perform an intensive analytical workload and don't want to cause a performance impact at the source Aurora cluster.

- You need to create a copy of the production DB cluster for a test environment.

Using the cloning mechanism, you won't be charged twice for the storage allocation. You'll be charged only for the additional changed data generated by the pages modified, as demonstrated in Figure 4.43.

Aurora supports up to 15 clones of a single Aurora DB cluster.

To clone an Aurora cluster, on Amazon RDS console, select the cluster to be cloned, select the Actions tab, and then select Create Clone (Figure 4.44).

FIGURE 4.44   Aurora cluster cloning

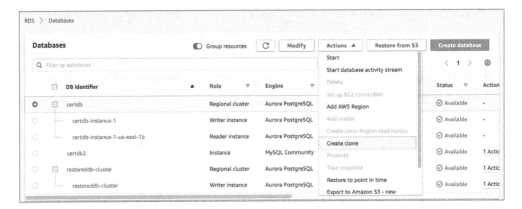

Auditing

Auditing is a requirement for environments that need to track database activities. For example, you can identify who (user/hostname) performed some statement, the specific SQL statement, the exact execution time, the IP address, and other information important to track what's going on with the data stored and how the data is being accessed by applications.

RDS offers the following methods to enable auditing the database activities according to the database engine:

- **Amazon Aurora:** `server_audit_logging` allows you to enable or disable the advanced auditing, available only in Aurora MySQL-Compatible, and `server_audit_events` allows you to specify which events to log.

  You can configure the following events in `server_audit_events`:

  - **CONNECT:** Records both successful and failed connections and disconnections and user information

  - **QUERY:** Records all queries in plain text, including queries that fail due to syntax or permission errors

  - **QUERY_DCL:** Records only data control language (DCL) queries (for example, `GRANT` and `REVOKE`)

  - **QUERY_DDL:** Records data definition language (DDL) queries (for example, `CREATE` and `ALTER`)

  - **QUERY_DML:** Records data manipulation language (DML) queries (`INSERT`, `UPDATE`, and `SELECT`)

  - **TABLE:** Records the tables that were affected by query execution

- **RDS for PostgreSQL:** You can employ the `pgaudit` extension. Once the extension is enabled, PostgreSQL will record the audit activities at `pgaudit.log`.

- **RDS for MySQL or MariaDB:** The MariaDB Audit plugin records events issued on the database—for example, connections, disconnections, queries, or tables queried.

To enable the MariaDB Audit plugin, you must create a custom option group and assign it to the database instance, as follows:

1. Create a custom option group or modify an existing custom option group.
2. Assign the MariaDB Audit Plugin option to the option group, and configure the option settings.
3. Assign the option group to the database.

You can also publish the audit logs to Amazon CloudWatch to monitor the events:

1. In the Amazon RDS Console, select the database in the display window.
2. Select the DB instance that requires exporting log to CloudWatch.
3. Choose Modify.
4. In the Log exports section, select Audit Log.

5. Choose Continue.

6. Review the summary of modifications, and select Modify Instance.

Database Activity Stream in Amazon Aurora

- Another alternative to monitor the database activity in Amazon Aurora is the Database Activity Streams (DAS) feature. Using DAS, you can monitor database activities in near real time. By combining monitoring tools, you can watch and audit activities in the database. SQL statements and CONNECT details are collected, and Aurora pushes the database activities to an Amazon Kinesis stream. From Kinesis, you can configure AWS services such as Amazon Kinesis Firehose and AWS Lambda to consume the activity stream.

DAS generates data in event records in JSON format. The JSON record stores a database connection's valuable information for an audit requirement, such as the following:

- `logTime`
- `clientApplication`
- `dbUserName`
- `databaseName`
- `remoteHost`
- `remotePort`
- `command`
- `commandText`
- `objectType`
- `objectName`
- `exitCode`
- `rowCount`
- `serverType`
- `serviceName`
- `serverVersion`
- `dbProtocol`
- `netProtocol`
- `errorMessage`

Security

Managing security for databases is crucial. At the conception of your database implementation, it's important to plan several aspects of security based on the security requirements of the business and applications.

The following resources are available to handle security in RDS databases:

- **VPC:** When you launch an RDS instance, choose the VPC with the most significant network access control for your business operation.

- **Security groups:** Employ security groups to manage which IP address or EC2 instance can reach the database. When you launch an RDS instance, you define the security group with the appropriate security rules to avoid undesirable access to the database. The security group is similar to a firewall and has rules specifying the protocol, port, and source IP address or another security group and the allowed rules.

- **Identity and access management (IAM):** Utilizing IAM, you can control the permissions to operate, create, describe, modify, and delete database instances, tag resources, or modify security groups.

- **Encryption at rest:** You can choose to secure your data at rest and in snapshots. Amazon RDS employs the industry-standard AES-256 encryption algorithm to encrypt the data hosted on the database server.

- **Encryption in transit:** To protect the data in transit, you can configure the TLS or SSL connection in Amazon RDS.

- **Transparent Data Encryption (TDE):** To encrypt tables or tablespace, you can configure the native encryption mechanism available in database engines such as Oracle or SQL Server TDE.

RDS Encryption in Transit

The industry-standard protocol Secure Sockets Layer (SSL) enables secure network connections between the client and server. Since version 3.0, the name changed to Transport Layer Security (TLS), but we frequently refer to the protocol as SSL. To encrypt your data in transit, you need to use SSL/TLS connections.

For SSL, you must configure SSL certificates for the data in transit encryption. The client must trust the AWS root certified authority (CA).

To enforce SSL, you must configure encryption in transit according to the database engine.

- **MariaDB or MySQL:** Execute the following command at the database engine:

  ```
  ALTER USER 'service_user'@'%' REQUIRE SSL;
  ```

- **PostgreSQL:** Change the parameter `rds.force_ssl` to 1 by updating the parameter group for the DB instance. Modifying this parameter requires a reboot.

- **Microsoft SQL Server:** Change the parameter `rds.force_ssl` to 1 by adjusting the parameter group for the DB instance. You can also encrypt specific connections. Modifying this parameter requires a reboot.

- **Oracle:** Amazon RDS supports Oracle native network encryption (NNE). You must add the NNE option to the option group to enable it. Changing this parameter doesn't require a reboot.

To connect using SSL, you need to configure the connection client side according to the database engine. To provide the SSL Trust certificate, download it from https:// s3.amazonaws.com/rds-downloads/rds-ca-2019-root.pem.

You need to provide SSL options to connect to the database.

For Microsoft SQL Server, append `encrypt=true` to your connection string to encrypt the connection from other SQL clients.

To use SSL on PostgreSQL:

```
$ psql -h postgresqldb1.xxxxxxxxx.us-east-1.rds.amazonaws.com -p
5432 "dbname=mydb1 user=service_user sslrootcert=rds-ca-2019-
root.pem sslmode=verify-full"
```

To connect using SSL on MariaDB:

```
mysql -h mysqldb1.xxxxxxxxx.rds-us-east-1.amazonaws.com --ssl-
ca=[full path]rds-combined-ca-bundle.pem --ssl-mode=REQUIRED
```

To connect using SSL on MySQL:

```
mysql -h mysqldb1..xxxxxxxxx.rds-us-east-1.amazonaws.com --ssl-
ca=[full path]rds-combined-ca-bundle.pem --ssl-mode=VERIFY_IDENTITY
```

If you don't configure an SSL connection in a DB instance with the SSL enforcement enabled, it will result in an error.

RDS Encryption at Rest

Amazon RDS–encrypted DB instances use the industry-standard AES-256 encryption, and the AWS Key Management Service (AWS KMS) manages the keys. All logs, backups, and snapshots are encrypted for an Amazon RDS–encrypted DB instance.

Enabling DB encryption on RDS doesn't require any change at the application level or even a connection to the DB instance.

You can encrypt both primary and read replicas.

The encryption must be defined at the launch time of the DB instance. You can't modify this configuration later.

If you need to encrypt an unencrypted DB instance, you must create a snapshot of the DB instance and then generate an encrypted copy of that snapshot. Then you restore the encrypted snapshot, and the new DB instance will be encrypted.

Another method to enable encryption at rest in RDS is using TDE for Oracle and Microsoft SQL Server. You can use the TDE option for Oracle, and you can use the `TRANSPARENT_DATA_ENCRYPTION` option for Microsoft SQL Server. This feature is available by configuring the option group.

The database performance might be affected if you enable TDE and encryption at rest together. To choose the best encryption method, consider the application, performance, and compliance requirements for the DB instance.

Migrating Databases

Migrating databases is a critical task and must be planned carefully according to the downtime supported by the application and the complexity of the migration process.

The first step is choosing the target engine database to identify if a migration tool is required or if a native migration method is available. Keep in mind that using the native engine tools usually is the simplest way to migrate compatible engines.

For an RDS for MySQL or RDS for PostgreSQL to Amazon Aurora migration, the easiest method is to create an Aurora read replica from the source RDS DB instance. Once the replica becomes synchronized, you can schedule a maintenance window, promote the Aurora read replica to a new stand-alone primary database, and make it available to the application.

 Chapter 12 explores several migration methods in detail.

Summary

Relational databases are widely used for applications. They're important for applications that require relational consistency among tables, constraint enforcement at database level, and transaction control (commit and rollback) guaranteed by the database engine.

Amazon RDS supports six important database engines and supports native migration methods.

Amazon RDS automates the most time-consuming manual tasks, unlocking the architects, administrators, and developers to enable innovation and performance for the databases with much more reliability than deploying databases on Amazon EC2.

You can use tools like Aurora cloning and read replicas as a strategy to reduce downtime and risk during maintenance windows. To implement better and reduce operational deployment errors, you can rely on CloudFormation, as described in Chapter 14, "Saving Time and Reducing Errors Automating Your Infrastructure."

Exam Essentials

Know how to handle high availability and scalability on RDS.   For high availability on RDS, you can rely on Multi-AZ, and you can rely on read replicas for scaling read operations. Especially on Amazon Aurora, the read replica will attend to both high availability and scaling read operations.

Know how to manage and troubleshoot on Amazon RDS.   Databases require the usual management tools for troubleshooting, tuning statements, and auditing. For tuning SQL statements, you can use Performance Insights. For tuning the database instance, you can better understand the problem by using enhanced monitoring. For auditing and logging ıcquiremonto, you can enable this operation according to the database engine. For managing and changing database instance parameters, in RDS you can use the parameter groups. For managing additional options in the database, you can configure using option groups.

Know how to migrate from RDS to Amazon Aurora with minimal downtime.   It is important to understand how you can easily migrate from Amazon RDS MySQL and PostgreSQL to Amazon Aurora using read replicas. This is the fastest method, is easiest to implement, and has little downtime.

Know how to manage backups.   Amazon RDS enables automatic backups and point-in-time restore; it also enables you to use snapshots for longer retention and for additional backup requirements. You can also enable AWS Backup integration with RDS snapshots.

Know the pricing model.   Amazon RDS lets you choose the pay-as-you-go pricing model for environments that you can stop and start when your workload requires (for example, staging environments or any other type of temporary environment) and also lets you use the reserved instance model for environments that you are sure will be active for longer periods of time and have better discounts. It's essential to know the difference between pay-as-you-go and reserved instances and when to choose each.

Know how to secure the data at rest and in transit.   Amazon RDS supports encryption at rest using the industry-standard AES-256 encryption and the KMS managed keys. RDS also allows the encryption-in-transit configuration to secure connections using the database engine's specific methods. For the exam, it is essential to have a clear understanding of managing encryption at rest, converting an unencrypted database to an encrypted one, and vice versa. It is also important to understand the steps to encrypt the connections for data-in-transit security.

Know important cloud-native features in Amazon Aurora.   Amazon Aurora features such as cloning, read replicas for horizontal scaling, and automatic failover will improve resilience and performance for transactional environments. It is essential for the exam to understand when specific Amazon Aurora features will be useful for the question in the proposed environment.

Exercises

For assistance and additional details to complete the proposed exercises, refer to Amazon RDS and Amazon Aurora documentation at `https://docs.aws.amazon.com/AmazonRDS/latest/AuroraUserGuide/CHAP_Aurora.html` and `https://docs.aws.amazon.com/AmazonRDS/latest/UserGuide/CHAP_GettingStarted.html`.

EXERCISE 4.1

Create an Amazon RDS MySQL and enable Multi-AZ

In this exercise, you will create an Amazon RDS MySQL database and enable Multi-AZ:

1. Log in as a user with Amazon RDS privileges in AWS Console.

2. Navigate to RDS Console.

3. Click on the "Create database" option.

4. In the "Engine options" section, select "MySQL."

5. In the "Engine Version" section, choose the appropriate MySQL version.

6. In the "Templates" section, choose "Dev/Test."

7. In the "Availability and durability" section, choose the "Multi-AZ DB instance" option.

8. In the "Settings" section, in the DB instance identifier section you can keep the default name or rename to `exercise-41-db-certification-<Account ID>`, it will be similar to `exercise-41-db-certification-123456789012`.

9. In the "Credential Settings", at the "Master username" section, you can keep the default admin or rename to a username more appropriate to your use case.

10. In the "Master password" section, define a password for your "Master username" and confirm the same password in the "Confirm master password" section.

11. In the "Instance configuration," at the "DB instance class" section, change to "Burstable classes (includes t classes)" and select the db.t3.micro instance class.

12. In the "Storage" section, change the "Storage type" to general purpose SSD (gp2).

13. In the "Allocated storage" section change to 20 GiB.

14. In the "Connectivity" section in the "Virtual private cloud (VPC) section, select the VPC or keep the Default VPC.

15. In the "DB subnet group" section you can keep the default subnet group or choose another.

16. In the "Public access" section select "No".

17. In the "VPC security group (firewall)" section, select "choose existing".

18. In the "Existing VPC security groups" section, select the default.

19. In the "Database authentication" section, choose the "Password authentication" option.

20. Click on "Create database".

Create an Amazon Aurora cluster

In this exercise you will launch an Amazon Aurora cluster (MySQL-Compatible) with a writer instance and an Aurora replica:

1. Log in as a user with Amazon RDS privileges in AWS Console.

2. Navigate to the RDS Console.

3. Click on the "Create database" option.

4. In the "Engine options", at the Engine type, choose Aurora (MySQL–Compatible).

5. In the "Available versions" section, select Aurora MySQL 3.02.2 (compatible with MySQL 8.0.23).

6. In the "Templates" section, choose the Dev/Test option.

7. In the "Settings", at the "DB cluster identifier", you can keep the default name or rename to `exercise-42-db-certification-<Account ID>`, it will be similar to `exercise-42-db-certification-123456789012`.

8. In the "Credential Settings", in the "Master username" section, you can keep the default admin or rename to a username more appropriate to your use case.

9. In the "Master password" section, define a password for your "Master username" and confirm the same password in the "Confirm master password" section.

10. In the "Instance configuration", at the "DB instance class", select "Memory optimized classes (includes r classes)", then choose the db.r6g.large instance class.

11. In the "Availability & Durability" section, select "Create an Aurora Replica or Reader node in a different AZ".

12. In the "Connectivity" section in the "Virtual private cloud (VPC)" section, select the VPC or keep the Default VPC.

13. In the "DB subnet group" section you can keep the default subnet group or choose another.

14. In the "Public access" section select "No".

15. In the "VPC security group (firewall)" section, select "choose existing".

16. In the "Existing VPC security groups" section, select the default.

17. In the "Database authentication" section, choose the "Password authentication" option.

18. Click on "Create database".

EXERCISE 4.3

Add an Amazon Aurora replica and modify the priority

In this exercise you will add an Aurora replica to the previous Aurora cluster and modify to a higher priority for failover situations:

1. Log in as a user with Amazon RDS privileges in AWS Console.

2. Navigate to RDS Console.

3. Select the `exercise-42-db-certification-123456789012` database.

4. In the "Actions" option, click on "Add reader".

5. In the "Settings", at the DB instance identifier, define a name like `replica-exercise-42-db-certification-123456789012`.

6. In the "Instance configuration", select "Memory optimized classes (includes r classes)", and choose db.r6g.large instance class.

7. In the "Additional configuration", at the "Failover priority" section, choose tier-0.

8. Select "Add reader".

Review Questions

1. The RDS database instance was rebooted and is having problems starting; you are getting errors on the parameter group due to incompatible parameter status. How can you safely fix this problem?

    A. Reset the parameter group to the default values, and reboot the instance.

    B. Select the incompatible parameter group of the instance, make a copy, select the parameter group actions, choose Edit, choose the valid parameter values, and save the changes. Reboot the instance without failover to apply the new values at the DB instance.

    C. Select the RDS database, and modify the DB to the default parameter group instead of the custom problematic parameter group.

    D. Remove the custom parameter group; it will force the instance to use the default parameter group.

2. You have a legal requirement to retain the RDS database backup taken on the last day of the month for two years. Which method is the most appropriate to meet the requirements?

    A. Configure the automatic backup retention for two years; then you'll be able to restore at any time within this period.

    B. Take a manual snapshot and configure the appropriate retention.

    C. Use the clone feature to keep regular database images.

    D. Export the database snapshot to S3.

3. The application team is detecting an odd behavior in the application and has asked you to help identify what SQL statements are consuming the most resources in the RDS database. Which feature will better assist this requirement quickly?

    A. Use Performance Insight, and check the top SQL session.

    B. Prefer a native migration tool according to the database engine. For example, for PostgreSQL, use pgbadger; or for MySQL, use MySQL EXPLAIN.

    C. Analyze the SQL statements' execution plan.

    D. Check the slow query logs exported on CloudWatch.

4. You received a request to validate a maintenance patch on the Amazon Aurora cluster. This is a critical application, and you must guarantee the minimal interruption time if something goes wrong, and the application must be returned to the previous structure. Which method will best attend to this requirement?

    A. Take a database snapshot. If something bad occurs, restore the snapshot.

    B. Restore from automatic backup to the point in time exactly previous to the maintenance.

    C. Launch a new Amazon Aurora cluster, and configure logical replication from the original cluster to the new Amazon Aurora cluster. If something goes wrong, point to the new cluster.

D. Create a clone of the database before performing the maintenance. If something bad occurs, quickly start the clone image and point the application to the clone database cluster.

5. Your team is working on the development of an application and has received the requirement to encrypt the data in transit between RDS for PostgreSQL and the application tier. How can you enable this?

 A. Require an SSL connection at the session layer.

 B. In your RDS for PostgreSQL instance, change the parameter `rds.force_ssl=1` in the parameter group, and reboot the instance. On the application side, download the certificate `rds-ca-2019-root.pem`, and for the connection define `sslmode=verify-full`.

 C. Select Native Network Encryption in the option group.

 D. Enable the parameter `rds.force_ssl=1` to enforce SSL.

6. You were requested to store the SQL statements issued by the user's connections in the Amazon Aurora database. This information must be stored for a long time, and after one year if the information is required, it's acceptable to wait some time to retrieve the information. Which option is the best alternative?

 A. Enable Database Activity Stream (DAS), store the JSON events in Amazon S3, and configure a life-cycle policy to move the files to infrequent access storage class after one year.

 B. Enable the MariaDB Audit Plugin option, creating a custom option group.

 C. Enable the `pgaudit` extension.

 D. Enable the `server_audit_logging` and `server_audit_events` advanced parameters on Amazon Aurora.

7. You received a request to attend to the audit requirement for your RDS for MySQL database. It's required to identify SQL statements issued in the DB instance and also to read this audit log from a management console to configure notifications. How can you answer this request?

 A. Enable the MariaDB Audit Plugin option, creating a custom parameter group.

 B. Enable the MariaDB Audit Plugin option, creating a custom option group. Add the MariaDB plugin option to the option group, configure the option settings, apply the option to the Database, and publish the audit logs to CloudWatch.

 C. Create a logon trigger that captures and stores the statements issued by the users.

 D. Enable Database Activity Streams (DAS).

8. Your customer has RDS for PostgreSQL and has decided to migrate to Amazon Aurora PostgreSQL. He has asked you which is the best option to reduce the downtime for the application.

 A. Using the `pg_dump` tool to connect to the RDS for PostgreSQL instance and generate a backup; create the Amazon Aurora PostgreSQL instance; use `pg_restore` to connect to Amazon Aurora PostgreSQL and restore the backup.

   B.   Create an Amazon Aurora read replica from the RDS for PostgreSQL; when the Amazon Aurora read replica lag reaches zero, promote the read replica, and connect the application to the newly promoted Amazon Aurora PostgreSQL.

   C.   Replicate from RDS for PostgreSQL to Amazon Aurora PostgreSQL using AWS DMS.

   D.   Use the pg_dump tool to connect to the RDS for PostgreSQL instance and generate a backup; copy the backup to Amazon S3; at the RDS Console, on the creation step, select the Restore From S3 option.

9. Your customer has a MySQL database on premises and has decided to migrate to Aurora MySQL. Which option is the best method to simplify and reduce downtime during the migration?

   A.   Create an Amazon Aurora MySQL instance; create an AWS DMS instance and configure the endpoints and migration task; then start the migration task to start loading the data from the MySQL on premises to Aurora.

   B.   Use mysqldump to extract the MySQL backup; copy the dump file to an EC2 instance; and use the MySQL client to connect to the Amazon Aurora MySQL instance and restore from the dump file.

   C.   Generate a backup from the source MySQL DB using the Percona XtraBackup tool, and copy the backup file to an S3 bucket. At the Amazon Aurora instance creation, select the Restore From S3 option, and select the S3 bucket where the backup file was uploaded. After the restore is completed, establish binlog replication from MySQL on premises to Amazon Aurora MySQL.

   D.   Create a read replica from MySQL on premises to Amazon Aurora MySQL. When the replication is completed and without any lag, switch the application to the new Amazon Aurora MySQL.

10. You have an Amazon RDS database unencrypted, and the company now needs to attend to a regulatory requirement of encryption at rest. What can you do to attend to this requirement?

   A.   Modify the database configuration to encrypt the DB instance.

   B.   It is not possible to modify the database.

   C.   Take a snapshot, copy the snapshot with the encryption option, and restore the encrypted snapshot; then you'll have an encrypted DB instance.

   D.   Create a read-replica with encryption and promote the read-replica.

Chapter 5

Low-Latency Response Time for Your Apps and APIs

THE AWS CERTIFIED DATABASE – SPECIALTY EXAM OBJECTIVES COVERED IN THIS CHAPTER MAY INCLUDE, BUT ARE NOT LIMITED TO, THE FOLLOWING:

✓ **Domain 1: Workload-Specific Database Design**
- 1.2 Identify strategies for high availability and disaster recovery solutions.
- 1.3 Database designs for scalability, compliance, and performance.
- 1.4 Take into consideration database solutions costs.

✓ **Domain 2: Deployment and Migration**
- 2.2 Be familiar with the migration strategies and data preparation steps.

✓ **Domain 3: Management and Operations**
- 3.1 Maintenance tasks and processes.
- 3.2 Backup and restore strategies.

✓ **Domain 4: Monitoring and troubleshooting**
- 4.2 Know how to identify and resolve common database issues.
- 4.3 Database performance optimization.

✓ **Domain 5: Database security**
- 5.1 Data encryption in transit and at rest.
- 5.3 The authentication and access control mechanisms.
- 5.4 Be aware of potential security vulnerabilities related to the database solutions.

In this chapter, you will learn about the main functionalities of Amazon DynamoDB and Amazon Keyspaces (for Apache Cassandra) and when to leverage them. You will also learn how to migrate, deploy, and operate workloads using DynamoDB or Keyspaces as the data store. The chapter will cover DynamoDB and Keyspaces security, scalability, and availability aspects. Finally, it will familiarize you with the following features of DynamoDB and Keyspaces:

- DynamoDB:
  - Local and global secondary indexes
  - On-demand and provisioned capacity modes
  - In-memory accelerator
  - Real-time event handling with DynamoDB Streams
  - Active/active global tables
  - Continuous backups
  - Autoscaling and burst capacity
- Keyspaces:
  - Clustering keys
  - On-demand and provisioned capacity modes
  - Static columns
  - Continuous backups
  - Consistency models

Getting Started with Modern Applications and NoSQL Databases

Before we start talking about the low-latency database systems on AWS, we need to mention that the application patterns and architectures have evolved significantly over the years and brought new challenges related to scalability, developer efficiency, performance, and total cost of ownership (TCO). This phenomenon is a consequence of the following trends related to the data:

Microservice and analytics   Organizations are moving from legacy monolithic applications to a modern microservices architecture. Microservices let organizations decouple complex problems into independent components so developers can build and operate in small groups with fewer dependencies and, therefore, respond more quickly to business chances. However, there are two implications in this trend.

- First, developers can pick the best tool to build those specific components, including the database layer.

- Second, because those microservices are independent from each other, there is a need for detailed monitoring and analytics capabilities to understand what's not working well between them.

Explosion of data   A lot of data is being generated every second worldwide. Companies already know that it is crucial to track and keep all that data, especially the data that comes from their business applications. However, that growth is also coming from data generated by smart devices such as smart homes, mobile phones, wearable technologies, connected cars, home appliances, industrial equipment, security systems, etc. Most high-end new cars are coming out with built-in cellular connections. Those connections alone account for one-third of mobile sign-ups with telecom cellular networks. Modern applications also generate data in real time, such as user behavior from mobile apps, purchase data from e-commerce sites, and data from social media applications.

DevOps and innovation   As companies need to innovate quickly to keep up with the competition, the IT velocity also changes, which is why most of them are transitioning to a DevOps model. This model leverages different tools to automate the software development life cycle and, as a consequence, improves the software delivery pace, which also affects the change rate of data and its structure.

Cloud application characteristics are very different from traditional applications. Users can easily be in the millions order of magnitude; data volumes can reach PB and EB levels on short notice. Performance is often measured in milliseconds and microseconds. On average, the app serves millions of requests per second and on big days processes tens of millions of requests per second. This application variance demands that systems can scale up, out, and in to maintain the right cost profile.

The workloads with these new requirements can be fulfilled only by using multiple purpose-built databases; in this chapter, we will focus on low-latency key-value and wide-column NoSQL databases on AWS, Amazon DynamoDB, and Amazon Keyspaces (for Apache Cassandra).

Amazon DynamoDB

Amazon DynamoDB is a cloud-native NoSQL database engine compatible with key-value and document databases created by AWS. It is a fully managed, multiregion, durable, and highly available service capable of delivering single-digit millisecond performance at any scale. The scale can be pretty impressive. There is a story about a media company supporting the 2017 Super Bowl and handling 10+ millions of transactions per second at the end of the game with their DynamoDB table. A more recent example is the Amazon 2020 Prime Day, where over the course of the 66-hour event, the retail application components running using DynamoDB made 16.4 trillion calls to the API, peaking at 80.1 million requests per second.

AWS does the heavy lifting related to running a massively scalable NoSQL database on behalf of the customer, allowing their software developers to focus on adding functionalities rather than managing infrastructure. Developers only need to learn the DynamoDB's API instead of having to become experts in advanced distributed database and compute concepts.

DynamoDB is also cost effective; the customers pay for the actual storage they are allocating and the read/write throughput values they have provisioned. When the application requires only a small portion of storage and compute, that small amount of capacity is what needs to be provisioned in the DynamoDB service. As the usage of the application grows and the required storage and throughput increase, DynamoDB keeps up by adding more capacity on the fly. This elasticity at the database layer enables the application to seamlessly grow to support millions of concurrent users making thousands of requests to the database every second.

Design Considerations

The common relational database model is nicely organized in human-readable components such as tables, columns, foreign keys, etc., and the data is related. It is modeled to reduce storage because decades ago the storage was expensive; now the storage is very cheap compared to compute power.

We step off into the world of aggregated items, essentially prebuilt items. Rather than running queries/joins across tables, these items are written as they will be fetched, making it very compute-cheap and fast to store and retrieve each one of them. This requires understanding the access patterns and writing the data appropriately, but the benefits are nearly limitless scale and consistent performance, which is precisely where Amazon DynamoDB excels.

Amazon DynamoDB Design

Rather than storing data in tables with rows and columns, DynamoDB stores data in tables with items and attributes, with one or two attributes chosen as the primary key.

The tables in DynamoDB are similar to those in other common database systems. They are collections of data organized in items.

A *DynamoDB item* is a collection of attributes that is uniquely identifiable among the other items in the table. It is similar to a row in traditional database systems.

A *DynamoDB attribute* is the fundamental data element in DynamoDB, something that does not need to be broken down any further. Attributes in DynamoDB are similar to columns in SQL database systems.

Additionally, each table can have secondary indexes, a cache layer, and read and write capacity units, among other features. Which feature to leverage for each table will depend on the database design.

There are six main tenets to consider when designing a DynamoDB database:

- **Use case:** The nature of the application, for example, a mobile app, a game backend, a product catalog, a session storage, or a cache system.

- **Access pattern:** The relation between read and write operations. What are the necessary query dimensions and aggregations?

- **Application type:** Whether the workload type resembles online transaction processing (OLTP) or online analytical processing (OLAP) behavior.

- **Define the data life cycle:** Time to live (TTL), backup, and archival.

- **Identify the primary keys:** How the inserts and gets are going to be done. How would the data spread among the partitions?

- **Data modeling:** Start with one table. This helps break that relational training, but it also helps reduce the number of round trips. Try to organize data to be returned as related collections under partition keys.

Table 5.1 describes the main difference between SQL and NoSQL databases.

TABLE 5.1   SQL and NoSQL Comparison

SQL	NoSQL
Normalized/relational	Denormalized/hierarchical
Ad hoc queries	Instantiated views
Scale vertically	Scale horizontally
Good for OLAP	Built for OLTP* at scale

Partition and Sort Keys

DynamoDB supports two different kinds of primary keys:

Partition Key   The partition key must be string, number, or binary. Each table can have only one partition key, and it is one of the attributes of the table that identifies each item individually, so it has to be unique. It's known as a *partition key* because DynamoDB uses its value as input to an internal hash function to evenly distribute data items across partitions. The output of the mentioned hash function determines the partition (physical device) in which the item will be stored.

Composite Key   The composite key consists of two attributes: a partition key and a sort key. Items with the same value for the partition key will be stored in the same partition, using the same hash function as the partition key in a sorted way. Using the attribute defined as the sort key. In a table with a partition key and a sort key, it's possible for two different items to have the same partition key value. Nevertheless, those two items must have different values as the sort key.

Most Amazon DynamoDB tables can benefit from using a composite key approach. Imagine a Book table described in items and attributes for an example of a table with a composite primary key (Author and Title). You can access any item in the Book and its regular attributes (such as genre, year, and language) directly if you provide the Author and Title values for that item. Figure 5.1 shows the previously described DynamoDB table.

FIGURE 5.1   DynamoDB table: Books

Primary Key		Data Attributes		
Partition Key	Sort Key	Attr 1	Attr 2	Attr 3
	Title 1	Genre: Fantasy	Year: 2019	Language: EN
	Title 2	Genre: Novel	Year: 2020	Language: EN
Author 1	Title 3	Genre: Fiction	Year: 2018	Language: FR
	Title 4	Genre: Romance	Year: 2021	Language: EN
	Title 5	Genre: Mystery	Year: 2018	Language: ES

The composite primary also provides extra flexibility when querying the data. For example, if you provide only the value for Author, DynamoDB retrieves all of the books by that particular author. To retrieve only a subset of books by a particular author, you can provide a value for Author along with a range of values for the book titles.

Migrating Your Data into DynamoDB

There are three main sources from which you can migrate data into a DynamoDB database:

- Plain-text files like JSON documents on Amazon S3
- NoSQL database like MongoDB and Cassandra
- RDBMS sources like MySQL

Let's go through an overview of the available options and good practices for each one of them.

Plain-Text Files

There are several options to migrate plain-text data. Let's review the five main ones.

If you can control the format and type of the file, the fastest and most cost-effective way to do it is by using a JSON file in a PutItem API payload-like format and use the `batch-write-item` AWS CLI operation to bulk load the data into the DynamoDB table, as in this example:

```
aws dynamodb batch-write-item --request-items file://ProductCatalog.json
```

If the data is on a random format in a random file type, the best way to do it is by using an AWS Lambda function. You need to load the data from the location where it resides—ideally on Amazon S3 due to the fast and seamless integration it has with AWS Lambda. Then, you can start putting the items into the DynamoDB table by using the SDK available in the language you use to code the Lambda function.

If the data is in a comma-separated value format in Amazon S3, you can use the AWS Database Migration Service (AWS DMS) to do the migration. To use S3 as a source for DMS, the source data files must be in CSV format, and you need to build a JSON mapping file for the tables and the columns for the DynamoDB target database.

If neither of the previous approaches can be done due to format or data volume constraints, you can use the Amazon EMR service to load data from Amazon S3 to DynamoDB. You can do this by using a source file in Apache Hive format, but it requires a deeper knowledge of AWS services, AWS APIs, and HiveQL.

You can also leverage AWS Glue to create and orchestrate ETL jobs in Python Shell or PySpark.

Amazon EMR and AWS Glue options can be used also to export data from Amazon DynamoDB into Amazon S3.

NoSQL Databases

Since DynamoDB is a NoSQL database, the migration from another NoSQL source should be seamless, especially if you use a tool like AWS DMS. It doesn't support live migration by using Change Data Capture (CDC) as it does when migrating a SQL database, but since the NoSQL database engine provides high read and write throughput by default, the migration time window is typically smaller than with regular SQL import and export migrations. When using DMS, you can choose NoSQL database sources like MongoDB and Cassandra databases.

For MongoDB, you will have available two migration modes:

- **Document mode:** When using document mode, AWS DMS migrates all the data within the JSON document into a single column named "_doc" in the target DynamoDB table.

- **Table mode:** When using table mode, AWS DMS scans the specified number of documents in the source MongoDB database and then creates a schema with all the keys and their types it found during the previous scan. Additionally, customers can use the object mapping feature in AWS DMS to transform the original data from MongoDB to the desired structure in DynamoDB.

To perform the migration from a MongoDB database to DynamoDB, AWS DMS connects to the MongoDB database, reads all the source data, and then transforms that data to load it into the DynamoDB table. If the MongoDB database contains sharded collections, the customers need to migrate each one of the shards separately.

If the source database is Cassandra, there is also an automated way to do this, but it needs to be done by a component of AWS DMS dedicated to schema conversions: the AWS Schema Conversion Tool (AWS SCT).

To use the SCT for a Cassandra migration, you need to use a special data extraction agent available exclusively for Cassandra. This agent is compatible with most of the current Cassandra database versions. To be able to execute the migration without impacting your original system, you need to convert the current Cassandra database to a data center cluster. All the migration tasks will run on the newly created data center.

Data extraction is performed directly from each binary .db file using the Cassandra driver and data extraction agents. During the extraction process, the data is transformed into .csv files, and the metadata is stored in task-setting and table-mapping JSON files. The AWS DMS tasks use those files for the migration process, so the customers need to upload all the files to an Amazon S3 bucket. The final step is to load each file from Amazon S3 to DynamoDB by using the AWS Schema Conversion Tool and an AWS DMS task.

SQL

You can use the AWS Database Migration Service as well for this kind of migration. However, because RDBMS table designs could be very different from those of DynamoDB and NoSQL, you will need some time to think about how to distribute your current data into several DynamoDB tables and indexes and then build a mapping JSON on the AWS DMS task. There are a few DMS options like "map-record-to-record" that will automatically create a corresponding attribute on the target DynamoDB table for each column on the source database, but it still can be a complicated process.

You can decouple the migration into two steps by using AWS DMS as well. You can first migrate the data from the RDBMS database into plain-text files on Amazon S3 and then create another DMS task from Amazon S3 to DynamoDB. In this way, you can have more control over the process and perform some manual transformation between, but it will also require you to build mapping files to accommodate the data in the target DynamoDB tables.

Query Considerations

There are two ways of getting the data out of DynamoDB: queries and scans.

Queries

A *DynamoDB query* finds items in the database based on the primary key value. Optionally, you can also provide the value for the sort key attribute to refine the result further. When using the sort key attribute, you can leverage comparison operators to cover more access patterns with a single attribute. DynamoDB also provides the attributes projection feature to reduce the amount of data being retrieved from the database, in a similar way to how "Select X, Y, Z from. . ." works in the SQL world.

Besides the primary and sort key conditions, you can query the data by using filters on other attributes. Let's consider the difference between filters and sort key conditions.

Imagine an IoT application where devices' sensors are sending updates to a table, as shown in Figure 5.2. The table is organized by DeviceID, so it has a well-distributed/high-cardinality key space. The sort key is the date so that queries can return items in the most recent order. The combination of the ID and the date define a unique item; there could be a new log inserted for each device every five minutes.

FIGURE 5.2   Devices DynamoDB table

Primary key		
Partition key: DeviceID	Sort key: Date	
d#12345	2020-04-24T14:40:00	State WARNING1
	2020-04-24T14:45:00	State WARNING1
	2020-04-24T14:50:00	State WARNING1
	2020-04-24T14:55:00	State NORMAL
	2020-04-11T05:50:00	State WARNING3
	2020-04-11T05:55:00	State WARNING3
d#54321	2020-04-11T06:00:00	State NORMAL

To retrieve only warning logs for device d#12345 with this design, you can query using a WHERE clause like DeviceID=d#12345 and then filter out all the updates that were normal.

Using SQL-like syntax, this would look like this:

```
SELECT * FROM DeviceLog
WHERE DeviceID = 'd#12345'
```

```
ORDER BY Date DESC
FILTER ON State=WARNING
```

Using the DynamoDB query API, it would look like this:

```
aws dynamodb query
--table-name DeviceLog
--key-condition-expression "#dID = :dID"
--no-scan-index-forward
--filter-expression "#s = :s"
--expression-attribute-names '{"#dID": "DeviceID", "#s": "State}'
--expression-attribute-values '{":dID": {"S":"d#12345"}, ":s":
{"S":"WARNING"}}'
```

Now, this would be OK, but most systems may have more than 99 percent of updates with a normal state and less than 1 percent of updates that are warning. In this case, when a query is run on 500 items, typically 495 of them will be filtered out and 1 percent of them will be returned. The filter expression is applied after the query, so DynamoDB will read all 500 items regardless of whether it returns 5 or 500.

This design can be improved by implementing a composite sort key by concatenating two attributes that you are interested in, as shown in Figure 5.3. Use the most general on the left and concatenate the more unique on the right. This enables the begins_with condition we will see next.

FIGURE 5.3   Sort key attribute concatenation

Primary key	
Partition key: DeviceID	Sort key: State#Date
	NORMAL#2020-04-24T14:55:00
d#12345	WARNING1#2020-04-24T14:40:00
	WARNING1#2020-04-24T14:45:00
	WARNING1#2020-04-24T14:50:00
	NORMAL#2020-04-11T06:00:00
	NORMAL#2020-04-11T09:30:00
d#54321	WARNING2#2020-04-11T09:25:00
	WARNING3#2020-04-11T05:50:00
	WARNING3#2020-04-11T05:55:00

This action of moving a regular attribute into the primary key as part of the sort key fundamentally changes the access pattern. Now, if there were 500,000 saved items in total and only 500 with a warning state and you only want to retrieve the items with "warning" state wherever the begins_with query is run, it will read and return *only* the warning items, making it very efficient.

You can achieve the previous in traditional SQL-like syntax as follows:

```
SELECT * FROM DeviceLog
WHERE DeviceID = 'd#12345'
ORDER BY Date DESC
BEGINS_WITH
    State='WARNING'
```

This is how it looks with the actual DynamoDB API:

```
aws dynamodb query
--table-name DeviceLog
--no-scan-index-forward
--key-condition-expression "#dID = :dID  AND begins_with(#s, :sd)"
--expression-attribute-names '{"#cId": "DeviceID", "#s": "State#Date"}'
--expression-attribute-values '{":cId": {"S":"d#12345"}, ":sd":
{"S":"WARNING#"}}'
```

As you can see, there are several ways to optimize the query operation times and the compute resources used for each one. Let's dive deep now into the other way to get data out of DynamoDB.

Scans

The scan operation always searches through all the data, so it can be less efficient than other DynamoDB operations like query, which targets the specific partition where the items are located. Once the full scan finishes, it filters out values to provide the result you want, basically adding an extra step for removing data from the result set.

To get faster response times, you design your tables and indexes in a way that your applications can use query instead of scan. (In the case of tables, you can also use the BatchGet-Item and GetItem APIs calls.)

Because the scan operation reads an entire page (the default value in DynamoDB is 1 MB), you can mitigate the impact of the full scan operation by setting a smaller page size, which you can do by using the limit parameter.

It is strongly recommended to not perform scans on a table that has "mission-critical" traffic. You can handle this load by rotating traffic hourly between two tables—one for critical traffic and the other for the querying of bookkeeping purposes.

Another option is to perform parallel scan operations. Many applications can benefit from using it rather than the typical sequential scans. For instance, an application that needs to process a large table of historical data can leverage a parallel scan. As a rule of thumb, the tables that can better benefit from parallel scans are those with more than 20 GB of storage.

If you enjoy running queries with SQL instead of an API-like request, you will be able to do so by using PartiQL, a SQL-compatible query language. This way you can easily interact with DynamoDB tables and run ad hoc queries using the AWS Management Console, NoSQL Workbench, AWS Command Line Interface, and DynamoDB APIs for PartiQL. PartiQL operations provide the same availability, latency, and performance as the other DynamoDB data plane operations.

Amazon DynamoDB Index Options

Modern applications usually have several access patterns that cannot be resolved by just using composite keys and attribute filters. Database indexes are a way to support more access patterns within the same table.

An *index* is a data structure that reduces the speed of retrieval queries on a database table at the cost of additional storage capacity and extra write operations. Amazon DynamoDB provides two index mechanisms to seamlessly evolve the database to meet new access pattern demands: a local secondary index (LSI) and a global secondary index (GSI).

- **Global secondary index:** A GSI can be created at any time and with any kind of primary key because it's a partition key, and a sort key can be different from the one in the original table. A query on a global secondary index can span all of the data in the base table, across all partitions. Another important thing is that the global secondary index has no size limitations regarding storage and has its own provisioned throughput settings apart from the table ones.

- **Local secondary index:** An LSI can be created only at table creation time, and the table must have a composite primary key. It is essentially an index that has the same partition key as the base table but a different sort key. A local secondary index works in a way that every partition of a local secondary index is scoped to an original table partition that shares the same partition key value. As a result, the total size of locally indexed items for any partition key value can't exceed 10 GB. Regarding throughput, the local secondary index shares the provisioned throughput settings with the base table.

Table 5.2 represents the main difference between the LSI and GSI.

TABLE 5.2   LSI vs. GSI

LSI	GSI
Create at table creation	Create at any time
Shares WCU/RCU with table	WCU/RCU independent of table
Collection size <= 10 GB	No size limits
Limit = 5	Limit = 20
Strong consistency	Eventual consistency

Each table in DynamoDB can have by default up to 20 global secondary indexes and 5 local secondary indexes. This can be increased, but it might not be a good idea. In general, you should keep the number of indexes at a minimum. Just create those for the attributes you need to query very often, because it can be more expensive in terms of storage and throughput than the actual performance improvement for the application.

Another tip is to use a global secondary index, whenever possible, over a local secondary index. The exception is when the application needs strong consistency in the query results, which a local secondary index can provide and a global secondary index cannot. Note that the GSI should have enough capacity units to accommodate the original table throughput; otherwise, it could generate throttling issues.

Let's go back to our IoT sensors table example. What happens when there is a new access pattern? What if the system has a requirement to fetch data logs from an operator between two dates?

By keeping values as top-level attributes, you can add a GSI to the table at any time. A GSI in practical terms is a view or a second table that DynamoDB keeps up to date for you.

Using the Operator field of our table as a GSI-partition key, as shown in Figure 5.4, is a good choice here, because it will maintain high cardinality for the primary key of the GSI (a requirement just like the base table). By adding this GSI, we are establishing an M:N relationship (many devices to many operators).

FIGURE 5.4   Operator global secondary index

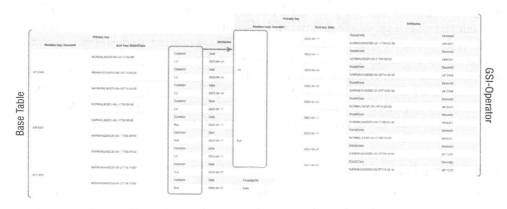

This is what a query for the logs of a given operator between two dates will look like in traditional SQL syntax:

```
SELECT * FROM GSI-Operator
WHERE Operator = 'Liz'
ORDER BY Date DESC
BETWEEN
      Date='2020-04-20' AND
            '2020-04-25'
```

This is what a query for the logs of a given operator between two dates will look like using the DynamoDB API:

```
aws dynamodb query
--table-name DeviceLog
--index-name GSI-Operator
--key-condition-expression "#op = :op AND #d  between :d1 AND :d2"
--expression-attribute-names '{"#op": "Operator" , "#d": "Date"}'
--expression-attribute-values '{":op": {"S":"Liz"} , ":d1":
{"S":"2020-04-20"}, ":d2":{"S":"2020-04-25"}}'
```

DynamoDB Capacity Modes

Another important point to consider when designing an Amazon DynamoDB table is the capacity mode. We have mentioned the terms *capacity* and *provisioned throughput* a couple of times in this chapter. Let's discover exactly what that means for Amazon DynamoDB.

DynamoDB comes with provisioned capacity mode as default, but it actually has two read/write capacity modes for processing each read and write operation on the tables.

On-Demand Capacity

On-demand capacity is the autopilot capacity option for Amazon DynamoDB. A pay-as-you-go billing option capable of serving from zero to thousands of requests per second without planning or provisioning capacity, DynamoDB instantly accommodates your work-loads as they ramp up or down at any given time. The on-demand mode instantly accommodates up to double the previous peak traffic on a table. For instance, if your table has a peak traffic of 3,000 reads per second, DynamoDB can accommodate up to 6,000 reads per second. Even if you need more than double your previous peak capacity, DynamoDB automatically allocates more capacity as your traffic volume increases to avoid throttling. Nevertheless, throttling can happen if you exceed double your previous peak within a 30-minute window.

Provisioned Capacity

Provisioned capacity mode requires you to specify the number of read and write operations per second the application needs from the table. This doesn't mean that you will only get up to that capacity; you can still use autoscaling techniques to adjust the table's provisioned capacity in response to traffic pattern changes. This feature helps customers to govern their DynamoDB capacity to stay at or below a defined request rate to save costs when there are some levels of predictability in the traffic.

The recommendation, if you are unsure about the table load the application will have, is to start with on-demand, monitor the table read and write capacity consumption for a period of time, and then decide whether you should switch to provisioned mode or continue using on-demand.

This capacity mode change can happen once every 24 hours. Consider that tables that use on-demand mode deliver the same single-digit millisecond latency, service-level agreement (SLA) commitment, and security that DynamoDB already offers for provisioned capacity—at a higher cost per granular read or write operation. The customers can choose on-demand capacity mode for new and existing tables without changing the API calls or the application code. Table 5.3 shows the main reasons to choose one mode or the other.

TABLE 5.3   On-Demand vs. Provisioned Capacity

On-Demand	Provisioned
Unpredictable spikes of application traffic	Predictable application traffic patterns
For new tables with unknown workloads	Applications with consistent traffic patterns
Ease of paying only for what you use	Can predict the capacity requirements to save costs

How does DynamoDB measure the capacity being provisioned? This is when the terms read capacity units (RCUs) and write capacity units (WCUs) come into play.

A *read capacity unit (RCU)* represents two eventually consistent reads or one strongly consistent read per second, as long as the item is up to 4 KB in size. If the item is more than 4 KB in size, it consumes the total size divided by 4 and rounded up to the next unit.

A *write capacity unit (WCU)* represents one write operation per second for an item up to 1 KB. If the application needs to write an item larger than 1 KB in size, DynamoDB consumes additional write capacity units the same way we explained before.

The current maximum DynamoDB item size is 400 KB; beyond that, you will need to redesign and split the table into smaller items. There is a special feature of DynamoDB that lets you run transactional reads and writes. We will get deeper into that later; for now, you just need to know that these transactional operations consume twice the capacity units for the same item size.

To put this in practical terms, suppose that you create a provisioned table with 4 RCUs and 2 WCUs. With these settings, the application could do the following:

- Perform strongly consistent reads of up to 16 KB per second (4 KB × 4 read capacity units)

- Perform eventually consistent reads of up to 32 KB per second (twice as much read throughput)

- Perform transactional read requests of up to 8 KB per second

- Write up to 2 KB per second (1 KB × 2 write capacity units)

- Perform transactional write requests of up to 1 KB per second

A single partition in a DynamoDB table can handle 3,000 reads and 1,000 writes per second. So, you might ask, how does DynamoDB handle millions of requests per second on a table, as we mentioned at the beginning of the chapter? Well, the answer is that the service allocates that many partitions on your table so it can handle millions of requests per second. As simple math, if the table needs to handle 2,000 writes per second, it requires two partitions.

Let's say for your upcoming event you know you need to handle 30,000 writes per second at peak load. To handle the peak load, switch to provisioned mode and allocate 30,000 WCUs prior to the event and switch back to your original table configuration. The advantage of doing this exercise is that DynamoDB repartitions the data in 30 partitions (one every thousand write operations)—thus, your table is now ready to handle your pick traffic without repartitioning your data during the actual event. Allocating the 30,000 WCUs will be very quick the next time. And if you use on-demand mode, it will be instant. If the application goes beyond the maximum provisioned capacity, the DynamoDB API will throw a ProvisionedThroughputExceededException error. The DynamoDB SDKs will automatically retry requests that receive this exception until your request is eventually successful, unless your retry queue is too large to finish. To mitigate the long queue issue, the AWS SDK implements an exponential backoff algorithm for better flow control.

Reserved Capacity

You may be familiar with other purchase options provided by different services, for instance Amazon Relational Database Service (Amazon RDS) reserved instances or Amazon EC2 compute saving plans. Amazon DynamoDB has a way to reserve the capacity as well to save costs even further.

With the DynamoDB Reserved Capacity option, you pay a discounted one-time up-front fee with a commitment to keep a minimum provisioned usage over the defined period of time. The reserved capacity is billed at the hourly reserved capacity rate. At the time of writing, the price for 100 RCUs is $0.0025 per hour in the US-EAST-1 AWS region. The same amount without the price discount would be $0.013 per hour. You may check the latest numbers in the official Amazon DynamoDB pricing page.

Besides the reserve capacity mode, DynamoDB provides a permanent free usage tier consisting of 25 GB of storage, 25 RCUs, and 25 WCUs. With these settings, you may be able to handle up to 200 million requests per month.

Other Features of DynamoDB

Let's explore some additional DynamoDB features.

Transactions

Despite DynamoDB being a NoSQL database, there can be access patterns that require ACID-like transactions. What is an ACID transaction in the database context? It is a sequence of database operations that can be perceived as a single logical one. This transaction has to satisfy the ACID properties (atomicity, consistency, isolation, and durability).

Normalized data structures are a primary driver for ACID requirements. With DynamoDB, many of these requirements are fulfilled simply by aggregating and storing all the information as single rows/items. Each single-item operation is ACID because no two operations could partially impact a row simultaneously. However, DynamoDB introduced transactions in 2018, which makes it very simple to ensure consistent changes across related items.

It works as an "all or nothing" operation. There is no concept of "rolling back." The application will not see a partial transaction that is then reverted. Once accepted, it will complete, or it will be rejected because one of its steps failed. If this happens, you can use an option called `ReturnValuesOnConditionCheckFailure` and then you can rebuild the operation.

You can include a client token when making a TransactWriteItems call to ensure that the request is idempotent. Making the transactions idempotent helps you prevent application errors if the same operation is submitted more than once. DynamoDB ensures that operations will be treated as idempotent for 10 minutes.

Like the rest of the operations with DynamoDB, the transactions can be used via API, and there is no additional cost for enabling this feature; it will just consume twice as many read and write capacity units per operation. With the transaction write API, the application can group together multiple Update, Put, Delete, and ConditionCheck operations—up to 100 unique items or 4 MB of data. The application can then submit the actions as a single TransactWriteItems operation that can either succeed or fail as an atomic unit.

Let's see a real-life example use of transactions. Consider the table design shown in Figure 5.5 to store information about a player in an online game.

FIGURE 5.5   Online game player data

Primary key		Attributes		
Partition key: GamerID	Sort key: Type			
Hammer57	Assets	Coins		
		1000		
	Rank	Level	Points	Tier
		87	4050	Elite
	Status	Health	Progress	
		90%	30	
	Weapon	Class	Damage	Range
		Taser	55-67	120

It is partitioned by GamerID. The game requirement is that whenever health is purchased, there are three simultaneous operations.

- The player must have 400 coins to purchase health.
- Set the health attribute value to 100 percent.
- Decrement the coins attribute value by the cost (400).

The payload for the `TransactWriteItems` operation will look like this:

```
{
"TransactItems" :  [ {
   "Update ": {
    "TableName": "Gamers",
    "Key" :{"GamerID" : {"S": "Hammer57"},
    "Type" : {"S" : "Status"}},
    "UpdateExpression" : "Set health = :nhealth",
    "ExpressionAttributeValues":{":nhealth":{"N":"100"}}
   },
  {
   "Update ": {
    "TableName": "Gamers",
    "Key" :{"GamerID" : {"S": "Hammer57"},
    "Type" : {"S" : "Assets"} },
      "ConditionExpression" : "coins > :cost",
      "UpdateExpression" : "Set coins = coins - :cost",
       "ExpressionAttributeValues" :{":cost":{"N":"400"}}
   }
 }]
}
```

These will all happen simultaneously, with an "all or nothing" approach. This could be more complex—and include up to 25 items. Perhaps the 400 coins are added to the inventory of the healer? Or, it checks to ensure that health is not already equal to 100 percent, etc.

Consider the following recommended best practices when using the DynamoDB transactions feature:

- The AWS SDK for DynamoDB handles the idempotency of the request on your behalf. If you are not using the SDK, you should include a `ClientRequestToken` attribute with the TransactWriteItems API call to ensure that the request remains idempotent.

- Enable autoscaling on the tables, or be sure that you have enough provisioned capacity to perform twice as many read and write operations for every item in your transaction.

- Try not to group operations together in a single transaction. For instance, if a transaction with eight operations can be decoupled into smaller multiple transactions without compromising the application's integrity, it is recommended to break it up into the smallest possible number. Simpler transactions are more likely to succeed and improve throughput.

- Multiple transactions updating the same items simultaneously can cause conflicts that cancel the transactions. We recommend following DynamoDB best practices for data modeling to minimize such conflicts.

- If a set of attributes is often updated across multiple items as part of a single transaction, consider grouping the attributes into a single item to reduce the scope of the transaction.

- Avoid using transactions for ingesting data in bulk. For bulk writes, it is better to use BatchWriteItem. It can handle up to 25 items with up to 16 MB in aggregated size within each operation.

In-Memory Acceleration

Most cloud-native and modern applications can work seamlessly within the single-digit millisecond latency that DynamoDB provides by default, but there may be some workloads that demand even lower latency from the database. For those cases, you can use DynamoDB Accelerator functionality and enjoy the 10x performance improvement at the same scale of up to millions of requests per second.

DynamoDB Accelerator (DAX) is a secure, scalable, fully managed, read-through/write-through caching service compatible with the DynamoDB API. It is designed to seamlessly add an in-memory cache layer to DynamoDB tables so the customer can benefit from ultra-fast in-memory operations. It supports server-side encryption with AES-256 and in-transit data encryption with TLS.

DynamoDB acceleration addresses these three core scenarios:

- It reduces the response times of eventually consistent read workloads from single-digit milliseconds to microseconds.

- It reduces the cache implementation complexity at the operational and application levels by providing a managed service that is API-compatible with DynamoDB. And in that way, it requires only minimal changes within an existing application.

- For read-heavy or spiky workloads, DynamoDB DAX provides cost savings by reducing the need to overprovision read capacity units. This works even better for applications that need to perform repeated reads for individual keys.

To be able to provide microsecond latency response times, DAX is deployed within an Amazon VPC environment that lets you add another layer of security via the ACL and SG.

DAX is a read-through/write-through cache engine that will intercept both reads and writes to the DynamoDB tables you define. Each DAX cluster can be assigned to one or many tables within the same AWS region. As a read-through caching system, when a read is sent to DAX, it will first see if that item is in the cache; if it is (cache hit), DAX will return the value with response times in microseconds scale. If the item is not in the cache (cache miss), DAX automatically fetches the item from the DynamoDB table, stores it in the cache for subsequent reads, and returns the value to the application. This is done transparently to the developer. Similarly, for writes, DAX first writes the value to DynamoDB, caches the value in DAX, and then returns success to the application. This way, reads after writes are available for cache hits, which further simplifies the application. With cache eviction handled by time-to-live (TTL) and write-through evictions, you no longer need the code to perform this task.

It is important to understand the eventual consistency models of both DAX and DynamoDB (by default) to ensure that your applications behave as expected. To ensure high availability, it's recommended that the DAX cluster be deployed across three availability zones. When your DAX cluster is up and running, it replicates the data to all of the nodes in the cluster. When an application performs a successful UpdateItem, the system will update the value of that item in the primary node of the cluster. That value is then replicated among the other nodes in the cluster with an eventual consistency model. As you might be thinking, in this scenario, it's possible for two clients to get different values when reading the same key from the same DAX cluster if they hit different nodes.

If you are building an application that will leverage DAX as a cache layer, that application should be designed in a way that can tolerate eventually consistent data. If the request specifies a strong consistent read, the DAX cluster will forward the request to the DynamoDB table and won't store its result on the cache. These applications can benefit directly by using DAX:

- Applications that require a microsecond-fast response time for reads, such as trading applications, social gaming, and real-time bidding.

- Applications that usually read some items more frequently than others, for example, an ecommerce application that has a one-day sale on a popular product. You can offload the read activity to a DAX cache layer until the sale promotion is over.

- Applications that are read-intensive and also cost-sensitive. With DynamoDB provisioned mode, the customer provisions the number of reads per second that the application requires. If the read activity increases, you can increase your tables' provisioned read throughput (at an additional cost). Another choice is to offload that read activity from the application to a DynamoDB DAX cluster and reduce the number of RCUs that you would purchase otherwise.

- Applications that usually perform repeated reads operations over a large set of data, such as a long-running forecast process using regional weather. That weather analysis could be performed against DAX cached data, saving a lot of RCU from the original table.

Time to Live

Time to live (TTL) is an item-level attribute represented as an epoch timestamp mark that indicates that the item can be deleted by an automatic background process, without consuming a provisioned capacity unit or causing extra costs. TTL is lazy, so expirations can take a couple of hours. There is a 48-hour upper bound of this behavior. Stale items can be easily removed from result sets using a filter expression on the epoch timestamp.

The following are typical TTL attribute use cases:

- Applications that store user usage or sensor data that is not relevant after a given period of time
- For analytics purposes, archive expired items to an Amazon S3 data lake via Amazon DynamoDB Streams and AWS Lambda
- Applications that need to retain data for a certain amount of time according to contractual or regulatory obligations

The following are best practices to consider when assigning TTL attributes to a table:

- Changing the TTL settings on a table can take up to one hour to propagate and also to allow the modification of any other TTL-related actions.
- Customers cannot modify the TTL to use a different attribute. It must be disabled and then reenabled with the new attribute or just done via a CloudFormation template.
- IAM policies can be used to prevent unauthorized modifications to the TTL attribute on an item or the configuration of TTL itself.
- Remember that this can be combined with the DynamoDB Streams feature to take some action whenever a record is deleted. There is a principal flag for TTL expired items; it is simple to "tier out" cool data from the table into an S3 data lake or archive.
- If data recovery feasibility is a concern, it is recommended that you back up your tables. DynamoDB offers fully managed table backup features like the DynamoDB on-demand backups and the continuous backups with point-in-time recovery (PITR).

It's important to be aware that if you specify a TTL for a table (for example, an attribute named expirationDate) but an item does not have any attribute with that name, the TTL process ignores the item.

DynamoDB Streams

Modern applications also follow modern architectures, and event-driven applications are very popular these days due to the increasing use of serverless compute and distributed systems.

DynamoDB Streams is like a change log that captures information about every modification to data items in the table. This is one of the powerful features of DynamoDB because it allows you to react to data changes in near real time without impacting the performance of your table.

For example, you can build a social media application that automatically sends notifications to mobile devices as soon as one contact uploads a new picture. DynamoDB Streams is integrated with AWS Lambda, which makes it easy to build a trigger-based application with a piece of code that automatically responds to events in DynamoDB Streams.

DynamoDB has two streaming models for CDC built in: Kinesis Data Streams for DynamoDB and DynamoDB Streams. Table 5.4 illustrates when to choose each one.

TABLE 5.4   DynamoDB Streams vs. Kinesis Data Streams for DynamoDB

Property	DynamoDB Streams	Kinesis Data Streams for DynamoDB
Data retention	24 hours.	Up to 1 year.
Kinesis Client Library (KCL) support	Supports KCL version 1.X.	Supports KCL versions 1.X and 2.X.
Number of consumers	Up to two concurrent consumers per shard.	Up to five concurrent consumers per shard. Customer can enable the enhanced fan-out feature and increase that number to 20.
Throughput quotas	Subject to throughput quotas by DynamoDB table.	Unlimited.
Record delivery model	Pull mode over HTTP by using GetRecords.	Pull mode over HTTP by using GetRecords. Customer can enable the enhanced fan-out feature, and Kinesis Data Streams pushes the records over HTTP/2 to the subscribers created by using SubscribeToShard.
Ordering of records	The stream records appear in the same order as the actual modifications executed to the item in the table.	Items can appear in a different order than in the DynamoDB table, so there is a timestamp attribute on each stream record that can be used to identify the actual order.
Duplicate records	No duplicate records can appear in the stream.	Duplicate records might occasionally appear.
Stream processing options	DynamoDB Streams Kinesis Adapter or AWS Lambda.	AWS Lambda, Kinesis Data Firehose, Kinesis Data Analytics, or AWS Glue Streaming ETL.

DynamoDB Streams can be turned on/off at any time without extra cost; the cost is per reading at $0.2 per 100,000 reads in us-east-1 at the time of writing. There's no reading cost at all if the reader is a Lambda function. DynamoDB Streams supports the following record views:

- NEW_IMAGE: Send the entire item as it is after being modified.
- OLD_IMAGE: Send the entire item as it was before it was modified.
- NEW_AND_OLD_IMAGES: Send both the new and old images of the item.
- KEYS_ONLY: Send only the key attributes of the modified item.

It is also important to see that items expired by TTL will have a new attribute to indicate that the item was expired by the system.

This is what a stream record looks like:

```
{
 'eventID': 'ba0aa41d6f9f2d64f',
 'eventName': 'MODIFY',
 'eventVersion': '1.1',
 'eventSource': 'aws:dynamodb',
 'awsRegion': 'us-east-1',
 'dynamodb': {
               'ApproximateCreationDateTime': 1546020023.0,
               'NewImage': {Full map of item goes here}
               'SequenceNumber': '11397370000000000001108655351',
               'SizeBytes': 116,
               'StreamViewType': 'NEW_AND_OLD_IMAGES'
       },
 'eventSourceARN': 'arn:aws:ddb:reg:acct:tbl/str/'
}
```

These are the appropriate use cases for DynamoDB Streams:

- You have a mobile application that needs to modify the data in a DynamoDB table at the rate of thousands of operations per second. On the other hand, you might have another application that captures and stores related data about those updates, providing real-time usage metrics for the first app.

- There is a financial application that updates stock market data in a DynamoDB table. At the same time, different applications are running in parallel tracks, and these changes in real time compute value-at-risk formulas and automatically rebalance portfolios based on each stock price movement.

- Industrial equipment or transportation vehicle applications need to handle IoT sensor information. That real-time data can be stored in a DynamoDB table and have different applications to monitor performance and send messaging alerts whenever a problem is detected. Furthermore, a customer can leverage that inbound data to predict any potential issues by implementing machine learning algorithms.

- A customer registration process workload for any application can store its data in a DynamoDB table. The event invokes another application via DynamoDB Streams that can send a welcome email to the new customer.

Consider the following recommended best practices when using DynamoDB Streams:

- DynamoDB Streams does not enforce consistency or transactional capability across the tables; those features must be handled at the application level. Also, there is a sub-second latency in every stream processing task as data is propagated into the stream.

You should take the previous factors into account when defining the SLA of your applications.

- All item-level changes will be sent to the stream, including deletes. The application should be able to handle each one of those operations.

- Avoid having more than two processes reading from a stream shard at the same time.

- Design your stream-processing layer to handle different types of failures. You should also define your processing application to be idempotent, which can allow you to safely retry each event.

- Try to catch different exceptions in your source code and decide if you want to retry them or put them in a dead letter queue (DLQ) for further analysis.

- We recommend that you consider using AWS Lambda for stream processing whenever possible. Lambda is serverless and therefore easier to manage and scale. Regarding Lambda optimization, set an appropriate batch size (up to 10.000) based on the type of transformation. For example, a simple copy could be 200 records, or complex difference-finder analysis may read only 20 records per call.

Global Tables

The global tables functionality uses DynamoDB's global footprint to provide you with a fully managed, multiregion, and multiwriter database that provides low-latency read and write performance for distributed global applications. Global tables replicate your DynamoDB tables automatically across your choice of AWS regions to provide local data access for the application. This feature eliminates the difficult task of replicating data between AWS regions and resolving update conflicts across each node, enabling customers to focus on their application's business logic.

When customers create a DynamoDB global table, the service actually creates several table replicas (one per AWS region) that DynamoDB treats as a single unit. All of the replicas share the same table name and the same primary key. Whenever an application performs a write operation to a replica table, DynamoDB propagates that update to the other replicas in the other AWS regions automatically by using log processors, as shown in Figure 5.6.

A global table's goal is to get the same copy of an item in every table worldwide. There are many replication flows running at a time in global tables version 2019.11.21. In fact, one replication pipeline is set up from each source region to each remote region so that in the event of failure in a remote region, only replication to that region is impacted, while the other replicas continue to replicate normally.

At the time of writing, two versions of DynamoDB global tables are available: version 2019.11.21 (latest) and version 2017.11.29. We recommend using the most recent one, which enables you to dynamically add new replica tables from a table populated with data. Besides that, it is more efficient and consumes less write capacity than the oldest one.

FIGURE 5.6   DynamoDB global tables' high-level architecture

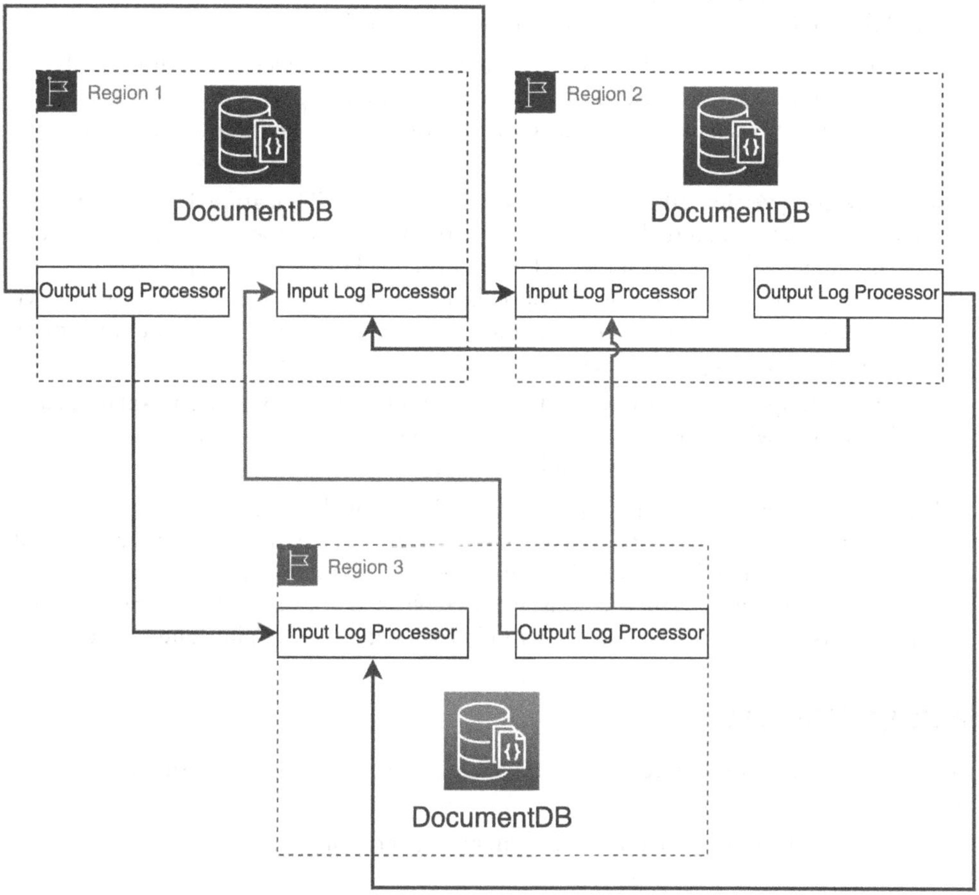

These are the appropriate use cases for DynamoDB global tables:

- Massively scaled applications with globally dispersed users. In such an environment, users expect very fast application performance.

- Mission-critical applications that require high availability, even in the unlikely event of isolation or degradation of an entire region.

Consider the following recommended best practices when using DynamoDB global tables:

- Global tables can be declared natively as infrastructure as code via CloudFormation without a custom resource since May 2021. This is the recommended way to deploy DynamoDB infrastructure, but you cannot convert a DynamoDB table into a

DynamoDB global table just by changing its type in the template. Doing so will result in the elimination of the DynamoDB table. For that reason, it is recommended to always use global table resources if your application might go global at some point.

- When using the latest available version of global tables, customers must either enable autoscaling on the table or use on-demand capacity. By doing so, you can be sure that the table will always have enough capacity to perform replicated writes across all regions of the global table.

- If you are using version 2019.11.21 and you also use the TTL feature, DynamoDB replicates TTL deletes to all replica tables. The initial TTL delete does not consume write capacity in the region in which the TTL expiry occurs. However, the replicated TTL delete to the replica table(s) consumes a replicated write capacity unit when using provisioned capacity, or replicated write when using on-demand capacity mode, in each of the replica regions, and applicable charges will apply.

- Transactional operations provide ACID properties (atomicity, consistency, isolation, and durability) only within the region where the original write operation was made. Transactions are not supported for global table replicas.

- The number of replicated write capacity units (WCUs) will be the same in all regions of the global table deployment. For instance, suppose that you expect 10 writes per second to a replica table in N. Virginia and 10 writes per second to a replica table in Oregon. In this case, you should expect to consume 20 replicated WCUs (or 20 replicated write request units, if using on-demand capacity) in each region, N. Virginia and Oregon.

Backup/Restore

Like many other database services in AWS, DynamoDB offers two ways to back up and restore the data.

- On-demand backups for long-term data archiving and compliance
- Continuous backups for PITR

On-Demand Backups

The on-demand backups allow you to create full backups of your DynamoDB tables' data, making it easy to perform data archiving and comply with the corporate and governmental regulatory requirements. Customers can back up tables from just a few megabytes up to hundreds of terabytes of used capacity, without impact on performance and availability across thousands of partitions. On-demand backup operations can process backup requests in seconds regardless of the total size of the DynamoDB tables so that customer don't have to worry about the orchestration of backup schedules or long-running processes.

It is important to consider that when you do a full table restore using on-demand backups, the destination table is configured with the same provisioned RCU and WCU as the original table, as it was at the time when the backup was requested.

When restoring a backup, you can assign the same value of the original table for these settings or change it as necessary.

- Global secondary indexes (GSIs)
- Local secondary indexes (LSIs)
- Billing mode
- Provisioned read and write capacity
- Encryption settings

There are other settings that need to be manually defined for each restored table:

- Autoscaling policies
- AWS IAM policies
- Amazon CloudWatch metrics and alarms
- Tags
- DynamoDB Streams settings
- TTL settings

Continuous Backups

In addition to the on-demand backups, you can enable continuous backups for point-in-time recovery. This gives you the ability to restore to any point in the last 35 days down to the per-second granularity. All the backups taken are automatically encrypted and retained until the customer explicitly deletes them. You can run backup and restore operations with a single click in the AWS Console or via a single API call.

The point-in-time recovery restoration process always restores the data to a new table and can be within the values for `EarliestRestorableDateTime` and `LatestRestorableDateTime`. The earliest is 35 days ago, and the latest is usually five minutes before the current time.

Like the on-demand backups, the point-in-time recovery operations don't affect performance or API latencies or consume any provisioned throughput on the table.

In the same way as with on-demand restores, you are able to modify the same group of settings when performing a restore and need to manually assign the other group of settings after the restore is done.

You can use the `describe-continuous-backups` command to get the current options for the PITR.

```
{
    "ContinuousBackupsDescription": {
        "PointInTimeRecoveryDescription": {
            "PointInTimeRecoveryStatus": "ENABLED",
            "EarliestRestorableDateTime": 1519257118.0,
            "LatestRestorableDateTime": 1520018653.01
        },
        "ContinuousBackupsStatus": "ENABLED"
    }
}
```

DynamoDB is also natively integrated with a fully managed, centralized backup solution: AWS Backups. You can leverage AWS Backups to schedule, copy, tag, and handle the life cycles of your backups automatically across all DynamoDB tables in the AWS organization from a centralized place while still being able to view and restore these backups from each DynamoDB console.

With AWS Backups for DynamoDB, you can automatically copy your backups to a different AWS region or AWS account, which allows you to fulfill your data protection requirements. AWS Backups also has an Audit Manager feature to find backup activity and resources that are not yet compliant with the centralized controls that you defined for your organization.

Consider the following recommended best practices when working with DynamoDB backups:

- Each time the customer creates an on-demand backup, all the data in the table is backed up. There is no limit regarding the number of on-demand backups that can be taken from a table.

- Be sure that you execute the backup process on the right table at the right time, because once it's initiated, it can't be paused or canceled, and the table cannot be deleted, until the backup is finished.

- You can schedule a recurrent backups request by using an AWS Lambda function and an Amazon Event Bridge rule.

- Restore operations can be more cost-efficient and faster if some or all indexes are excluded from being created on the restored table.

- When planning for a disaster recovery process (DRP), the overall recovery time objective (RTO) related to a restore operation (based on more than 95 percent of the customers) should be less than an hour.

- If you disable PITR and later reenable it on a table, you reset the `EarliestRestorable DateTime` attribute from which you can recover that table. In other words, you will lose the potential 35 days of history stored at that point.

- You can enable point-in-time recovery on each local replica of a global table. When you restore the table, the backup restores to an independent table that is not part of the global table.

- While a restore operation is in progress, you can't modify or delete the IAM policies that grant the IAM principal permission to perform the restore; if you did, it would throw an error.

Scalability

Before talking about Amazon DynamoDB scalability, we need to cover some differences between scaling SQL and NoSQL databases.

In relational databases, the data is usually normalized. To enable join operations, you are usually tied to a single storage unit in a single system. That makes you dependent on the performance of the hardware specs of the server. To improve performance in that scenario, you can create read replicas or add cache layers, but that approach works only for read operations, and you may still run out of head room. That's why SQL databases are usually only able to scale up.

NoSQL databases were specifically designed to overcome those scalability issues. You can scale out data and workload using distributed clusters and shards running on low-cost hardware. All that can be achieved without sacrificing throughput or latency for all the operations. Therefore, by using NoSQL, businesses can scale virtually without limit. Of course, that limitless scalability doesn't come for free; you need to bend one of the CAP theorem pillars.

Figure 5.7 will help you remember the CAP theorem and where Amazon DynamoDB fits in.

FIGURE 5.7 CAP theorem and AWS database service affinity with each pillar

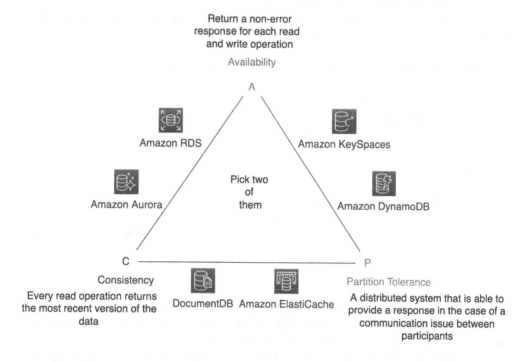

Autoscaling

We talked before about the on-demand provisioning mode of Amazon DynamoDB and how it can scale up to millions of transactions per second. Let's focus now on the provisioned capacity mode and the autoscaling feature. If you are familiar with the autoscaling of Amazon EC2 instances, this is similar. DynamoDB leverages the AWS Application Auto Scaling service to automatically adjust the provisioned throughput capacity in response to actual traffic patterns. This enables a table to dynamically handle sudden changes in traffic.

You take advantage of autoscaling policies to provision capacity when your application demands it and avoid unnecessary overprovisioning. The scaling policy contains a target utilization of the provisioned throughput at a point in time. It uses a target tracking algorithm to adjust the provisioned throughput of the table or global secondary indexes up or down in response to actual request volumes so that the actual capacity utilization remains at or near your target utilization. The target utilization can go from 20 percent to 90 percent of the read or write capacity.

The autoscaling modifies the provisioned capacity only when the request rate is sustained for a period of several minutes to keep the target utilization at or near the desired value most of the time. What happens to sudden spikes on the workload?

Amazon DynamoDB provides flexibility in your per-partition provisioning by providing some burst capacity. Whenever the application is not fully using a partition's throughput, DynamoDB stores a portion of that unused capacity (five minutes at time of writing) for later bursts or background maintenance tasks.

This kind of surge, represented in Figure 5.8, is what actually happened in the 2017 Super Bowl game as we mentioned at the beginning of this chapter.

FIGURE 5.8   2017 Super Bowl game's DynamoDB traffic surge

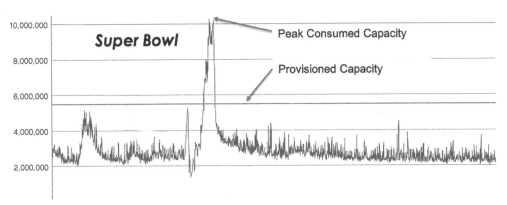

As mentioned previously, DynamoDB spread the provisioned capacity evenly across all partitions. What happens in terms of scaling and burst when some items are more requested than others, causing what is usually called a *hot partition*?

Amazon DynamoDB also handles this for you without any additional cost by using the adaptive capacity feature. To better accommodate uneven access patterns, the adaptive capacity enables your application to continue reading and writing to hot partitions without being throttled, as long as that traffic does not exceed your table's total provisioned capacity or the partition's maximum capacity.

If this uneven access pattern becomes normal, then DynamoDB rebalances your partitions such that frequently accessed items don't reside in the same place. This can go as granular as a single item for a whole partition if necessary.

Scaling is achieved through partitioning and the number of partitions is calculated based on the following two formulas, whatever happens first:

- By capacity = (Total RCU / 3000) + (Total WCU/1000)
- By size = Total Size / 10 GB

As you may guess with the first formula, each partition delivers 1,000 writes/second and 3,000 reads/second.

Consider the following recommended best practices when working with DynamoDB autoscaling:

- The frequently accessed items isolation feature doesn't work with tables with local secondary items or with DynamoDB Streams.

- DynamoDB autoscaling doesn't prevent customers from manually modifying the provisioned throughput settings for a table. These manual adjustments don't affect any existing CloudWatch alarms that are related to autoscaling either.

- If DynamoDB autoscaling is enabled for a table that has one or more global secondary indexes, it is highly recommended that autoscaling is also configured for those indexes. The Apply Same Settings To Global Secondary Indexes option can do this automatically.

- When using AWS CloudFormation templates to create scaling policies, customers should manage the scaling policies from AWS CloudFormation so that the resources are in sync with the stack template. If you change scaling policies from DynamoDB or Application Auto Scaling, they might get overwritten with the values from the AWS CloudFormation template.

Security

Amazon DynamoDB is a fully managed serverless service, so if you recall the Shared Responsibility Model from Chapter 2, there are only a few tasks that the customers need to take care of regarding security: identity access management and data protection. AWS provides all the tools and features to seamlessly manage both of them.

Access Management

Amazon DynamoDB depends on IAM for access control. You need credentials to use the DynamoDB APIs, and those credentials must have permissions to access each resource within it, such as a table, an index, or DynamoDB Streams.

Two types of principals can be used to grant access to DynamoDB resources: users and roles. The user can be a regular IAM user or an IAM group. We strongly recommend not using the root user for these purposes. The other principal is a role; the role is intended to be assumable by anyone who needs it and doesn't have long-term credentials such as a password. The IAM roles, instead, use temporary credentials to grant access to the following options:

- Federated user existing in another identity provider (IDP) such as AWS SSO, another SSO provider, or a corporate directory.

- AWS Service that needs to access the data inside a DynamoDB table or its configuration, typically the application layer. This can be an AWS Lambda function or the Application Auto Scaling service to modify the provisioned capacity.

- Applications on Amazon EC2 instances that need credentials to access DynamoDB data. The application running on EC2 can use an IAM role that is attached to the instance to get the temporary credentials to access DynamoDB APIs. Though you can store an IAM user access key inside the virtual machine, the role option is the recommended method.

One thing is the authentication before the DynamoDB API, and another is the permissions that the principal has authorization for. When granting permissions for DynamoDB, you decide who is getting what permissions, the resources they get permissions for, and what specific actions you want to allow on those resources.

These permissions are granted through policies. You can view policies like gates, and you can create different gates to different parts of your "property." DynamoDB is compatible only with identity-based policies that can be attached to IAM entities, like an IAM role or an IAM user.

The following is an IAM policy example to allow data management operations in the Books DynamoDB table:

```
{
    "Version": "2012-10-17",
    "Statement": [
            {
            "Sid": "DynamoDBTableAccess",
            "Effect": "Allow",
            "Action": [
                "dynamodb:BatchGetItem",
                "dynamodb:BatchWriteItem",
                "dynamodb:ConditionCheckItem",
                "dynamodb:PutItem",
                "dynamodb:DescribeTable",
                "dynamodb:DeleteItem",
                "dynamodb:GetItem",
                "dynamodb:Scan",
                "dynamodb:Query",
                "dynamodb:UpdateItem"
            ],
```

```
        "Resource": "arn:aws:dynamodb:us-west-2:123456789012:table/Books"
    }
  ]
}
```

Each DynamoDB resource belongs to an AWS account, but you can use IAM roles to grant cross-account access to each resource.

In addition to the regular policies, you can define granular access control on items based on the primary key, as well as attributes using conditions.

The following AWS IAM policy example allows data management operations over the Title, Language, and Genre attributes of the DynamoDB Books table.

```
{
    "Version": "2012-10-17",
    "Statement": [
        {
            "Effect": "Allow",
            "Action": [
                "dynamodb:GetItem",
                "dynamodb:BatchGetItem",
                "dynamodb:Query",
                "dynamodb:PutItem",
                "dynamodb:UpdateItem",
                "dynamodb:DeleteItem",
                "dynamodb:BatchWriteItem"
            ],
            "Resource": ["arn:aws:dynamodb:*:*:table/Books"],
            "Condition": {
                "ForAllValues:StringEquals": {
                    "dynamodb:Attributes": [
                        "Title",
                        "Language",
                        "Genre"
                    ]
                },
                "StringEqualsIfExists": {"dynamodb:Select":
"SPECIFIC_ATTRIBUTES"}
            }
        }
    ]
}
```

DynamoDB Accelerator (DAX), on the other side, is designed to work together with DynamoDB. However, DAX and DynamoDB have separate access control mechanisms. Both services use IAM to implement their respective security policies, but the security models for DAX and DynamoDB are different. You can grant a user access to a DAX cluster but not to the DynamoDB table itself and viceversa.

Figure 5.9 represents a user that doesn't have a policy to access a DynamoDB table directly, but it can access a DAX cluster, which in turn has access to the table itself.

FIGURE 5.9 Accessing DynamoDB data through DAX

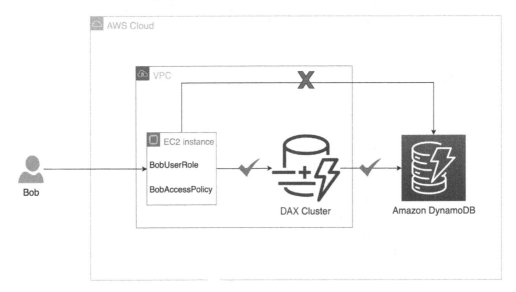

Data Protection

In addition to permissions (via IAM), which is the fundamental way of protecting your data, you should protect it against the following other events:

- **Data corruption:** To avoid this kind of event, you can enable point-in-time recovery and design your tables to minimize the risk of corruption by keeping a local table replica for mission-critical data, or you can apply policies that only allow you to insert new items instead of updating them, in other words, some kind of append-only strategy.

- **Disasters:** DynamoDB provides a highly durable storage infrastructure replicated across three availability zones but for some mission-critical workloads that might not be enough and need extra protection. You can use DynamoDB global tables for disaster recovery purposes and on-demand backup and restore.

- **Disclosure:** This one is easy: it is done by data encryption. Amazon DynamoDB supports two kinds of data encryption: at rest and in transit. All data stored in DynamoDB is fully encrypted at rest by default using its own keys for free. When creating a table, you have the option to use AWS KMS Customer Managed Keys (CMKs) or AWS Managed Keys stored on KMS as well, but this option might incur KMS charges. The encryption of the storage layer happens transparently with minimal impact on the performance and without the need to change the application code.

DynamoDB encryption at rest includes data in a table, local and global secondary indexes, streams, global tables, backups, and DAX clusters.

Regarding the protection of the data in transit, DynamoDB uses Transport Layer Security. We recommend using TLS 1.2 or greater. Clients must also support cipher suites with Perfect Forward Secrecy (PFS). Additionally, you must sign requests using an access key ID and a secret access key that are associated with an IAM principal.

Besides the protection of the protocol, you can protect the channel of communication. What do I mean by that? DynamoDB APIs are public by default, but if your DynamoDB client resides within an Amazon VPC, you can create a VPC endpoint to privately connect to the DynamoDB API without traversing the public Internet. On top of that, you can add a condition to the IAM policy to allow access to the DynamoDB resources only from that specific VPC endpoint, as you can see in the following example:

```
{
    "Version": "2012-10-17",
    "Statement": [
        {
            "Sid": "AccessFromSpecificEndpoint",
            "Action": "dynamodb:*",
            "Effect": "Deny",
            "Resource": "arn:aws:dynamodb:region:account-id:table/*",
            "Condition": { "StringNotEquals" : { "aws:sourceVpce":
"vpce-11aa22bb" } }
        }
    ]
}
```

The channel protection does not only apply from clients within a VPC; you can also use Dynamo DB securely from on-premises networks via an AWS site-to-site VPN connection or an AWS Direct Connect connection.

Monitoring

Once you have your database up and running, you need to be sure that it continues that way. You can do that by monitoring. This is an important part of maintaining the reliability, availability, and performance of your DynamoDB resources. AWS provides several tools and services for monitoring DynamoDB to respond to potential incidents and to troubleshoot specific errors.

To be able to set up the right autoscaling thresholds, first you need to understand the performance baseline of your application. The best way to do that is by measuring performance at various times and under different load conditions. You can do that by observing the Amazon CloudWatch metrics available for DynamoDB. These metrics are delivered in near real time and retained for a period of time (up to 15 months), so you can access historical information for a better analysis of how the database is performing. Table 5.5 shows some examples.

TABLE 5.5 Amazon CloudWatch Metrics Available for DynamoDB

Use Case	Metric
Rate of TTL deletions on a table	You can monitor `TimeToLiveDeletedItemCount` over the specified time period.
Provisioned throughput being used	For this, customers can monitor the `ConsumedReadCapacityUnits` or `ConsumedWriteCapacityUnits` metrics over the specified time period.
Requests exceed the provisioned throughput quotas	`ThrottledRequests` is incremented one by one if any event within a request exceeds the provisioned throughput quota. Then, to gain insight into which operation is throttling a request, you should compare the `ThrottledRequests`, `ReadThrottleEvents`, and `WriteThrottle Events` metrics for the table and its local secondary indexes.
System errors	Customers can monitor the `SystemErrors` metric to determine whether any requests returned an HTTP 500 (server error) code.
Provisioned capacity usage	`AccountProvisionedWriteCapacityUtilization` displays the percentage of provisioned write capacity units utilized by an account.
Read data bandwidth out of your tables or streams	You can monitor `ReturnedBytes` to get the number of bytes returned by `GetRecords` operations during the specified time period.

You can get these metrics for a given dimension as well, for instance, per the following:

- **Operation:** PutItem, GetItem, DeleteItem, Query, Scan, etc.
- **Operation type:** Read or write
- **StreamLabel:** Limits the metrics to a specific DynamoDB stream
- **TableName:** Limits the metrics to a specific DynamoDB table

Another important element is to be aware if any of those metrics are in an undesired state. For that you can use Amazon CloudWatch Alarms to watch a single metric over a time period and perform some actions based on the values of the metric relative to a given threshold.

You can also integrate Amazon Event Bridge (formerly known as CloudWatch events) to capture an event generated by DynamoDB and route them to a target function or a DynamoDB Stream to capture the state information and take corrective action.

Figure 5.10 represents a rule to send a message to an Amazon SNS topic and get notified every time that a table DDL operation is performed.

FIGURE 5.10   DynamoDB event notification rule

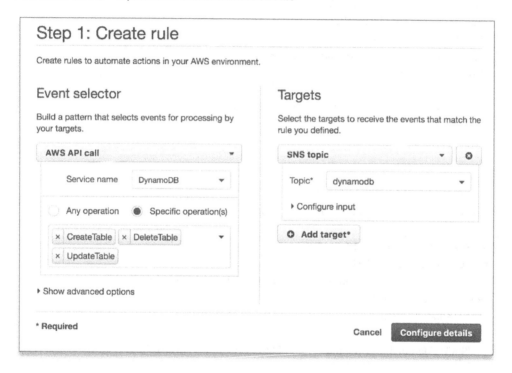

As you probably already know, AWS CloudTrail keeps track of every API operation performed on AWS, and since DynamoDB works exclusively via API calls, CloudTrail is the main logging mechanism available for DynamoDB. The API requests captured by CloudTrail include requests from the DynamoDB web console and API client requests to the DynamoDB control plane API.

If you haven't created a CloudTrail trail yet, you can still view the most recent DynamoDB events in the CloudTrail console in Event history.

Amazon CloudTrail stores the log information on Amazon S3 by default. Once on S3, you can use Amazon Athena queries to identify trends and further isolate activity by attribute, such as the source IP address, event type, error code, or IAM principal.

The following JSON represents a CloudTrail entry for DynamoDB `GetItem` operation:

```json
{
  "eventVersion": "1.08",
  "userIdentity": {
    "type": "Root",
    "principalId": "123456789101",
    "arn": "arn:aws:iam::123456789101:root",
    "accountId": "123456789101",
    "accessKeyId": "AKIAIOSFODNN7EXAMPLE",
    "sessionContext": {
      "attributes": {
        "creationDate": "2021-06-09T22:15:24Z",
        "mfaAuthenticated": "false"
      }
    }
  },
  "eventTime": "2021-06-09T22:19:30Z",
  "eventSource": "dynamodb.amazonaws.com",
  "eventName": "GetItem",
  "awsRegion": "us-east-1",
  "sourceIPAddress": "192.0.2.1",
  "userAgent": "aws-internal/3 aws-sdk-java/1.11.1022 Linux",
  "requestParameters": {
    "tableName": "dev",
    "key": {
      "PK": "Recording|RE445def6510c9ed7979c5b9a03f62d61a"
    },
    "consistentRead": true
  },
  "responseElements": null,
  "requestID": "I8I6AF2O99VTFIDU5S44GDJ363VV4KQNSO5AEMVJEXAMPLE",
  "eventID": "6accd126-d6c4-444d-9141-7ccc939fc1c3",
  "readOnly": true,
  "resources": [
    {
```

```
    "accountId": "555555555555",
    "type": "AWS::DynamoDB::Table",
    "ARN": "arn:aws:dynamodb:us-east-1:555555555555:table/dev"
  }
 ],
 "eventType": "AwsApiCall",
 "apiVersion": "2012-08-10",
 "managementEvent": false,
 "recipientAccountId": "555555555555",
 "eventCategory": "Data"
}
```

For a more robust monitoring solution, you can send CloudTrail events to Amazon CloudWatch Logs to enable a near real-time analysis of the traces. Once the events are on CloudWatch Logs, you can create filters to raise an alarm in case something strange is going on—for example, like the filter in Figure 5.11 that identifies when someone is attempting an unauthorized operation.

FIGURE 5.11   CloudWatch Logs filter example

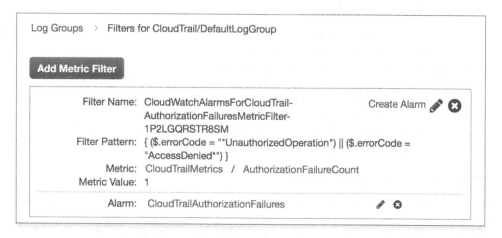

Another interesting Amazon CloudWatch feature is Contributor Insights for Amazon DynamoDB. This is a diagnostic tool for seamlessly identifying the most frequently accessed items on your table or index. The Contributor Insights feature helps customers to understand who or what is impacting their system and application performance by highlighting outliers, finding traffic patterns, and ranking the top-heavier system processes.

Amazon Keyspaces

Amazon DynamoDB is not the only AWS NoSQL database service capable of millisecond response times at millions of transactions per second. Apache Cassandra is an open-source, wide-column, transactional database designed to handle large amounts of data, and is considered by many in the world to be one of the top 10 database engines. You can use Amazon Keyspaces (for Apache Cassandra) to support your application within a few clicks and lines of code without the need to provision, patch, or manage servers.

Keyspaces is a managed service that is scalable and highly compatible with the Apache Cassandra 3.11.2 version at the time of writing. Like DynamoDB, Keyspaces is serverless, so you pay as you go only for the resources that you use. The service also automatically scales tables up and down in response to the actual application traffic. Customers can build applications that can serve up to thousands of requests per second while keeping virtually unlimited storage and throughput.

When you use Keyspaces, it will appear as a nine-node Apache Cassandra cluster and supports all commonly used Cassandra data-plane operations, such as creating keyspaces and tables, reading data, and writing data.

Design Considerations

For both SQL and NoSQL databases, how you model your data is critical to achieve optimal performance. Amazon Keyspaces is no exception. An inefficient data model can significantly impact its performance. Let's review some design considerations.

Like most NoSQL databases, in Cassandra Query Language (CQL), there are no joins despite it being a SQL "like" query language. Therefore, Cassandra table design should be done while thinking about the shape of the data and business use cases. This might result in denormalization with data duplication. You should design each Cassandra table specifically for each particular access pattern, as you do with DynamoDB.

Partition and Clustering Keys

Data is stored as a key-value pair in partitions, which are in turn organized into tables and keyspaces.

The *Cassandra keyspace* groups related tables that are relevant for one or more applications in a similar way as tablespaces do in the relational world.

The *Cassandra table* is the primary data structure for Amazon Keyspaces and its made-up rows and columns. A subset of those columns is used to partition and ultimately to place the data.

The partitions system works very similar the way it works in DynamoDB regarding the number of partitions used to store the data and how that data is distributed across the partitions by using the partition key. For this reason, how you build the partition key can have a significant impact on the performance of the queries.

The primary key can be composed the same way as in DynamoDB, but in Cassandra, the sort key has a different name (clustering column), and it can use several columns at the same time. If the clustering column has more than one column, the sorting order is executed in the same order in which the columns are listed in the clustering column definition, from left to right.

This ability to add extra columns to the sort key makes it easier to shard the data than in DynamoDB because all you need to do is create a new column with a random number and add it to the sort key.

Static Columns

Another particular feature of Keyspaces is the static column. The value stored in this column type is shared across all rows in a partition. When customers update the value of the column, Amazon Keyspaces applies that change automatically to all rows within the partition.

This static data is associated with Cassandra logical partitions and not with individual rows. Logical partitions can have virtually unlimited capacity by distributing data across several physical storage partitions. As a consequence, Amazon Keyspaces counts write operations on static and nonstatic data separately. Furthermore, writes that include both static and nonstatic data require additional overhead to provide data consistency.

If customers perform a mixed write operation on both nonstatic and static data, they will generate two separate write operations (one for each type). This applies the same way to both capacity modes (on-demand and provisioned read/write).

Keys and Rows Sizing

Partition keys can store up to 2,048 bytes of data. Each column in the partition key needs to contain up to 3 bytes of metadata that count toward the 1 MB row size limit.

Each row can store up to 850 bytes of clustering column data. Each clustering column requires up to 4 bytes for metadata that also count toward the 1 MB row size limit.

When calculating the total size of each row, you should consider the previously mentioned partition key and clustering column metadata.

Migrating Your Data into Keyspaces

As of this writing, Amazon Keyspaces is not yet compatible with the AWS migration and data movement services as DynamoDB is. Therefore, to migrate your current data to Keyspaces, you need to use native tools or ETL services. Let's explore an example of each.

The native tool available for homogeneous data migration is `cqlsh`. With the shell tool for CQL, you can use the `COPY FROM` command to migrate from a CSV file into the Keyspaces table. The file header must match the column names on the target Keyspaces table to work. This approach has minimal options available, is single process, and has throughput and connection limitations.

If the migration can't be done via `cqlsh`, you can use the Amazon EMR service to accomplish it. Since Amazon EMR is an ETL-like service, you need to explore the data source structure first and transform it into any Apache Hadoop–compatible file format like HDFS, for example. Once on a Hadoop-compatible format, you can use a Cassandra connector like Spark Cassandra to open a session and execute the migration commands. This option allows you to run complex data transformations during the migration; it is distributed and has scalable throughput.

The other option is to use a third-party tool for the migration. One of the more popular is DataStax Bulk Loader. With DataStax Bulk Loader, you can do bulk migrations using a CSV file such as the native tool or a complex migration with a transformation-like approach by using Amazon EMR.

The migration is more cost effective if you use provisioned capacity instead of on-demand. Therefore, you need to know how much throughput capacity to provision for the table receiving the data. For an accurate estimation, you need to consider two variables: how much data you will load and how fast you want to load it. You can use the following formulas to do the calculations:

$$\text{Capacity per row} = \text{ceiling}\left(\text{average size of each item} / 1024\right)$$

For example, for an average item size of 1,950, you will get the following:

$$\text{Ceiling}\left(1950 / 1021\right) = 2.0$$

$$\text{WCU} = \left(\text{number of items to load} / \text{time in seconds}\right) * \text{capacity per row} *$$
$$1.10 \left(\text{an extra} 10\% \text{ for buffer}\right)$$

For example, for 1.300.600 lines to be loaded in 5 minutes, you will need the following:

$$\left(1.300.600 / 300\right) * 2 * 1.10 = 9537 \text{ WCUs}$$

Query Considerations

Like DynamoDB, Keyspaces automatically paginates the results from SELECT statements when the data to return exceeds 1 MB in size. The application can process the first page, then the second page, and so on. Cassandra clients should always check for pagination tokens when executing the SELECT queries that return more than one row.

Because the pagination of the results is based on the number of row reads necessary to process a request and not the actual rows to be returned, there is a chance that some pages may be empty.

For instance, if you set PAGE SIZE to 20 and Keyspaces evaluates 80 rows to process a SELECT query, Amazon Keyspaces will return four pages. If only a subset of the rows matched your query, some pages may have fewer than 10 rows.

Keyspaces Capacity Modes

Amazon Keyspaces has two throughput capacity modes: on-demand and provisioned. Customers can choose each table's throughput capacity mode to optimize the price of each read and write operation based on the predictability and variability of their workload.

On-Demand Mode

This is the default Keyspaces throughput mode where you pay for only the requests that your application actually performs. You do not need to specify the throughput capacity in advance. With on-demand mode, Amazon Keyspaces can scale the capacity for the table up to any previously reached traffic level instantly, just like DynamoDB, and then back down when application traffic decreases. This mode instantly accommodates up to double the previous peak traffic on a table; however, you might get "insufficient throughput capacity" errors if you exceed twice the previous peak capacity within 30 minutes.

Amazon Keyspaces charges you for the read and write operations that your application performs on your tables in terms of read request units (RRUs) and write request units (WRUs).

One RRU represents one LOCAL_QUORUM read request or two LOCAL_ONE read requests, for a row up to 4 KB in size, which is similar to DynamoDB's strongly and eventually consistent read operations.

One WRU represents one write for a row up to 1 KB in size. All writes are processed with the LOCAL_QUORUM consistency model, and there is no additional charge for using lightweight transactions (LWTs).

Lightweight transactions in Apache Cassandra leverage linearizable consistency to ensure a transaction isolation level similar to the serializable level offered by relational databases.

You can enable on-demand capacity mode for new and existing tables. Figure 5.12 represents the max throughput change with new peaks.

FIGURE 5.12   Amazon Keyspaces traffic peak example

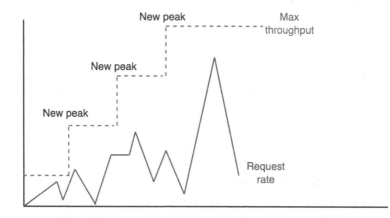

Provisioned Mode

With provisioned throughput capacity mode, customers specify the number of reads and writes per second that they are expecting to get from the application in the form of read capacity units (RCUs) and write capacity units (WCUs), which is similar to DynamoDB.

One RCU in Keyspaces represents one LOCAL_QUORUM read per second or two LOCAL_ONE reads per second, for an item up to 4 KB in size. For instance, if your row size is 8 KB, you will require 2 RCUs to perform one LOCAL_QUORUM read per second, and 1 RCU if you require a LOCAL_ONE read.

One WCU in Keyspaces represents one write per second for an item up to 1 KB in size. All writes use the LOCAL_QUORUM consistency model, and there is no additional charge for using lightweight transactions (LWTs) the same way as we described the WRU earlier.

The provisioned throughput value is the maximum amount of throughput capacity an application can consume from a specific table. If your application exceeds that provisioned throughput capacity, you might get insufficient capacity errors. To avoid those errors, you can enable autoscaling to increase and decrease the provisioned capacity automatically. You can optimize the price if you have predictable application traffic and can forecast your table's capacity requirements.

You can change the table capacity mode once per day as you learn more about the workload access patterns or, perhaps, when you expect to have a large burst in traffic from a major event that you anticipate will drive a lot of extra traffic.

When you change a table from provisioned capacity to on-demand capacity mode, Amazon Keyspaces internally makes several changes to the structure of the table and partitions. This process can take several minutes to complete. During the ongoing switching period, the table delivers the previously provisioned WCU and RCU values.

When switching from on-demand capacity mode to provisioned capacity mode, the Keyspaces table delivers throughput that is consistent with the last peak reached when the table was configured with on-demand capacity mode.

Consistency Models

The consistency models are specific for each operation executed on the database, whether reads or writes. Before getting into the consistency level, let's understand those available for Amazon Keyspaces first.

- LOCAL_QUORUM: The local quorum means that the transaction will be approved once the majority of replicas in the coordinator site have already confirmed the transaction. Since Keyspaces replicates the data three times on each availability zone, the LOCAL_QUORUM waits for the confirmation of two replicas.

- LOCAL_ONE: The LOCAL_ONE waits for one replica of the coordinator site to acknowledge the operation before confirming the transaction to the client.

- ONE: This will confirm the transaction whenever any replica acknowledges it.

Amazon Keyspaces replicates all write operations three times across multiple availability zones for durability and high availability and uses only the LOCAL_QUORUM consistency level.

Regarding the read operations, Keyspaces supports the three consistency levels: ONE, LOCAL_ONE, and LOCAL_QUORUM. The first two levels can improve the performance and availability of your read requests, but the response might not reflect the results of a recently completed write.

Each write operation up to 1 KB will consume a WCU or WRU, and each read operation with LOCAL_QUORUM consistency up to 4K will consume RCU or RRU depending on the configured throughput capacity mode.

If you use LOCAL_QUORUM for both reads and writes, you can emulate a strong consistency model for your queries, but of course, this doesn't come for free. In addition to the additional response latency, there is more usage of the provisioned capacity for the cluster. Table 5.6 will help you see the difference.

TABLE 5.6 Amazon Keyspaces Capacity per Consistency Level

Consistency Level	Capacity
ONE	0.5 RCUs
LOCAL_ONE	0.5 RCUs
LOCAL_QUORUM	1 RCU

Use Cases

Amazon Keyspaces use cases are similar to Amazon DynamoDB ones with regard to low latency and the ability to process data at high speeds with single-digit-millisecond latency. These applications can be industrial equipment maintenance, trade monitoring, fleet management, and route optimization, but it is better when the customers are already using Apache Cassandra or have experience working with CQL. For instance:

- You can build applications on AWS using the open-source Cassandra drivers and APIs available for several programming languages, such as Ruby, Java, Node.js, Python, PHP, Microsoft .NET, C++, Go, and Perl.

- You can move your Cassandra workloads to the cloud to avoid the heavy lifting of managing Cassandra tables yourself. With Amazon Keyspaces, customers can deploy, secure, and scale Cassandra-compatible tables in the AWS without managing or provisioning infrastructure.

Best Practices

When using Amazon Keyspaces, consider the following best practices:

- The on-demand capacity mode can accommodate traffic requests up to twice as much as the previous peak. For instance, suppose that an application's traffic pattern typically goes from 10,000 to 20,000 strongly consistent reads per second, where 20,000 reads per second is the previously reached traffic peak. In this scenario, the service recommends that you to wait for at least 30 minutes before going up to a new peak of 80,000 reads per second.

- New tables with the on-demand capacity mode or tables switched to on-demand mode will have a default RRU peak of 6,000 and a WRU of 2,000.

- When using AWS CloudFormation templates to create scaling policies, customers should manage the scaling policies from AWS CloudFormation so that the resources are in sync with the stack template. If you change scaling policies from Amazon Keyspaces or Application Auto Scaling, they might get overwritten with the values from the AWS CloudFormation template.

- When doing a migration to Keyspaces, try to break it down into smaller components. There are several division criteria to consider; it can be by keyspace or table, or by data itself, for instance: by category, by date, or by groups of user and products. When running the actual migration, avoid using batches with all the items on the same partition and with a maximum of 30 statements. Rather, create more new connections rather than more requests in the same connection. It's also a good idea to stop the CloudWatch metrics when the migration is running.

- Don't name new tables the same as any previously deleted one. If a new table is created with the same qualified name, the deleted table will no longer be restorable.

- As is the case with DynamoDB, while a restore is in progress, don't modify or delete the IAM policies that grant the IAM principal permission to perform the restore.

Backups

The Cassandra snapshot and increment backup process requires heavy lifting and increases in cost as the cluster grows. Besides that, the open-source third-party backup systems for Apache Cassandra are very complex and require deep expertise to work with.

Amazon Keyspaces offers point-in-time recovery (PITR) to help protect your tables from accidental write or delete operations. With PITR, you can restore a table's data to any second in time since the PITR option was enabled up to the last 35 days. If a customer deletes a table with point-in-time recovery enabled, they can query for the deleted table's data for up to 35 days (at no additional cost). There is also an option to restore it to the state it was in just before the point of deletion. A table recovery using the PITR feature does not impact the table's performance or availability, nor does it consume additional throughput capacity. The restores are done in a new table; PITR doesn't overwrite existing tables.

The PITR option is enabled by default when you create the table via the web console. Amazon Keyspaces uses two timestamps to maintain the time frame for which restorable backups are available for a table the same way as DynamoDB does.

- **Earliest restorable time:** This marks the time of the earliest available restorable backup. The earliest restorable backup can go back to 35 days ago or to when the PITR feature was enabled, whichever is more recent. The maximum backup range of 35 days can't be modified.

- **Current time:** The timestamp for the latest restorable backup is the current time at the operation request time. If no timestamp is provided during a restore, the current time is used.

If you disable and then enable the PITR option, you will lose the earliest restorable time and thus the previous history. A table doesn't have to be active in order to be restored. Customers can also restore deleted tables if the PITR option was enabled on the deleted table and the deletion occurred within the last 35 days.

Scalability

As mentioned in the capacity mode overview, Amazon Keyspaces also has autoscaling features. This is done by using the Application Auto Scaling service to increase and decrease a table's read and write capacity on your behalf. This service works through autoscaling policies to define a target utilization related to the specific services it's supporting. The target utilization is the relation of consumed capacity units to the provisioned capacity units at a given point in time, expressed as a percentage value. The automatic scaling feature uses a target tracking algorithm to adjust the provisioned throughput capacity of the table upward in response to increasing traffic and downward once the peak is over.

As with Amazon DynamoDB, when customers create a scaling policy, the Application Auto Scaling service creates two pairs of Amazon CloudWatch alarms. Each alarm represents your upper and lower boundaries for provisioned and consumed throughput values. The Application Auto Scaling service only modifies the capacity of the table when the actual workload runs higher (or lower) for a sustained period of several minutes. To handle the small sudden spikes in the traffic, Keyspaces has the same burst feature we reviewed in DynamoDB.

Security

As Amazon Keyspaces is a managed serverless service, the shared responsibility model bar is very high because AWS manages the infrastructure, operating system, application server, and scalability on your behalf. You only need to take care of data encryption and access control.

Data Encryption

Customers can protect their data in transit and at rest. Amazon Keyspaces is compatible with encryption at rest by using 256-bit Advanced Encryption Standard (AES-256). This encryption helps secure the data from unauthorized access to the underlying storage layer. The Keyspaces engine encrypts and decrypts the table data transparently without performance impact or extra costs. Customers can use an AWS managed key without extra costs or can use their own keys via AWS KMS, but extra charges may apply. The key type used can be changed at any time.

Regarding encryption in transit, Keyspaces only accepts secure connections using Transport Layer Security (TLS), no matter what you use as the client, such as the Cassandra Client Driver or the cqlsh tool.

Access Control

Amazon Keyspaces supports two ways to authenticate client requests. One is through service-specific credentials, which are the username and password credentials that Cassandra typically uses for authentication and access control but are associated with a specific IAM user. The other method uses an authentication plugin for the DataStax Java Driver for Cassandra. The plugin allows you to use temporary credentials when connecting to Amazon Keyspaces by signing the API requests using the access key that you specify when you configure it.

Like DynamoDB, Keyspaces only supports identity-based policies and not resource-based policies. With IAM identity-based policies, customers can specify allow or deny actions on resources as well as the conditions under which those actions are allowed or denied. If there are several condition elements in a statement or multiple keys affected with a single condition, AWS evaluates them using a logical AND operation. If there are multiple values for a single condition key, on the contrary, AWS evaluates the condition using a logical OR operation.

The permission for the statement will be granted only after all the conditions are met.

You can add conditions on resources up to the table level:

```
arn:${KeySpacePartition}:cassandra:${AWSRegion}:${AWSAccount}:/
keyspace/${KeyspaceName}/table/${TableName}
```

You can replace the TableName or KeyspaceName value with wildcards if you want to increase the scope of the resource condition.

There is also the option to use placeholder variables when writing policy conditions. For instance, customers can grant an IAM user permission over a resource only if it is tagged with the same IAM username.

Keyspaces uses IAM service-linked roles. This kind of role is a unique type of IAM role that is linked directly to the Amazon Keyspaces service and includes all the permissions that the service requires to leverage all the necessary AWS services on your behalf. For instance, a service-linked role makes setting up autoscaling easier because you don't have to manually add the necessary IAM permissions for it.

The default method to access Amazon Keyspaces is through AWS-published APIs. Clients must support at least Transport Layer Security (TLS) 1.0 and a cypher suite compatible with Perfect Forward Secrecy (PFS). If you need to access Amazon Keyspaces privately without leaving the Amazon network, you can use a VPC interface endpoint powered by AWS PrivateLink. AWS PrivateLink enables this by using an elastic network interface with private IP addresses in your VPC so that network traffic does not leave the Amazon network.

Consider the following recommended best practices when working with Keyspaces access control:

- Get started by using AWS managed policies to grant your employees all the permissions they need to work with Keyspaces. These policies are already available in every account and are maintained and updated by AWS.

- When you create custom policies, comply with the least privilege best practices, and grant just the minimum permissions required to perform that particular task.

- For extra security settings, require IAM users to use multifactor authentication (MFA) to access sensitive resources or API operations. For example, delete or disable Cloud-Watch metrics and autoscaling features.

- Use policy conditions for extra security. Define the conditions under which the identity-based policies grant access to a given resource. For instance, customers can write conditions to allow only a range of IP addresses to call the APIs. You could also write conditions to allow requests only within a specified date or time range to avoid critical business hours or to require the use of SSL or MFA for extra security.

- Prefer to use IAM roles when using Amazon Keyspaces within an AWS service that uses or can use a role, like applications running on EC2 instances or a microservice on AWS Lambda.

- Enable encryption at rest; with AWS Managed Keys you won't incur extra charges. Consider using client-side encryption if the Keyspaces table stores sensitive or confidential information.

Monitoring

The AWS Console for Amazon Keyspaces offers a preconfigured dashboard showing the latency and errors aggregated across all tables in an account, but that isn't enough to maintain the reliability, availability, and performance of Amazon Keyspaces.

Like every AWS service, Keyspaces is integrated with Amazon CloudWatch to send raw system and operation data to be processed and converted into readable, near-real-time metrics. It's near real time because all metrics for Keyspaces are aggregated and reported every minute.

Like all other metrics, Keyspaces metrics can be added to a CloudWatch dashboard and are stored within CloudWatch for 15 months so that you can access historical information and gain insights on how the service is performing. Customers can also set alarms when the metrics reach certain thresholds and send notifications or take actions according to the data.

Table 5.7 covers some of the most important metrics available for Keyspaces.

TABLE 5.7   Amazon CloudWatch Metrics Available for Keyspaces

Metric	Description
ConsumedReadCapacityUnits and ConsumedWriteCapacityUnits	Shows the number of read and write capacity units consumed over the specified time period.
ProvisionedReadCapacityUnits and ProvisionedWriteCapacityUnits	Shows the number of provisioned read and write capacity units for a table.

(continues)

TABLE 5.7   Amazon CloudWatch Metrics Available for Keyspaces *(continued)*

Metric	Description
PerConnectionRequestRateExceeded	Requests to Amazon Keyspaces that exceed the per-connection request rate quota. Each connection to Amazon Keyspaces endpoints can support up to 3,000 requests per second. As a workaround, the clients can create multiple connections concurrently to increase the throughput.
ReturnedItemCount	Corresponds to the number of rows that a multirow SELECT query returns during the specified time period. Multirow SELECT queries do not contain a fully qualified primary key like a full table scan or a range query.
SystemErrors	Shows the requests to Amazon Keyspaces that generate an internal ServerError during the specified time period.
UserErrors	Shows the number of requests to Amazon Keyspaces that generate an InvalidRequest error during the specified time period. This kind of error usually indicates a client-side error regarding parameters and resource names.

Like all other AWS services, Amazon Keyspaces will store all API call traces on Amazon CloudTrail; remember that this also includes web console actions and CLI commands.

Summary

This chapter covered the necessary concepts and features of Amazon DynamoDB and Amazon Keyspaces to be able to identify the right use cases for both and to understand how to translate the applications requirement to the deployment options of these services. You will be able to design the DynamoDB or Keyspaces databases to be highly available, scalable, secure, and performant. We showed you the available tools to monitor and troubleshoot possible database issues and talked about how to optimize the performance even further. You also gained a general understanding of how to operate the DynamoDB and Keyspaces databases in terms of backups, maintenance tasks, and security configurations.

Exam Essentials

Know the right database for each use case.   The technology is no longer evolving toward modern application development, microservices, distributed system, and NoSQL databases; it is already there, and there are only a few laggards left behind. It is crucial to know which database type is best suited for each use case, especially managed and serverless ones like DynamoDB and Keyspaces.

Understand the right deployment and migration options.   Not all applications are born cloud-native. Most of them are still legacy on-premises ones. That's why it is important to know what are the available migration and deployment configuration tools for Amazon DynamoDB and Amazon Keyspaces.

Understand Amazon DynamoDB and Keyspaces management and operations.   Once you have your application running, you need to keep it in that state, and the database is an important part of it. You need to know the available features and services to help manage and operate Amazon DynamoDB and Amazon Keyspaces, including scaling, backup/restore, performance optimization, and maintenance.

Know the available monitoring and troubleshooting tools.   Everything fails all the time. Be familiar with the AWS monitoring and logging services available for Amazon DynamoDB and Keyspaces. Know how to identify and resolve the potential issues and optimize the database performance.

Strengthen the security for Amazon DynamoDB and Keyspaces.   Security is a priority for most organizations, so it is important to understand the security mechanism that you should leverage to secure your data in transit and at rest and implement a robust access control in Amazon DynamoDB and Keyspaces.

Exercises

If you need assistance in completing the following exercises, please refer to the Amazon DynamoDB developer guide at docs.aws.amazon.com/amazondynamodb/latest/ developerguide/GettingStartedDynamoDB.html.

Create a DynamoDB Table and Populate It

In this exercise, you will create a new DynamoDB table.

1. Sign in to the AWS Management Console with a user with the right DynamoDB permissions and open the DynamoDB console.

2. Navigate to the DynamoDB console dashboard with the left menu button Dashboard or Tables.

3. Click the Create Table button.

4. Enter the basic table information such as the name, the partition key, and the sort key.

5. Leave Default Settings checked and click the Create Table button at the bottom-right side of the screen.

6. You will go automatically to the table screen and see a message similar to this: "Creating the [table_name] table. It will be available for use shortly."

7. Once the table is successfully created, go to the Explore Items section on the top menu and select the recently created table.

8. Click the Create Item button located on the right of the interface and enter some values for the primary and sort keys. You can also add other new attributes as desired. Note that you can use two views, a form or the JSON view.

9. Click the Create Item button at the bottom right of the screen.

10. Repeat the previous step as many times as you want to populate the table with sample items.

Create a Global Secondary Index

In this exercise, you will create a GSI for the table created in the previous exercise.

1. In the DynamoDB console, navigate to the tables view with the left menu button Tables.

2. Click the recently created table from the list.

3. Go to the Indexes tab on the top-right side of the screen.

4. Click the Create Index button and select a partition key for the index among the existing attributes. Remember that the GSI can be different from the main table. You will notice that the index name will autocomplete.

5. Leave the rest of the default values and click the Create Index button at the right bottom of the dialog. You will see the index being created in the Indexes section of the table.

EXERCISE 5.3

Query the Data on Your Table

In this exercise, you will query the data you created in Exercise 5.1.

1. In the DynamoDB console, navigate to the tables view with the left menu button Tables.

2. Go to the Explore Items section at the top right and select the recently created table from the table list.

3. Expand the Scan/Query Items section to visualize the query interface.

4. Enter some of the partition key values you inserted in Exercise 5.1 and click Run.

You will see that the result page changes to fit the search criteria you used.

EXERCISE 5.4

Clean Up the Created Resources

In this exercise, you will delete the table and index you created in the previous exercises.

1. In the DynamoDB console, navigate to the tables view with the left menu button Tables.

2. Click the recently created table from the list.

3. Go to the Indexes tab on the top right side of the screen.

4. Select the GSI you created and click the Delete button on the right of the screen. Finally, confirm the delete action by typing **delete** in the pop-up window.

5. Once the GSI is deleted, click the Actions drop-down list at the top right of the screen and choose the Delete Table option. Finally, confirm the delete action by typing **delete** in the pop-up window, leaving the other options with the default values.

6. Wait for a few seconds and check that the table has been deleted successfully.

Review Questions

1. A company is developing an IoT application using DynamoDB as the database for device event data. The application needs to archive all event data older than 60 days automatically on Amazon S3. What is the best way to implement this?

    A. Create an Amazon EventBridge rule to be executed every day and trigger a Lambda function to perform a query and move to S3 the items with a timestamp greater than 60 days.

    B. Create a new DynamoDB table every 60 days and archive the old DynamoDB table.

    C. Enable TTL on the DynamoDB table and set the expiration timestamp in the TTL attribute when putting the item. Enable Stream on the table to capture the TTL deletions and send those items to Amazon S3 for archiving.

    D. Enable TTL on the DynamoDB table and set the expiration timestamp in the TTL attribute when putting the item. Create on-demand backups of the data every 60 days.

2. A development team needs to build an AWS Lambda function to communicate with Amazon DynamoDB. What is the most secure method of providing the Lambda function access permissions to the DynamoDB table?

    A. Create an IAM role and an IAM policy granting the necessary access permissions for the AWS Lambda service. Assign the IAM role to the DynamoDB table.

    B. Create a DynamoDB user and password, store the credentials in Secret Managers, and use it in the Lambda Function.

    C. Create an IAM user with programmatic access keys. Grant the necessary DynamoDB permissions policies to that user and use the keys in the Lambda function.

    D. Create an IAM role and an IAM policy granting necessary access permissions for AWS Lambda service. Assign the IAM role to the Lambda function.

3. A company is developing a mission-critical application. There is a requirement to store the data in two AWS regions in active-active mode. What is the best solution for these requirements?

    A. Amazon Aurora with the Global Database option

    B. Amazon RDS with Multi-AZ and read replicas in the other regions

    C. Amazon DynamoDB with Global Tables

    D. Amazon Aurora with the multimaster cluster

4. A large enterprise is currently migrating to the cloud, and it has several workloads running Apache Cassandra. They want to do a migration of their 100 TB of data on Cassandra to a serverless deployment option that will let them save costs and reduce operational overhead. There is a requirement to do the migration within the least amount of time to reduce downtime. What is the best approach to accomplish the migration requirements?

    A. They need to do a heterogeneous migration to DynamoDB since it is the only compatible NoSQL database with a serverless mode on AWS.

    B. They should migrate to Amazon Keyspaces (for Apache Cassandra) and use `cqlsh` to build the import jobs.

   C. Use the third-party tool DataStax Bulk Loader (DSBulk) to migrate the on-premises cluster to Amazon Keyspaces with on-demand capacity mode.

   D. Create an Amazon Keyspaces cluster with provisioned capacity and build the migration process using Amazon EMR.

5. An ecommerce application stores the inventory of available items for purchase on the website. Each item is uniquely identified by a stock keeping unit (SKU) number. The DynamoDB table contains additional attributes such as Type, Manufacture Date, Manufacturer Name, Country of Origin, and Price. The application must get the item information on each purchase. Another component produces reports for a list of sales for each country. Which of the following is the best combination for indexes and keys for both access patterns?

   A. Table Partition Key=Manufacture Date

   Table Sort Key=SKU

   GSI Partition Key=Manufacturer Name

   GSI Sort Key=Country of Origin

   B. Table Partition Key=SKU

   Table Sort Key=Type

   GSI Partition Key=Country of Origin

   GSI Sort Key=Manufacturer Name

   C. Table Partition Key=SKU

   Table Sort Key=Type

   GSI Partition Key=Random Prefix

   GSI Sort Key=Country of Origin

   D. Table Partition Key=SKU

   Table Sort Key=Type

   GSI Partition Key=Manufacture Date

   GSI Sort Key=Country of Origin

6. A payment transaction application stores its data in DynamoDB. A business unit sends a new requirement to the development team where the application has to perform strongly consistent queries on an attribute that is not the partition key. How can the team approach this problem?

   A. Create a new DynamoDB table.

   B. Create a new GSI on the current table.

   C. Create a new LSI on the current table.

   D. Create a DynamoDB DAX cluster and use it on the front of every get operation.

7. Select the AWS NoSQL databases that always provide strong consistency read operations within their options. (Choose three.)

   A. Amazon Neptune

   B. Amazon Keyspaces

   C. Amazon DynamoDB

   D. Amazon DocumentDB

8. A company is having budget problems and needs to optimize the DynamoDB database performance without incurring extra costs. A database specialist has to identify frequently accessed keys. What service can the specialist use to achieve this in the most cost-effective way?

   A. Analyze CloudTrail events history in Amazon S3 with Amazon Athena.

   B. Enable DynamoDB Performance Insights and review the usage of the database.

   C. Use AWS X-Ray to trace the DynamoDB requests and find what is the most used key.

   D. Create a CloudWatch Contributor Insight rule to find the outliers among all the logs.

9. A high-performance application is currently using Amazon DynamoDB as the database system, with a maximum item size of 5 KB. The application needs to perform 50 strongly consistent reads and 10 writes per second all the time. What are the required RCUs and WCUs to accommodate the application traffic in the provisioned throughput capacity mode?

   A. 50 RCUs and 25 WCUs

   B. 50 RCUs and 50 WCUs

   C. 100 RCUs and 25 WCUs

   D. 100 RCUs and 50 WCUs

10. A DBA was asked to truncate a DynamoDB table. What's the most effective way to do it?

    A. Use the CLI command `truncate-table` with the right parameters.

    B. Use the DynamoDB truncate API operation with the right parameters.

    C. Use the CLI command `scan` and iterate through all the items using the CLI command `delete-item`.

    D. Delete and re-create the table with the same options as before.

Chapter

6

Document Databases in the Cloud

THE AWS CERTIFIED DATABASE - SPECIALTY EXAM OBJECTIVES COVERED IN THIS CHAPTER MAY INCLUDE, BUT ARE NOT LIMITED TO, THE FOLLOWING:

✓ **Domain 1: Workload-Specific Database Design**

- 1.2 Determine strategies for disaster recovery and high availability.
- 1.3 Design database solutions for performance, compliance, and scalability.
- 1.4 Compare the costs of database solutions.

✓ **Domain 2: Deployment and Migration**

- 2.2 Determine data preparation and migration strategies.
- 2.3 Execute and validate data migration.

✓ **Domain 3: Management and Operations**

- 3.1 Determine maintenance tasks and processes.
- 3.2 Determine backup and restore strategies.
- 3.3 Manage the operational environment of a database solution.

✓ **Domain 4: Monitoring and troubleshooting**

- 4.2 Troubleshoot and resolve common database issues.
- 4.3 Optimize database performance.

✓ **Domain 5: Database security**

- 5.1 Encrypt data at rest and in transit.
- 5.2 Evaluate auditing solutions.
- 5.3 Determine access control and authentication mechanisms.
- 5.4 Recognize potential security vulnerabilities within database solutions.

When you modernize your application, you need to modernize your database too; it's not one size fits for all. Modern applications need different databases flavors, one of which is the document database. In this chapter, you will learn what a document database is and how to work with document databases in AWS. You'll also learn how to use document databases in cloud architectures, as well as use MongoDB on AWS and Amazon DocumentDB.

Introducing Document Databases

A document database is a nonrelational database that stores data as structured documents. Documents can be represented by Extensible Markup Language (XML) or JavaScript Object Notation (JSON) formats in most cases. *Extensible Markup Language (XML)* is a markup language that allows users to define their own tags and structure data in a hierarchical manner. *JavaScript Object Notation (JSON)* is a text-based data format that is designed to store and exchange data in an organized, human-readable way. JSON is often used in web applications for transferring data between the client and the server. One of the major benefits of JSON is its flexibility, as you can change the structure of documents (add or remove fields) without worrying about a schema definition. The flexible data model is also one of the key benefits of using document databases. In the following example, a JSON-like simple document describes a user:

```
{
    id: "2301",
    user: "derek",
    status: "enabled",
    groups: [ "sports", "news" ]
}
```

The preceding code snippet enables you to store unstructured or semistructured data as a document. The document structure, or *schema*, provides nested key-value pairs, which is how documents are stored in a document database. With these characteristics and natural APIs for agile development, document databases are a great option for user profiles, real-time Big Data, and content management use cases. An *application programming interface (API)* is a set of routines, protocols, and tools used to build software applications. An API specifies how software components should interact, allowing developers to create modular, reusable code that can be integrated into other applications.

Some of the benefits of using document databases include the following:

- Documents correspond to native data types in several programming languages (e.g., Python dictionaries or JavaScript objects)
- Indexing
- Flexible schema
- Replica sets (mirror instances)
- Sharding (distributed data)

There are a variety of document databases, including Amazon DocumentDB, Amazon DynamoDB, CouchDB, Couchbase, and MongoDB. MongoDB is by far the most popular and used document database to date. In MongoDB, documents are represented in a JSON-like format called Binary JSON (BSON). BSON uses a key-pair way to store data. *CouchDB* is an open-source, document-oriented NoSQL database. It uses JSON to store data, JavaScript as its query language, and HTTP for an API. *Couchbase* is an open-source, distributed NoSQL database. It uses a distributed architecture to provide scalability, high availability, and performance. Couchbase supports various data models including key-values, JSON documents, and search indexes. It also has an extensive API for interacting with the database. *MongoDB* is an open-source, document-oriented NoSQL database. It stores data in flexible, JSON-like documents, allowing for a dynamic schema. MongoDB also has an extensive API for interacting with the database, making it easy to build and scale applications.

Because of this particular structure, document databases use a different terminology than relational databases. A group of documents form a *collection*. In relational databases this is known as a *table*. Each record in a collection is a document, and the structure between documents can be the same or not. Typically, all documents in a collection have a similar or related purpose. Table 6.1 compares the terminology used by document databases, especially for MongoDB, with the terminology used by relational databases.

TABLE 6.1   Terminologies of Relational vs. Document Databases

Relational Databases	Document Databases
Database	Database
Table	Collection
Row	Document
Column	Field
Primary Key	ObjectID
Nested table or object	Embedded document

Document databases are not ideal when the relationships between multiple entities are important for your application or if there are a lot of foreign keys or joins.

Because it is multiplatform, MongoDB is accepted among enterprise environments with modern tools for management and data modeling like Compass, Robo3T, Studio 3T, and MongoView. MongoDB is also schema-free, which means documents can have any structure, even in the same collection. However, it's important to have a good schema design based on application requirements.

Another feature of MongoDB is scalability. It can easily scale within and across multiple locations. MongoDB can scale with no downtime and without changing your application. The architecture of your MongoDB installation will depend on the scale at which you want to operate. You have two options:

- **Stand-alone instances:** Mongod (primary daemon process) will handle requests, manage data access, and perform background management operations. With this option, you have only one instance, which is good for development and testing but should not be used in a production environment, because it cannot guarantee high availability or automatic failover in a disaster scenario. *Mongod* is a daemon process for MongoDB, an open-source document-oriented NoSQL database. It is the primary component of a MongoDB system and is responsible for managing data stored in collections and databases.

- **Replica sets:** These are groups of mongod processes that maintain multiple copies of the data and perform automatic failover for availability. In this scenario, you have multiple instances, with one instance (primary) acting as the primary member (node) and the other instances acting as secondary members (replicas). The primary member receives all write operations, while replicas can serve read-only traffic. If the primary member fails, one of the secondary members is automatically elected to the primary role. You cannot serve any write operations until the election completes successfully, but you can serve to read requests.

The time limit in milliseconds for detecting when a replica set's primary is unreachable when you have higher values results in slower failovers, just as lower values result in faster failover. Either way, the primary node will be impacted.

MongoDB offers read-after-write consistency when you read from the primary instance, which means that read and write requests are issued to a primary member of the replica set. Applications and clients can read from the replicas, but a read preference must be specified, and this operation is eventually consistent.

MongoDB has native sharding. Sharding is a way to distribute data across multiple machines. This is helpful to support large data sets and high-throughput operations. Only one server can fit or match in terms of CPU, memory, and disk capacity. There are two options for scaling:

- **Vertical:** This involves increasing the capacity of a single server, such as adding a CPU, adding memory, or adding storage spaces. This can be a good fit for a small or medium environment but has some limitations. In the cloud, you pay as you go, which means larger instances will cost you more; another limitation is downtime. To increase capacity and/or change your Amazon EC2 family type, you must stop the machine.

- **Horizontal:** This involves dividing your data set and load across multiple servers. With this scenario, every machine handles a subset of the data set, providing better efficiency over a single server. There is a limitation: increased complexity in infrastructure and maintenance for deployment.

As mongod is a primary daemon for MongoDB, mongod acts as a query router to determine in which shard a query must be run. A config server stores metadata and configuration settings for the sharded cluster. These two elements are key to have sharding along with MongoDB, because it will surpass the hardware limitations of a single server, without adding complexity to the application. As shown in Figure 6.1, MongoDB automatically balances the data in the shared cluster as the data grows or the size of the cluster increases or decreases.

FIGURE 6.1   Sharding in MongoDB

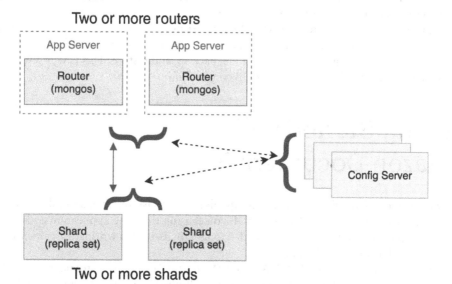

MongoDB supports indexing, which is a way to efficiently query your data set without needing to perform a collection scan, meaning scanning every document in a collection. MongoDB indexes are similar to other database systems. MongoDB defines indexes at the collection level and supports indexes on any field or subfield of the documents.

When you create an index, MongoDB can use the index to limit the number of documents it must inspect in a query.

```
>db.COLLECTION_NAMME.createIndex ({KEY:1})
```

Because of its flexible data model and indexing capabilities, MongoDB can be a great fit for both transactional and analytical workloads.

In AWS, you can run MongoDB in two ways:

- Using Amazon EC2 with MongoDB installed
- Using Amazon DocumentDB (with the MongoDB compatibility)

There is a third way: MongoDB Atlas is a fully managed document database service in the cloud, built by the MongoDB team, but this is beyond the scope of the AWS Database exam.

You can install and manage MongoDB in Amazon EC2. EC2 is a service that provides compute capacity in the cloud, and it is aligned with the shared responsibility model. AWS takes care of the infrastructure, hypervisor, and facilities, and you are responsible for patching, managing the operating system, data, encryption, and so on. AWS offers a Quick Start reference deployment for MongoDB Community Edition version 3.2 or 3.4, where you can rapidly deploy a MongoDB cluster. The *AWS Shared Responsibility Model* is an agreement between customers and AWS that outlines the security responsibilities of each party in running and using the cloud service. It states that the customer is responsible for their own application, data, and operating system security, while AWS is responsible for the security of the cloud service, infrastructure, and physical resources.

Also, you can create a cluster or stand-alone server using your system administrator skills, but this can be a complex and hard task, especially if you want to create multiple replica sets, as it is hard to manage, maintain, upgrade, backup, and restore. This is why AWS created Amazon DocumentDB (with MongoDB compatibility).

Getting Started with Amazon DocumentDB

Amazon DocumentDB (with MongoDB compatibility) is a fast, reliable, and fully managed database service. With Amazon DocumentDB you can run the same application code and use the same drivers and tools that you use with MongoDB. As of this writing, DocumentDB is compatible with MongoDB 3.6 and 4.0.

With the launch of MongoDB 4.0, Amazon DocumentDB supports atomic, consistent, isolated, and durable (ACID) transactions across multiple documents, statements, collections, and databases. *ACID* is a set of properties that guarantees transaction integrity in a database system. It ensures that data is consistent and reliable even if the system crashes or errors occur. Common use cases for transactions include financial processing, fulfilling and managing orders, and building multiplayer games. Transactions simplify application development by enabling you to ACID operations across one or more documents within an Amazon DocumentDB cluster.

Amazon DocumentDB is compatible with the MongoDB 3.6 and 4.0 APIs; however, it does not support every MongoDB feature. To see a list of supported APIs, refer to docs .aws.amazon.com/documentdb/latest/developerguide/mongo-apis.html.

Amazon DocumentDB is a cluster, and you can have from 1 up to 16 instances. One of those instances acts as a primary, supporting read and write requests, and the others are replicas, supporting read-only requests. Instances are distributed across subnets (i.e., AZs) within the subnet group assigned to the cluster. You can have only one subnet group per cluster. This is a collection of subnets within an Amazon VPC, and it must have at least two subnets associated, which means at least two availability zones for each cluster. A *cluster* is a group of computers that are connected and work together to provide better performance, scalability, and availability than would be possible with a single computer. *Amazon Virtual Private Cloud (Amazon VPC)* is a cloud computing service that provides an isolated virtual network in the AWS cloud. AWS users can launch Amazon EC2 instances and other AWS services in Amazon VPC to leverage the scalability, reliability, and availability of the AWS cloud while maintaining control of their sensitive data. *Availability zones* are a high-availability offering from AWS that provides fault-tolerant and scalable deployments of applications.

Like MongoDB, the Amazon DocumentDB cluster has two instance roles: the primary instance and the replica instance. The primary instance executes all the data modifications on the cluster volume and performs both read and write operations. Replica instances perform read-only operations; you can have up to 15 replica instances across multiple AZs. DocumentDB must have one primary instance; replica instances are optional.

The Amazon DocumentDB cluster is sitting on a region, which means sitting on a VPC with subnets, but Amazon DocumentDB stores data in a cluster storage volume, which is a single virtual volume that uses solid-state drives (SSDs). As shown in Figure 6.2, this cluster volume makes six copies of your data, distributed across three AZs. This helps ensure your data is highly durable and available. DocumentDB will consider the data durable when the storage layer acknowledges the persistence of at least four copies out of six; this is known as *write quorum*. Now, for read operations, DocumentDB needs two copies out of six; this is known as *read quorum*.

FIGURE 6.2 Amazon DocumentDB architecture

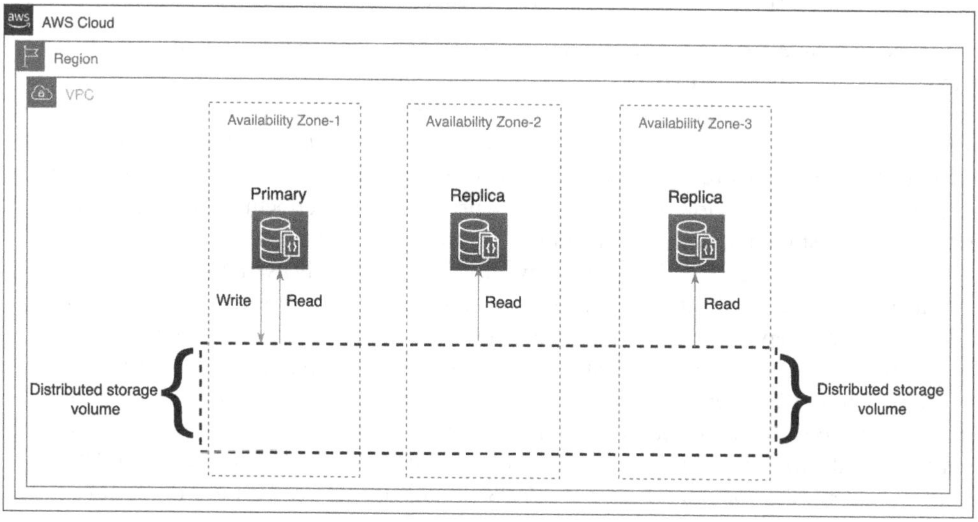

The DocumentDB cluster storage size scales automatically from 10 GB to 64 TB (the maximum cluster size as of this writing) as the amount of data increases. The storage is fault-tolerant and self-healing. DocumentDB uses a log-structured at storage layer passing incremental log records from the instance (compute) to the store layer, very similar to the Amazon Aurora architecture. *Amazon Aurora* is a relational database service provided by AWS that is designed to be compatible with MySQL and PostgreSQL; it provides the security, reliability, scalability, and availability of commercial-grade databases at a fraction of the cost.

In a DocumentDB cluster, the primary and replica instances can have different instance classes, and you can scale in or out to meet the demand. The cluster's storage scales independently of the instances. To serve multiple connections, Amazon DocumentDB has three endpoints, as you can see in Figure 6.3, and each endpoint has a unique DNS name followed by a colon and the port number (default value is 27017).

- **Cluster endpoint:** This is the endpoint that you will use to connect to the cluster's current primary instance. It can be used for read and write operations. The Amazon DocumentDB cluster has only one cluster endpoint.

  `sample-`**`cluster`**`.cluster-111111111111.us-east 1.docdb.amazonaws.com:27017`

- **Reader endpoint:** This is a read-only endpoint that load balances across all available replicas in the cluster. If a cluster has only one instance, then the primary instance will be the target of both the cluster and reader endpoints.

  `sample-cluster.cluster-`**`ro`**`-111111111111.us-east 1.docdb.amazonaws.com:27017`

- **Instance endpoint:** This endpoint connects to a specific instance within a cluster. Both primary and replica instances have their own instance endpoints, but the same premise remains: the primary instance endpoint is for write and read operations, and the replica instance endpoint is only for read operations.

  `sample-`**`instance`**`.111111111111.us-east-1.docdb.amazonaws.com:27017`

It is recommended to connect using the cluster endpoint in replica set mode, which enables your SDK to auto-discover the cluster arrangement as instances get added or removed from the cluster. Each Amazon DocumentDB cluster consists of a single replica set with the default name rs0, and this cannot be changed. A *software development kit (SDK)* is a set of tools and resources designed to help developers create software applications. It typically includes a collection of APIs, libraries, prewritten code, documentation, and other resources to assist them in creating customized software solutions.

An Amazon DocumentDB cluster can have up to 15 read replicas and has a default approach as an async replication, which means that even though replicas share the same underlying storage layer, there is typically a replication lag of fewer than 100 milliseconds. Because the replica lag can vary depending on the rate of data change, it is recommended to monitor the *ReplicationLag* metrics on Amazon CloudWatch, especially on high write activity operations. *Amazon CloudWatch* is a monitoring and observability service provided by AWS that allows you to monitor, store, and access data and logs related to your AWS resources and applications running on the AWS cloud, edge services, and/or on premises.

FIGURE 6.3   Amazon DocumentDB architecture endpoint

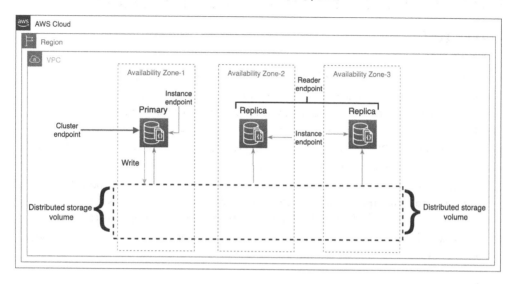

As previously mentioned, you can set the read-preferred option for a specific query or as a default option in your MongoDB driver. Amazon DocumentDB supports the following read preference options:

- **Primary:** This option ensures that all reads are routed to the cluster's primary instance; if the primary instance is unavailable, the read operation fails. Use this preference when read-after-write consistency is necessary over high availability and read scaling.

- **PrimaryPreferred:** This option also ensures that read operations are routed to the primary instance, but if the primary instance fails over, the client routes requests to a replica. Use this option for use cases that prioritize read-after-write consistency over read scaling but still need high availability. This is a recommended option.

- **Secondary:** This option ensures that all reads are routed to a replica, never the primary instance. If a cluster does not have a replica, the read request fails. Use this option when you want to prioritize the primary instance for write throughput over high availability and read-after-write consistency.

- **SecondaryPreferred:** This option also ensures that reads are routed to a read replication, but only if one or more replicas are active. If there are no read replicas, the read request is routed to the primary instance. Use this option for reading scaling and high availability over read-after-write consistency. This is also a recommended option for read use cases.

- **Nearest:** This option of reading preference routes is based only on the measured latency between the client and all instances in the cluster. Use this option when you want to prioritize the lowest possible read latency and high availability over read-after-write consistency and read scaling.

Logged into an Amazon DocumentDB cluster, this is how you specify one of the preceding options. Change the option in `readPref` to the value you want.

```
db.example.find().readPref('nearest')
```

Creating an Amazon DocumentDB Cluster

To create an Amazon DocumentDB cluster, perform the following steps:

1. Before you begin, make sure that the AWS region you are logged into supports Amazon DocumentDB. See docs.aws.amazon.com/documentdb/latest/ developerguide/regions-and-azs.html#regions-and-azs-availability.

2. Avoid using the VPC default: before creating your cluster, create a corresponding VPC with at least two subnets in different subnets.

3. Create a corresponding security group for your cluster. Make sure that port 27017 (you can choose another port number in DocumentDB) is open within the security group itself and can be reached from the application servers or your on-premises servers.

4. If you will not use the default KMS key, make sure you create a key through the AWS KMS console or API before starting this process.

 Clusters that you create using the console have encryption at rest enabled by default. Clusters that you create using the AWS CLI have encryption at rest disabled by default. Therefore, you must explicitly enable encryption at rest using the --storage-encrypted parameter. In either case, after the cluster is created, you can't change the encryption at rest option.

5. Open the Amazon DocumentDB console and click Launch Amazon DocumentDB.

6. Select a unique name for your cluster.

7. Select your engine version. At this moment, DocumentDB supports versions 3.6.0 and 4.0.0.

8. Select your instance class.

9. Select the number of instances for your cluster. Note that all instances will be the same instance class selected in the previous step. You can modify the instance class later. The number can vary from 1 to 16. (One instance will have the primary role.)

10. In the Authentication step, type your master username and password. The master username cannot be *admin*.

11. Choose Show Advanced Settings.

12. Select the Amazon VPC created in step 2.

13. Select the subnet group. If you did not create a subnet group, Amazon DocumentDB creates one for you with one subnet available per AZ. It is recommended that you create a subnet group before this step.

14. In VPC security groups, select the security group created in step 3.

15. At Cluster Options, select a port that should be used to connect to the cluster. By default, it is 27017.

16. In the Cluster Parameter group, if you did not have a parameter group, the Amazon DocumentDB will create a default. Be aware that you cannot modify any parameters in a default parameter group. Therefore, it is highly recommended that you create parameter groups accordingly before setting this step. Each parameter group must be on the same engine version of the cluster.

17. By default, encryption is enabled by AWS KMS managed key aws/rds, but you can change this key for a key created in step 4.

18. Backup retention by default is one day; this is the retention for automated backup of your cluster. You can change this to a value up to 35 days. Also, change the backup window accordingly in UTC time.

19. In Logs Exports, select Audit And Profiler Logs so the logs can be delivered to Amazon CloudWatch Logs. Note that this is the first of two steps—you also must enable these logs in your parameter group within your cluster.

20. Amazon DocumentDB is a fully managed service, but you need to set maintenance windows for modification or patches that can be applied to instances in the cluster. Modification in general in the cluster will be applied during these windows.

21. As a best practice, add tags so that it's easier to manage your resources and identify the costs related to it.

22. For production clusters, enable deletion protection.

23. A disclaimer will show an estimated hourly cost for the cluster. The value will depend on the instance class size and the number of instances that you are using for the cluster. Double-check the class size and number of instances, and click Create Cluster. In a few minutes your new Amazon DocumentDB cluster will be created.

Amazon DocumentDB Architecture

For Amazon DocumentDB failover scenarios, a replica is automatically promoted to be the new primary during disaster recovery. Amazon DocumentDB flips the CNAME of the DB instance to point to the replica and promotes it, which means that failovers occur automatically. A *canonical name (CNAME)* record is a type of resource record in the Domain Name System (DNS) that maps one domain name (an alias) to another (the canonical name). There is a minimal downtime of 30 seconds for failover to a replica. If you do not have a replica, creating a new instance could take less than 10 minutes; it is highly recommended for a production environment to have at least three replicas across multiple AZs. It is also recommended that Amazon DocumentDB replicas use the same instance class as the primary instance.

You can control which replica instances are preferred as failover targets. You put preference ranges from 0 for the highest priority to 15 for the lowest primary in each replica instance. This means, if a primary instance fails, the replica with the highest preference is promoted to the new primary instance. You can modify the priority of a replica at any time. If two or more replicas in the same cluster have the same preference, then the largest instance replica is promoted to primary. If the replicas are the same size and have the same priority, a random replica instance in the same promotion tier is promoted.

Table 6.2 provides guidelines for an Amazon DocumentDB deployment configuration to meet specific availability. Plan according to your goals.

TABLE 6.2   Availability of Amazon DocumentDB

Availability Goal	Total Instances	Replicas	Availability Zones
99%	1	0	1
99.9%	2	1	2
99.99%	3	2	3

Amazon DocumentDB has a service level agreement (SLA). You can find more information at aws.amazon.com/documentdb/sla.

You can force your Amazon DocumentDB cluster to fail over to verify your application's behavior or test the availability during a real failover event. To initiate a manual failover, in the AWS console within the Clusters page, choose the Failover action on the Actions menu, as shown in Figure 6.4.

FIGURE 6.4   How to fail over your DocumentDB cluster

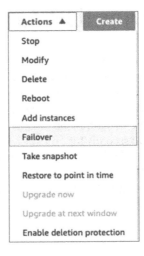

This option also can be done through the AWS CLI by executing the `failover-db-cluster` command. It is good practice to have a process to test the failover of your cluster, at least once every six months, to understand how your application will respond and how long the process takes.

Amazon DocumentDB supports cross-region instance replicas using global clusters. A global cluster allows you to have up to five read-only secondary regions from one primary region. Amazon DocumentDB automatically replicates asynchronously the data to the secondary regions using a dedicated infrastructure with less than one second of latency. For more information, visit `docs.aws.amazon.com/documentdb/latest/developerguide/global-clusters.html`.

Also, Amazon DocumentDB supports AWS CloudFormation for provisioning and deployment. *AWS CloudFormation* is a service that allows users to create and manage a collection of related AWS resources in an orderly and predictable fashion. It uses templates written in JSON or YAML to describe infrastructure and provides versioning and rollback options. It can be used through the AWS Management Console, AWS CLI, or SDKs. This can be used as a cross-region disaster recovery plan and to have a blueprint using infrastructure as a code, but make sure you always define recovery strategies in line with your RTO and RPO needs. *Infrastructure as code (IAC)* is a practice that treats infrastructure and its configuration as code, rather than as manual processes. This allows for the automated provisioning and management of infrastructure, as well as version control, testing, and collaboration on infrastructure changes.

The *recovery time objective (RTO)* is the amount of time within which a business process must be restored after a disaster to avoid unacceptable consequences associated with the disruption.

The *recovery point objective (RPO)* is the amount of time that might pass during a disaster before the quantity of data lost is not tolerable by the business. For more information, visit `docs.aws.amazon.com/AWSCloudFormation/latest/UserGuide/AWS_DocDB.html`.

Security

Security is an important topic for exam and real-life application environments. Security is a shared responsibility between AWS and the customer. This section describes common topics in document databases.

Access Control

MongoDB has a default authentication mechanism called the Salted Challenge Response Authentication mechanism (SCRAM), which Amazon DocumentDB also supports. You can use AWS IAM to manage DocumentDB resources and built-in roles for DB users with role-based access control (RBAC) and always enforce the least privilege principle. SCRAM is a password-based authentication mechanism that uses a combination of hashing, salting, and challenge-response protocol to provide secure authentication.

AWS IAM is a web service from Amazon Web Services (AWS) that enables you to securely control access to AWS services and resources for your users.

RBAC is a method of regulating access to computer or network resources based on the roles of individual users within an organization. In RBAC, users are assigned to specific roles, and those roles are then associated with certain permissions or access levels to various resources.

The *principle of least privilege (POLP)* is a security concept that states that an entity (such as a user or program) should have the minimum set of permissions or access rights necessary to perform its intended function. The idea behind this principle is to reduce the attack surface and potential for damage in case of security breaches. By giving users or programs only the access they need to perform their specific tasks, the risk of accidental or malicious misuse of those privileges is minimized.

You can connect as the master user to Amazon DocumentDB, which you created when you launched the cluster, and also create additional users as required using `db.createUser`.

```
db.createUser(
    {
        user: "sample-user",
        pwd: "database123",
        roles:
            [{role: "readWrite"}]
    }
)
```

For more information, visit `docs.aws.amazon.com/documentdb/latest/developerguide/role_based_access_control.html`.

Data Protection

There are certain features, such as encryption at rest with AWS Key Management Services keys, that Amazon DocumentDB shares operational technology with Amazon RDS and Amazon Neptune. You should grant permissions to a user following the least privilege principle. *AWS Key Management Service (KMS)* is a secure and convenient tool for managing encryption keys. It allows customers to securely encrypt data stored in the cloud and manage access control to their encryption keys.

Amazon Relational Database Service (RDS) is a fully managed service provided by Amazon Web Services (AWS) that makes it easy to set up, operate, and scale a relational database in the cloud. RDS supports multiple database engines including Amazon Aurora, PostgreSQL, MySQL, MariaDB, Oracle, and Microsoft SQL Server.

Amazon Neptune is a fully managed graph database service provided by Amazon Web Services (AWS). It is designed to make it easy to build and run applications that work with highly connected data, such as social networks, recommendation engines, and fraud detection systems.

Regarding network security, Amazon DocumentDB is VPC-only, which means that it can be used only in private subnets. For access within a corporate network, you must have a hybrid connection, such as a VPN or AWS Direct Connect, to connect from an on-premises host, or you can use an Amazon EC2 or AWS Cloud9 as a jump server with a MongoDB shell installed. A *virtual private network (VPN)* is a technology that allows users to create a secure connection to another network over the Internet. This can be used to access resources on a private network, such as a company's internal network, while connected to the INTER-NET from a remote location.

AWS Direct Connect is a service provided by AWS that allows users to establish a dedicated network connection from their on-premises data centers to AWS. This connection can be used to transfer data between the two environments with lower latency and higher throughput than a traditional Internet connection.

A *jump server*, also known as a *jump box* or a *bastion host*, is a secure intermediate host or an intermediary device that is used to access and manage other devices on a network. It is typically used as a secure way to access a private network from an external location, such as remote employees connecting to a company's internal network.

Amazon DocumentDB is an AWS service that follows the shared responsibility model. In terms of data protection, two approaches should be followed: encryption at rest and encryption in transit.

- **At rest:** An Amazon DocumentDB cluster uses AWS KMS to retrieve and manage encryption keys. If you do not specify an AWS KMS key identifier at the launch process, Amazon DocumentDB will use the default AWS managed service customer master key (CMK). The CMK is a unique encryption key used to protect data stored in the Amazon Web Services (AWS) cloud.

  You can enable or disable encryption at rest only at the time the Amazon DocumentDB cluster is created. If a cluster is encrypted, then all instances, automated backups, snapshots, and indexes will be encrypted with the same CMK.

 You cannot change the CMK in a cluster after you have already created it.

- **In transit:** Amazon DocumentDB cluster endpoints use Transport Layer Security (TLS) to encrypt data in transit. *TLS* is a cryptographic protocol that provides secure communication over a computer network. To enable TLS, you must set the `tls` parameter in the cluster parameter group. By default, encryption in transit is enabled for newly created Amazon DocumentDB clusters. To connect over TLS, you must download the certificate (public key) from AWS and pass the certificate key while connecting to the cluster. The public key can be downloaded at `s3.amazonaws.com/rds-downloads/rds-combined-ca-bundle.pem`.

Other Features

An Amazon DocumentDB cluster has a feature to enable cluster deletion protection. This feature prevents the accidental deletion of your cluster. It is a best practice to have this feature enabled in all production clusters.

To avoid saving usernames and passwords as plaintext in code, it is highly recommended to use vault manager credentials, such as AWS Secrets Manager. *AWS Secrets Manager* is a service provided by AWS that allows users to store and manage sensitive information, such as passwords, database credentials, and API keys. It rotates, stores, and encrypts your passwords with a simple API request. For more information, visit docs.aws.amazon .com/secretsmanager/latest/userguide/rotating-secrets-documentdb.html.

The Amazon DocumentDB service complies with several security standards, including PCI DSS, ISO 9001, 27017, 27018, SOC 1/2/3, and HIPAA. For more information, you can download the compliance reports available in AWS Artifact. *AWS Artifact* is a secure repository of compliance reports and security documents provided by AWS. It provides customers with easy access to the latest reports on AWS services and helps them easily manage their compliance needs.

Backup and Restore

The data in the Amazon DocumentDB storage layer is continuously backed up to Amazon S3 in real time for *point-in-time recovery (PITR)* purposes, which means that instance (compute) node performance is unaffected, as shown in Figure 6.5. PITR is a feature of some database management systems that allows for restoring a database to a specific point in time. This can be useful for recovering from data loss or corruption or for undoing data changes that were made by mistake. The maximum retention period is 35 days; if you need more retention time, you will need to do a manual snapshot. Amazon DocumentDB automated

FIGURE 6.5   Amazon DocumentDB's backup architecture

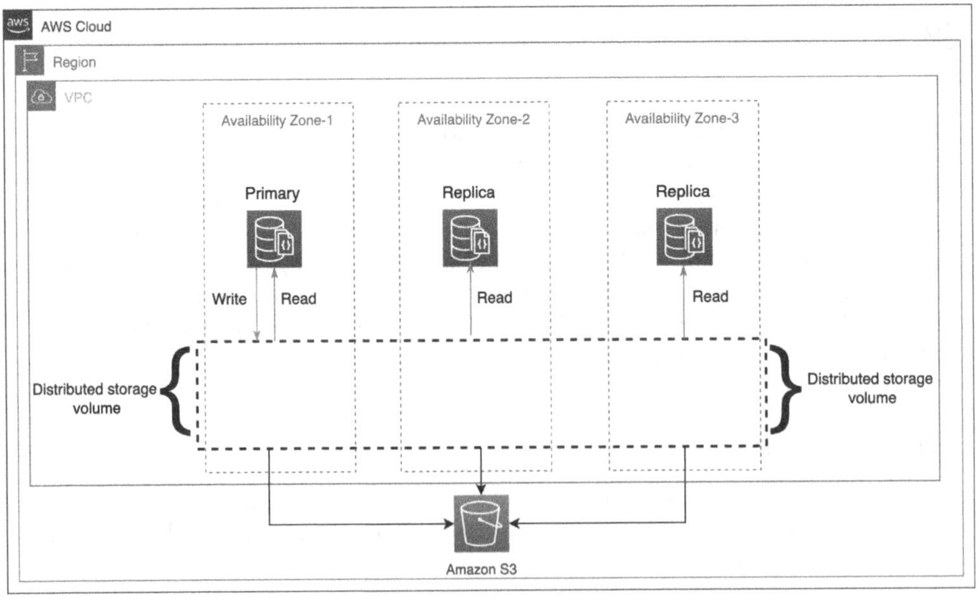

backup is enabled by default, with a default backup retention period of one day, and you cannot disable it. Choose your backup retention period according to your recovery point objective (RPO).

The first backup is full and the subsequent backups are incremental. When you want to restore a point in time, you need to stipulate a time between the earliest and latest restore times.

Your backup can be restored only to a new Amazon DocumentDB cluster. This new cluster can have the same or different instance classes from the original. Also, you can restore an unencrypted snapshot to an encrypted cluster, but not the other way round. To restore a cluster from an encrypted snapshot, you must have access to its AWS KMS key.

When you delete an Amazon DocumentDB cluster, you can take a final snapshot, and this will be persisted as long as the user chooses, together with the manual snapshots. However, all automated backups for the point-in-time restore will be deleted.

For sharing purposes, you can share snapshots across AWS accounts within the same AWS region. Also, you can copy manual or automatic snapshots within the same AWS region or to a different region but in the same AWS account. At this time, sharing an encrypted DB snapshot publicly is not supported. For private sharing, you also must share the customer master key to the target account through the AWS KMS policy. For more information, visit `docs .aws.amazon.com/kms/latest/developerguide/key-policy-modifying .html#key-policy-modifying-external-accounts`.

Figure 6.6 shows that if you want to share an automated backup, you must first copy and then share the snapshot. You cannot share a snapshot encrypted using the default AWS KMS key of the account (alias `aws/rds`).

FIGURE 6.6   Sharing snapshots in Amazon DocumentDB

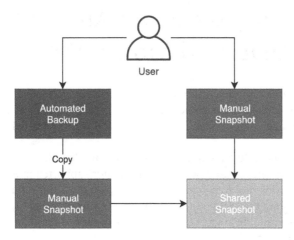

This feature of sharing between AWS accounts can be suitable to share data between your several environments such as production, development, test, staging, and so on.

Amazon DocumentDB supports copying an automated backup or manual snapshot to any AWS supported region.

Performance and Scaling

One of the key scaling benefits for MongoDB is sharding, but Amazon DocumentDB does not support it; instead, it offers read replicas, vertical scaling, and storage scaling.

Why is sharding not necessary in Amazon DocumentDB? Sharding is important when you want to do the following:

- **Scale reads:** In DocumentDB, you can add up to 15 read replicas.
- **Scale writes:** In DocumentDB, you can easily resize your instances with very low impact.
- **Scale storage:** As mentioned, the storage layer in DocumentDB scales automatically up to 64 TB and is decoupled from the compute instances.

Besides, you can scale up a replica independently from other replicas. This is typically for analytical workloads. If you have problems identifying slow queries, you can use profiler logs to dive deep and/or use the explain command, as follows:

```
db.runCommand({explain:{<query document>}});
```

If your cluster is having performance issues, with mongoshell you can use the following command to list all the activity:

```
Db.adminCommand({currentOp: 1, $all: 1});
```

Once you have identified which operation is facing problems, you can kill it:

```
Db.adminCommand({killOp: 1, op: <opid of running or blocked query>});
```

Compatibility between Amazon DocumentDB and MongoDB

Amazon DocumentDB has compatibility with MongoDB 3.6 and 4.0. The life of MongoDB 3.6 ends in April 2021. Amazon DocumentDB does not follow the same life cycles as MongoDB. Therefore, you can use Amazon DocumentDB 3.6 with MongoDB 3.6 drivers, applications, and tools.

The Amazon DocumentDB Compatibility tool examines log files from MongoDB to determine whether any queries use operators that are not supported in Amazon DocumentDB. You can use this tool to produce a simple report of the use of unsupported operators and save all log lines that were not supported to an output file for further investigation. More information is available at github.com/awslabs/amazon-documentdb-tools/tree/master/compat-tool.

Migrating from MongoDB to Amazon DocumentDB

You can migrate your MongoDB databases to Amazon DocumentDB. First, you must assess which version of MongoDB your current cluster is. For that, you should use the `db.version()` command. The version must be 3.x or greater.

AWS Data Migration Service (AWS DMS) is a service to help with homogeneous and heterogeneous migrations between different database platforms. AWS DMS supports MongoDB versions 3.x and 4.0 as a database source, as well as many popular databases as a target for data replication, including Amazon DocumentDB. Bear in mind that AWS DMS does not migrate indexes, only data. You must manually create your indexes in DocumentDB. It is recommended to create them before migrating the data. There is a GitHub repository with tools that can help with MongoDB to DocumentDB migration tasks, including index validation and creation. For more information about the Amazon DocumentDB Index Tool, go to `github.com/awslabs/amazon-documentdb-tools`.

Besides AWS DMS, common MongoDB utilities such as `mongodump`, `mongorestore`, `mongoimport`, and `mongoexport` can be used in migrations. Figure 6.7 shows the migration strategies.

- **Online:** An online migration uses AWS DMS and can support change data capture (CDC) mode to replicate changes from the source database. This approach is recommended to reduce downtime in the environment. *Change data capture (CDC)* is a technique used to identify and capture changes made to data in a database. This can include inserts, updates, and deletes.

- **Offline:** This can be achieved via the Amazon DocumentDB Index Tool and the `mongodump` and `mongorestore` tools. The Amazon DocumentDB Index Tool allows you to check the dumped indexes for compatibility and pre-create the indexes on the target Amazon DocumentDB cluster. Executing this process can reduce overall restore time because the indexes can be populated in parallel while restoring. It is recommended to first create your indexes in Amazon DocumentDB before performing the migration. This strategy might have a long downtime period, as you can't use the databases while the export and import processes are running.

- **Hybrid:** A hybrid approach combines both online and offline strategies. It uses `mongodump` and `mongorestore` tools to migrate the data from the source MongoDB to Amazon DocumentDB cluster, and it uses AWS DMS with CDC mode to replicate changes. This is the most complex of the three approaches, but it balances speed and downtime.

You can migrate your Amazon DocumentDB cluster from 3.6 to 4.0, using AWS DMS or utilities such as `mongodump`, `mongorestore`, `mongoimport`, and `mongoexport`.

FIGURE 6.7   Migration strategies from MongoDB to an Amazon DocumentDB cluster

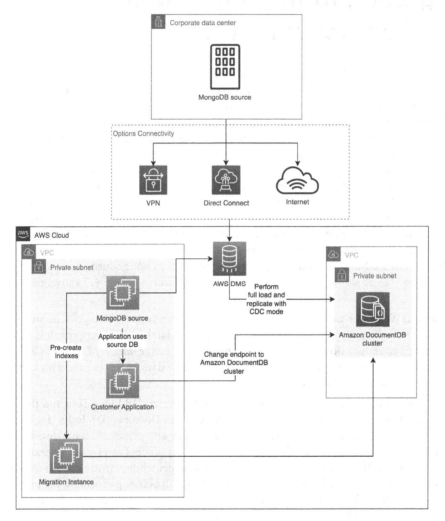

Amazon DocumentDB Monitoring

Amazon DocumentDB integrates with Amazon CloudWatch, Amazon CloudTrail, and third-party solutions like New Relic and Datadog. Amazon CloudWatch uses operational metrics to monitor the status and health of your cluster, and alarms can be set up to receive notification if a metric value breaches a specific threshold that you specify. Some key metrics are CPUUtilization, FreeableMemory, VolumeReadIOPS, VolumeWriteIOPS, WriteIOPS, ReadIOPS, DatabaseConnections, DatabaseTransactions, NetworkThroughput, and VolumeBytesUsed. Amazon CloudWatch can monitor the cluster by Reader or Writer role, by whole-cluster metrics, and by instance metrics.

For log purposes, Amazon DocumentDB will request during the launch process to publish audit and profiler logs to Amazon CloudWatch Logs. They should be enabled if you want to publish any logs regarding the audit and profiler of your cluster. To support auditing of the operations performed, you need to enable `audit_logs` in the parameter group of the cluster; by default, it is disabled. When the audit parameter is enabled, the logs record data definition language (DDL) statements; authentication, authorization, and user management events are exported to Amazon CloudWatch Logs as JSON documents. Table 6.3 details some of the auditing supports by Amazon DocumentDB.

TABLE 6.3 Events That audit_logs Deliver to Amazon CloudWatch Logs

Event Type	Category
authCheck	Authorization
authenticate	Connection
createDatabase	DDL
createCollection	DDL
createIndex	DDL
dropCollection	DDL
dropDatabase	DDL
dropIndex	DDL
createUser	User Management
dropAllUsersFromDatabase	User Management
dropUser	User Management
grantRolesToUser	User Management
revokeRolesFromUser	User Management
updateUser	User Management

To find the audit logs for your cluster, open the Amazon CloudWatch console, make sure that you are in the same AWS region as your Amazon DocumentDB cluster, and choose `/aws/docdb/yourClusterName/audit`. The respective instance names will have auditing events for each of your instances within your cluster.

The profiler logs need to be enabled in the parameter group of the cluster; by default, it is disabled. These logs will detail the operation performed on the cluster and help to identify slow operations and improve query performance. At launch or by modifying your cluster, you can enable Audit and/or Profiler logs and be published to Amazon CloudWatch Logs.

In addition, the following parameter groups can be set:

- `profiler`: Enables profiling for slow operations. It is disabled by default.

- `profiler_sampling_rate`: Sampling rate for logged operations.

- `profiler_threshold_ms`: Operations longer than this value will be logged.

- `Change_stream_log_retention_duration`: Duration of time in seconds that the change stream log is retained and can be consumed. The default is 10,800 seconds, or 180 minutes.

- `ttl_monitor`: Enables time to live to monitor. This is enabled by default.

- `tls`: Enables/disables TLS connection over to the cluster; it is enabled by default.

As usual, API calls are logged with CloudTrail, but for certain management features, Amazon DocumentDB uses operational technology that is shared with Amazon RDS. Filter in the AWS CloudTrail console at the event source from `rds.amazonaws.com` to see the appropriate events from the Amazon DocumentDB APIs.

Naturally, when choosing an instance type, you must be aware of the workload's performance requirements. You must estimate the number of vCPUs, memory, and connections your application needs. For baseline performance reasons, you can monitor the Amazon CloudWatch metrics of your cluster to evaluate whether it meets or exceeds expectations. You can use the following key metrics:

- Network throughput

- Write throughput

- Read throughput

- Replica lag

You can mix your cluster with different instance classes, but be aware that for failover purposes it is recommended to configure the failover priority for each instance.

Amazon DocumentDB has an Events Subscriptions feature where you can add a subscription to a certain source type event that is present on the Events page. The subscription can be an existing Amazon SNS topic, or you can create a new topic and recipient email to receive the notifications. The event may be related to instances, security groups, parameter groups, clusters, and cluster snapshots. You can subscribe to only one of the source types at a time. Each event subscription consumes events from all or the specific sources mentioned. Each source type has event categories, and you may include all or specific categories. These specific categories vary depending on the source type. This is a good option for monitoring and notifying the cluster's stakeholders about issues or informational messages that can lead to preventive or corrective actions. Furthermore, because the Event Subscriptions feature relies on Amazon SNS, you can do any sort of automation triggering AWS Lambda or putting on a queue with Amazon SQS.

The subscription to DocumentDB's events may be created through the AWS management console or the AWS CLI using `create-event-subscription`.

Developing with Amazon DocumentDB

An Amazon DocumentDB cluster does not have public access. Therefore, you need a jump server to connect with the cluster. You can use the jump server in the cloud, within the same VPC, or from a VPC that can reach the cluster's VPC, as well as on premises. For this, a hybrid connection is necessary.

In AWS, you can use AWS Cloud9 or Amazon EC2 as a jump server to connect to your cluster. You can also use tools such as Robo3T or Studio3T and a command-line tool like `mongoshell`.

All new DocumentDB clusters have TLS enabled by default. You can disable it in the cluster parameter group using the `tls` parameter. To connect to a cluster with TLS enabled using `mongoshell`, you use the following command:

```
mongo --ssl --host sample-cluster.node.us-east-1.docdb.amazonaws.com:27017
--sslCAFile rds-combined-ca-bundle.pem --username <sample-user> --password
<password>
```

This is how to connect to your cluster without TLS:

```
mongo --host mycluster.node.us-east-1.docdb.amazonaws.com:27017 --username
<sample-user> --password <password>
```

An important feature in DocumentDB is change streams. This provides a time-ordered sequence of change events that occur within your cluster's collections. The retention period by default is three hours, but you can extend it up to seven days through the cluster parameter group in the `change_stream_log_retention_duration` parameter. The Amazon DocumentDB change streams feature is disabled by default, but you can enable it at any time; be aware that could incur additional charges. For more information about this feature, please check in `docs.aws.amazon.com/documentdb/latest/developerguide/change_streams.html`.

When to Use DynamoDB vs. DocumentDB

Chapter 4, "Transactional Databases on AWS," mentioned that Amazon DynamoDB supports both key-value and document models. Some key points distinguishing between DocumentDB and DynamoDB are flexibility and performance.

Amazon DynamoDB is designed for workloads that need variable throughput or infinite scale. Access patterns should be known up front. DynamoDB provides differentiated features such as global tables and DynamoDB Accelerator. The performance could handle millions of requests per second with multiple writers and reads, and last but not least, DynamoDB is serverless with pricing that varies between on-demand or provisioned capacity units.

Amazon DocumentDB is designed around the flexibility of the document model with compatibility with the MongoDB APIs and workloads that need known query operation to run ad hoc queries. DocumentDB is a cluster with a single write that can handle tens of thousands of writes per second and multiple readers that can handle millions of reads per second. DocumentDB is priced by instance, storage, backup, and I/O.

Another key factor is that you can store a document of up to 16 MB in Amazon DocumentDB. To store a large document in DynamoDB, you would have to break it down in smaller pieces, as an item in Amazon DynamoDB can be only up to 400KB in size.

The decision about which AWS services you should use will depend on the facts discussed, the application, the technical and business requirements, the costs, and the overall purpose of the services.

Amazon DocumentDB Pricing

Amazon DocumentDB pricing is based on the following dimensions. There is no up-front cost and no minimum fee.

- On-demand instances
- Database I/O
- Database storage
- Backup storage

Amazon DocumentDB is billed per second for instances, with a 10-minute minimum billing period. You can stop your cluster for up to seven days when you do not need to access it. This is a good option for development and test environments because you can pause them on the weekend. You are not billed for cluster instances when the cluster is stopped.

Amazon DocumentDB replicates your data six times across three AZs, but you pay for only a single copy, with pricing at $0.10 GB/month (may vary among AWS regions). Also, the data transferred across multiple AZs between cluster instances is free. The I/O of the cluster automatically scales, and you pay $0.20 per 1 million requests (may vary among AWS regions). Be aware, when you enable features such as TTL and change streams, that they incur I/O costs when data is written, read, and deleted. If you are not using those parameters for a particular reason, disable them to reduce costs.

You are not billed for sharing snapshots between accounts. Nevertheless, you may be charged for the snapshots, as well as any clusters that you restore from shared snapshots.

For more information about pricing, visit `aws.amazon.com/documentdb/pricing`.

Summary

MongoDB is a powerful document database that can be deployed on Amazon EC2, but it can be difficult to manage, scale, upgrade, and maintain. Amazon DocumentDB is a managed service that gives you the ability to create and manage a cluster easily. It has compatibility with MongoDB 3.6 and 4.0; however, it does not follow the life-cycle policies of MongoDB.

With Amazon DocumentDB, you can have 1 to 15 instances in your cluster that automatically balance the addition or reduction of instances on demand. These processes are done in a few minutes, and there is no need to copy your hundreds of gigabytes to one instance or another, as one of the key features of Amazon DocumentDB is that the cluster volume is decoupled from the computational part and automatically grows in size on demand. This gives you great flexibility and cost benefits without compromising on performance.

It offers an SDK for most common languages, allowing developers to build applications to interact easily with the collections.

You can secure your cluster access using IAM policies and encryption at rest and in transit. Also, you can audit through AWS CloudTrail and Amazon CloudWatch Logs and see profiler performance with Amazon CloudWatch Logs and Metrics.

Exam Essentials

Understand what a document database is.   The knowledge of what a document database and its advantages are will be key for driving architectural decisions, as well as for the exam.

Know how the architecture of Amazon DocumentDB works.   Using Amazon DocumentDB allows you to handle different architectures because it gives you options depending on your workload's scope. So, knowing how the architecture of Amazon DocumentDB works will give you options to match with scenario requirements and its particularities.

Know how to migrate from MongoDB to Amazon DocumentDB.   AWS DMS is the way that we can migrate online from this source and target; other built-in options can be used, depending on the scenario. Be aware of the migrations options for online, offline, and hybrid modes.

Know how to enable audit and profiler logs in the Amazon DocumentDB cluster.   AWS CloudTrail and profiler logs with Amazon CloudWatch Logs are the way to monitor and manage access control and determine slow queries to an Amazon DocumentDB cluster.

Know when Amazon DocumentDB is a good fit for an architecture.   AWS exams are case scenario questions, so knowing how and when to use Amazon DocumentDB is essential for this exam. Also, it helps to know the differences between Amazon DocumentDB and similar services, such as Amazon DynamoDB, but remember the purpose of each AWS service.

Exercises

For assistance in completing the following exercises, refer to the Amazon DocumentDB developer guide at docs.aws.amazon.com/documentdb/latest/developerguide/what-is.html.

EXERCISE 6.1

Create a Secure Amazon DocumentDB Cluster

In this exercise, you will create an Amazon DocumentDB cluster uniquely in AWS, with encryption enabled.

1. Log in as a user with Amazon DocumentDB privileges in the AWS Console.

2. Navigate to the DocumentDB console.

3. Click the Create button.

4. For the cluster identifier, you can use the default name or rename it in this format: <Account ID>-exercise-6-db-certification. It would look like this: 123456789012-exercise-6-db-certification.

5. Select the engine version. The default is 4.0.

6. Select an instance class of db.t3.medium. The default is db.r6g.large.

7. Select the number of instances. The default is 3.

8. Enter a master username and master password and a confirmation.

9. Select Show Advanced Settings.

10. Make sure Encryption-at-rest is set to Enable.

11. Advance to the page bottom and click Create Cluster to confirm the creation, with the selected options.

EXERCISE 6.2

Apply a Custom Parameter Group in Your Cluster

When you create an Amazon DocumentDB cluster, it will use the default parameter group, but you cannot modify this parameter group. To customize your cluster, you need to create a parameter group and apply it.

1. In the Amazon DocumentDB console, go to Parameter Groups and click Create.

2. For Name, use db-certification-pg.

3. For Family, use the name of your Amazon DocumentDB cluster's engine.

4. For Description, use **This is a custom parameter group**, and click in Create.

5. Enter your custom parameter group and modify a parameter, like audits_logs.

6. Select audit_logs, click Edit, and change the value to Enabled.

7. For When To Apply Modifications, select Apply Immediately.

8. For Clusters, select your cluster and click Actions and Modify.

9. For Cluster Parameter Group, select db-certification-pg.

10. Advance to the page bottom and click ModifyCluster to confirm the modification, with the selected options, and apply immediately.

Review Questions

1. A DBA needs to access and monitor all data definition language for Amazon DocumentDB. The DBA already enabled the `audit_logs` parameter in the cluster parameter group. What should the DBA do to automatically collect the database logs?

   A. Enable DocumentDB to export the logs to Amazon CloudWatch Logs.

   B. Enable DocumentDB to export the logs to AWS CloudTrail.

   C. Enable DocumentDB events to export the logs to Amazon CloudWatch Logs.

   D. Enable change streams on Amazon DocumentDB.

2. Which of the following AWS services should you use to migrate from MongoDB to Amazon DocumentDB with minimum downtime?

   A. AWS Database Migration Service

   B. AWS VM Import/Export

   C. AWS Cloud9

   D. AWS Server Migration Service

3. An Amazon DocumentDB can have up to ___ instance replicas.

   A. 1

   B. 6

   C. 10

   D. 15

4. An Amazon Document cluster can have up to ____ primary instance(s).

   A. 2

   B. 3

   C. 1

   D. 6

5. Which is a key difference between MongoDB and Amazon DocumentDB?

   A. Amazon DocumentDB is a fully managed service, while MongoDB is a document database that you should manage yourself.

   B. They are the same thing; Amazon DocumentDB is a software as a service of MongoDB.

   C. Amazon DocumentDB follows the software life cycle of MongoDB.

   D. MongoDB supports change streams, and Amazon DocumentDB does not.

6. Which are the key benefits of document databases? (Choose two.)

   A. Flexible schema

   B. Horizontal scaling

   C. Support for joins

    D. Instance resizing capabilities

    E. CSV support

7. Which metric should you monitor to know about replication between replica instances?

    A. DBClusterReplicaLagMaximum

    B. DatabaseConnections

    C. BufferCacheHitRatio

    D. SwapUsage

8. Which option should you enable in the cluster parameter group to get slow query operations?

    A. `audit_logs`

    B. `profiler`

    C. `ttl_monitor`

    D. `profiler_threshold_ms`

9. A CSO determines that all data storage must be encrypted at rest. The company requires the solution to be cost-effective and operationally efficient. How can you encrypt an unencrypted Amazon DocumentDB cluster with minimum operational costs?

    A. This is not possible.

    B. Take a snapshot of the unencrypted cluster and restore it in a new cluster with encryption enabled with AWS KMS.

    C. Modify the cluster and enable encryption.

    D. Use AWS DMS to migrate to an encrypted cluster.

10. Which feature can you use to be notified when something occurs in your Amazon DocumentDB cluster?

    A. Events

    B. Parameter groups

    C. Change streams

    D. Events subscription

Chapter

7

Better Places Than Databases to Store Large Objects

**THE AWS CERTIFIED DATABASE –
SPECIALTY EXAM OBJECTIVES COVERED
IN THIS CHAPTER MAY INCLUDE, BUT ARE
NOT LIMITED TO, THE FOLLOWING:**

✓ **Domain 1.0: Workload-Specific Database Design**

- 1.1 Select appropriate database services for specific types of data and workloads.

- 1.3 Design database solutions for performance, compliance, and scalability.

- 1.4 Compare the costs of database solutions.

✓ **Domain 5.0: Database Security**

- 5.1 Encrypt data at rest and in transit.

- 5.3 Determine access control and authentication mechanisms.

This chapter discusses how to deal with workloads that need to store large objects as binary or text files. AWS has services that can work with database services to process and store data.

When choosing the technology to accommodate different kinds of data for an application, before cloud computing, we used to use a single service with hundreds of features such as queue services, email services, and large objects (LOB). Databases have been the common place to store everything for decades.

Today, with cloud computing services such as AWS, when we analyze the performance, compliance, scalability, and costs of a solution, we usually find that there are specific services for each purpose that are faster, cheaper, more reliable, and more scalable for each of those features, as well as easier to manage and integrate.

Databases and Large Objects

Relational databases were built to handle transactions, so their default units of read and write from and to the disks, called *block size*, are usually small (8–64 KB). This means each read or write will deal with records to write or read in this granularity of 8 KB.

When we look at NoSQL databases, they also usually have small units of reads and writes, as in Amazon DynamoDB, where the read capacity unit (RCU) is 4 KB and the write capacity unit is 1 KB, or Apache HBase, which defaults to a 64 KB block size.

Table 7.1 shows some popular databases' default block sizes. When you put records larger than the block size in a database, the records are split into several blocks as a chain. As you may expect, this causes overhead when reading from and writing to the database.

TABLE 7.1   Some popular databases' default block sizes

Database engine	Default block size for reads and writes
PostgreSQL	8 KB
MySQL	16 KB
MS SQL Server	64 KB
Oracle Database	8 KB

Database engine	Default block size for reads and writes
Amazon DynamoDB	1 KB WCU 4 KB RCU
MongoDB	4 KB OS dependent
Apache HBase	64 KB

Most relational databases allow you to read a group of multiple blocks in a single read operation to spend fewer operational system resources, and some of them allow you to choose larger block sizes such as 32 KB or 64 KB.

To optimize this and to allow databases to store larger objects, database engines have the concept of large objects. *LOB* databases have a particular structure to store the large objects and a pointer in a table to find out where each LOB is stored physically.

With this approach, most databases use these common types of LOB:

- **CLOB**: Stores long text fields.
- **NCLOB**: Similar to CLOB; uses characters from the national character set.
- **BLOB**: Stores binary objects—for example, media files.
- **BFILE and GridFS**: Files stored out of the database file structure directly in the filesystem.

We have support for different LOB types in each database engine, as shown in Table 7.2.

TABLE 7.2   Support for LOB types

Database engine	LOB support
PostgreSQL	BLOB and CLOB
MySQL	BLOB
MS SQL Server	BLOB, CLOB, and NCLOB
Oracle Database	BLOB, CLOB, NCLOB, and BFILE
Amazon DynamoDB	Binary
MongoDB	GridFS
Apache HBase	MOB (Medium size Object)

With LOB support, the storage of large objects inside the database is feasible, but the object storage services offered by cloud services are cheaper and not dependent on database compute power.

Introducing Amazon S3

In 2006 AWS introduced an *object storage service* called Amazon Simple Storage Service (Amazon S3), which is a storage layer that provides APIs to store and interact with objects as files, such as backup files, media files (pictures, movies, and audio), compressed sets of application files, big data files, logs, and many others. Amazon S3 is designed to have 99.999999999 percent durability by offering six copies of each object spread among different availability zones.

When we look at different databases and compare their ability to store large objects, we find that they may not be the best option for this kind of object.

- Object store services like Amazon S3 cost less than 25 percent of a dedicated disk volume attached to an instance if we consider the Standard class. This cost can go down to 4 percent of the cost of the attached volume if we consider the Glacier class.

- Amazon S3 objects are replicated to at least three availability zones by default with no further setup, which makes it cost even less compared to replicating your database storage.

- As opposed to what happens in an instance-attached store volume, there is no need to allocate and pay for storage areas when you are not using them and are expecting to receive new objects. In Amazon S3, you are charged for the amount of storage your objects really use.

- The central processing unit (CPU) consumption of Amazon S3 is included in the service, so there is no need to manage concurrency with other database workloads to store and retrieve the objects; this is the opposite of what happens in a database instance. There are no explicit limitations on the number of objects in Amazon S3, as there are in some databases, such as LOBs per instance or per database.

Many commercial and open-source software applications are already aware of these benefits and have created plugins for Amazon S3. One example is the Amazon S3 plugin for the WordPress media library, which can store videos, images, audios, and PDF documents.

Amazon S3 comes with storage classes, and objects can have their lifecycles automatically managed by lifecycle policies. When using lifecycle policies, objects are moved from one tier to another after a custom-defined number of days in one tier, keeping the same object key.

The following storage classes are available:

- *Amazon S3 Standard* is the default class for Amazon S3 objects; it is designed for frequent access and high durability (99.999999999 percent).

- *Amazon S3 Standard-IA* is the infrequent access class of Amazon S3 with high durability. It was designed for data accessed infrequently that needs to be retrieved quickly when requested.

- *Amazon S3 OneZone-IA* is the Amazon S3 class for infrequent access, with only one-zone durability. It was designed for objects that can be re-created in the case of losing one AWS availability zone (AZ).

- *Amazon S3 Glacier* is a low-cost class of an Amazon S3 object store for long-term data that is intended to be accessed or restored rarely.

- *Amazon S3 Deep Archive* is an Amazon S3 class for data that is very rarely retrieved but is needed for legal/compliance obligations.

- *Amazon S3 Intelligent Tier* is an automatic decision of best-of-class for S3 objects based on the access pattern detected. It uses a mix of access patterns automatically managed between the classes: Standard, Standard-IA, S3 Glacier, and S3 Deep Archive.

Choosing the class and the lifecycle is a matter of how often the data needs to be retrieved after it is stored. Table 7.3 shows S3 storage classes and the use cases that may take advantage of each one.

The Standard class has the highest price for storage, but you don't pay for retrievals, which means it's good for data you use frequently.

TABLE 7.3 Amazon S3 options

Storage class	Use case	Keep here if:
S3 Standard	Frequent low-latency access.	Frequency >= 2 times a month
S3 Standard-IA	Infrequent access with high durability. The data is accessed infrequently but needs to be retrieved quickly.	Frequency <= 1 time a month
OneZone-IA	For infrequent access, with only one-zone durability. You need to re-create objects in the case of losing one AZ. For use cases where you can re-create the data.	Frequency <= 1 time a month
S3 Glacier	Long-term backups, rare to access.	Frequency <=1 time in 4 months
S3 Deep Archive	Very rarely retrieved but necessary for legal/compliance obligations.	Frequency <=2 times a year
Intelligent Tier	You can't tell previously what the frequency of your data access is, and you want S3 to decide based on the access pattern detected. Mixed access patterns automatically managed between the classes: Standard, Standard-IA, S3 Glacier, and S3 Deep Archive.	Frequency = unknown

For the database exam certification, you should be aware of the S3 capabilities for keeping backups, moving data from on-premises facilities, storing asset files such as SQL files, and keeping large objects that can have different access patterns.

Costs of Amazon S3 vs. Elastic Block Storage

Each Amazon S3 class has a different set of costs: storage cost (price per gigabyte), requests and retrievals (price per 1,000 requests and gigabytes retrieved), and data transfer (from one region to another or from S3 to the Internet).

The cost of objects stored in S3 is mainly composed of the storage and data retrievals, as the request operations cost a few cents per thousands of operations. AWS prices can change over time, but Table 7.4 compares the S3 classes for North Virginia (us-east-1) as of September 12, 2022.

TABLE 7.4   Amazon S3 storage class costs—first 50 TB

Amazon S3 storage class	Storage per GB	Data retrievals per GB	Time to retrieve data	Copies to AZs
Standard	$0.0230		Low latency	>=3 AZs
Standard-IA	$0.0125	$0.01	Low latency	>=3 AZs
OneZone-IA	$0.01	$0.01	Low latency	1 AZ
S3 Glacier				
Expedited		$0.03	1–5 minutes	>=3 AZs
Standard	$0.004	$0.01	3–5 hours	
Bulk		$0.0025	5–12 hours	
S3 Deep Archive	$0.00099			>=3 AZs
			12 hours	
Standard		$0.02		
Bulk		$0.025		
S3 Intelligent - Tiering	$0.0230			

Source: Adapted from AWS, https://aws.amazon.com/s3/pricing

Amazon Relational Database Service (RDS) has three storage options:

- **General Purpose SSD (gp2/gp3):** Volumes offering a low cost for nonintensive I/O workloads
- **Provisioned IOPS (io1/io2):** Volumes recommended for I/O-intensive and consistent workloads with low latency
- **Magnetic:** Volumes used for backward compatibility only; not recommended for new workloads

Large objects in Amazon RDS can be stored in SSD storage, as they are usually not accessed frequently, even for magnetic storage options. The problem with magnetic is that you cannot choose to put only large objects on it; all your database data of that instance must reside on magnetic if you choose it, so you may end up with some performance issues for other tables.

Table 7.5 shows the RDS storage prices for the PostgreSQL engine for North Virginia (us-east-1) on September 12, 2022.

TABLE 7.5 RDS storage costs

RDS storage	Storage per GB	Provisioned IOPS per IOPS	Cost per 1 million requests
EBS	$0.115		
IOPS	$0.125	$0.10	
Magnetic	$0.10		$0.10

Source: Adapted from AWS, `https://aws.amazon.com/rds/postgresql/pricing`

To compare the strategy of using LOB objects inside databases versus Amazon S3, consider the following scenario:

- Your application has 200 objects, such as images and PDF documents, every month.
- There is a business need for AZ failure recoverability.
- The average object size is 512 MB.
- Documents and images are accessed at a rate of 20 objects per day.
- Thirty days after the object creation, the object is stored in Amazon S3; the objects are infrequently accessed, at a rate of two objects accessed per day.
- After 90 days, objects are maintained only for auditing purposes and are rarely accessed, at a rate of one object per month.

We used an AWS calculator to simulate the cost. Costs can change, but in general the proportion stays the same.

- **Amazon S3 Standard = 2.51 USD/month.** This is the class we chose for the first month in which the objects are created.
    - We are considering one month of Standard (200 objects × 512 MB × 1 month) = 100 GB.
    - It will require 200 PUTs to store the objects.
    - It will request 20 GETs per day × 30 days = 600 GETs per month.
    - It will retrieve 600 GETs × 512 MB = 300 GB per month.
    - The cost of storage is calculated by 100 GB × 0.023 USD/GB = 2.30 USD per month.
    - The cost of PUT requests is calculated by 200 PUT requests per month × 0.0000005 USD per request = 0.001 USD.
    - The cost of GET requests is calculated by 600 GET requests per month × 0.00000004 USD per request = 0.0002 USD.
    - The cost of select data returned is calculated by 300 GB select data returned per month × 0.0007 USD select data returned = 0.21 USD.

    The total cost of Standard is the sum of the preceding items:

    2.30 USD + 0.001 USD + 0.0002 USD + 0.21 USD = 2.51 USD/month

- **Amazon S3 Standard-IA = 1.55 USD/month:** This is the S3 storage class we chose for objects older than 30 days in S3.
    - We are considering one month of Standard-IA (200 objects × 512 MB × 1 month) = 100 GB.
    - It will require 200 lifecycle transitions per month.
    - It will request 2 GETs per day × 30 days = 60 GETs per month.
    - It will retrieve 60 GETs × 512 MB = 30 GB per month.
    - The cost of storage is calculated by 100 GB × 0.0125 USD/GB = 1.25 USD per month.
    - The cost of GET requests is calculated by 60 GET requests per month × 0.000001 USD per request = 0.0001 USD per month.
    - The cost of lifecycle requests is calculated by 200 lifecycle requests per month × 0.00001 USD per request = 0.002 USD per month.
    - The cost of select data returned is calculated by 30 GB per month × 0.01 USD = 0.30 USD per month.

    The total cost of Standard-IA is the sum of the previous items:

    1.25 USD + 0.0001 USD + 0.002 USD + 0.30 USD = 1.55 USD/month

- **Amazon S3 Glacier = 0.41 USD/month:** This is the class we chose for compliance 90 days after object creation.
  - We are considering one month of Glacier (200 objects × 512 MB × 1 month) = 100 GB.
  - It will require 200 lifecycle transitions per month, after 90 days.
  - It will request 1 GET × 1 month = 1 GET per month.
  - It will retrieve 1 GET × 512 MB = 0.5 GB per month.
  - The cost of storage is calculated by 100 GB × 0.004 USD/GB = 0.40 USD per month.
  - The cost of lifecycle transition requests is calculated by 200 requests per month × 0.00003 USD / request = 0.006 USD (lifecycle)/month.
  - The cost of a GET request is calculated by one request per month × 0.00003 USD = 0.00003 USD.
  - The cost of select data returned is calculated by 0.5 GB per month × 0.01 USD = 0.005 USD per month.

  The total cost of Glacier is the sum of these items:

0.40 USD + 0.006 USD + 0.00003 USD + 0.005 USD = 0.41 USD/month

When using databases in AWS, you will be required to use Elastic Block Storage (EBS) SSD or Provisioned IOPS volumes to store data and objects.

Now we can compare the cost of the same scenario using EBS storage attached to the instance's solution. We chose the less expensive SSD EBS disk and considered a multi-AZ deployment, where there is a storage volume in one availability zone and another one in a second availability zone for high availability.

- Amazon EBS, SSD = 23.00 USD/month.
  - One month of EBS (SSD) (200 × 512 MB × 1 month) = 100 GB.
  - 100 GB per month × 0.23 USD × 1 instance = 23.00 USD (storage cost) per month.

As shown in Table 7.6, the AWS costs for object storage in S3 for our one-year example are advantageous—23 times less compared to EBS volumes. You can play with the AWS calculators to get used to this kind of comparison and understand the cost perspective of this scenario.

Pay attention to the words in the AWS certification exam questions to clarify what is being asked. You will usually see four possible answers, but they will have qualifiers like *lowest cost, highest performance, lowest effort to manage,* or *most secure.* When looking for the cost perspective, getting familiar with the costs of the services you are studying is key to understanding the side costs, such as requests for Amazon S3 using the calculator we used (calculator.aws) and the old AWS calculator (calculator.s3.amazonaws.com/index.html).

TABLE 7.6   Cost comparison for one month of data stored for one year

Storage	1st month	2nd month	3rd month	4th+ month	One year [1st+2nd+3rd+(4th x 9)]
Amazon S3	**2.51**	**1.55**	**1.55**	**0.41**	**9.30**
Standard	2.51				
Standard-IA		1.55	1.55		
Glacier				0.41	
EBS, multi-AZ	**23.00**	**23.00**	**23.00**	**23.00**	**276.00** (29 times S3 cost)
SSD	23.00	23.00	23.00	23.00	

Moving LOBs to Amazon S3

Now that you know where to put your LOBs to have a cost-effective solution, let's start moving the large objects to Amazon S3.

Creating an S3 Bucket

We start by creating a *bucket*—that is, a logical space where you can store objects. Note that every bucket name must be unique globally; it doesn't matter if it's accessible only in your account. The bucket will reside in one region of your preference, where most of your other AWS resources may be located, which means that there will be no data transfer costs between S3 and other AWS services in that region.

To enforce that your bucket name is unique and avoid naming conflicts, you can add a unique value such as an account ID, which provides an easy way to find it in the AWS Console. At the top right, click the login name to open a menu where you can copy the account ID.

Say that your account ID will be 123456789012; you can use different methods to create an S3 bucket with a suffix of mylobs-certification in the us-east-2 region.

- In the AWS Console, navigate to the S3 services with the (Ohio) us-east-2 selected and click Create Bucket, as shown in Figure 7.1.

- In the AWS command-line interface (CLI), use the `s3 mb` (make bucket) function.

```
aws s3 mb s3://123456789012-mylobs-certification --region us-east-2
```

- Use the AWS SDK. For example, use `boto3` to interact with S3, which is the SDK library for the Python language.

```python
import boto3
s3 = boto3.client('s3', region_name='us-east-2')
s3.create_bucket(Bucket='123456789012-mylobs-certification')
```

FIGURE 7.1   S3 bucket creation console

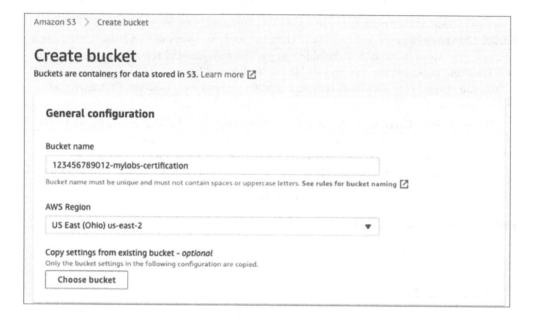

If you create a bucket name like s3://mylobs, where s3:// is a prefix for S3, no other bucket named s3://mylobs will exist in any other AWS account globally. Anyone in the world who tries to create the next s3://mylobs bucket will get an error message. So, a best practice is to include the account ID in your bucket name—for example, 123456789012-mylobs-certification.

Putting or Uploading Objects

Objects reside in buckets, and you can add a *path* to them. For example, if I have a set of pictures from New York taken in 2019 that I named `picny1.jpg`, `picny2.jpg`, `picny3.jpg`, and `picny4.jpg`, I can add a prefix before the image names as a path to organize the data. For example, I use `s3://123456789012-mylobs-certification/2019/us/new-york/pics`, so each object will be named as follows:

```
s3://123456789012-mylobs-certification/2019/us/new-york/pics/picny1.jpg
s3://123456789012-mylobs-certification/2019/us/new-york/pics/picny2.jpg
s3://123456789012-mylobs-certification/2019/us/new-york/pics/picny3.jpg
s3://123456789012-mylobs-certification/2019/us/new-york/pics/picny4.jpg
```

It's important to recognize that you have two components for every object in S3: the bucket `123456789012-mylobs-certification` and the object key `us/new-york/pics/picny4.jpg`. Keep in mind that the object key is the way you will refer to any object inside an S3 bucket, and it has the full path inside the bucket and filename.

You can upload your files from remote machines or your own machine to Amazon S3 as follows:

▪ Using the AWS Console, navigate to S3 Services and open the bucket you created to create three folders inside it, as shown in Figure 7.2. Create a us folder inside the bucket, then a new-york folder, and then a pics folder. Folders are logical representations of object keys; you need to create them only if you are using the Console to upload files.

Upload the files to the pics folder, as shown in Figure 7.3.

FIGURE 7.2   Creating the folder

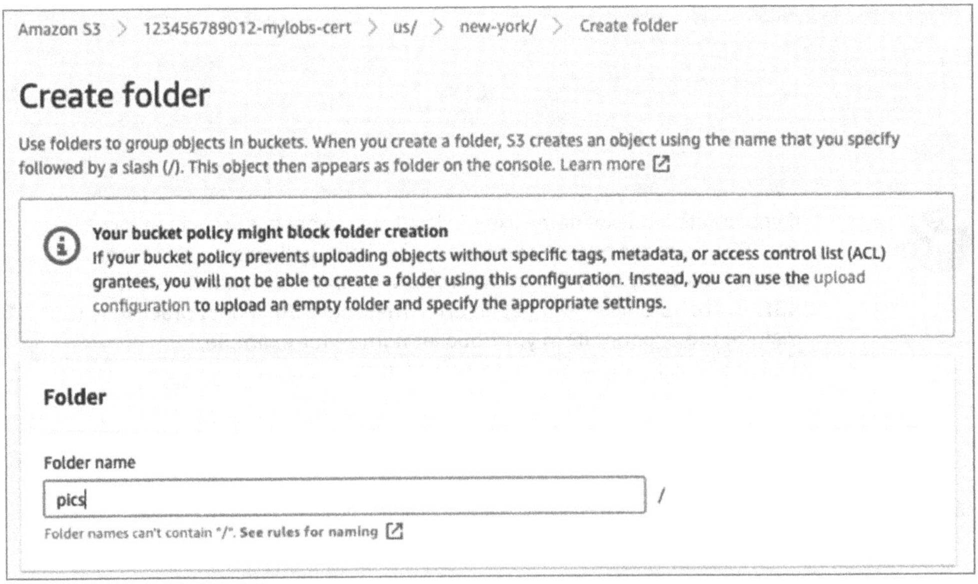

Amazon S3 > 123456789012-mylobs-cert > us/ > new-york/ > Create folder

Create folder

Use folders to group objects in buckets. When you create a folder, S3 creates an object using the name that you specify followed by a slash (/). This object then appears as folder on the console. Learn more ☑

ⓘ **Your bucket policy might block folder creation**
If your bucket policy prevents uploading objects without specific tags, metadata, or access control list (ACL) grantees, you will not be able to create a folder using this configuration. Instead, you can use the upload configuration to upload an empty folder and specify the appropriate settings.

Folder

Folder name

```
pics
```
/

Folder names can't contain "/". See rules for naming ☑

FIGURE 7.3   Uploading the files

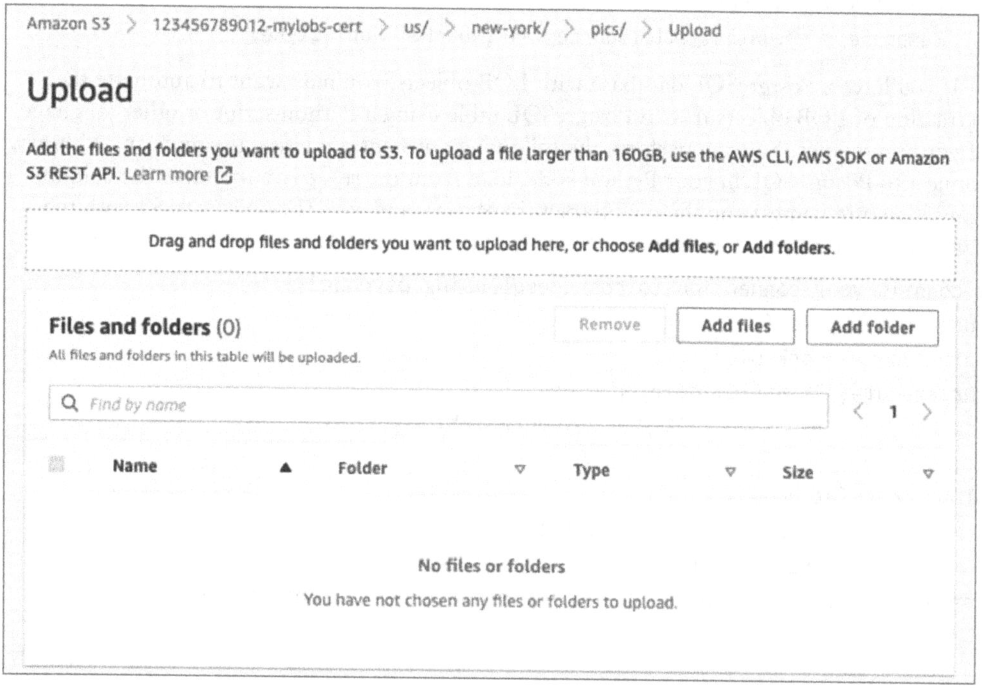

Amazon S3 > 123456789012-mylobs-cert > us/ > new-york/ > pics/ > Upload

Upload

Add the files and folders you want to upload to S3. To upload a file larger than 160GB, use the AWS CLI, AWS SDK or Amazon S3 REST API. Learn more ⎋

> Drag and drop files and folders you want to upload here, or choose **Add files**, or **Add folders**.

Files and folders (0)   Remove   **Add files**   **Add folder**
All files and folders in this table will be uploaded.

Q Find by name   ⟨ 1 ⟩

	Name ▲	Folder ▽	Type ▽	Size ▽

No files or folders

You have not chosen any files or folders to upload.

- With the AWS CLI, you don't need to create folders, as S3 commands automatically handle the folder path as a key to the objects.

    Using s3 cp (copy function for the S3 bucket), copy the file to a complete S3 path.

    ```
    aws s3 cp picny1.jpg s3://123456789012-mylobs-certification/2019/us/
    new-york/pics/
    ```

    Copy all images from a local directory in one AWS CLI command using the s3 cp --recursive (copy object to bucket) function.

    ```
    aws s3 cp . s3://123456789012-mylobs-certification/2019/us/new-york/
    pics/ --recursive
    ```

- Using the AWS SDK (for example, upload_fileobj in Python boto3), you also don't need to create folders.

    ```
    import boto3
    s3 = boto3.client('s3', region_name='us-east-2')
    bucket = '<your bucket>'
    picture_name = 'picny1.jpg'
    local_path='<local directory>/'
    s3_path = 'us/new-york/pics/'
    ```

```
source file=local_path+picture_name
object_key = s3_path+picture_name
response = s3.upload_file(source_file, bucket, object_key)
```

If you have a PostgreSQL database with LOB objects, you may want to automate the extraction of LOB objects from a PostgreSQL table using a Python script or other language of your preference. You can perform the following automation: Using the `psycopg2` library, connect to PostgreSQL in your Python code, load from the `my.picture` table the column names (picture names) and the piclob (picture object), and save the objects to S3 with the path set and add the picture name as the filename.

```
# conn is your connection to postgresql using psycopg2
cur = conn.cursor()
path='us/new-york/pics/'
cur.execute(""" SELECT name, piclob
                    FROM my.pictures""")


blob = cur.fetchone()
        object_key = path + blob[0]
        picture = blob[1]
response = s3_client.upload_fileobj(picture, bucket, object_key)
```

Indexing LOBs in Amazon S3

You now have your objects inside S3. A common pattern to create an index for the objects in S3 using SQL databases is to *create a table as select*, which is the creation of a new table based on a `SELECT` statement, with only the other columns, not the LOB, from your old table. Then add two new columns as text, `s3bucket` and `s3key`, as they are commonly used separately in the AWS API.

Table 7.7 shows the column values of a table named `Pictures`.

TABLE 7.7 Representation of a relational table

id (pk)	Name (index)	City	s3bucket	s3key	Other columns
1	subway0002	New York	123456789012-mypics	us/new-york/subway/subway0002.jpg	a b c
21	dog0012	New York	123456789012-mypics	us/new-york/dogs/dog0012.jpg	a b c

id (pk)	Name (index)	City	s3bucket	s3key	Other columns		
22	dog0003	New York	123456789012-mypics	us/new-york/dogs/dog0012.jpg	a	b	c
50	people0010	New York	123456789012-mypics	us/new-york/people/people0010.jpg	a	b	c
60	trees0001	New York	123456789012-mypics	us/new-york/trees/trees0001.jpg	a	b	c
61	trees0025	New York	123456789012-mypics	us/new-york/trees/trees0025.jpg	a	b	c

Indexes in relational databases are useful for querying exact items with a better response time. For relational databases, it's common to have an integer identification number (ID) as the primary key that will be used in join operations. In this case, you can create an index on the Name and City columns. The Name and City columns will be indexed, and the query to quickly retrieve a key to an S3 object for the object name people0010 of New York City would be as follows:

```
SELECT 's3://'||s3bucket||'/'||s3key as s3_bucket_key
FROM pictures
WHERE name = 'people0010' and city='New York';
============
query result
============
s3_bucket_key  s3://123456789012-mypics/us/new-york/people/people0010.jpg
```

A cost-effective way to save and retrieve objects in S3 is to keep them indexed in NoSQL databases and store two attributes (s3bucket and s3path) along with a key. Different from relational databases, the main index for a NoSQL database is its primary key; so, if you use Amazon DynamoDB, you have the option to use a composite, concatenating two attributes as a partition key and another as a sort key. Table 7.8 illustrates how it would be stored in an Amazon DynamoDB table named Pictures.

TABLE 7.8   Representation of a DynamoDB table

Name (pk)	City (sk)	s3bucket	s3key	Other attributes		
subway0002	New York	123456789012-mypics	us/new-york/subway/subway0002.jpg	a	b	c
dog0012	New York	123456789012-mypics	us/new-york/dogs/dog0012.jpg	a	b	c
dog0003	New York	123456789012-mypics	us/new-york/dogs/dog0012.jpg	a	b	c
people0010	New York	123456789012-mypics	us/new-york/people/people0010.jpg	a	b	c
trees0001	New York	123456789012-mypics	us/new-york/trees/trees0001.jpg	a	b	c
trees0025	New York	123456789012-mypics	us/new-york/trees/trees0025.jpg	a	b	c

In our modeling, the DynamoDB table keys Name (partition key) and City (sort key) uniquely identify a record and can be retrieved in one-digit milliseconds (refer to Chapter 5, "Low Latency Response Time for Your Apps and APIs"). A GET operation using the AWS CLI would be as follows:

```
aws dynamodb get-item \
    --table-name picture \
    --key '{"Name": {"S": "people0010"},"City": {"S": "New York"}}' \
    --projection-expression "s3bucket, s3key"
============
get-item result
============
{
    "Item": {
        "s3bucket": {
            "S": "123456789012-mypics"
        },
  "s3key": {
            "S": "us/new-york/people/people0010.jpg"
        }
    }
}
```

Your application now can use the result from the get-item CLI call and perform a GET operation in S3 to retrieve the picture.

If you have lots of files that tend to have the same name, use an application immutable universally unique identifier (UUID) library for the language you chose to generate unique names for the object keys.

Additional S3 Features

We have explained some concepts of Amazon S3, the storage classes and their use cases, and the resilience and costs associated with each class. But there are some other important concepts and features of S3 that you need to learn.

Backup and Dump Files

As a database administrator, you need to know that Amazon S3 is the first place to think of when dealing with large backup files. AWS-managed services also use this strategy, but they perform it to AWS internal-only S3 buckets.

So if you have a PostgreSQL pg_dump file, MySQL mysqldump, Oracle RMAN backup, or MS SQL Server .bak, you may want to store these files in S3.

Amazon RDS also provides access from your instances to Amazon S3 with the following:

- **MySQL on Amazon RDS:** Supports files created with Percona XtraBackup and then uploaded to S3.

- **PostgreSQL on Amazon RDS:** An aws_s3 PostgreSQL extension to export or import data to S3.

- **Oracle on Amazon RDS:** S3 integration that enables you to use features such as Oracle Data Pump along with S3. The S3 integration is also useful to extract backups in RMAN format. At this time, RDS provides backups only; you cannot restore them in RDS.

- **MS SQL Server on Amazon RDS:** To load backup data from S3 to an RDS SQLServer, you can use backup files (.bak), supported with the SQLSERVER_BACKUP_RESTORE option in the RDS option group. You can also enable the S3_INTEGRATION option in the RDS option group to use files from S3 to perform bulk inserts into a SQL Server database.

Other Use Cases

Amazon S3 is used by AWS analytics tools such as Amazon EMR, AWS Glue jobs, Amazon SageMaker, and Amazon QuickSight, as well as by migration tools such as AWS Database Migration Service (AWS DMS). A standard pattern is to use S3 as data lake storage.

You can use the following tools to extract data from a database to the data lake with minimal code effort:

- AWS Glue jobs, created on Glue Studio
- AWS DMS for change data capture (CDC) or full load
- Amazon Data Pipeline ETL tool
- Sqoop and s3distcp on Amazon EMR

Sharing content via S3 is a common practice, but always keep in mind that database content may require a private-only bucket.

Also consider the following use cases:

- **Scripts:** S3 is a good place to share and reuse content using an S3 bucket as asset provider, as S3 can support versioning. You can enable it to update files with new versions and roll back to previous versions. Common shared scripts include the following:
  - SQL routine or custom monitoring that needs to be scheduled
  - AWS CLI (shell scripts) or infrastructure scripts to create snapshots or clones
  - Export dump scripts
  - Backup scripts for EC2 or on-premises databases
- **Backups:** You can store backup files, backup pieces, and dump files (especially when dealing with database migration to the cloud). S3 can store very large backup files, up to 5 TB each.

Other AWS services are integrated into Amazon S3 to perform data movement from an on-premises environment to Amazon S3, including the following:

- **AWS Storage Gateway:** Creates an extension of S3 as gateway systems, such as filesystems, tapes, or volumes, with the option of caching data locally.
- **AWS Transfer for SFTP:** Can be used to move large files, backup files, and dump files from an on-premises environment or other remote facilities in a secure way to Amazon S3.
- **AWS DataSync:** Can be used to copy data from on-premises storage as Network File System (NFS) or Server Message Block (SMB) to Amazon S3 buckets.
- **AWS Snow family:** Physical devices that you can order to copy high volumes of data from your on-premises datacenter into them and send them back to AWS. They can be from as few as 8 TB in Snowcone to several petabytes in Snowmobile.

Pay per Usage and Scalability

Amazon S3 is a managed service, and you interact with buckets and objects in S3 through an API. There are zero provisioning requirements to store objects; you only create a bucket with no objects.

After you have a bucket (not paid), you start to put objects in it, where you pay per USD cent per thousands of PUT operations. When you have some files, you will pay per gigabyte per month usage ($0.0230 USD/GB for the Standard class).

If you delete files, S3 will stop charging for the space the files used to have.

Suppose that you start with the sum of 1 MB. You can easily scale to gigabytes, terabytes, and exabytes. (One *exabyte* is 10^{18} bytes, or 1,000,000,000,000,000,000 bytes.)

Each object (file) can be as large as 5 TB, so Amazon S3 supports very large objects, sometimes database backup files.

Availability and Durability

You will find in the Amazon S3 documentation that it is designed for extremely high durability (11 nines), and this is achieved using several copies of each S3 object across multiple systems. As shown in Figure 7.4, each object has at least six copies automatically created when you put the objects in S3.

FIGURE 7.4   S3 bucket resilience and durability

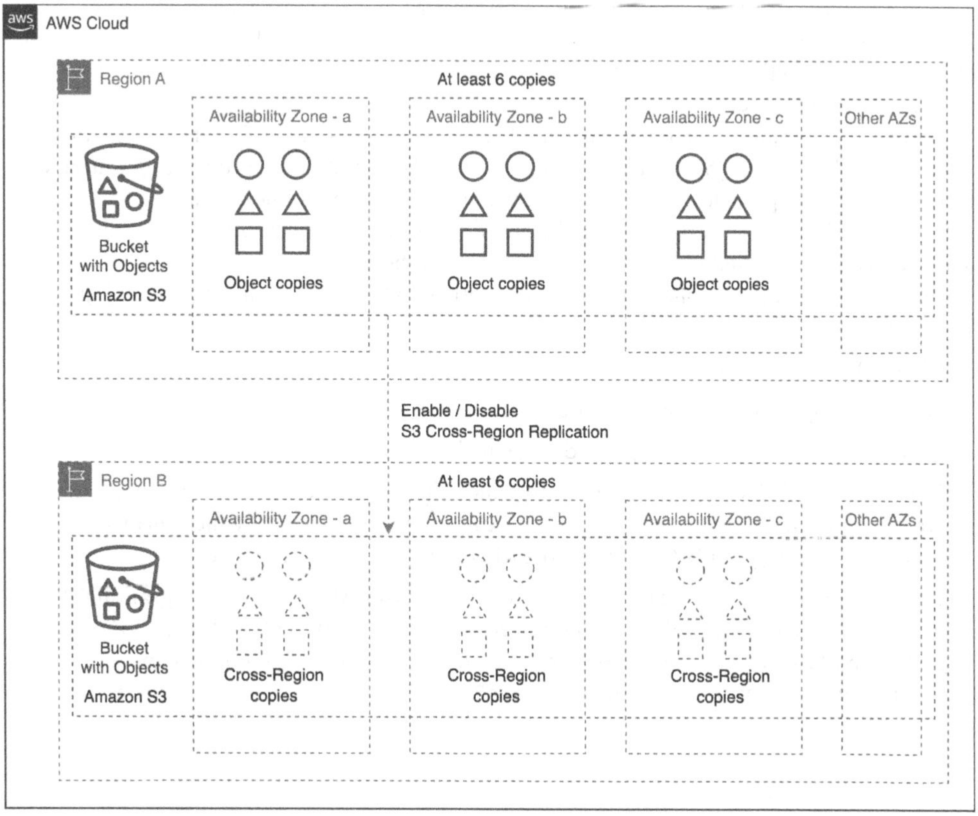

So, S3 is a highly durable object store, which means the chances of losing a file are mostly related to bad operations you perform, not the infrastructure.

But being highly durable doesn't mean S3 has 100 percent availability. Not losing an object is different from being able to always access the object, and S3 is designed for 99.99 percent and 99.9 percent availability for S3 Standard and Standard-IA, respectively.

As shown in Figure 7.4, to increase availability and have an even more reliable storage infrastructure, S3 allows you to build a cross-region replication, which enables a fast recovery not only in the case of AZ failure but also from an entire region failure.

Security

Amazon S3 has several security features such as data encryption and access control. You will learn in this section how to protect your data using standard features.

Access Control

Amazon S3 access relies on AWS Identity and Access Management (IAM). It can be as sharp as you need—for example, allowing specific put operations to your application and denying delete operations to the same application, while allowing another application read-only access to the same objects.

You can set a policy at the bucket level, which means this is the main set of rules for that bucket, limited to 20 KB JSON. To refine it, you can also set individual policies granting or blocking users, groups, roles, or specific actions in a bucket and a bucket path.

Amazon S3 bucket, user, or role policies should follow the least privilege principle, in which everything is denied except what really needs to be allowed.

You create Amazon S3 policies as you create other IAM policies with the following components:

- **Effect:** Allow or Deny.
- **Action:** S3 operations such as `PutObject`, `GetObject`, and `ListObjects`.
- **Principal:** User or role to be granted or denied.
- **Resource:** The bucket or bucket path to which this permission applies; resources are *Amazon Resource Name* (ARN), and you can use the * wildcard, which means every object inside that path before the wildcard will be applied in the policy.

The following is an example of a bucket policy that uses Allows as Effect, granting the policy to two roles as principals (`arn:aws:iam:us-east-1:012345678901:role/MyAppRole` and `arn:aws:iam:us-east-1:012345678901:role/Audit`) and enables it to put and get objects as the action (`s3:PutObject` and `s3:GetObject`) to the bucket (my-bucket-022022022) in any path inside it, represented by the resource (arn:aws:s3:::bucket-022022022/*) with the wildcard * at the end.

```
{
  "Version":"2012-10-17",
  "Statement":[
    {
        "Sid":"MyFirstBucketPolicy",
        "Effect":"Allow",
      "Principal": {"AWS": ["arn:aws:iam:us-east-1:012345678901:role/
MyAppRole","arn:aws:iam:us-east-1:012345678901:role/Audit"]},
        "Action":["s3:PutObject","s3:GetObject"],
        "Resource":"arn:aws:s3:::bucket-022022022/*"
    }
  ]
}
```

If you want to apply dynamic rules in a bucket policy to allow it to filter what users can be allowed, you can have specific dynamic paths for users in the resource, which means that different users would have different permissions for bucket paths. This is achieved using the policy's Condition attribute for the user group policy, filtering by string with the StringLike clause.

If you need to share a bucket with another AWS account, you can specify the principal of the bucket policy as the other account ("AWS":"123123123123").

Amazon S3 now has a configuration that can block public access. It's highly recommended that you turn on the Amazon S3 Block Public Access option, unless you have a good reason to allow public access and are totally confident that you have no sensitive data in your bucket. You can use Amazon Macie to look for sensitive information before you open access to the public.

Data Encryption

Amazon S3 allows you to easily set up encryption to your bucket, so there is no excuse to not do so. There are four options to enable data encryption at rest on S3 buckets, and only new data uploaded after encryption setup will be encrypted.

- **At rest:**
  - **Client-side encryption:** You can encrypt the data with some security package on your side before uploading it to S3 and then get an object and decrypt it on your side again.
  - **Server-side encryption with Amazon S3–managed keys (SSE-S3):** This uses a strong encryption cipher, Advanced Encryption Standard (AES-256), to encrypt data on the S3 side using a key from the AWS Key Management Service (KMS).

- Server-side encryption with an AWS KMS key stored in the AWS Key Management Service (SSE-KMS): This differs from SSE-S3 only because it uses a customer-created key, and you can use this with different groups of users and access patterns.
- Server-side encryption with customer-provided keys (SSE-C): This follows the same concept, but now you provide the keys by yourself using software or an appliance and use this key in AWS.

- In transit:
  - S3 enables you to use HTTPS (TLS) for in-transit encryption. You can enforce this behavior by specifying the condition `aws:SecureTransport` in your bucket policies.

Summary

This chapter discussed strategies for offloading large objects from databases to the large-scale object store called Amazon S3.

The 99.999999999 percent durability of S3 is one of the key features to rely on for backing up and storing application objects such as photos, videos, and documents.

S3 costs are very attractive, and S3 storage classes for less frequently accessed objects can lower these costs even more.

An AWS SDK is available for most common languages and allows developers to build applications that interact easily with the objects.

You can secure your bucket access using IAM policies and encryption at rest and in transit.

Exam Essentials

Know the basics of S3 costs compared to EBS costs.   When talking about strategies of moving databases to AWS and database migration, it is key to know that Amazon S3 is a cost-effective solution to substitute LOB segments as well as to handle backup and dump files.

Know the different storage classes in S3.   Amazon S3 has an option to handle different frequencies of access to get a lower cost for nonfrequent or even rare access. So, if you put a backup file in S3 that will be used just in the case of compliance, you can set up an S3 lifecycle policy to move the object to a lower-cost storage class, such as Infrequent Access, Glacier, or Deep Archive.

Know how to prevent access to objects with IAM.   AWS IAM enables you to manage access control to an S3 bucket, an S3 path, and an S3 key (the singular object), with very granular options. You can set up different approaches based on each group of user permissions to list, put, get, and prevent access from nonauthorized sources.

Know how to encrypt data with different levels of security.   Amazon S3 enables you to use its default encryption, starting with TLS in transit encryption, but also to use AWS KMS keys and custom keys. This allows you to build different strategies of encryption that also help in granting specific groups the ability to decrypt the data.

Exercises

For assistance in completing the following exercises, refer to the S3 User Guide at docs .aws.amazon.com/AmazonS3/latest/userguide/Welcome.html.

EXERCISE 7.1

Create a Secure S3 Bucket for Your LOBs

In this exercise, you will create an Amazon S3 bucket uniquely named in AWS, with encryption enabled.

1. Log in as a user with S3 privileges in the AWS Console.

2. Using the service menus, go to the S3 console.

3. Click the Create Bucket button.

4. Define your bucket name as <Account ID>-exercise-7-db-certification. It should look like this: 123456789012-exercise-7-db-certification.

5. Select a region such as us-west-2 or us-east-2 to create it.

6. Ensure that the option Block All Public Access is selected.

7. For the Default Encryption option, select Enable and choose the Amazon S3 Key (SSE-S3) Encryption option.

8. At the bottom of the page, click Create Bucket to confirm the creation, with the selected options.

EXERCISE 7.2

Create a Lifecycle Rule for Your S3 Bucket

In this exercise, you will enable a lifecycle policy in your bucket to save money with objects that are infrequently accessed and also objects maintained for compliance reasons moving objects to Standard-IA after 30 days and to Glacier after 90 days.

1. Click the bucket you created in Exercise 7.1 to open the options.

2. Click Management to open the lifecycle options.

3. Click the Create Lifecycle Rule button.

4. Enter **Lifecycle for LOBs at Lifecycle** as the rule name.

5. Select This Rule Applies To All Objects In The Bucket and confirm your acknowledgment.

6. For lifecycle rule actions, select Transition Current Versions Of Objects Between Storage Classes.

7. Select Standard-IA and 30 days. This is the minimum time to transition to Standard-IA.

8. Click Add Transition.

9. Select Glacier as the storage class, and select 90 days. The number of days needs to be 30 days more than the value for the Standard-IA rule.

10. Check the Acknowledge button and click Create Rule.

EXERCISE 7.3

Enable Versioning for S3

In this exercise, you will enable versioning, so if someone uploads a file with the same name, S3 will keep the previous version of the file in the background and enable you to roll back to this previous version.

1. Use the bucket you created in Exercise 7.1, and click it to open the options.

2. Go to the Properties tab.

3. At the Bucket Versioning session, click Edit.

4. Check the Enable button and click the Save Changes button to complete the versioning configuration.

Review Questions

1. A customer is trying to reduce costs by migrating from a simple on-premises Oracle database that handles user profiles in an application to AWS. What is the most cost-effective solution to store the profiles with profile photos that is currently stored in Oracle BLOB segments?

   A. Create an RDS for Oracle and keep using an Oracle blob to store profile photos, since RDS for Oracle supports blob segments.

   B. Create an RDS for the PostgreSQL database, convert the schema, and migrate everything from Oracle to PostgreSQL using the AWS Database Migration Service.

   C. Create an RDS for the PostgreSQL database, convert the schema, and migrate everything except the LOB segments from Oracle to PostgreSQL using the AWS Database Migration Service. Create a script to move the pictures to Amazon S3 and index them in the table in PostgreSQL.

   D. Create an RDS for the PostgreSQL database, convert the schema, and migrate everything except the LOB segments from Oracle to PostgreSQL using the AWS Database Migration Service. Create a script to move the pictures to an Amazon EBS volume and index them in the table in PostgreSQL.

2. What are examples of the storage classes available in S3?

   A. S3 Standard, S3 Standard-IA, Deep Storage and PCI Compliance

   B. Standard, Standard One-Zone IA, Deep Storage and PCI Compliance

   C. S3 Standard, S3 Standard-IA, S3 Glacier, and S3 Glacier Deep Archive

   D. Standard, Standard One-Zone IA, Long-Term Archive, and S3 One-Zone Infrequent Access

3. A customer is starting to use S3 to store large objects but is concerned about badly written routine overwrite files. What is the easiest and cheapest way to implement a track version for overwritten objects in a way that the old version of files is recoverable?

   A. Index the files in S3 in a DynamoDB table, enable S3 encryption, create a routine that checks object existence before writing it, and append a hash with the object key if it already exists.

   B. Use a UUID library to generate unique names for your files to avoid the chances of being overwritten, and enable bucket versioning for bad routines error prevention.

   C. Use a UUID library to generate unique names for your files to avoid the chances of being overwritten and enable cross-region replication to replicate the objects.

   D. Index the files in S3 in a DynamoDB table, enable S3 encryption, create a routine that checks object existence, and replicate it to another region to keep a version of it.

4. Which of the following are valid encryption at rest options for an S3 bucket?

   A. Amazon S3-Managed Keys (SSE-S3) with AES-256.

   B. AWS Key Management Service (SSE-KMS).

   C. Server-Side Encryption with Customer Master Keys (CMKs).

   D. Server-Side Encryption with Customer-Provided Keys (SSE-C).

   E. All the above are valid.

5. What is an S3 object key?

A. An object key is a necessary key to gain access to the object for a user

B. An object key or key name is the object tag you need to retrieve before accessing the object.

C. An object key is an optional parameter to identify a key to retrieve your object.

D. An object key or key name uniquely identifies the object in an S3 bucket.

6. What is an invalid object size for a single object in S3?

A. 1 byte

B. 5 TB

C. 1 PB

D. 0 bytes

7. In terms of the cost per gigabyte of Amazon S3 objects, what is the correct *ascending* order of storage classes, from the lowest to highest price?

A. S3 Standard, S3 Infrequent Access, S3 One Zone IA, S3 Glacier, S3 Glacier Deep Archive

B. S3 Glacier Deep Archive, S3 Glacier, S3 One Zone IA, S3 Infrequent Access, S3 Standard

C. S3 Glacier, S3 Glacier Deep Archive, S3 Standard, S3 One Zone IA, S3 Infrequent Access

D. S3 Glacier Deep Archive, S3 Glacier, S3 Standard, S3 One Zone IA, S3 Infrequent Access

8. Considering S3 resilience, what is true?

A. Objects in S3 are automatically replicated across availability zones in a region, unless you use S3 One-Zone Infrequent Access.

B. You may need to manually copy S3 objects if you would like to have redundancy copy in a region.

C. Objects in S3 are automatically replicated across regions unless you use S3 One-Zone Infrequent Access.

D. You can set up cross-region replication so S3 will keep only one physical copy of the file in each region.

9. How can you allow list and read-only access to objects in your S3 to a user from another account (AccountB) with the least privilege necessary?

A. Set up the following bucket policy:

```
{
    "Version": "2012-10-17",
    "Statement": [
        {
```

```
            "Effect": "Allow",
            "Principal": {
                "AWS": "arn:aws:iam::AccountB:user/AccountB_UserName"
            },
            "Action": [
                "s3:GetObject",
                "s3:PutObject",
                "s3:PutObjectAcl",
                "s3:ListBucket"                   ],
            "Resource": [
                "arn:aws:s3:::YourAccountBucketName/*",
                "arn:aws:s3:::YourAccountBucketName"
            ]
        }
    ]
}
```

B. Set up the following bucket policy:

```
{
    "Version": "2012-10-17",
    "Statement": [
        {
            "Effect": "Allow",
            "Principal": {
                "AWS": "arn:aws:iam::AccountB:user/AccountB_UserName"
            },
            "Action": [
                "s3:GetObject",
                "s3:ListBucket"
            ],
            "Resource": [
                "arn:aws:s3:::YourAccountBucketName/*",
                "arn:aws:s3:::YourAccountBucketName"

            ]
        }
    ]
}
```

C. Set up the following bucket policy:

```json
{
    "Version": "2012-10-17",
    "Statement": [
        {
            "Effect": "Allow",
            "Principal": {
                "AWS": "arn:aws:iam::AccountB:user/*"
            },
            "Action": [
                "s3:GetObject",
                "s3:ListBucket"
            ],
            "Resource": [
                "arn:aws:s3:::YourAccountBucketName/*",
                "arn:aws:s3:::YourAccountBucketName"

            ]
        }
    ]
}
```

D. Set up the following bucket policy:

```json
{
    "Version": "2012-10-17",
    "Statement": [
        {
            "Effect": "Allow",
            "Principal": {
                "AWS": "arn:aws:iam::AccountB:user/AccountB_UserName"
            },
            "Action": [
                "s3:*"
            ],
            "Resource": [
                "arn:aws:s3:::YourAccountBucketName/*"
            ]
        }
    ]
}
```

10. How can you provide in-transit TLS encryption to put or get objects from S3 with low effort?

A. Use the AWS CLI or AWS SDK that provides authentication and encryption in transit with S3.

B. Create an API gateway and a Lambda function to receive the requests and deal with the put and get to and from S3.

C. Create a Beanstalk application to perform the put and get and a public load balancer with a certificate to receive the requests.

D. Use a CloudFront and a bucket policy to accept requests only from it.

Chapter

8

Deliver Valuable Information at the Speed Your Business Needs

This chapter describes how to address different business speed requirements with AWS databases for analytics, time-series, and operational data.

Tools have been used more and more to extract information for business decisions. With cloud services, business intelligence (BI) has been empowered, with data arriving faster and being delivered in near real time for business decision-makers.

Different businesses require different response times when an event is generated to the business. For example, an e-commerce application or website that delays a recommendation 5 seconds may lose the opportunity to catch a user's attention, because they have already clicked another banner, but the same 5-second wait for an analysis of your last five years of sales may be OK.

For the different database flavors, AWS has launched different options to deliver business information with managed services.

Information Latency

Information latency is the time from the event being generated to the time it's available for your business decision. The event can be a sequence of clicks, a single click, a photo upload, the change in value of a stock in the market, or thousands of other kinds of events.

The Internet of Things (IoT) and Global Position System (GPS) technology have created new use cases for image recognition algorithms. Enterprises can rely on sensors and alerts to trigger actions. A simple application, for example, is to interact with customers using messages or pop-ups that display discounts to their smartphones as they get close to a store.

As you can expect, companies have a small window of time to interact with their customers and business problems and to really make valuable decisions and take actions for them. For example, this can be the time the customer enters the mall until the time the customer decides to leave the mall. Or it can be the time when a customer interacts with products on your website to the time they leave the website. If the application misses this window of time, it loses the opportunity to extract the full value from the data.

Figure 8.1 represents the value of the information for a business from the time an event has been generated to the complete business action. The concept, introduced in 2002 by Richard Hackathorn (www.researchgate.net/publication/228815719_Current_practices_in_active_data_warehousing), highlights that the value of the information for the business decreases when the response of the business action is delayed.

FIGURE 8.1   Information latency

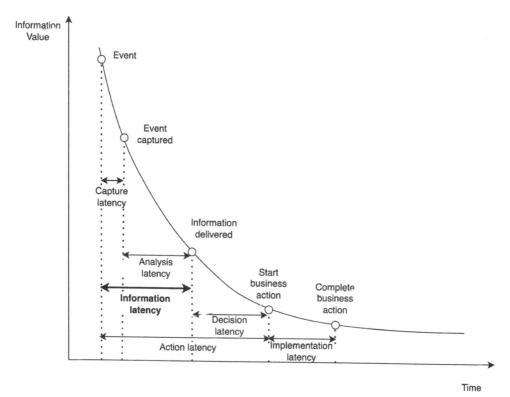

Considering the time elapsed between an event and the business action reacting to it, database solutions can influence the *information latency*, which is the time it takes for the information about the event to be ready for a business decision, we will use this concept for the rest of this chapter.

As shown in Figure 8.2, speeding up the response time usually requires a higher infra-structure cost, so there is a trade-off.

For example, if you analyze 1 TB of information that arrived in the last 24 hours using Amazon Redshift Spectrum to read the data, you can use a different frequency to read it—for example, every day, every hour, or every minute. For all frequencies, it will cost USD $5 per terabyte of data scanned, plus the cost of a small job to trigger during each frequency. Considering that the job used to trigger the action of data processing uses the minimal time usage of 1 minute, using AWS Glue Python Shell, it would cost the following:

- USD $0.44 per hour ÷ 60 min/hour = USD $0.00733 × 1 execution for the daily rate

- USD $0.00733 × 24 executions = USD $0.1759 for the hourly rate

- USD $0.0073 × 1440 executions = USD $10.555 in a per minute rate

Adding the USD $5 costs per terabyte of data scanned, reading the data using Redshift would cost from USD $5.00733 to USD $15.555 per day, depending on the frequency of the job.

FIGURE 8.2   Solution cost comparison based on information rates

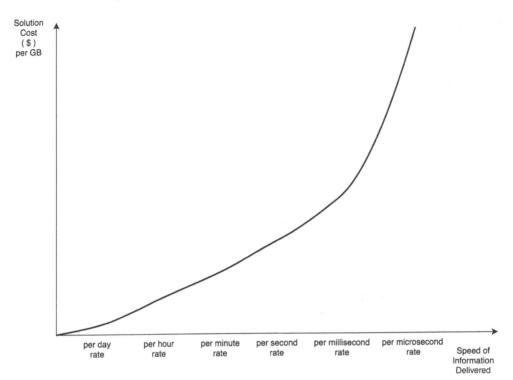

For the same 1 TB, if you need a faster response time, from seconds to a few milliseconds, and you choose Amazon Timestream, it will cost USD $0.05 per 1 million writes of 1 KB multiplied by 1073.74 millions of KB to write 1 TB, which equals USD $53,687, plus a per scan price of USD $0.01 per GB scanned times 1024 GB, which equals USD $10.24, for a total of USD $63.927.

When you're getting a microsecond response time, performing queries and calculations is challenging because each calculation needs to occur close to the event that triggered the action. If you used a cache environment to store the data, and assuming the data would be removed after one day, you would need a cluster of seven instance types of m4.10xlarge just to store the data. This would cost USD $15,902.32 per month or USD $530.07 per day.

So, in this example of 1 TB, the costs vary from a fraction of a dollar to $530 for the same amount of data with different information latency.

All the prices of the preceding examples were taken from the AWS website in October 2022.

To deliver information extremely quickly, we need to provide infrastructure and streaming technologies that have higher cost; if the business decisions can wait to extract value from the data, there are batch and microbatch technologies that are very cost efficient.

Because of network communications latency, if we need faster information, we need to put closer to the business event infrastructure that is capable of handling the event and transform it into information for the business, such as what happens in the example of Amazon Go stores.

This chapter addresses three different database solutions with different characteristics, as shown in Table 8.1.

For near real-time analysis over time-series data, there are specific database engines, such as Amazon Timestream, that are able to perform time-windowed queries and advanced analytics.

TABLE 8.1 Database Engines for Analytics, Time-Series, and Operational Data

Database Engine	AWS Service	Information Latency	Use Case
Time-series database	Amazon Timestream	Milliseconds	IoT Operational data Time-series analytics
Data warehouse	Amazon Redshift	Minutes to hours	Analytics of any complexity Historical analysis
Search engine	Amazon Open-Search Service	Milliseconds to seconds	Operational data Text search Simple queries

Search engines, such as Amazon OpenSearch, provide a fast granular ingestion capability and the ability to index your data to perform complex searches and timeline analysis.

If your business needs powerful analytical functions, such as comparing business results among hundreds of different channels and locations for the past six months, that allow a few minutes of information latency, you can use a data warehouse, such as Amazon Redshift. The information latency is higher, but the analytical capabilities and cost are lower for large amounts of data.

Data Warehouses

Data warehouses are enterprise systems specializing in data analysis and reporting. They are composed of large computational machines dedicated to storing and combining aggregated information, extracted from transactional environments. They have been in place since the 1970s to help businesses make decisions based on information. The concepts are old but still useful for many enterprises.

Extract, transform, and load (ETL) is the process that extracts data from transactional environments, aggregates it in a business view, and loads it into a data warehouse. It usually is performed on a dedicated machine that sits between the transactional database and the data warehouse. As shown in Figure 8.3, the data warehouse information flow starts with the ETL process.

1. Connect to the sources with ETL tools (for example, Pentaho Data Integration, Informatica PowerCenter, Matillion, Talend, or AWS Glue).

2. Map the data sources, schemas, and tables.

3. Create jobs to extract the data from the source systems and save them in a staging area.

4. Add steps to transform the data with a job.

   a. Combine tables to enrich the data.

   b. Perform a quality check on the information.

   c. Create business views of the data, adjusting the naming conventions and data types.

5. Add the job's final step to load the data into the data warehouse.

6. Schedule the job for a period when the source system is not being used intensively to avoid concurrency with transactional operations.

FIGURE 8.3 Data warehouse environment diagram

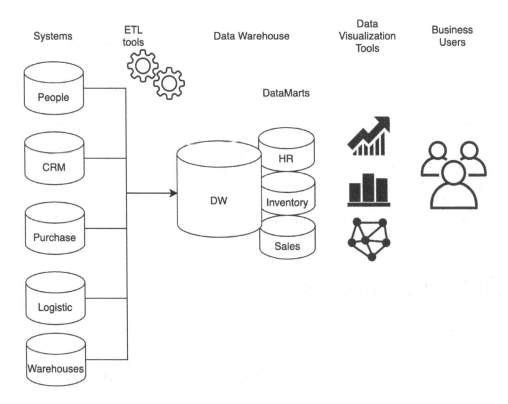

As an established standard inside the data warehouse, the information is separated into *data marts* that represent the business unit's data domain with all the information this business unit needs.

The business users use powerful analytics tools with data visualization capabilities, such as Tableau, QlikView, and Amazon QuickSight, to create graphic dashboards that represent the main metrics for their businesses, usually called *key performance indicators* (KPIs), and also discover trends and make business projections.

It happens that the ETL process usually to extract data from the systems by querying large amounts of data that may affect the transaction operations, which used to be done during the night batch job schedules.

Scheduling tools help operations by allowing jobs to run in parallel and also in sequence with dependencies.

With all this complexity, in a standard data warehouse you will see "D-1" (the current day minus one day) information. Unfortunately, due to the capacity of ETL tools and the data warehouse itself, it's not uncommon to see some D-2 environments that have information from about two days ago.

With less intrusive extraction tools using change data capture (CDC), it's possible to perform "all day" operations, extracting data from the source systems without affecting their performance.

Database Engines for Data Warehouses

To deal with information at scale from different sources and serve the business areas in large data warehouse systems, the hardware (CPU, memory, and disk) in a single machine is not enough for large companies.

The *massively parallel processing (MPP)* architecture uses several machines that work in parallel, orchestrated by a process, to speed up the analysis of very large datasets, taking advantage of several sets of CPU, memory, and storage to perform data operations, as shown in Figure 8.4.

FIGURE 8.4   MPP architecture

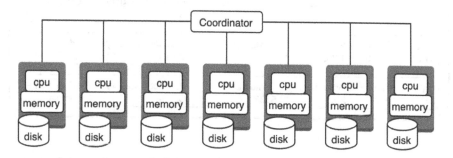

MPP data warehouses can receive more workloads and still deliver the information at a reasonable information latency rate. Using several computational nodes and software intelligence to use the nodes in parallel to process queries has become the standard.

In the MPP architecture, the data is split into different nodes, usually using a key with good cardinality and then a key to group similar data inside the blocks.

Data marts and the business user queries aggregate data by column and do not care much about the details of a single record. Instead of picking a single transaction of a customer in a store, for example, business analysts usually query for the total sales in stores and compare the sales for a period of time, such as which products, categories, or brands were sold the most, for example.

To aggregate data with the Structured Query Language (SQL) using aggregate functions (SUM, COUNT, AVG) grouped by a few columns, it makes sense to store data in a columnar format. Say we have a table that has 50 columns, and the system is querying information about only 3 columns. Then when summarizing or counting the results of column sales by column, month, and product, the system will read fewer storage blocks using a columnar storage format, actually only 3/50 of potential blocks, compared to a line record storage format, where it would need to read all 50 columns and then filter the 3 columns used in the query.

MPP databases use a columnar format, so performing Select * from is terribly bad usage of them, because instead of reading a few column blocks, you will read *all* column blocks. In other words, you will be wasting CPU, memory, and disk operations.

Figure 8.5 shows the difference between three records stored in a line record format and stored in a columnar format. The advantage of columnar format for aggregating data is that you can read only the blocks of the columns you are using in your query. For example, Dates and Product Name discover the number of products you have sold by date, instead of reading all the columns from the line records (OLTP pattern) and then discarding the ones you don't need.

FIGURE 8.5   Line record storage vs columnar storage formats

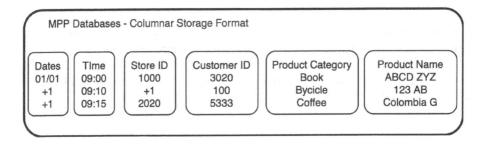

The block size is also larger compared to online transactional database (OLTP) relational databases. Using columnar format and querying aggregated data benefits from large block sizes, so instead of using an 8 KB block size (a common size in many OLTP databases), MPP databases usually use 512 KB or 1 MB block size. This means each physical read can contain a large number of records of a single column.

Appliances were a good way to solve the problem for on-premises data centers, but since cloud computing is being used more and more, data warehouses benefit from the cloud. We can find a great variety of software and hardware built together to deliver MPP databases. The following are good examples:

- Teradata

- IBM Netezza

- IBM Infosphere Balanced Warehouse, based on DB2

- EMC Greenplum appliance

- Oracle Exadata

- Vertica (Dell/EMC)

After the introduction of cloud computing, companies launched their data warehouses in the cloud, so we are now seeing some of the appliance leaders with great solutions built on top of AWS. Examples include Teradata (Teradata Vantage on AWS) and Greenplum (Pivotal Greenplum on AWS), and some new ones are Snowflake and Vertica (Vertica by Hour).

For the certification exam, you must know Amazon Redshift, a PostgreSQL-based database specifically designed for OLAP and BI applications. Amazon Redshift is the AWS solution for data warehouses that uses the modern concept of a data lakehouse.

A *data lakehouse* is an architecture with a single access point that provides joins between the data that is inside the data warehouse, Amazon Redshift, for example, and the data that resides in Amazon S3, acting as a data lake. You will learn more about this later in this chapter.

Amazon Redshift has been the managed service choice in AWS to migrate from on-premises data warehouses to the cloud. AWS has also developed tools to make it easy to migrate.

Migrating Data Warehouses to Amazon Redshift Using AWS SCT

The AWS Schema Conversion Tool (AWS SCT) converts database schemas and can migrate data from traditional data warehouses to Amazon Redshift.

AWS SCT is a client tool that you can install in a machine running Microsoft Windows, Apple macOS, Ubuntu, or Fedora Linux. It facilitates the migration to Amazon Redshift by converting the schemas from supported source systems to Amazon Redshift and migrating the data using SCT data extractors.

The following are some of the supported sources for schema migration:

- Greenplum Database (version 4.3 and later)

- Microsoft SQL Server (version 2008 and later)

- Netezza (version 7.0.3 and later)
- Oracle (version 10 and later)
- Teradata (version 13 and later)
- Vertica (version 7.2.2 and later)

AWS SCT facilitates the migration to Amazon Redshift by performing the following steps (see Figure 8.6):

1. Map the source DW schema and create conversion SQL statements for the schema. (You can create rules to change names and data types in this step.)

2. Migrate the schema to Redshift, creating tables and other database objects; you can filter the objects to be migrated.

3. Extract data from the source data warehouse and store it in an AWS Snowball device on premises that will be loaded into Amazon S3, or directly send it into an S3 bucket.

4. Load the data from the S3 bucket into Amazon Redshift with the COPY command.

FIGURE 8.6   SCT schema and data migration to Redshift

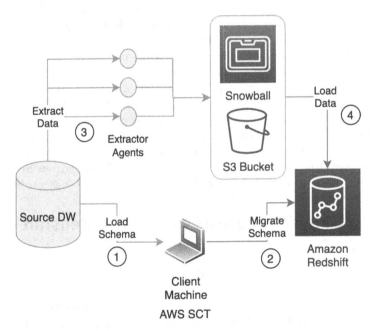

Besides the schema and the data, you may want to convert the ETL jobs you run on premises to AWS Glue. The job conversion can be done with the AWS SCT ETL convertor.

AWS SCT also provides a schema migration for other databases; this will be discussed in Chapter 12, "Migrating Your Data to AWS."

AWS Snowball is a storage device with high-speed connectivity that AWS provides in case you need to move large amounts of data and there is limited network traffic bandwidth. Each device can handle 50–80 TB, depending on the version. AWS sends the device to you; then you connect it to your network using RJ45, SFP+, or SFP+ (with optic) connectors. You transfer the data, send it back to AWS, and AWS loads your data into an S3 bucket or EBS volumes. AWS Snowball Edge is a version where you transfer data and also run code on premises, and AWS Snowcone is a simple option for volumes up to 8 TB.

Amazon Redshift

Amazon Redshift is a robust, fully managed AWS service for data warehouses. It creates all the cluster infrastructure and manages cluster nodes for you to load data and analyze tens of gigabytes to perabytes of data.

When migrating data warehouse workloads to AWS, Amazon Redshift is the top-of-mind service. Although there are options to perform queries for reports, such as Amazon Aurora with read replicas, when the workload has analytics characteristics with large volumes, then the columnar storage format and the MPP architecture of Amazon Redshift are keys to delivering performance at low cost.

Redshift Cluster Architecture

Amazon Redshift cluster architecture is based on MPP concepts with columnar data storage and efficient data compression per column (see Figure 8.7).

The *leader node* is where the client applications connect, using JDBC or ODBC connectors. The leader node receives the queries, parses and builds an execution plan, and then distributes the compiled code of this plan to the compute nodes.

Compute nodes are where the data and processing are distributed, with dedicated CPU, memory, and disks attached to each one. Every compute node has a group of slices that are the smallest unit of Redshift; slices are units of CPU, memory, and disk space used to parallelize processing and storage.

So even if you have only one compute node, the data as well as the processing will be distributed among the *slices*.

As your data and workloads grow, you can add more nodes to a Redshift cluster.

Table Design in Redshift

Amazon Redshift supports several different table models, such as star schema, snowflake schema, third normal form (3NF), and denormalized tables. It's easy to bring working models from other data warehouses to Redshift without changing table modeling.

FIGURE 8.7 Redshift architecture

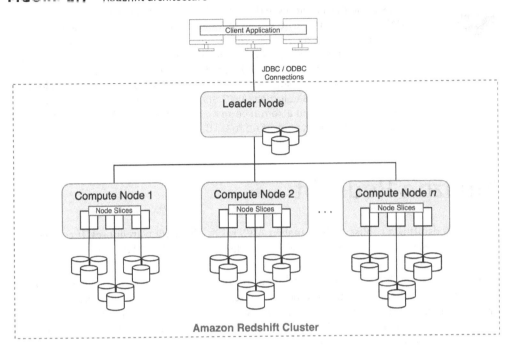

One important thing to know about table relationships and constraints is that you should define the primary key and foreign key constraints between tables wherever appropriate for the table models mentioned, such as star schema, snowflake, and 3NF. Even though they are informational only, they don't enforce data uniqueness; for example, the query optimizer uses those constraints to generate more efficient query plans.

To get all the benefits from the Redshift architecture, we need to distribute the data among the compute nodes and slices. This way, when you issue a query, the work is distributed among the slices using parallelism.

Distribution style is a table attribute in Redshift that tells Redshift how to distribute data among Redshift cluster nodes; it can be set to EVEN, KEY, ALL, or AUTO. We can specify a distribution style during table creation; otherwise, Redshift will use the AUTO distribution.

Figure 8.8 illustrates the distribution styles, using an alphabetic column example for the distribution key that will determine where to put the records in the slices according to their values. It also shows that Distribution Even will store the records in a round-robin fashion in the slices, without taking the value into consideration, and that Distribution All will save all the records in all the nodes.

FIGURE 8.8   Redshift distribution style

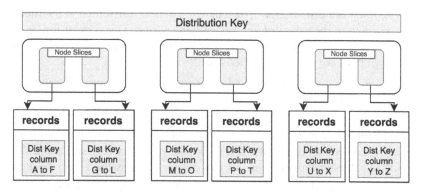

Distributed according to the sort value order of Distribution Key

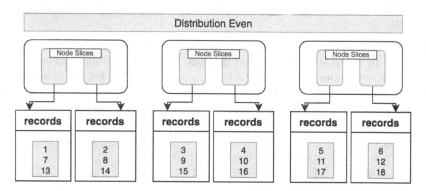

Distributed in a round-robin fashion, numbers are the arrival order of records.

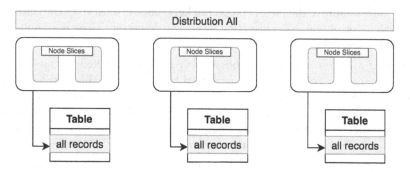

Each node has a full copy of the table.

The following are the Redshift distribution style options:

- *Key distribution* is a distribution style where the data is distributed in the slices and nodes according to the values of one key-chosen column. This is great for large tables such as fact tables, and if you distribute a pair of tables by their joining keys, the matching values of both are physically stored together.

- *All distribution* is a distribution style where every node has a copy of the entire table. It's ideal for small dimension tables that you frequently join with fact tables. As each node has a copy of it, the storage requirement is multiplied by the number of nodes.

- *Even distribution* is a distribution style where the data is distributed in the slices and nodes in a round-robin fashion, without taking the values into consideration. You may use it if your table doesn't perform joins, such as one big denormalized table design pattern.

- *Auto distribution* is a distribution style that lets Redshift decide automatically between the ALL, EVEN, and KEY distribution styles, based on your table size and queries, so data will be distributed based on the style that better fits the data and query profile of the table.

After deciding the distribution style, you should decide on the *sort key*, which is how the data will be ordered inside the data blocks that were distributed by the distribution key.

Sort keys are important for the queries. For example, if you are interested in queries using ranges of dates, using the date column as the sort key can reduce the number of blocks needed for a query, as all the dates in a small range will be in a single or few blocks, instead of having them split in several blocks not ordered.

You should always use sort keys for frequently used columns in your WHERE clauses that could filter the number of data blocks to retrieve.

Redshift lets you create two types of sort keys.

- *Compound sort keys* is the preferred sort key method for a Redshift table. Data is ordered by a list of columns, in the order in which they are listed in the compound key definition. To improve the use of compound keys, put the most frequently used columns in the WHERE or GROUP BY clauses first in the key definition. There is a limit of 400 sort key columns per table.

- *Interleaved sort keys* is a more flexible sort key method for a Redshift table that gives equal weight to the columns in the interleaved key definition. This method is used when a query uses restrictive predicates on secondary sort columns. However, AWS recommends not using an interleaved sort key on columns with monotonically increasing attributes, such as identity columns, dates, or timestamps. There is a limitation of eight columns per table when using interleaved sort keys.

You can also set SORTKEY AUTO for your table definition. This allows Redshift to choose the best sort keys based on your query behaviors.

As a columnar database, Redshift can use *compression encode*, which is the type of compression that will be applied for each column; there are different encoding algorithms available according to column data types (see Table 8.2), and you can let Redshift manage the encode for the tables using the ENCODE AUTO option for tables, which is the default.

TABLE 8.2   Compression Encodings and Data Types

Compression Encoding	Keyword in CREATE TABLE and ALTER TABLE	Data Types
Raw (no compression)	RAW	All
AZ64	AZ64	SMALLINT, INTEGER, BIGINT, DECIMAL, DATE, TIMESTAMP, TIMESTAMPTZ
Byte dictionary	BYTEDICT	SMALLINT, INTEGER, BIGINT, DECIMAL, REAL, DOUBLE PRECISION, CHAR, VARCHAR, DATE, TIMESTAMP, TIMESTAMPTZ
Delta	DELTA	SMALLINT, INT, BIGINT, DATE, TIMESTAMP, DECIMAL
	DELTA32K	INT, BIGINT, DATE, TIMESTAMP, DECIMAL
LZO	LZO	SMALLINT, INTEGER, BIGINT, DECIMAL, CHAR, VARCHAR, DATE, TIMESTAMP, TIMESTAMPTZ, SUPER
Mostlyn	MOSTLY8	SMALLINT, INT, BIGINT, DECIMAL
	MOSTLY16	INT, BIGINT, DECIMAL
	MOSTLY32	BIGINT, DECIMAL
Run-length	RUNLENGTH	SMALLINT, INTEGER, BIGINT, DECIMAL, REAL, DOUBLE PRECISION, BOOLEAN, CHAR, VARCHAR, DATE, TIMESTAMP, TIMESTAMPTZ
Text	TEXT255	VARCHAR only
	TEXT32K	VARCHAR only
Zstandard	ZSTD	SMALLINT, INTEGER, BIGINT, DECIMAL, REAL, DOUBLE PRECISION, BOOLEAN, CHAR, VARCHAR, DATE, TIMESTAMP, TIMESTAMPTZ, SUPER

Encoding saves storage space by compressing the data. It also optimizes read and write operations by reducing the number of storage blocks required for the same data.

Although you can explicitly set up encodes for your table columns, it's a good idea to let Redshift calculate and suggest the best encoding for you, as it does by default when you use the COPY command to load data for the first time.

ENCODE AUTO is the default for tables and columns whenever you don't specify other encode types. With ENCODE AUTO Redshift will manage compression encoding for the columns in the table.

Loading Data into Redshift

Performing a single-row insert is bad for Redshift. As discussed previously, Redshift is a columnar database, so every row you add in a table, with 10 columns, for example, will actually perform 10 entries, in 10 different 1 MB blocks of storage.

So, to optimize load performance and Redshift block usage, avoid performing isolated insert operations.

Redshift optimizes load operations with the following commands:

- COPY: This command is used to load data from files, usually from an Amazon S3 bucket. You can use parallelism, using cluster slices to load data from the files. When you have data in a number of files that is a multiple of the cluster slices count, you optimize parallelism, as every slice will always be handling a file and loading it to Redshift until all the files are done.

- INSERT as SELECT: This command performs a bulk insert into an existing table, optimizing the write operation with efficient block usage and using parallelism.

- CREATE TABLE as SELECT: This command creates a table from a result set of a SELECT statement, performing a bulk insert similar to INSERT as SELECT.

The Redshift COPY command is very flexible, allowing you to load data from Amazon S3, Amazon DynamoDB, and Amazon EMR, as well as from an SSH remote connection. When loading data from Amazon S3, the Redshift COPY command supports several file types and compressions: AVRO, JSON, BZIP2, GZIP, LZOP, PARQUET, ORC, ZSTD, CSV, DELIMITED, FIXED WIDTH, and SHAPED FILE.

If you need to encrypt data on the client side, before loading the data into Redshift using the COPY command, you can use an AWS KMS customer-managed symmetric key (KMS-CMK) to encrypt the data, add the ENCRYPTED keyword along with the compress format in the FORMAT parameter (GZIP, LZOP, BZIP2, or ZSTD), and perform the load using COPY.

To parallelize the work of the COPY command, you need to split the data you want to load into several files. Each *slice* of Redshift will be able to load a file at a time, so if you have 16 slices in a cluster, you should split your data into a multiple of 16 files, in a way that every slice is working until the load is ended in a fast and parallelized way.

Remember, however, that you should not keep file size too small; it should be at least 1 MB and ideally up to 1 GB after compression. If you have a large dataset to load, you can use a larger file size than 1 GB, but keep in mind that you should parallelize the load using multiple files to use the cluster resources and speed up the operation.

You should always authorize COPY commands using IAM roles to allow access to the data source, although it's possible to use IAM credentials.

The following is an example of a COPY command that loads the data from all the files that are in the specified path in Amazon S3 using an IAM role:

```
copy my_student_table
from 's3://mybucket_name/path_for_files/'
iam_role 'arn:aws:iam::<aws-account-id>:role/<role-name>'
region 'us-east-1;
```

The IAM role used in the COPY command needs to have permission to list and read files from the specified path. You can be specific and point to a single file or use a manifest file with a list of files.

The following is an example of the COPY command using a manifest file:

```
copy my_student_table
from 's3://mybucket_name/student.manifest'
iam_role 'arn:aws:iam::<aws-account-id>:role/<role-name>'
manifest;
```

The following is an example of a manifest file where four files with the path url need to be loaded for the operation to succeed:

```
{
  "entries": [
    {"url":"s3://mybucket_name/student01", "mandatory":true},
    {"url":"s3://mybucket_name/student02", "mandatory":true},
    {"url":"s3://mybucket_name/student03", "mandatory":true},
    {"url":"s3://mybucket_name/student04", "mandatory":true}
  ]
}
```

Data Lakes in AWS

AWS has a well-known architecture for data lakes—that is, Amazon S3 to store the data, AWS Glue Data Catalog to catalog data objects as tables and databases (using a hive meta-store), and AWS Lake Formation to control access for IAM groups and roles (see Figure 8.9).

FIGURE 8.9   AWS data l architecture

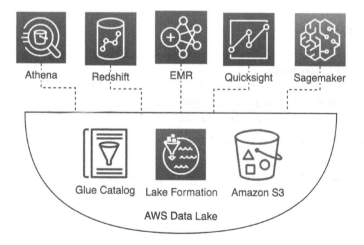

For some data sources, such as Apache Avro, Apache ORC, Apache Parquet, JSON, Binary JSON, XML, Amazon Ion, Apache log, Combined Apache log, Linux kernel log, Microsoft log, Redis log, Ruby log, and CSV files, AWS Glue Data Catalog can map tables with hive metastore definitions using a crawler. After cataloging the tables, it allows them to be queried with Amazon Athena (with Presto engine), Amazon EMR (Spark and Presto), and Redshift Spectrum.

Redshift Spectrum

Redshift Spectrum allows Redshift to query data from an AWS data lake in Amazon S3, over structured and semistructured data.

The Redshift Spectrum servers are a set of servers that work independently and along with the Amazon Redshift cluster.

You can point Redshift Spectrum to the AWS Glue Data Catalog using an external schema, and you can attach an IAM role to this schema to be granted access to databases and tables using AWS Lake Formation.

```
CREATE EXTERNAL SCHEMA my_student_schema
FROM DATA CATALOG DATABASE 'my_db' region 'us-east-1'
IAM_ROLE 'arn:aws:iam::<redshift-account-id>:role/<spectrum-role>';
```

Redshift Federated Queries

Redshift federated queries allow you to integrate queries from Amazon Redshift on live data in external databases with queries across your Amazon Redshift and Amazon S3 environments.

Federated queries can work with external databases in Amazon RDS for PostgreSQL and Amazon Aurora PostgreSQL and Aurora MySQL Compatibles.

Data Lakehouse

A *data lakehouse* architecture uses a data warehouse in conjunction with a data lake and other sources (see Figure 8.10).

With Amazon Redshift, you can use Redshift Spectrum and federated queries to access external tables and join them with internal Redshift tables.

Suppose you have the following three tables:

- **Redshift table:** `redshift.transactions`
- **Amazon S3 table:** `s3.transactions_hist`
- **RDS for PostgreSQL table:** `rds.transactions_online`

FIGURE 8.10   AWS data lakehouse architecture

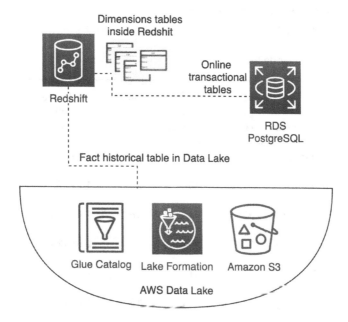

You can create a view that unites the three tables:

```
CREATE VIEW transactions AS
  SELECT t_id, t_date::date , t_type, t_value
  FROM s3.transactions_hist
  UNION ALL SELECT * FROM redshift.transactions
  UNION ALL SELECT * FROM rds.transactions_online
    with no schema binding;
```

Then you can join the view with dimensions:

```
SELECT tr.t_id, tr.t_date , tp.t_description, tr.t_value
FROM transactions as tr
LEFT OUTER JOIN redshift.type_t as tp
ON tr.t_type = tp.t_type;
```

Redshift Cluster Node Types

AWS offers three Redshift cluster node types:

- **Dense compute:** Nodes with SSD storage, with 160 GB (dc1.large and dc2.large) or 2.56 TB per node (dc1.8xlarge and dc2.8xlarge)

- **Dense storage:** Nodes with HDD storage, with 2 TB (ds2.large) or 16 TB per node (ds2.8xlarge)

- **RA3:** Nodes with an independent storage layer up to 32 TB (ra3.xplus) and 128 TB (ra3.4xlarge and ra3.16xlarge) per node

Table 8.3 shows detailed information about each node type for Redshift.

TABLE 8.3 Redshift Node Types

Node Type	Node Size	vCPU per Node	RAM (GB) per Node	Slices per Node	Nodes per Cluster (Range)	Max Storage (TB)
Dense Compute	dc1.large	2	15	2	1 to 32	5
	dc2.large	2	15	2	1 to 32	5
	dc1.2xlarge	32	244	16	2 to 128	326
	dc2.2xlarge	32	244	16	2 to 128	326
Dense Storage	ds2.xlarge	4	31	2	1 to 32	64
	ds2.8xlarge	36	244	16	2 to 128	2,048
RA3	ra3.xplus	4	32	2	2 to 16	1,024
	ra3.4xlarge	12	96	4	2 to 32	8,192
	ra3.16xlarge	48	384	16	2 to 128	16,384

Notice that Redshift clusters with the RA3 node types have the largest scalability in terms of RAM and storage. The storage for RA3 nodes is provided and priced separately from the nodes as Redshift Managed Storage.

Redshift Monitoring

Amazon CloudWatch is the central monitoring for AWS services, and Redshift is also supported with tens of metrics.

The Redshift console also displays several metrics from CloudWatch, such as CPU utilization, which is displayed for each node. This helps to check whether all the clusters are being used or only a few nodes are working.

One thing to notice is that Redshift will try to use the cluster for heavy queries. Sometimes we can see a high usage (above 95 percent of CPU), and the expected behavior is that peaks last for a few seconds to minutes. If the cluster is being used for a very long period with high usage, then it is time to evaluate resizing the cluster.

Metrics about queue utilization and query wait time are also available on a Redshift console, so it's good to check how queues are set and adjust them as needed.

With CloudWatch alarms you can set alarms triggered by thresholds reached and send the alert to an Amazon Simple Notification Service (Amazon SNS) topic or run an AWS Lambda function that reacts to your alarm.

> CPU utilization for Redshift is key to getting benefits from its multinode architecture. We want to see all the nodes working, especially for large queries and loads (COPY commands). If you see an unbalanced usage of CPU among the nodes for queries, you can look at the tables involved in the queries and verify the distribution style and distribution keys. If you see this behavior for load operations, you should split the number of files you have into multiple slices in the cluster so that each will be handled by a slice.

Redshift Scalability

As previously demonstrated in Table 8.3, the scalability can vary according to the node type. If you use a cluster with the largest Redshift RA3 node size (ra3.16xlarge), it can have up to 6,144 vCPUs, 48 TB of RAM, and 16,384 TB of storage.

To scale your cluster, you can perform the following operations:

- **Elastic resize:** This can be used to change the cluster configuration in terms of the number of nodes, node type, or both. An elastic resize can take between 10 and 15 minutes. During a resize operation, the cluster is read-only. If you're changing the number of nodes only, the connections are kept open, but the queries are temporarily paused. There are growth and reduction limits on the number of nodes, based on the current node number and type: four times for RA3 xlarge nodes, two times for other node types. An elastic resize has some limitations: it is available only for clusters in a Virtual Private Cloud (VPC) network, and dc2, ds2, and ra3.xplus nodes support only two times the growth and a one-half reduction, as opposed to ra3.4xlarge or ra3.16large nodes for which you can resize up to four times the current size or a one-quarter reduction. To check the available resize possibilities for your cluster, you can use the `describe-node-configuration-options` AWS CLI command with the `--action-type resize-cluster` parameter.

- **Classic resize:** If the elastic resize is not available according to the number of node restrictions described previously, use a classic resize to change the node type, number of nodes, or both. The operation can take hours or last up to several days, depending on your data size. Note that the source cluster will be read-only during a resize operation.

- **Snapshot, restore, and resize:** You can make a copy of your cluster to keep it available during a classic resize. Then, resize the new cluster. You will need to copy the very recent data ingested in the old cluster, if any, after the migration completes.

You can upgrade from dense compute or dense storage to an RA3 node. The operation is performed by taking a snapshot, creating a new cluster RA3 from the snapshot, and renaming it to the old cluster name.

You can automate the operation of upgrading to RA3 by performing an elastic resize.

You may encounter a few examples of Redshift environments where the customer uses more than one cluster at the same time using some of these options:

- Using PgBouncer, an open-source, lightweight, single-binary connection pooler for PostgreSQL, in front of two Redshift clusters in different availability zones, and letting PgBouncer control each cluster access. Check AWS git github.com/awslabs/pgbouncer-rr-patch for details.

- Dual load using the same ETL process for both clusters.

- Dedicate a different group of user to each cluster.

Workload management (WLM) enables you to define queues of queries with rules to limit the number of Redshift resources or cluster time they can use; then you associate groups of users to route their queries to the appropriate queue's runtime.

To get started with WLM, you can use Automatic WLM, which creates up to eight queues and sets memory and concurrency to automatic. Then you can define a priority for the queues you need based on the business requirements. Queries can be assigned based on database user groups, and you can use a query monitor rule (QMR) to limit long-running queries.

Manual WLM is also available. With this option you set up the queues and create the routing rules for user groups and query groups. You also control the memory and concurrency for each queue.

There is also a queue for fast-running queries, called *short query acceleration* (SQA), which is useful to avoid having short-running queries waiting in a common queue. This is enabled by default.

The Concurrent Scaling feature may help with peaks of load for Redshift clusters.

When you enable Concurrent Scaling for a queue using WLM, you can support virtually unlimited concurrent users; with this option Redshift adds additional cluster capacity to process peaks of read and write queries.

Although concurrency scaling supports COPY, INSERT, DELETE, and UPDATE statements, in some cases, the write statements are not sent to the concurrency-scaling cluster, such as CREATE TABLE or ALTER TABLE.

Redshift Security

To protect data in a Redshift cluster, you should create Redshift clusters inside nonpublic subnets in your VPCs and connect to Amazon VPC through a VPN or AWS Direct Connect connection, unless you have a good reason to deploy it in a public subnet.

Redshift is secured by *security groups* that will allow traffic only from well-known applications. You will explicitly set up security group rules that allow ingress traffic from other security groups or IP ranges to access your Redshift cluster.

You should also use *Amazon S3 VPC endpoints* so that Redshift will privately access data In S3 for the ETL process to load or unload. The Amazon Redshift API also can be used through a VPC endpoint (AWS PrivateLink).

It is important to know that you can enable storage encryption if you have requirements for encryption at rest. Redshift allows you to set up an AWS Key Management Service to manage the encryption keys.

With Redshift encryption at rest enabled, the data stored on disks within a cluster and the Amazon S3 backups of Redshift data will be encrypted with Advanced Encryption Standard (AES-256).

It's always possible to encrypt the data before sending it to Redshift with *client-side encryption* of your preference, but with this option the management of encryption process, keys store, and related tools is all yours.

Data tokenization is popular nowadays to mask or obfuscate table column values that should not be public or seen by users or groups of users for data security purposes. Personal identifiable information (PII) or protected health information (PHI) can be tokenized with Amazon Redshift user-defined functions (UDFs) using AWS Lambda functions.

There are also native Redshift functions such as SHA2 that can be used in database views to provide hash values for people not authorized to view the information.

The following is an example of a VIEW with a hash function for PII information:

```
CREATE OR REPLACE VIEW <hashed_view> AS
SELECT sha2(name, 256) AS name,
sha2(email, 256) AS email,
transaction_timestamp,
transaction_id,
transaction_type,
transaction_value
FROM <original_table>;
```

With the preceding VIEW example, if you grant only this view to a group of data scientists, they would have data to analyze but would not know who this data belongs to.

For audit purposes, Redshift has two levels of traceability:

- **CloudTrail** is available for API calls that change or interact with a Redshift cluster, with rich information about the origin of the call such as IP address, interface, and IAM role or user.

- **Database audit logging** is available for database events such as *connection log*, *user log*, and *user activity log*. The last one logs each query before running it. You need to set the parameter enable_user_activity_logging to true. The *audit* log destination is Amazon S3 with managed keys encryption (AES-256).

Redshift Data Resilience and Backup

Redshift is backed up by default with a snapshot every 8 hours or 5 GB of changing data per node. The default retention policy is 24 hours, but you can modify it. To disable automatic snapshots, you can set the retention policy to zero.

For RA3 node–type clusters, you cannot disable automated snapshots, so you can set the retention from 1 to 35 days.

For some use cases (for example, after a data load completion), you may want to schedule snapshots, which can be as specific as days of the week and times or as generic as every 12 hours. (The limits are from every 1 hour to every 24 hours.)

Manual snapshots can be triggered using the Redshift API or Redshift console. This is useful when you need to trigger snapshots in a script, and their retention can be specifically set for each manual snapshot.

If you have a set of tables that doesn't need to be backed up (because you re-create them every day, for example), you can set the table with the BACKUP NO parameter. This will exclude the table from snapshots. The default is set to include the table.

For restore operations, you can use table granularity, restoring, for example, a single table from the snapshot to your cluster.

If you need to create a multiregion failover scenario, you can set Redshift automated snapshots to be written also in another region.

You can restore the whole cluster from a snapshot and can use this process to also change the node type or node number of your cluster using the following AWS CLI command, for example:

```
aws redshift restore-from-cluster-snapshot
--region us-west-2
--snapshot-identifier student-cluster-change011-snapshot
--cluster-identifier student-cluster-123456789012
--node-type ra3.4xlarge
--number-of-nodes 4
```

To verify which cluster node types and node numbers would be the best options for your Redshift snapshot to be restored on, you can use the Redshift AWS CLI command describe-node-configuration-options. This command will list all the available configurations, NodeType and NumberOfNodes, that you can use to restore your snapshot with an estimated disk utilization percentage for each configuration.

Redshift snapshots are stored in an AWS internal managed S3 not shown in your account as S3 objects, and you can only access them using Redshift's API. This means that every snapshot is available in any availability zone of the region your cluster is in, and in any availability zone of another region if you set up the automated cross-region snapshot replication copy.

So if your current cluster is in the us-east-1 region at the availability zone a (us-east-1a), you can restore a snapshot in any other availability zone of that region—us-east-1b, us-east-1c, and so on.

And if you enabled Redshift to automatically copy snapshots to another region, such as us-west-2, you would be able to restore in any availability zone of us-west-2, for example, us-west-2a, us-west-2b or us-west-2c.

You can use the Redshift UNLOAD operation to extract logical backups of tables directly to Amazon S3.

Time-Series Databases

Time-series databases are intended to store and query data records that are in a *time-series* format, which basically means a set of data points that have a timestamp and values associated to each timestamp.

Historically, time-series databases have been used for industrial equipment measurement with a set of sensors, such as rotation per minute, temperature, and pressure, that can be correlated to a good function and performance of a transformation machine or line of production.

Today's common use cases include the following:

- Financial stock prices over time

- Metrics of infrastructure utilization, such as CPU and memory of an application over time

- IoT sensor measurements over time, such as temperature or humidity

- Application measurements, such as user activity interaction over time

With the popularization of the IoT, devices are generating time-series data all the time. For example, Table 8.4 is a set of sensors installed in a bicycle, where for each timestamp we have a measurement of temperature, bike speed, and wind speed.

TABLE 8.4   Time-Series Data Example

Timestamp	Temperature (Celsius)	Bike Speed (kph)	Wind Speed (km/h)
2021-08-01 10:37:00.000	23.41	39.8	5.0
2021-08-01 10:37:00.045	23.52	39.9	5.0
2021-08-01 10:37:00.120	23.52	39.9	5.0
2021-08-01 10:37:00.231	23.50	40.1	4.9
2021-08-01 10:37:00.309	23.45	40.2	4.9
2021-08-01 10:37:00.343	23.01	40.2	4.9
2021-08-01 10:37:00.402	22.99	40.1	4.8
2021-08-01 10:37:00.522	22.94	40.1	4.8
2021-08-01 10:37:00.600	22.92	40.1	4.7

(continues)

TABLE 8.4   Time-Series Data Example *(continued)*

Timestamp	Temperature (Celsius)	Bike Speed (kph)	Wind Speed (km/h)
2021-08-01 10:37:00.621	22.41	40.2	4.7
2021-08-01 10:37:00.720	22.50	40.1	4.7
2021-08-01 10:37:00.800	22.59	40.3	4.7
2021-08-01 10:37:00.920	22.51	40.0	4.7
2021-08-01 10:37:01.009	22.46	40.0	4.7
2021-08-01 10:37:01.343	22.03	39.9	4.9
2021-08-01 10:37:01.402	21.99	39.8	5.0
2021-08-01 10:37:01.522	21.94	39.8	5.1
2021-08-01 10:37:01.600	21.92	39.9	5.1

You can use a relational database for time-series data or even a NoSQL database such as Apache Cassandra or Apache HBase with proper table modeling, but a time-series database usually offers statistical functions to facilitate the analysis of time-series data and the data life cycle.

Several time-series databases are available to install and manage, including the following:

- Apache Druid
- Apache Pinot
- InfluxDB
- Apache Kudu
- Prometheus
- Riak-TS
- RDDtool

For the purpose of the AWS Certified Database Specialty certification, you should know that AWS has a fully managed time-series database, Amazon Timestream.

Amazon Timestream

Amazon Timestream is a fully managed AWS database service for IoT and operational application data that is stored as time-series data points. It's accessible using a JDBC driver and SQL.

As shown in Figure 8.11, the Amazon Timestream services use the following terminology:

- **Database:** A container for *tables*.

- **Table:** The unit to store and query a set of time-series *records*.

- **Record:** A single data point in a time series.

- **Timestamp:** The moment that a given record was collected. Timestream supports time-stamps with nanosecond granularity.

- **Dimension:** A pair of dimension name and dimension value that describes the time-series metadata—for example:

  - The device ID for IoT sensors identifies the sensors the measure came from; Device 00001 data points will have `DeviceID` as the dimension name and `00001` as the dimension value.

  - For the stock exchange, `StockID` can be the dimension name and `AMZN` the dimension value.

  - For AWS resource metrics, you can use `Resource ARN` as the dimension name and the resource ARN value as the dimension value—for example, `Resource ARN"="arn:aws:s3:::my_corporate_bucket/*`.

- **Measure:** The value being measured. Examples are the temperature or humidity reading, the stock price, or the number of gigabytes stored in S3. Measures consist of measure names and measure values. Consider the following examples:

  - `"stock price" = 100` is the actual stock price at a point in time, for a `"StockID"`.

  - `"temperature" = 70` and `"humidity" = 0.55` are measures for a given `DeviceID` at a specific timestamp.

  - For CPU utilization, the measure name is `CPU utilization`, and the measure value is the actual CPU utilization.

FIGURE 8.11   Amazon Timestream logical structure

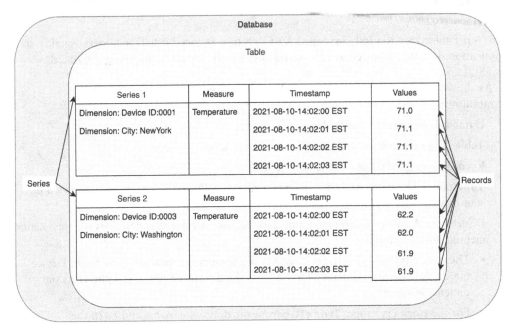

Amazon Timestream Architecture

The Amazon Timestream architecture has three main layers. Ingestion happens fast using the ingestion layer to an in-memory fault-tolerant store, replicated to three AZs in the storage layer, and can then be queried using the query layer, as shown in Figure 8.12.

- **The layer** is the layer we interact with through JDBC or the AWS SDK to query time-series data inside a Timestream table. It has a fleet of dedicated workers.

- **The storage layer** is the layer for data persistence. There are two types of storage layer:

  - The in-memory storage layer is used for ingestion and queries with a horizontal scalability. It stores time-series data in a fault-tolerant in-memory structure, which will then be written to the magnetic store.

  - The magnetic (persistent) store storage layer is used for queries. You can set a retention period for data to reside in a magnetic store.

- **The ingestion layer** is the layer we use in the AWS SDK to ingest time-series data. It works independently from the query layer. Data is replicated to three AZs, and duplications are detected.

FIGURE 8.12   Amazon Timestream logical structure

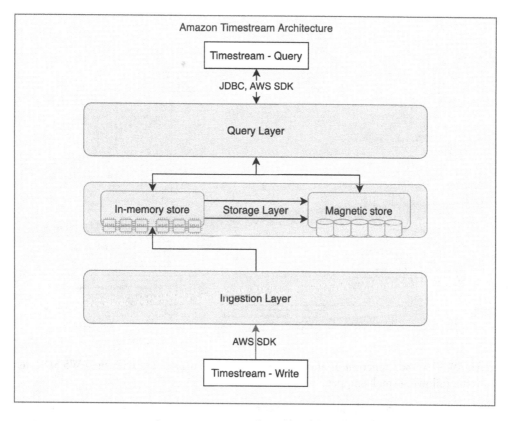

Amazon Timestream has a concept of *cellular architecture*, a small unit of the infrastructure that holds a copy of your data, so when you interact with Timestream, it has a virtual endpoint called *discovery endpoint* that will redirect your interaction to the *cellular endpoint*, that is, the Timestream cell that holds your data. This concept is shown in Figure 8.13 wherein each cell is a Timestream unit.

With cellular architecture, AWS enables scalability and avoids a single point of failure for the Amazon Timestream architecture.

Loading Data into Amazon Timestream

Amazon Timestream can receive data natively from some sources within AWS services.

- AWS IoT core rules can be configured to send data to Amazon Timestream.

- An Amazon Kinesis Data Analytics for Apache Flink data connector can be used to load data from Amazon Kinesis Data Analytics, Amazon MSK, Apache Kafka, and other streaming technologies directly into Amazon Timestream.

FIGURE 8.13 Amazon Timestream cellular architecture

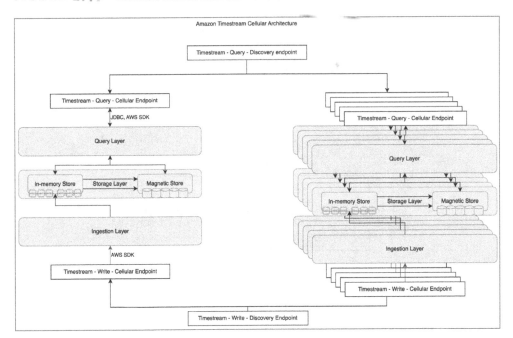

- An AWS Lambda function or another application can ingest data with the AWS SDK, as in the following small snippet:

```
write_client = session.client('timestream-write', config=Config(read_timeout=20,
max_pool_connections = 5000, retries={'max_attempts': 10}))
result = write_client.write_records(DatabaseName=Constant.DATABASE_NAME,
TableName=Constant.TABLE_NAME,                              Records=records,
CommonAttributes={})
```

There are also connectors such as Prometheus or Amazon SageMaker Data Wrangler to send data to Amazon Timestream.

Querying Data from Amazon Timestream

Amazon Timestream offers a JDBC driver for connections, enabling it to be connected from a wide variety of tools, from SQL clients to analytics tools.

The query language supports the standard SELECT statements and WITH clause and has a variety of options for aggregate functions. The following example calculates the average temperature for every 30 seconds in sensors from 'NewYork' for the last two hours:

```
SELECT city, BIN(time, 30s) AS binned_timestamp, ROUND(AVG(measure_
value::double), 2)
AS avg_temperature
FROM "certification".Rides
```

```
WHERE measure_name - 'temperature'
    AND city = 'NewYork'
    AND time > ago(2h)
GROUP BY city, bin(time, 30s)
ORDER BY binned_timestamp ASC
```

You can see that we use special time functions that are commonly used in time-series databases but not present in many standard SQL databases, such as the ago function, which returns a timestamp interval from a time unit behind (2 hours in the example) until now, and the bin function, which has nothing to do with binary conversion (as in MySQL) but instead is a rounded timestamp interval, usually to group data in a time-based window—in our case, one window of aggregation for every 30 seconds.

The Amazon Timestream tables' data can also be consumed from Amazon QuickSight, Amazon SageMaker, and Grafana.

Amazon Timestream Monitoring

There are fewer Amazon Timestream metrics on CloudWatch than for Amazon Redshift or Amazon OpenSearch Service—because you don't have to worry about nodes and because there are fewer parameters or queues to tune.

Metrics available for Timestream include SuccessfulRequestLatency, SystemErrors, UserErrors, and CumulativeBytesMetered, for the DatabaseName, TableName, and Operation dimensions. The metrics are used to monitor the response time, errors, and workload for a given table and database.

Amazon Timestream Scalability

Timestream scales very well. You don't need to add nodes, and you don't need to make new configurations to accommodate new workloads. Each layer scales automatically for peaks and new workloads.

The scale model is different from Redshift and Amazon OpenSearch Service, which are based on adding or changing nodes. It's closer to DynamoDB on-demand provisioning, where the infrastructure automatically accepts new throughputs.

Amazon Timestream doesn't set a limit on the throughput for ingestion or query concurrency. It has some limits, however. Examples of limits that you may consider for scale in the exam include the following:

- **Time data remains in memory:** 1 to 8,766 hours, default is 6 hours

- **Time data remains in persistent store:** 1 to 73,000 days

- **Per account databases:** Up to 500

- **Per account tables:** Up to 50,000

- **Records write in a single WriteRecords API call:** 100

- **Query result set size:** Up to 5 GB

- **Query execution time:** Up to 1 hour

Amazon Timestream Security

Timestream has encryption set up by default.

- **At-rest** encryption is set by default with an AWS KMS key, which can be managed by Timestream or your own custom key.

- **In-transit** encryption is in place for all communications to and from Timestream, using Transport Layer Security (TLS) encryption.

AWS IAM is used to grant access to Amazon Timestream with identity-based policies, as in the following example:

```
{
    "Version": "2012-10-17",
        "Statement": [
                {
                        "Effect": "Allow",
                        "Action": [
                                "timestream:Select",
                                "timestream:ListMeasures"
                        ],
                        "Resource": "arn:aws:timestream:us-east-
1:<account_ID>:database/study/table/student"
                }
        ]
}
```

Amazon Timestream does not support resource-based IAM policies, but you can use tag-based access control, as in the following policy, which allows access only to the tables that are tagged with Owner with a value equal to the username:

```
{
    "Version": "2012-10-17",
    "Statement": [
        {
            "Sid": "ReadOnlyAccessTaggedTables",
            "Effect": "Allow",
            "Action": "timestream:Select",
            "Resource": "arn:aws:timestream:us-east-
1:123456789012:database/study/table/*",
            "Condition": {
                "StringEquals": {"aws:ResourceTag/Owner": "${aws:username}"}
            }
        }
    ]
}
```

API calls to Amazon Timestream are captured by AWS CloudTrail for table change operations, not for query or write records.

To access Timestream from your applications in a VPC, you should create a VPC endpoint for Timestream and then apply policies to allow the action you need to this endpoint.

Amazon Timestream Data Resilience and Backup

Amazon Timestream achieves data resilience by replicating the data to three AZs by default.

It is important to know that the service doesn't offer point-in-time recovery or snapshots to extract backups from your tables. If you have some requirements, you may want to extract data and put it on Amazon S3, for example.

Amazon OpenSearch Service

OpenSearch is not a topic of this certification exam, but it's here because it's a related topic. You can skip this section if you're focused on the exam only.

AWS has a managed service search engine, the Amazon OpenSearch Service, that provides an installation of OpenSearch Dashboards. The service is based on OpenSearch, an open-source search engine powered by Apache Lucene and derived from Elasticsearch 7.10.2 and Kibana 7.10.2.

Amazon OpenSearch Service has gained several features such as SQL syntax support to interact with the data, available in the OpenSearch project, or the Ultrawarm storage technology based on OpenSearch's own storage layers. You will learn in this chapter about the basics of Amazon OpenSearch Service.

Amazon OpenSearch Service Domain Architecture

Although you can launch a publicly accessible Amazon OpenSearch Service domain, it is highly recommended that you keep your cluster inside a VPC and then create an application load balancer on top of it, if you need to expose your domain to the Internet.

Amazon OpenSearch Service domain architecture is based on nodes, as shown in Figure 8.14, and at least one data node is required to have a domain. Ultrawarm nodes and dedicated master nodes are optional.

Loading Data to Amazon OpenSearch Service

Elasticsearch has a long history of receiving data from Logstash. This strategy usually uses Beats, a free open platform to send data to Logstash or Elasticsearch. You can find tens of convenient types of beats in the community, such as filebeats, metricbeat, packetbeat, and winlogbeat, each one specialized on the source format. You can use this strategy with Amazon OpenSearch Service as well.

FIGURE 8.14 OpenSearch domain architecture

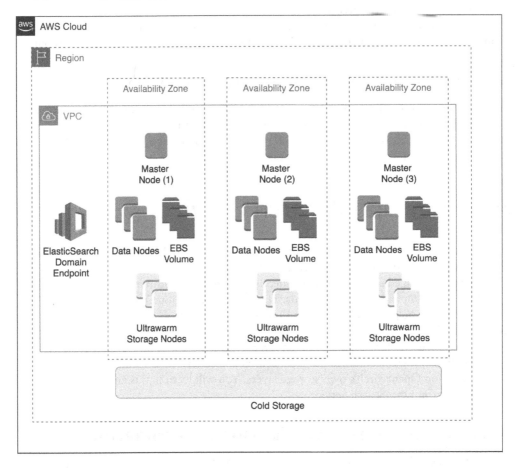

Of course, there are several ways to load data from other AWS services like Amazon Kinesis Data Firehose, Amazon CloudWatch Logs with an AWS Lambda function, AWS IoT, Amazon Kinesis Data Streams, and Amazon API Gateway with an AWS Lambda function.

Searching for Data in Amazon OpenSearch Service

To search for data, Elasticsearch APIs provide a simple way to interact with indexed data in Amazon OpenSearch Service.

A simple call would be a GET on the Amazon OpenSearch Service domain URL followed by /search_?/q=, as in the following examples:

- A query that searches for the word *certification* in all indexes and fields of the search-mystudent-domain domain:

  ```
  GET https://search-mystudent-domain.us-east-
  1.es.amazonaws.com/_search?q=certification
  ```

- A query that searches for the word *certification* in the my_student_index index and only in the title field of this domain:

```
GET https://search-mystudent-domain.us-east-1.es.amazonaws.com/
my_student_index/_search?q=title:certification
```

You can use the SQL interaction with Amazon OpenSearch Service as in the following example:

```
SELECT author, book_name, book_description
FROM books
WHERE address = MATCH_QUERY('Jeff')
```

For the certification exam you don't need to master search syntax, but as Elasticsearch has an expressive usage, it would be good to explore other interesting search possibilities, such as KNN search, asynchronous search, or custom packages (dictionaries).

Amazon OpenSearch Service Monitoring

Several metrics are collected by Amazon CloudWatch for Amazon OpenSearch Service, and some of them are displayed in Amazon OpenSearch Service's own console.

Amazon OpenSearch Service Scalability

Amazon OpenSearch Service domains can be scaled to handle a heavier workload or more data, so you can scale a domain by adding more data or Ultrawarm nodes, increasing EBS storage size and changing node types.

Amazon OpenSearch Service Security

Launching an Amazon OpenSearch Service domain inside a VPC is always the best option. Using domains inside a VPC actually uses one Elastic Network Interface (ENI) for each data node with a private IP address, and you protect the access to them using *VPC security groups*.

Encryption at rest using AWS KMS is also available for the Amazon OpenSearch Service, and this includes all indexes, logs, swap files, application directories, and automated snapshots.

Amazon OpenSearch Service uses node-to-node TLS 1.2 encryption inside the VPC by default.

Amazon OpenSearch Service Data Resilience and Backup

Amazon OpenSearch Service sets a replica of each index using one replica by default for the indexes, but you can increase them to a desired *number_of_replicas*. This is useful to prevent data lost in the case of node failure.

In a production domain environment running in a multi-AZ configuration, the replicas of index shards will be distributed in different availability zones and also prevent data lost in the case of AZ failures.

Automated hourly snapshots are provided for Elasticsearch version 5.3 or later by Amazon OpenSearch Service, and manual snapshots can be taken to prepare for a recovery or when moving data from one cluster to another; as the snapshots are stored in Amazon S3, standard S3 charges apply.

Summary

This chapter introduced the information latency concept and three information systems that can be used in different approaches: Amazon Redshift for a data warehouse with an information latency of minutes, Amazon Timestream for near real-time latency with advanced features considering time-series data, and Amazon OpenSearch Service for near real-time ingestion, processing, and search engine functionality.

All three systems can be used to extract information through complex or simple queries.

For time-series data, such as IoT sensor data or infrastructure metrics that you want to store and analyze, Amazon Timestream is a natural choice. For large datasets of historical multidimensional data and for traditional data warehouses, Amazon Redshift is the best option. For full-text engine and operational data with near real-time latency, Amazon Open-Search Service is the best option.

Amazon Kinesis Firehose is a streaming tool that can be used to load data into Amazon Redshift, using the proper COPY command, and to load data into Amazon OpenSearch Service, performing a buffering layer for the records to be loaded and optimizing the write operations.

Amazon Kinesis Data Analytics for Flink can be used to ingest data to Amazon Timestream and Amazon OpenSearch Service. AWS Lambda functions also can be used for this purpose.

All three services—Redshift, OpenSearch, and Timestream—support encryption at rest and in transit. Amazon OpenSearch Service and Amazon Redshift provide private access inside a VPC by default, and Amazon Timestream provides private access via a VPC endpoint.

AWS IAM is used to grant and prevent access to Amazon OpenSearch Service, Amazon Timestream, and the Amazon Redshift Data API. Regular database grants can be used to grant object permissions to users and user groups in Redshift, which allows you to set up fine-grained access.

Exam Essentials

Know that AWS offers analytics capabilities on managed service databases for different use cases. Amazon Redshift offers a full data warehouse, plus a flexible way to join internal data with data lake data. Amazon Timestream provides a fast, near real-time ingestion and analysis of time-series data.

Understand that database solutions for analytics have different information latency. When choosing services for different information latency requirements, note that Amazon Timestream is faster than Redshift and OpenSearch, because it ingests data in-memory, but it fits only for time-series data.

Amazon Redshift has a higher information latency compared to Timestream and Open-Search, due to its columnar storage format. It cannot handle direct inserts well and uses the COPY command to enforce a copy of data on Amazon S3 before it goes to Redshift. In terms of information latency, Amazon OpenSearch is between Timestream and Redshift, as you can ingest data directly to it, so it's faster than Redshift, but the acknowledgment and availability of data take longer than Timestream.

Choose the right tool for the right job. Although all the use cases presented in this chapter could be addressed by a regular relational database like MySQL, when we scale the solution, the price, performance, and effort to build are really better if we choose the proper databases, such as Amazon Redshift, Amazon Timestream, and Amazon OpenSearch, to perform complex analysis with multidimensional queries, time-series queries, and search jobs.

Know how to build a security environment for analytics databases. Using VPC private subnets for Amazon Redshift and Amazon OpenSearch Service and using VPC endpoints for Amazon Timestream, along with encryption at rest and in transit, are the keys to start building a secure analytical environment. Security groups should allow only specific applications that need to query and ingest data, filtering them by their security group or source IP address in case they are on premises.

Exercises

For assistance in completing the following exercises, refer to the User Guides at docs
.aws.amazon.com/redshift/latest/dg/welcome.html, hdocs.aws.amazon.com/
timestream/latest/developerguide/what-is-timestream.html, and docs.aws
.amazon.com/opensearch-service/latest/developerguide/what-is.html.

EXERCISE 8.1

Create an Amazon Redshift Cluster

This exercise guides you through how to launch and load data into a Redshift cluster.

1. Open the Amazon Redshift console at `console.aws.amazon.com/redshift`.

2. Choose the N. Virginia (us-east-1) AWS region to create the cluster.

3. Choose CLUSTERS, and then click Create Cluster.

4. In the Cluster Configuration section, specify values for Cluster Identifier, Node Type, and Nodes.

   - Use the cluster identifier **myfirstcluster**.

   - Select Production for the question *What are you planning to use this cluster for?* (Otherwise, you cannot specify the size by yourself.)

   - Set Node Type to dc2.large.

   - Configure a cluster of two nodes by setting Nodes to 2.

5. Select some sample data and check Load Sample Data.

6. Use the following values:

   - Admin username: Type **student**.

   - Admin user password: Type a value for the password.

7. Select Cluster Permissions. Do not set any IAM role now, as you will not need it for the exercise, because we are not accessing data in S3.

8. Click Create Cluster.

Do not skip Exercise 8.6, where you'll destroy your cluster and avoid unwanted costs.

EXERCISE 8.2

Use the Query Editor to Create and Interact with a Table

In this exercise, you'll interact with a Redshift cluster using its own editor. You need to complete Exercise 8.1 before completing this exercise.

1. At the Redshift console (`console.aws.amazon.com/redshift`), choose QUERY EDITOR, version 1.

2. Click Connect To Database in your cluster.

3. Use temporary credentials and then enter the values that you used when you created the cluster, as follows:

   - Cluster: Choose myfirstcluster.

   - Database name: Type **dev**.

   - Database user: Type **student**.

4. Click Connect.

   Notice that you have the following sample tables in the `public` schema:

   - `category`

   - `date`

   - `event`

   - `listing`

   - `sales`

   - `users`

   - `venue`

5. Expand each table by clicking the small triangle before it so you can examine its columns.

6. Examine the data of each table by clicking . . . (three dots) beside the table. Choose to preview the data.

   You may need to scroll down to see the results.

7. Repeat steps 5 and 6 until you are done with every table.

8. Type the following SELECT statement to discover the top 50 buyers among all the events, and click Run to execute it:

```
SELECT lastname||', '||firstname, event.eventname, total_quantity
FROM   (SELECT buyerid,eventid, sum(qtysold) total_quantity
         FROM  sales
         GROUP BY buyerid, eventid
         ORDER BY total_quantity desc limit 50) Q, users, event
WHERE Q.buyerid = users.userid AND
Q.eventid = event.eventid
ORDER BY Q.total_quantity desc;
```

9. Click the plus sign (+) to open a new tab.

10. Type the following SELECT statement and click Run to get the venue's available seats as emptyseats according to the sales by date:

```
SELECT q.dateid, venue.venuename, total_quantity, venueseats,
case
when venueseats>0 then venueseats-total_quantity
else null
end as emptyseats
FROM    (SELECT eventid,dateid, sum(qtysold) total_quantity
         FROM  sales
         GROUP BY dateid, eventid) Q, venue, event
WHERE Q.eventid = event.eventid
AND event.venueid = venue.venueid
ORDER BY total_quantity desc limit 50;
```

11. Click Clear.

Use the Query Editor to Insert Data and Export ResultSet

Perform this exercise to download results and manipulate data using the editor. You need to complete Exercise 8.1 first.

1. At the Redshift console (console.aws.amazon.com/redshift), choose EDITOR.

2. Click Connect To Database in your cluster.

3. Use temporary credentials and then enter the values that you used when you created the cluster, as follows:

   ▪ Cluster: Choose myfirstcluster.

   ▪ Database name: Type **dev**.

   ▪ Database user: Type **student**.

4. Click Connect.

5. Choose Public for the schema to create a new table based on that schema.

6. Type the following statement and click Run to execute it:

```
create table books(
bookname varchar (60),
bookauthor varchar(60)
);
```

7. Choose Clear.

8. Type the following statement and click Run to add rows to your table:

```
insert into books values
('Book Example','John Doe'),
('My exercises','Mike Doe');
```

9. Choose Clear.

10. Type the following simple query to retrieve the data:

```
select * from books;
```

The query displays the results:

bookname.	bookauthor
Book Fxample	John Doe
My exercise	Mike Doe

11. Click Export to download the query results as a CSV, TXT, or HTML file.

EXERCISE 8.4

Take a Manual Snapshot of Your Cluster

In this exercise, you will create a Redshift manual snapshot that is useful before significant changes as a backup of that exact time or to create a new cluster from this snapshot. You need to complete Exercise 8.1 first.

1. At the Redshift console (`console.aws.amazon.com/redshift/`), click Clusters.

2. Click the check box to select your cluster, myfirstcluster.

3. With your cluster selected, click Actions and then Create Snapshot.

4. Type a snapshot identifier: **manual-snapshot-1**.

5. Select a snapshot retention: 1 day.

6. Create a snapshot.

EXERCISE 8.5

Explore the Resize Options for Your Cluster

In this exercise, you will practice how to resize a Redshift cluster. You need to complete Exercise 8.1 before doing this exercise.

1. At the Redshift console (`console.aws.amazon.com/redshift/`), choose Clusters.

2. Click the check box to select your cluster, myfirstcluster.

3. With your cluster selected, click Actions and then Resize.

4. Select Elastic Resize.

5. Explore the Node Type option.

    Notice that only a few options are available based on your current cluster size: `ds2.xlarge`, `ra3.xplus`, `ra3.4xlarge`, `dc2.large`.

    For each node type, you can explore the number of nodes available; for example, for the ra3.xplus, you can use only two or four nodes; for `ra3.4xlarge`, you can use two, three, or four nodes.

6. Choose Cancel.

EXERCISE 8.6

Destroy Your Cluster

Perform this exercise to avoid unwanted costs and destroy the Redshift cluster you created to practice. Do not skip this exercise.

1. At the Redshift console (`console.aws.amazon.com/redshift`), click Clusters.

2. Click the check box to select your cluster, myfirstcluster.

3. With your cluster selected, click Actions and then Delete.

4. Uncheck Create Final Snapshot.

5. Click Delete Cluster.

EXERCISE 8.7

Create an Amazon Timestream Database

In this exercise, you will practice how to create a Timestream database and use a sample dataset.

1. Go to Amazon Timestream console at `console.aws.amazon.com/timestream/home`.

2. Click Create Database.

3. Choose Sample Database so that you can play around with the data.

4. Type a name for the database: **sampleDB**.

5. Choose IoT Sample Data Sets.

6. Check the Single-Measure button for the type of time-series records.

7. Click the Create Database button.

    A green message will appear at the top level of your AWS console: "Successfully created database sampleDB. Next, run a sample query in the Query Editor."

EXERCISE 8.8

Run Sample Queries on Amazon Timestream

In this exercise, you will use the Timestream Query Editor to interact with the data.

1. Click the Run Sample Query button in the upper right of the Timestream console.

2. Select a sample query of your choice from the list of sample queries, making sure to choose queries with an "IoT" value for the Scenario attribute.

    Amazon Timestream will load the query into the Query Editor.

3. Click Run.

4. Examine the query structure. Most of the queries aggregate the measures by a time-stamp type column.

5. For queries with a `bin` function, change the aggregation time by using the bin with the time you want.

6. For queries with the `ago` function, choose a short period of time to see changes in the query result.

7. Click the Sample Queries tab to choose another query, run it, and repeat the steps of changing the `ago` and `bin` function parameters.

EXERCISE 8.9

Delete Your Amazon Timestream Database

Perform this exercise to avoid unwanted costs and destroy the Timestream database you created to practice. Do not skip this exercise.

1. Click Tables in the upper left of the Amazon Timestream console.

2. Select the IoT table you created along with the database in Exercise 8.7.

3. Click Delete.

4. Confirm the deletion by typing **delete** in the text box, and click the Delete button.

5. Click Databases in the upper left of the Amazon Timestream console.

6. Select the sampleDB database you created in Exercise 8.7.

7. Click Delete.

8. Confirm the deletion by entering **delete** in the text box, and click the Delete button.

EXERCISE 8.10

Create an Amazon OpenSearch Service Domain

In this exercise, you will create an OpenSearch domain.

1. Go to the OpenSearch Service console at `console.aws.amazon.com/es/home`.

2. Click Create A New Domain.

3. Type an OpenSearch domain name: **myfirstdomain**.

4. Leave Enable Custom Endpoint unchecked.

5. Choose Development And Testing for the deployment type.

6. Choose the latest OpenSearch version and then click Next.

7. Leave Auto-Tune enabled.

8. Choose the t3.small.search instance type, select 1-AZ for availability zones, and set the value of number of nodes to 1.

9. Leave Data Nodes Storage at the default.

10. Do not enable dedicated master nodes.

11. Click Next.

12. Select Public Access for the network setup.

This is for the exercise only; do not use this option with real data.

13. Click the Enable Fine-Grained Access Control button.

14. Create a master user.

- Choose a master username.

- Choose a master password.

For now, ignore the SAML authentication and Amazon Cognito authentication sections.

15. For Domain Access Policy, choose Only Use Fine-Grained Access Control. In this tutorial, fine-grained access control handles authentication, not the domain access policy.

16. Keep the encryption settings at their default values.

17. Ignore the tags option and click Create.

18. Confirm your domain configuration and choose Confirm.

New domains typically take 15–30 minutes to initialize but can take longer depending on the configuration. After your domain initializes, make note of its endpoint.

EXERCISE 8.11

Log In to Your Amazon OpenSearch Service Domain

In this exercise, you will explore a sample data set inside OpenSearch.

1. Go to the OpenSearch Service console and select your domain.

2. Click the OpenSearch Dashboards URL link.

3. Use your master user credentials.

4. Click the Add Data button to play with the sample data.

5. Select the Global Tenant check box and click Confirm.

6. Select Sample eCommerce orders by clicking Add Data.

7. Click View Data to explore the dashboards based on the e-commerce data.

8. Use [eCommerce] Controls to filter data by manufacturer, category, or quantity.

9. Select Discover in the top-left corner menu to view the raw data.

EXERCISE 0.12

Delete Your Amazon OpenSearch Service Domain

In this exercise, you will remove the OpenSearch domain you created to avoid the costs of unused domains.

Do not skip this exercise.

1. At the OpenSearch console, select your domain.

2. Click Delete.

3. Type the name of your domain in the text box to confirm the deletion.

4. Click the Delete button.

Review Questions

1. Your customer wants to build a traditional data warehouse in AWS and is concerned about the possibility of keeping their star schema design required by their business users' dashboard. What is a possible solution?

   A. The customer can use Amazon Timestream and bring their star schema design; they can also use primary keys and foreign keys to improve their query plans.

   B. There is no feasible solution, as the options for data warehouses in AWS don't support star schema table modeling.

   C. The customer can use Amazon Redshift and bring their star schema design; they can also use primary keys and foreign keys to improve their query plans.

   D. The customer can use Amazon Redshift, although it supports only denormalized tables. It's possible to create views and simulate primary keys and foreign keys to improve visibility for business users.

2. You are working on a project that will handle millions of events per minute coming from thousands of Internet of Things (IoT) device sensors, and it will be required to compare device sensors over time values using statistics such as average, mean, and standard deviation. What is a managed service solution with low cost to address this requirement?

   A. Use AWS IoT to receive sensor data. Install a time-series database in containers using the managed service AWS Fargate and create an AWS Lambda function to ingest the data in the time-series database. Perform the queries using a SQL client with a JDBC driver.

   B. Directly ingest the data into Amazon DynamoDB and use DynamoDB APIs to perform queries over the time-series data.

   C. Use AWS IoT to receive sensor data, and create an Amazon Timestream database and table to receive the data. Create a rule in AWS IoT to ingest the data into a Timestream table. Perform the queries using a SQL client with a JDBC driver or the Amazon Timestream console.

   D. Use AWS IoT to receive sensor data, and create an Amazon Neptune database and table to receive the data. Create a rule in AWS IoT to ingest the data into a Neptune table. Perform the queries using a SQL client with a JDBC driver or Amazon Neptune console.

3. You talked to a customer who has a multiterabyte on-premises data warehouse using commercial databases and wants to migrate to AWS. The customer asked you for a simple solution, with a single endpoint, that can address scalability for further growth without hours of downtime; it's a goal also to reduce current storage costs. Choose the option that best addresses the customer's needs.

   A. Offload the storage to S3 and enable access to the data through AWS Storage Gateway for the on-premises environment. Activate Dynamic Migration Services to migrate to Amazon Redshift while converting the database objects with the AWS Object Conversion Tool (OCT).

   B. Convert and migrate their database objects using the AWS Schema Conversion Tool (SCT), along with its data extractor agents, to Amazon Redshift. Use Redshift managed storage for frequent data access, use Amazon S3 for historical infrequent data access, use

Redshift Spectrum to query the data, use concurrency scale for peak scale needs, and use elastic resize for increasing nodes.

C. Create an Amazon Aurora MySQL database, enable read-replica for reporting, migrate the data using AWS Transfer family services to Amazon S3, use the COPY command to load the data from Amazon S3 to Aurora, and keep the historical data in Amazon S3 to be accessed with an AWS Lambda function.

D. Migrate their database objects using the Schema Conversion Tool (SCT), along with its data extractor agents, to Amazon Redshift. Use Redshift SSD storage for frequent data access, use Redshift HDD storage for historical infrequent data access, use elastic resize for peak scale needs, and use concurrency scale for increasing nodes.

4. A customer who already uses Amazon Redshift has a website and wants to collect streaming data to enable analysts to query the data along with other Redshift tables. The customer requires a low-code and easy to set up solution to load the data to Redshift and enable retry in case of failure. What is the best approach?

A. Ask the customer to stream the data to an Apache Kafka installed in an EC2 instance, and create Kafka consumers with Fargate to ingest data on Redshift.

B. Ask the customer to stream the data to Amazon S3; create an AWS Lambda function using the COPY command, triggered by S3; and ingest the data to Redshift.

C. Ask the customer to stream the data to an Amazon Kinesis Data Firehose and enable Amazon Redshift as a destination for Kinesis Firehose.

D. Create an Amazon API Gateway backed by an AWS Lambda function that inserts the data into Redshift and stream the data to the API Gateway.

5. You need to load 100 GB from flat files to an Amazon Redshift cluster from your on-premises environment. Your Redshift cluster is a four-node ra3.4xlarge, with 48 vCPU, 16 slices, and 384 GB. You need to optimize network bandwidth to transfer the data and load the data as fast as you can. What are the steps you would perform to load this data?

A. Create a single file compressed with BZIP2. Transfer the file to an Amazon S3 bucket with the AWS CLI. Load the file using the COPY command using the PARALLEL parameter, directly from Amazon S3.

B. Create a single file compressed with GZIP. Transfer the file to Amazon S3 bucket with the AWS CLI. Load the file using the COPY command using a manifest file from Amazon S3.

C. Create files in a multiple of 384, compressed with BZIP2; calculate a size of a few kilobytes per file generated of compressed data. Transfer the files to an Amazon S3 bucket with the AWS CLI to a common path. Create a manifest file and load the files using the COPY command directly from Amazon S3.

D. Create files in a number multiple of 16, compressed with BZIP2; calculate a size of few gigabytes per file generated of compressed data. Transfer the files to an Amazon S3 bucket with AWS CLI to a common path. Create a manifest file and load the files using the COPY command directly from Amazon S3.

6. Your customer is concerned about security and wants to encrypt the data you need to load into an Amazon Redshift cluster. How could you use encryption on the client side and load this data to Amazon Redshift with minimal effort?

   A. Encrypt the data on the client side using an AWS KMS customer-managed symmetric key (CSE-CMK), and compress the data with GZIP. Load the data to Amazon S3, use an Amazon EC2 instance, and uncompress the data before loading it to Amazon Redshift.

   B. Encrypt the data on the client side using an AWS KMS customer-managed symmetric key (CSE-CMK), and compress the data with BZIP2. Load the data into Amazon S3, and use the COPY command with the appropriate ENCRYPTED BZIP2 parameters to load the encrypted, compressed files into Amazon Redshift.

   C. Encrypt the data on the client side using LUKS for encryption, and compress the data with GZIP. Load the data into Amazon S3, use an Amazon EC2 instance, and uncompress the data before loading it into Amazon Redshift with the COPY command.

   D. Encrypt the data using a key generated by you, and compress the data using BZIP2. Load the key into the Redshift Key Manager. Use the COPY command along with ENCRYPTED, and use the BZIP2 format parameters to load the data into the Redshift cluster.

7. What are the optimized ways to load external data to Redshift from files and from streaming?

   A. Load files into Amazon S3 and then use the COPY command for data in files and use Amazon Kinesis Data Firehose for streaming data.

   B. Use an AWS Lambda function to load data into Redshift for files in Amazon S3 or streaming using INSERT row by row.

   C. Use an AWS Lambda function to load data to Redshift for files in Amazon S3 or streaming using the UPSERT command.

   D. Load files into Amazon S3 and then use the COPY command for data in files and Amazon Kinesis Data Analytics for streaming data.

8. Consider you are migrating workloads to AWS and now need to define what are best choices of target databases for cost efficiency for your data warehouse, for your time-series data, and for operational logs and dashboards. What AWS services would you use for each workload?

   A. Use Amazon Redshift for a data warehouse, Amazon Aurora for time-series data, and Amazon OpenSearch Service with Kibana for operational logs and dashboards.

   B. Use Amazon Aurora for a data warehouse, Amazon DynamoDB for time-series data, and Amazon OpenSearch Service with Kibana for operational logs and dashboards.

   C. Use Amazon Neptune for a data warehouse, Amazon Timestream for time-series data, and Amazon OpenSearch Service with Kibana for operational logs and dashboards.

   D. Use Amazon Redshift for a data warehouse, Amazon Timestream for time-series data, and Amazon OpenSearch Service with Kibana for operational logs and dashboards.

9. Your customer asks you to create a database in AWS to handle time-series data with two very different payloads with different retention time requirements. The database should scale from a few records per second in the development phase to thousands of records per second in production. The customer would like to perform comparison between periods using SQL queries to gather statistics on the data with a data latency of a few milliseconds. What would be an easy, cost-efficient way to deliver this database?

A. Using Amazon Timestream, create a standard database for the application, and create a single table to handle both the different payloads with a customized data retention per payload. Use autoscaling groups for Amazon Timestream.

B. Using Amazon DynamoDB, create a single table to handle both the different payloads with a customized TTL per payload, and set up an on-demand table for capacity planning.

C. Using Amazon Redshift, start with a single-node environment and add more nodes when you need them. Create a routine to delete old data using an AWS Lambda function based on a column timestamp.

D. Using Amazon Timestream, create a standard database for the application, and create one table for each of the different payloads, with the proper data retention set up for each table. It will scale automatically.

10. You have an Amazon Timestream table and need to improve performance for queries using the latest 24 hours. You need to retain the data for only 1 month in the table. What is the best approach with a low cost?

A. Set the memory store retention to 24 hours and magnetic store retention to one month.

B. There's no way to improve performance in Amazon Timestream.

C. Create a DAX in front of Amazon Timestream to improve performance and set the DAX TTL to 24 hours.

D. Set magnetic store retention to 24 hours and memory store retention to 1 month.

Chapter

9

Discovering Relationships Using Graph Databases

THE AWS CERTIFIED DATABASE – SPECIALTY EXAM OBJECTIVES COVERED IN THIS CHAPTER MAY INCLUDE, BUT ARE NOT LIMITED TO, THE FOLLOWING:

✓ **Domain 1: Workload-Specific Database Design**

- 1.1 Select appropriate database services for specific types of data and workloads.
- 1.2 Determine strategies for disaster recovery and high availability.
- 1.3 Design database solutions for performance, compliance, and scalability.

✓ **Domain 2: Deployment and migration**

- 2.2 Determine data preparation and migration strategies.

✓ **Domain 3: Management and Operations**

- 3.2 Determine backup and restore strategies.
- 3.3 Manage the operational environment of a database solution.

✓ **Domain 4: Monitoring and Troubleshooting**

- 4.3 Optimize database performance.

✓ **Domain 5: Database Security**

- 5.3 Determine access control and authentication mechanisms.

Most developers used to choose relational databases for several purposes; in fact, they were the only choice available for most applications. Relational databases are efficient for storing transactional data. However, modern applications have scalability, performance, and the ability to handle the data format requirements appropriately. Exploring highly connected data use cases requires more specific data stores, so graph databases have taken over.

Graph databases can store highly connected nodes, properties, and relationships. They can explore similar attributes or properties much faster, enabling the correlation of data according to similar characteristics.

Graph Databases

Graph databases are used to store highly connected data and enable navigation in those relationships.

Graph databases store the information inside *nodes* (also named *vertices*). These nodes can be anything such as a person, a company, a product, or food. Graphs also enable the creation of a relationship between nodes with a direction representing a meaningful correlation between the nodes, like a relationship that means that a person likes a certain kind of food.

The relationships are the predicates or edges. Edges represent the relationships between entities/vertices in the property graph data model, and the edges must have a label name and a direction. A *predicate* is used to state the predicate of a statement in the RDF model.

Each edge has a type and direction from one vertex (starting from) to another (destination).

Both vertices and edges may have additional properties to hold characteristics. For example, a node or vertex representing a person may have properties such as name, age, weight, and height. And the predicate or edge that represents the relationship (`works_for`) between a person and a company may have the property job role.

These databases connect specific data points (nodes/vertices) and create relationships (predicates/edges) in graphs that users can access with queries. Nodes can represent customers, companies, or any data to represent relevant information.

Graph databases manage relationships between nodes using edges, so users can easily understand the relationship and consequently more quickly explore the data. A relational database would require recursive SQL queries for this use case, and performance could degrade as the table size grows or the number of recursions increases, whereas graph databases store both the nodes and predicates as part of the data structure; as a result, this data exploration has better performance compared to a relational implementation.

Figure 9.1 shows how graph databases store data. The nodes in light gray and dark gray represent the people; the lines represent the friendship (edges) between the nodes. The edges represent only the friendship among this group of people, but you can create many different relationships among the nodes.

FIGURE 9.1   Graph databases storing data

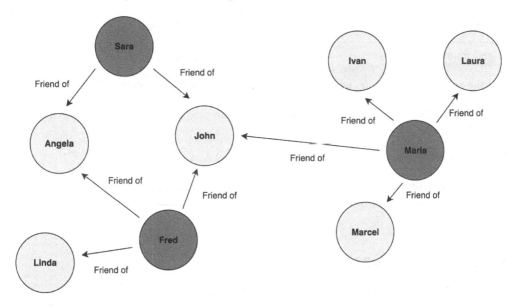

When to Use Graph Databases

Relational databases and graph databases are developed to run different application requirements.

Relational databases are very efficient for the following:

- Handling highly transactional application requirements.

- Applications that require primary keys, foreign keys, and the other constraints (check and not null, for example) implemented in the RDBMS database.

- Applications that require data lock control during transaction execution. For example, a billing application must manipulate data from different tables and keep the data integrity of the entire transaction.

- Applications that require the SQL language.

Graph databases are very efficient for the following:

- Modeling data interconnections and writing complex queries that extract real-world information from the graph
- Retrieving billions of rows to explore the relationships among the nodes
- Discovering similar patterns of relationships

Table 9.1 compares graph and relational databases.

TABLE 9.1   Comparing Graph and Relational Databases

Graph Databases	Relational Databases
Highly connected data	Complex models
Relationships represented by edges	Relationships represented by foreign keys
Programming languages: Gremlin, RDF, and Cypher	Programming language: declarative SQL
Flexible schema	Rigid schema
Graph traversal performance	SQL query performance

Common Use Cases

Graph databases are beneficial to develop the following:

- **Personalization and recommendations:** Graph databases are appropriate for handling relationships between information such as customer preferences, friends, and purchase history in a graph and query it to make personalized and relevant recommendations. A usual case is to make product suggestions to a consumer based on which products are purchased by other consumers who follow that same football team and have similar purchase histories. Or, you can identify people who have a friend in common but don't yet know each other and make a friendship recommendation.

- **Knowledge graphs:** The graph model is appropriate for identifying highly connected datasets. One example is to map tax policies and their differences across different countries. When an organization wants to go into a new region, it can recommend the set of tax policies that applies to that company.

- **Fraud detection:** A graph data model helps use relationships to process financial and acquisition transactions in near real time to detect fraud patterns more quickly. Neptune can execute efficient graph queries to identify relationship standards like multiple people associated with a personal email address or people using the same IP address but located at different physical addresses.

- **Network/IT operations:** Graph data models are appropriate for storing the connections of your network and use graph queries to answer questions like how many hosts are using a specific application. Amazon Neptune can hold and query billions of events to manage and secure your network. If you detect an event that is an anomaly, you can use Amazon Neptune to quickly understand how it might affect your network by querying a graph pattern using the attributes of the event. You can query the Amazon Neptune graph to discover additional devices that may be affected. A typical use case is detecting a malicious file on a host. Amazon Neptune can locate connections between the hosts that shared the malicious file and track the original host that downloaded it for the first time.

- **Life sciences:** You can use graph databases to store disease and gene interaction models and search for graph patterns within protein pathways to find other genes that may be associated with a disease. You can model chemical compounds as a graph and query for similar patterns in molecular structures.

Amazon Neptune

Amazon Neptune is a fast, reliable, fully managed database service that enables you to develop and run applications that require exploring highly connected data.

Amazon Neptune is a purpose-built, scalable graph database engine optimized for keeping billions of relationships and querying the graph with millisecond latency.

High-Level Architecture

An Amazon Neptune database cluster must have one primary database instance (writer), and you can add up to 15 read replica database instances.

The Amazon Neptune instances in a cluster share the same managed storage layer. The storage accessed by Amazon Neptune is natively reliable and highly available.

Figure 9.2 represents the Amazon Neptune architecture. At the bottom, the purpose-built shared storage is distributed across three availability zones, having two copies of each protection group in each availability zone. In total, Amazon Neptune cluster has six copies of each protection group. The middle part represents the Amazon Neptune cluster instances having one mandatory primary/writer instance and 15 additional optional read replica instances. The Amazon Neptune cluster makes the writer and reader endpoints available for the Gremlin and SPARQL query languages, from where the apps can reach the graph database instance and retrieve the data.

FIGURE 9.2 Amazon Neptune architecture

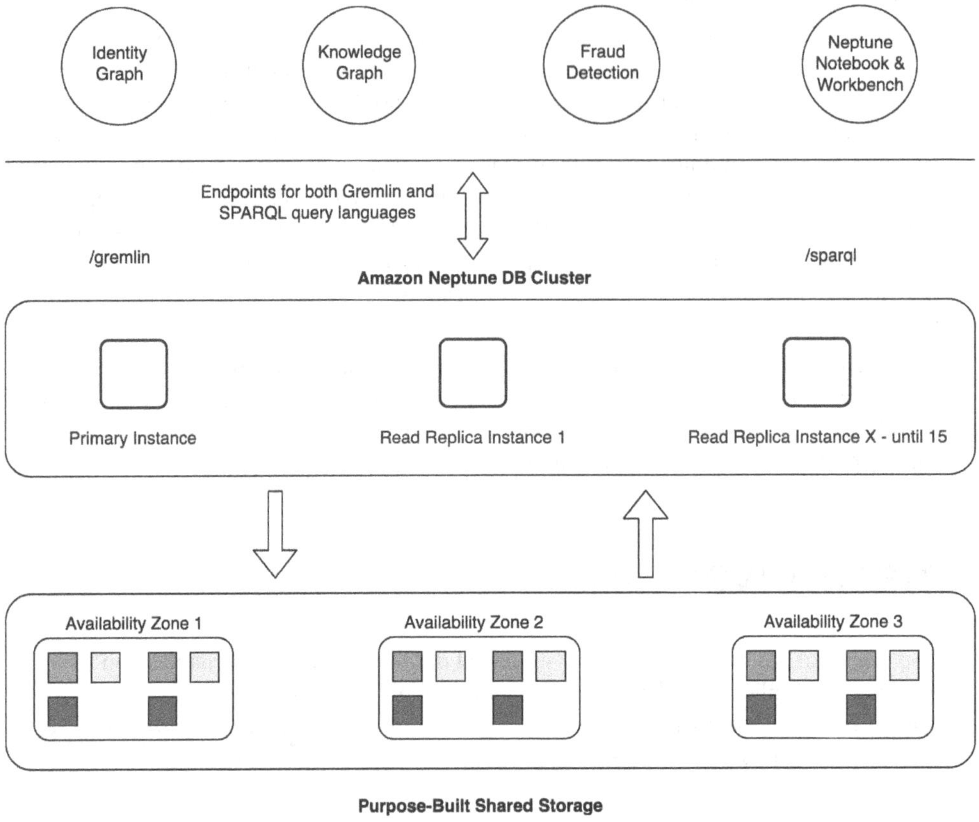

Graph Models and Query Languages
=================================

Graph Models and Query Languages

Amazon Neptune supports the following graph models and languages:

- **Property graph:** The *property graph data model* represents graph elements by *vertices* (nodes) and *edges* (relationships). *Vertices* represent entities from the real world in the domain. Edges represent the relationships between entities/vertices, and the edges must have a label name and a direction. In this model, edges without two connecting vertices aren't allowed. The property graph API is the open standard Apache TinkerPop project. It provides the imperative traversal Gremlin programming language. Gremlin is the language to write traversals on property graphs, and several open-source and vendor implementations support it.

- **W3C's RDF:** *Resource Description Framework (RDF)* encodes the resource descriptions in subject-predicate-object triples format. While the property graph model chunks data into record-like vertices and edges, RDF creates a fine-grained domain representation of the data. RDF adopts the Semantic Web standard defined by the W3C. The SPARQL query language for RDF allows users to write declarative graph queries to explore data from RDF graph models.

Developers prefer property graphs because they are used to relational models. Information architects prefer RDF because of the flexibility for modeling complex information domains. There are several existing public domains in RDF—for example, Wikidata and PubChem (a database of chemical molecules).

- **openCypher**: Neo4j developed the Cypher Query Language and open-sourced it in 2015. openCypher supports HTTPS endpoints and the Bolt protocol. The Bolt protocol is a statement-oriented client-server protocol initially developed by Neo4j and licensed as the Creative Commons 3.0 Attribution-ShareAlike. It's client-driven, meaning that the client always initiates message exchanges.

Property-graph query language is a query language inspired by the SQL language. Gremlin and openCypher are property-graph query languages. They're used for different purposes and also complement each other.

Figure 9.3 represents the same friendship initially used as an example among Marcel, Maria, Laura, and other people in this chapter. Examples of query languages include Gremlin, SPARQL, and openCypher, using the representation of friendship.

FIGURE 9.3 Graph databases storing data

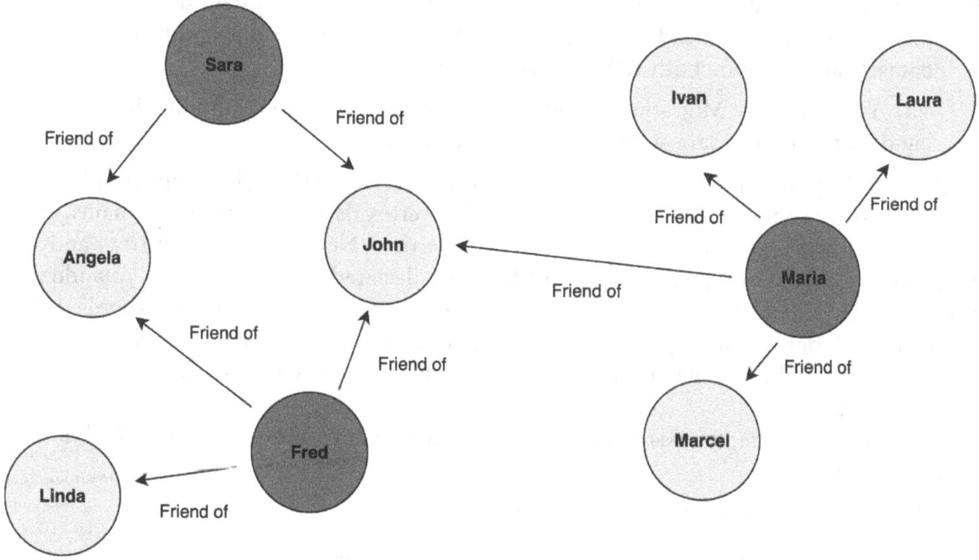

The following is an example of the query using Gremlin to return the names of the friends of Marcel's friends:

```
g.V().has('name', 'marcel').out('friend').out('friend').values('name')
```

The following example uses a SPARQL query to return the names of the friends of Marcel's friends:

```
prefix : <#>

select ?names where {
  ?howard :name "Marcel" .
  ?howard :friend/:friend/:name ?names .
}
```

The following example demonstrates openCypher:

```
MATCH (user:User {name: 'Marcel'})-[r1:FRIEND]-()-[r2:FRIEND]
-(friend_of_a_friend)
RETURN friend_of_a_friend.name AS fofName
```

Using and Extracting Data from Amazon Neptune

Amazon Neptune offers the following methods to load graph data into it:

- You can use SPARQL INSERT statements or Gremlin addV and addE steps for small datasets. *addV* is a Gremlin statement to add vertices. *addE* is a Gremlin statement to add edges.

- The bulk loader command is faster for loading large amounts of data from external files and has less overhead than the query-language commands. It's optimized for large datasets and supports both RDF and Gremlin data.

- The AWS Database Migration Service (AWS DMS) is also a good option when importing data from other data sources like Amazon RDS.

Amazon Neptune allows you to query data using Gremlin, SPARQL, or openCypher.

Let's explore some examples using Gremlin. The vertex designates entities/domains, and the edges define directional relationships between vertices. Neptune Gremlin Vertex and Edge IDs are always of type String. If the ID is not declared in Gremlin when you add a vertex or edge, Gremlin generates a UUID and converts it to a string. The user-supplied IDs are supported, but they are optional in normal usage. However, the Neptune Load command requires all IDs to be specified using the ˜id field in the Neptune comma-separated values (CSV) format.

The following example adds a vertex with a label (person) and a property called name with value marcel:

```
g.addV('person').property('name', 'marcel')
```

The following example adds a vertex with a custom ID with a value of 1:

```
g.addV('person').property(id, '1').property('name', 'marcel')
```

Do not put quotation marks around the ˜id keyword.

The following example changes the property or adds a property if it doesn't exist:

```
g.V('1').property(single, 'name', 'teo')
```

When the single cardinality is declared, it adds a new value to the property, but only if it doesn't already appear in the set of values. If you didn't specify single, it appends the value to the property name. In this example, the command changed the property name of the vertex with id=1 from marcel to teo. We can confirm the change:

```
g.V('1').hasLabel('person').values('name')
==>teo
```

Let's return the value to marcel.

```
 g.V('1').property(single, 'name', 'marcel')
```

Let's also insert some additional vertices.

```
g.addV('person').property(id, '2').property('name', 'maria')
g.addV('person').property(id, '3').property('name', 'laura')
g.addV('person').property(id, '4').property('name', 'ivan')
g.addV('person').property(id, '5').property('name', 'john')
g.addV('person').property(id, '6').property('name', 'fred')
g.addV('person').property(id, '7').property('name', 'linda')
g.addV('person').property(id, '8').property('name', 'angela')
```

Here we're adding an edge because marcel (ID 1) is Maria's friend (ID 2):

```
g.V('1').addE('friend').to(__.V('2')).property('weight', 0.5).iterate()
```

Let's check who is Marcel's friend:

```
g.V().has('name', 'marcel').out('friend').valueMap()
==>{name=[maria]}
```

All statements other than the last statement must end in a terminating step, such as .next() or .iterate(); otherwise, they won't run.

Use .iterate() whenever you don't need the results to be serialized.

All statements are sent together and included in a single transaction and will succeed or fail together.

Using the following command, you can run a traversal to return all the vertices having the label person:

```
g.V().hasLabel('person').values('name')
==>maria
==>laura
==>john
==>ivan
==>angela
==>marcel
```

```
==>fred
```

```
==>linda
```

The following command will run a traversal and return key-value pairs for all vertices that marcel is a "friend of."

```
g.V().has('name', 'marcel').out('friend').valueMap()
==>{name=[maria]}
```

Storage Architecture

Amazon Neptune architecture is reliable, durable, and fault tolerant.

Amazon Neptune data relies on a cluster volume, a storage layer available to the compute nodes as a single virtual volume that uses solid-state disk (SSD) drives.

The storage layer in Amazon Neptune has the same architecture as the storage layer for Amazon Aurora. Amazon Neptune relies on a shared storage architecture that scales automatically, distributed across three availability zones. The cluster volume can grow to 128 tebibytes (TiB).

The Amazon Neptune storage volume uses Non-Volatile Memory Express (NVMe) SSD-based drivers. This storage volume's logical block (segment) allocates 10 gigabytes (GB). Each segment is replicated into six copies, distributing two copies to each of the three availability zones (AZs).

Data Resilience

Amazon Neptune automatically identifies defeats in the disk volumes within the virtual cluster volume.

When a segment of the disk volume fails, Neptune instantly fixes that segment, using the data from the other available disk volumes. This self-healing feature guarantees that the data in the repaired segment is current.

This self-healing architecture avoids data loss and minimizes the condition of restoring a point in time from a disk failure situation.

Read Replicas

Each Amazon Neptune database cluster must have one primary node that supports read/write operations. You can add up to 15 read replica instances to run the read-only queries.

The read replica instances need not be the same instance class as the primary node.

The read replica instances read the same shared storage cluster as the primary, as represented in Figure 9.4; therefore, the read replica instances return the queried data with a minimal lag, usually much less than 100 milliseconds.

FIGURE 9.4   Read replicas

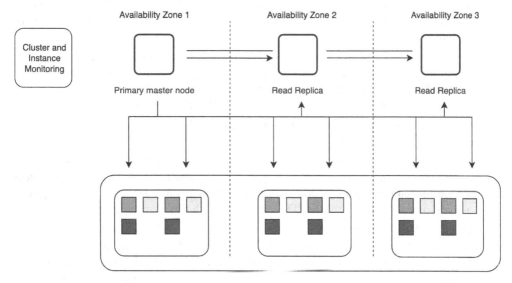

Purpose-Built Shared Storage

Amazon Neptune uses the endpoint method to make it transparent to the application connections so that you don't have to keep a fixed hostname in the application code or write specific failover logic for forwarding connections when some database instances are unavailable.

The following endpoints are available in an Amazon Neptune database cluster:

- **Cluster endpoint:** A *cluster endpoint* connects the primary database instance for that database cluster. Each Amazon Neptune database must have one primary database instance and its respective cluster endpoint.

   The cluster endpoint provides failover for reading/writing connections to the database cluster. The applications must use the cluster endpoint for all write operations (inserts, updates, deletes, and modifications on schemas by data definition language). You can configure the cluster endpoint for reading operations (queries), but for better scalability and readiness for scaling out read operations we strongly recommend using the reader endpoint.

   If the primary database instance fails, Amazon Neptune automatically fails over to an available read replica if there's one available. The failover process occurs with minimal service interruption; the database cluster keeps answering connection requests to the cluster endpoint from the newly promoted primary database instance.

- **Reader endpoint:** A *reader endpoint* connects the Amazon Neptune database cluster to one of the available read replicas for that database cluster. Each Amazon Neptune database cluster always has a reader endpoint, even if you don't add a read replica to the cluster, and it will connect to the primary instance. Whenever the database cluster has more than one read replica, the reader endpoint forwards the connection request to one read replica.

The reader endpoint works by round robin, routing the connections to the available read replicas. Each time you call the reader endpoint, you resolve the DNS and get a different IP address and establish a connection to this new IP. After confirming a connection, the cluster sends all the requests to the same IP address (host).

To potentially connect to a different read replica, the client must create a new connection to enforce the DNS resolution.

Some client software might cache the DNS resolution and use the IP address for all connections. This behavior will direct all requests to the same host, which can be a problem for round-robin routing and failover situations. Disabling any DNS caching configuration is recommended to force the DNS resolution each time.

- **Instance endpoint:** An *instance endpoint* connects to a specific database instance. Each database instance in the cluster has its unique endpoint. Using the instance endpoint allows the application to connect to a particular instance of the database cluster. This strategy might be appropriate when the cluster and reader endpoints are not the best alternatives.

- **Custom endpoints:** Custom endpoints manage the connection to a set of database instances you choose. When you connect to the endpoint, Amazon Neptune will choose one of the compound selected instances and handle the connection.

  The custom endpoint isn't available by default in an Amazon Neptune database cluster until you create one.

Scalability

Amazon Neptune architecture decouples the compute and storage layers and allows the scaling of instances and storage independently.

- **Storage scaling**—Storage in Amazon Neptune grows automatically up to 128 TiB in all supported regions except China and GovCloud, which is limited to 64 TiB. For engine releases earlier than release 1.0.2.2 (2020-03-09), however, the size of cluster volumes is limited to 64 TiB in all regions. When you create a Neptune database cluster, the cluster allocates a single segment of 10 GB. As the volume of data grows the current storage, Neptune automatically extends the cluster volume by adding new segments of 10 GB. The storage size is checked hourly to determine the storage costs. You're charged only for the space actually allocated. However, when Neptune data is removed, such as by using a drop query like `g.V().drop()`, the overall allocated space remains the same. Unused allocated space is then reused automatically when the amount of data increases in the future.

The storage costs are based on the "high water mark" (the maximum amount allocated to your Amazon Neptune database cluster at any time during its existence). Avoid ETL practices that create large amounts of temporary information or that load large amounts of new data before removing unneeded older data.

- **Instance scaling:** You can scale the instance class according to the workload requirements by modifying each database instance in the database cluster and choosing instances with more vCPUs and memory. Amazon Neptune supports several optimized database instance classes.

- **Read scaling:** For horizontal scaling, you can add more instances for read-only operations; each Amazon database cluster supports up to 15 read replicas. In the read replicas, you can load balance the read operations for your application.

Availability

To ensure high availability, it's recommended that you create one or more read replica instances that have the same database instance class as the primary instance and are located in a different availability zone than the primary instance.

Having one or more read replicas increases the availability of your cluster. In the case of failure of the primary node, Amazon Neptune automatically fails over to one of the read replica instances to primary with a priority that you can specify using the failover tier configuration. While promoting a read replica to primary, there's a brief interruption on the read replica while the promoted instance is rebooted. Read and write operations running on the primary instance will fail with an exception.

If the Amazon Neptune cluster doesn't have any read replica, in failure situations, the database cluster remains unavailable until the primary instance has been re-created. Re-creating an instance takes considerably longer than promoting a read replica.

For multiregion replication requirements, Amazon Neptune allows the global database to replicate across multiple AWS regions. An Amazon Neptune global database enables low-latency reads in the remote region and fast recovery if a failure impacts an entire AWS region, which is a rare situation.

Amazon Neptune global database enables replicating the cluster up to five different regions. Only read replicas will be available in the secondary regions, and in each region, you can launch up to 16 read replica instances.

 You can't create an encrypted read replica instance from one unencrypted cluster. And vice versa: you can't create an unencrypted read replica instance for an encrypted Amazon Neptune database cluster.

Failover Policy

You can configure the failover tier at the read replica instances. Read replica instances with lower values in the failover tier configuration have a higher preference to be promoted to primary in failure situations.

If the read replica instances have the same failover tier value, Amazon Neptune will promote the replica that is the same size as the primary instance.

You can modify the failover tier for a read replica instance at any time.

Security

The AWS shared responsibility model applies to Amazon Neptune. This model describes that AWS is responsible for protecting the global infrastructure that runs the AWS cloud. You are responsible for maintaining control over your content in this infrastructure.

For data protection purposes, it's recommended that you protect the AWS credentials and set up user accounts with AWS Identity and Access Management (IAM).

You can only create an Amazon Neptune database cluster in the Amazon Virtual Private Cloud (VPC) service deployed with a minimum of two subnets and with a minimum of two availability zones; this strategy will guarantee the instances' deployment across at least two availability zones and will minimize the impact in the unlikely failure of an availability zone. The storage volume is always distributed in three availability zones to reduce data loss and increase availability. The Amazon Neptune endpoints are accessible only within that virtual private cloud. The Figure 9.5 represents the security group deployment method to access the Amazon Neptune database cluster.

FIGURE 9.5   Security group

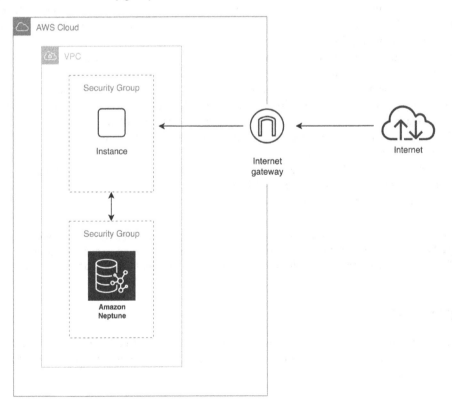

You need to create a security group to allow the EC2 instance that requires access to the Amazon Neptune database cluster within the VPC.

You can set up different ways to connect to your Amazon Neptune cluster:

- By connecting to the Amazon Neptune cluster from an Amazon EC2 instance in the same VPC

- By accessing your Amazon Neptune cluster from an Amazon EC2 instance in another VPC, using a VPC peering connection (network connection between VPCs)

- By accessing your Amazon Neptune cluster from a private network

Using IAM, you can authenticate to the Amazon Neptune database cluster or instance. Enabling the IAM database authentication requires all the HTTP requests to be signed using AWS Signature Version 4.

Amazon Neptune only allows Secure Sockets Layer (SSL) connections through HTTPS to any instance or cluster endpoint since engine version 1.0.4.0.

For security reasons, always use HTTPS instead of HTTP to connect to Amazon Neptune endpoints.

Amazon Neptune automatically provides SSL certificates for your Neptune database instances when you create new instances. There's no need to request any certificates.

Amazon Neptune permits you to protect data at rest by encrypting the data and using the AWS Key Management Service (AWS KMS) for the keys management for encrypting and decrypting operations.

All logs, backups, and snapshots are encrypted once the cluster encryption is enabled.

You can encrypt a cluster when creating it by using the AWS Neptune console; select Yes in the Enable Encryption section. If you don't define a KMS key during this step, Amazon Neptune uses the default Amazon RDS encryption key (aws/rds). Different AWS regions have other default encryption keys.

Note the following important tips:

- You cannot convert an unencrypted database cluster to an encrypted one. However, you can restore an unencrypted database cluster snapshot to an encrypted database cluster. To accomplish this conversion, you must set a KMS encryption key when restoring from the unencrypted database cluster snapshot.

- You cannot convert an unencrypted database instance to an encrypted one. You can only enable encryption for a database instance when you create it.

- You can't modify an encrypted database instance to disable encryption.

- You can't have an encrypted read replica of an unencrypted database instance or an unencrypted read replica of an encrypted database instance.

- You must encrypt read replicas with the same key as the source database instance.

Automatic Backup and Restore

Amazon Neptune automatically backs up your cluster volume and retains the backups for the backup retention period. The backup in the Amazon Neptune database cluster is continuous and incremental, so you can quickly recover the database to any specific date and time within the backup retention period. There's no performance impact or interruption of database service while the Amazon Neptune database cluster takes the backup. When creating or modifying, you can determine the backup retention from 1 to 35 days in the cluster configuration. You can take manual snapshots and manage their retention period.

For restoring the database from a previous timestamp, you can choose to restore from the automatic backup or from a snapshot (if snapshots were taken manually previously). During the restore process, a new Amazon Neptune database cluster will be launched with the chosen backup data.

To check the latest and earliest restorable time for a database instance, look for the Latest Restorable Time or Earliest Restorable Time values.

Amazon Neptune deletes its automated backups simultaneously when you delete a database cluster. Amazon Neptune does not delete manual snapshots during cluster deletion. You won't be able to restore this Amazon Neptune cluster at a later time unless you choose to create a final database snapshot manually.

Monitoring

Amazon Neptune enables native mechanisms for monitoring the cluster usage, performance, and service health.

- **Instance status:** Using curl, you can check the instance status. If the instance is healthy, the following command will return the status, startTime, dbEngineVersion, and query language available in the cluster, as well as other important information.

  ```
  curl -G https://your-neptune-endpoint:port/status
  ```

- **Amazon CloudWatch:** Using Amazon CloudWatch, you can observe by AWS Console, Cloudwatch API, or AWS command line (CLI) the percentage of CPU utilization, the average number of I/O disk writes, and the number of requests waiting in the input queue pending execution.

- **Audit log files:** When enabling audits in Amazon Neptune cluster, you can download data from the console to review information such as the timestamp, the IP address, or the hostname that originates the user connection, the connection type (Websockets, HTTP_POST, HTTP_GET, or Bolt), authentication information, the HTTP header, and the payload (Gremlin, SPARQL, or openCypher query).

- **Publishing logs to Amazon CloudWatch Logs:** You can enable publishing audit logs to Amazon CloudWatch to perform near-real-time analysis, create alarms, and view metrics.

- **AWS CloudTrail:** AWS CloudTrail exclusively logs events for Neptune Management API calls, such as creating an instance or cluster.

- **Event notification subscriptions:** You can enable the Simple Notification Service (SNS) for notifications when an Amazon Neptune event occurs. You can subscribe to event categories: availability, backup, failover, configuration change, failure, and others.

- **Tagging:** You can add tags with descriptions to the Amazon Neptune database cluster resources and track the usage based on tags.

Summary

Graph databases enable you to explore highly connected data. They support modern applications, such as recommendation engines, fraud detection, and others.

Amazon Neptune enables graph databases in a fast, secure, reliable, and scalable platform, enabling your applications to explore graph data models very efficiently.

Exam Essentials

Understand the Amazon Neptune architecture and purpose-built storage. Amazon Neptune relies on cloud-native architecture, with a durable and high-performance storage layer distributed across three availability zones; it keeps two copies on each AZ, which are six copies of each protection group segment.

Understand the graph models and query languages that you can use in Amazon Neptune. To explore the highly connected data, you can choose the property graph data model using the Gremlin or openCypher languages or using RDF via the SPARQL language.

Understand how to load data into Amazon Neptune. To load graph data into Amazon Neptune, you can use SPARQL INSERT statements or Gremlin addV and addE statements. For large datasets, you can use the bulk load command. It supports both RDF and Gremlin data. You can also use AWS Database Migration Service to migrate from other data sources.

Know how to scale and improve availability using read replicas in Amazon Neptune. Amazon Neptune cluster has one primary and writer node and allows it to scale out, adding up to 15 read replicas. The read replicas are available to balance read operations and failover in case of an eventual loss of the primary node. You can also modify the instance type to allocate more CPU and memory for your cluster.

Know how to secure your Amazon Neptune database cluster. You can rely on the VPC and security group configuration to restrict the connection to allowed sources. Use AWS IAM to authenticate the connections to the Amazon Neptune cluster.

Review Questions

1. Which query languages are currently supported on Amazon Neptune?

   A. Gremlin, openCypher, and SPARQL

   B. Structured Query Language (SQL)

   C. Python

   D. Pyspark

2. You received a requirement to host data for a large retail online store, make this data available for a product recommendation engine application, and build a fast and high-availability architecture. Which database is the best solution?

   A. RDS PostgreSQL

   B. Amazon DynamoDB

   C. Amazon Neptune

   D. Amazon Keyspaces

3. You have an Amazon Neptune database cluster with only one primary node that processes all write and read operations, and now the cluster is struggling with read operations. What is the best alternative to improve the performance and high availability of your cluster?

   A. Add a read replica to your Amazon Neptune cluster.

   B. Create another Amazon Neptune cluster, create a task using DMS to replicate the data to the new cluster, and connect the reading applications to this new cluster.

   C. Change the instance to an instance type with more vCPU and memory capacity.

   D. Add a read replica to your Amazon Neptune cluster, and change the application to connect the read-only operations to the read replica endpoint.

4. Your Amazon Neptune cluster has two read replicas configured with different instance types. In an eventual failure of the writer instance, how can you ensure that the cluster will promote the instance with more VCPUs?

   A. Configure the instance with more VCPUs with the lowest value in the failover tier.

   B. Configure the instance with more VCPUs with the highest value in the failover tier.

   C. There's nothing to configure; the Amazon Neptune cluster will always promote the instance with more VCPUs.

   D. There's nothing to configure; the Amazon Neptune cluster will always randomly choose the instance to promote.

5. You received the requirement to ensure the Amazon Neptune cluster replication in a second AWS region. How can you achieve this requirement with the lowest RTO and RPO?

   A. Enable Neptune Streams.

   B. Configure Database Migration Service replication.

   C. Enable Global Database for your Amazon Neptune cluster.

   D. It is not possible to replicate cross-region.

6. You received the requirement to encrypt your existing unencrypted Amazon Neptune cluster. How can you meet this requirement?

   A. Modify the cluster configuration and choose Apply Immediately.

   B. Modify the cluster configuration and choose Apply The Maintenance In The Next Maintenance Window.

   C. It is not possible to modify the instance encryption configuration.

   D. Take a snapshot, and set a KMS encryption key when restoring from the unencrypted database cluster snapshot. The newly restored cluster will be encrypted.

7. You received the requirement to encrypt data in transit for all your databases including the Amazon Neptune clusters. You have newer versions and clusters prior to version 1.0.4.0. How can you meet this requirement? (Choose two.)

   A. For all Amazon Neptune clusters starting from 1.0.4, there's nothing to do; SSL is the only option.

   B. For all Amazon Neptune clusters prior to 1.0.4, you can meet this requirement by modifying the cluster to use a newer parameter group.

   C. It is not possible to encrypt data in transit for an Amazon Neptune cluster.

   D. For all Amazon Neptune clusters prior to 1.0.4, you can't enable encryption in transit.

8. You are in charge of building a recommendation engine that will suggest products for customers while navigating the website. For the developers programming, using SQL queries is very easy, and according to your historical customers' purchase data, you are going to model the customers and products by vertices and the relationships by edges. Which is the best graph data model to store your data?

   A. Relational model.

   B. Property graph data model.

   C. Resource Description Framework.

   D. Convert the data to S3 in Parquet format, and explore the data using Athena.

9. You're in charge of inserting in your Amazon Neptune cluster that uses the property graph data model a large dataset already extracted to an external file. Which is the fastest method for loading large datasets?

   A. Perform the insert using addV and addE steps.

   B. Perform the bulk loader command.

   C. Configure Database Migration Service replication.

   D. Perform the insert using the SPARQL INSERT statement.

10. You are in charge of supporting a promotional campaign that will issue queries for the recommendation engine. You don't want to impact the production environment with two read replicas and have decided to launch a new read replica to accommodate this specific campaign. Which is the easiest method to ensure that this specific workload will connect to the new read replica launched?

    A. Your only option is to connect to the cluster endpoint.

    B. Connect to the reader endpoint, and it will connect to the new read replica.

    C. Connect to the instance endpoint for the new read replica instance.

    D. Configure a custom endpoint, and manage the connection to this new instance.

Chapter

10

Immutable Database and Traceable Transactions

THE AWS CERTIFIED DATABASE – SPECIALTY EXAM OBJECTIVES COVERED IN THIS CHAPTER MAY INCLUDE, BUT ARE NOT LIMITED TO, THE FOLLOWING:

✓ **Domain 1: Workload-Specific Database Design.**

  ▪ 1.3 Design database solutions for performance, compliance, and scalability.

✓ **Domain 4: Monitoring and troubleshooting.**

  ▪ 4.2 Troubleshoot and resolve common database issues.

  ▪ 4.3 Optimize database performance.

✓ **Domain 5: Database security.**

  ▪ 5.1 Encrypt data at rest and in transit.

  ▪ 5.3 Determine access control and authentication mechanisms.

In this chapter, you will learn about blockchain technology—specifically, centralized ledgers and the related AWS service, *Amazon Quantum Ledger Database (Amazon QLDB)*. The chapter also highlights QLDB main features and how they can be leveraged within your blockchain application. You will also learn how to deploy, secure, monitor, and operate workloads using Amazon QLDB.

Have you ever faced the challenge of versioning a database? How is it handled with a traditional relational database? A good database designer probably would go for a separate table that replicates the original table, plus some column with a time mark to keep track whenever the data is updated. When new data arrives, a new record is inserted into the history table with the data snapshot before the update. Another approach can be to use a data warehouse and store all the versions of the data in an aggregated way.

Any solution based on relational databases would be very complex since they cannot seamlessly prevent tampering with old data, not to mention that the whole setup and operation add extra complexity and time. The best solution for this scenario is to use blockchain technology. In this chapter, we will also cover the main centralized ledger use cases.

Amazon Quantum Ledger Database

When would it be appropriate to use Amazon Quantum Ledger Database? There are two possible scenarios.

In the first, multiple parties need to work with a centralized, trusted authority to maintain a complete and verifiable record of transactions. An example is a retail customer looking to connect its suppliers with a centralized ledger that maintains a transparent and verifiable history of information related to the movement of a product through its supply chain.

In the second, multiple parties transact in a decentralized manner without the need for a centralized, trusted authority. An example is a consortium of banks and credit houses looking to perform cross-boundary transfer of assets among each other, without a centralized authority acting as a broker.

If you require a centralized ledger that records all application data changes and maintains an immutable record of these changes, AWS provides the ledger database known as Amazon QLDB.

Amazon QLDB is a new kind of database that eliminates the need for the full development effort to create your own ledger-like applications. QLDB is a fully managed database that provides an immutable and cryptographically verifiable transaction log, owned by a trusted central authority. It can be used to record every change in application data and maintain a complete and verifiable history.

With QLDB, the data change history is immutable, meaning it cannot be modified or deleted, and by using cryptography, you can easily verify that no modifications have occurred to your application data. QLDB uses an immutable transaction log, called a *journal*, that records every change in application data and maintains a complete and verifiable history.

QLDB is easy to use because it provides to developers a familiar application programming interface (API) that is similar to Structured Query Language (SQL), a flexible document data model, and full transaction support. QLDB also has streaming capability that provides near real-time flow of data from a QLDB table, allowing you to develop event-driven workflows, perform real-time analytics, and replicate data to other AWS services to do further data processing such as advanced analysis.

QLDB is also serverless, so it scales automatically to support the demands of your application, and you pay only for what you use. There are no servers to manage, and there is no read or write limit to configure. Figure 10.1 shows the high-level architecture.

FIGURE 10.1   High-level architecture of Amazon QLDB

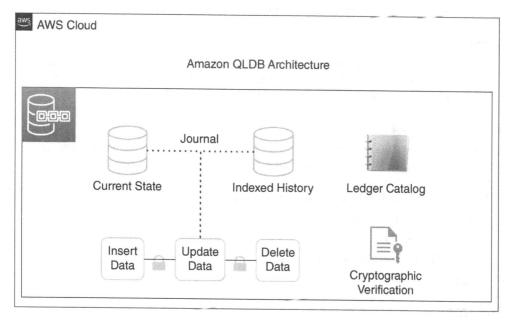

Amazon QLDB Components

If you have experience with relational database management systems (RDBMS) and SQL, you will find some analogies with QLDB components (see Table 10.1).

TABLE 10.1   Relational and QLDB

Relational	QLDB
Database	Ledger
Table	Table
Row	Document
Column	Document attribute
Index	Index
SQL	PartiQL
Audit logs	Journal

Ledger

An Amazon QLDB *ledger* is a set of tables with documents and a journal that keeps the complete, immutable history of changes to each document within the tables.

Table

Tables belong to a ledger and contain a collection of document revisions from the journal, similar to a materialized view. Tables support optional indexes on document fields; the indexes can improve performance for queries that make use of the equality operator.

System Catalog

For each table in an Amazon QLDB ledger, there is a system-assigned unique ID. You can find a table's ID, the index list, and other metadata by querying the system catalog table: `information_schema.user_tables`.

The following metadata fields are available for query:

- `tableId`: The unique ID of the table
- `name`: The table name
- `index`: The ID, the attribute, and the status for each index
- `status`: The table's current status, ACTIVE or INACTIVE

Documents

Data records within QLDB tables consist of revisions of QLDB documents. These documents use a specific format called Amazon Ion and represent a single version of a sequence of documents identified by a unique ID.

Amazon Ion is a superset of JSON format that adds additional data types, type annotations, and comments. Those documents don't need to comply to any particular schema, allowing you the flexibility to build applications that can easily adapt to changes.

QLDB supports documents that contain nested JSON elements and also gives you the ability to write queries that reference and include these nested elements.

Journal

The ledger is built on an append-only log called a *journal*. As transactions are committed to the ledger, they're organized into blocks and appended to the journal. Each block contains only one transaction.

Once committed and appended, blocks can't be modified or overwritten, which gives you an immutable record of every insert, update, and delete ever committed to the ledger and access to every revision of every document at all times.

Query Engine

The purpose of Amazon QLDB is to work as a high-performance online transaction processing (OLTP) immutable database with full ACID transaction support. To fulfill this role, the data needs to be accessed by some query language.

To this end, QLDB provides real-time table views based on the information stored in the journal. These views can be queried by using a subset of PartiQL operations. PartiQL is an open standard query language that supports SQL-compatible access to relational, semistructured, and nested data, while remaining independent of any particular data source or schema.

To run PartiQL queries in QLDB, you can use one of the following:

- The Query Editor on the AWS Management Console for QLDB
- The command-line QLDB shell
- An AWS-provided QLDB driver to run queries programmatically

Cryptographic Verification

To prove that the transaction history is immutable, Amazon QLDB provides a cryptographic verification feature that enables it to mathematically prove the integrity of the entire transaction history.

What exactly is this verification feature?

After a client writes data to the ledger, Amazon QLDB calculates a hash of the data using the SHA-256 hash algorithm and stores it along with the data. At a high level, verifying data in Amazon QLDB is done by recalculating the hash for the data you want to verify and comparing it to the hash that was stored at the time when the data was written.

You might be thinking, how can we verify the integrity of the entire database then?

Validating all the records one by one isn't a choice because an attacker with low-level access to the database could tamper with the data and its hash at the same time, and it would be difficult to discover.

To overcome this issue, QLDB uses a hash chaining mechanism. Hash chaining is the process of applying a cryptographic hash algorithm to another hash, creating a hash of a hash. The records in the database are sorted sequentially, and each data record hash depends on the hash of the record before it, so changing the data in one record affects the hash of that record and the hash of every other record that comes after it. This proves not just the contents of each document, but also that each document is where it belongs in the database in sequential order. Notice that the chain example in Figure 10.2 has two transactions per block, but Amazon QLDB stores only one transaction per block in a one-to-one relationship.

FIGURE 10.2 Hash chain example

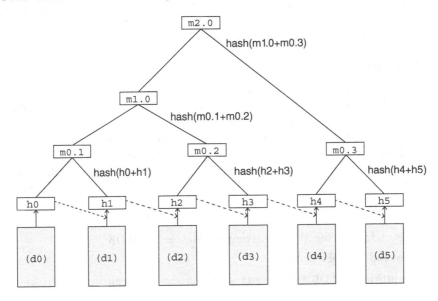

To make verifications more efficient, QLDB organizes the hashes using a Merkle tree. A *Merkle tree* is a binary tree data structure whose leaf nodes contain a single data hash and whose nonleaf nodes contain a hash of their two child node hashes, as shown in Figure 10.3.

Working with Amazon QLDB

As with all databases, the ledger doesn't fulfill any use case on its own; it needs to be integrated into an application that requires the immutable and auditable features to be built in.

FIGURE 10.3 QLDB Merkle tree implementation

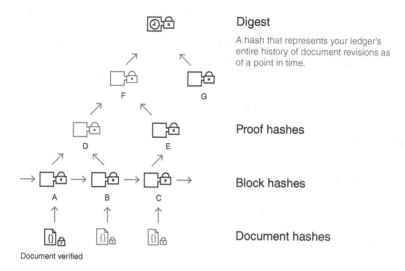

PROOF

Digest

A hash that represents your ledger's entire history of document revisions as of a point in time.

F G

Proof hashes

D E

Block hashes

A B C

Document hashes

Document verified

Application Integration

To connect to Amazon QLDB and transact with the data in the ledger, the app can use the Amazon QLDB API, the AWS SDK for QLDB, or the QLDB driver provided by AWS.

The driver provides a high-level abstraction layer above the transactional data API (QLDB session). It handles the SendCommand API calls including all the necessary parameters, session pool management, and retry policies.

In addition, the driver uses Amazon Ion libraries to enable support for handling Ion data when running transactions. These libraries also take care of calculating the hash of Ion documents, which QLDB requires to check the integrity of data transaction requests.

The driver is open source and currently available for the following programming languages:

- Java
- .NET
- Go
- Node.js
- Python

Amazon QLDB doesn't have the same concept of a traditional relational connection over TCP because transactions are sent via HTTP request and response messages. The analogous concept to an RDBMS connection is an *active session*. QLDB supports one actively running transaction per session.

The QLDB driver maintains and manages a pool of sessions for the clients. When the application asks the driver to run a transaction, the driver chooses a session from the pool and uses it. If the transaction fails because of a session error, the driver uses another session to retry the transaction. Essentially, the driver offers a fully managed session pool experience.

The QLDB driver automatically retries the transactions when common exceptions occur. You can implement a retry policy to configure how many retries to attempt before the transaction aborts and the session returns to the pool.

Besides the number of attempts, the retry policy also can be used to define the backoff strategy. The backoff is exponential, uses a minimum delay of 10 milliseconds and a maximum delay of 5000 milliseconds, and has equal jitter.

Querying the Data

Amazon QLDB provides access to the documents by keeping a subset of the data on table views. These are real-time views, so they're always available for applications to query by using PartiQL statements.

In addition to these queryable views, you can query the revision history of your data by using the built-in history function.

Besides the traditional basic query operations, QLDB allows you to run projections, filters, and some traditional ANSI SQL functions such as AVG, COUNT, SUM aggregates, COALESCE, EXIST, NULLIF conditionals, SUBSTRING, CHAR_LENGTH, and TRIM string operations, among other functions and categories.

The following query shows a select projection and a filter based on a string list containing predicates:

```
SELECT
    v.Make,
    v.Model,
    r.Owners
FROM
    VehicleRegistration AS r JOIN Vehicle AS v
ON
    r.VIN = v.VIN
WHERE
    r.VIN IN ('1N4AL11D75C109151', 'KM8SRDHF6EU074761')
```

Proof of Integrity of the Data

You can easily request proof of integrity from Amazon QLDB by requesting a digest. A *digest* is a cryptographic representation of the entire journal at some point in time. When one is requested, QLDB generates a digest as an output file, from which you can verify the integrity of the data that was committed at a prior point in time. If you recalculate the hashes by starting with a revision and ending with the digest, you prove that your data has not been tampered with in between.

QLDB also has a feature to assist you in the verification process. It is done by requesting a digest with the ID and block address of the document revision to verify.

The ID and address can be retrieved with the following PartiQL query example:

```
SELECT metadata.id, blockAddress FROM table_name
WHERE some_criteria
```

With that ID, you can use the QLDB console verification page, and the service will automate the hash verification process by returning a result page showing the content of the proof for the specified document revision and digest. Figure 10.4 shows an example of a verification result page.

FIGURE 10.4   Block reference example

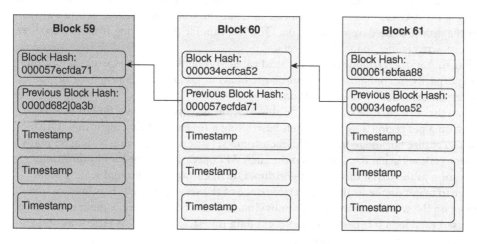

Amazon QLDB also supports event-driven architectures by providing continuous journal stream capability. This data streaming can be integrated with Amazon Kinesis to process real-time journal data.

Backup and Durability

Like all other AWS services, Amazon QLDB is built on the AWS Global infrastructure and shares the same level of resilience. In addition, Amazon QLDB has some backup features.

The managed service comes with a feature that provides on-demand journal export to an Amazon S3 bucket. Once the journal is on S3, you can access its contents in your ledger for various purposes including analytics, auditing, data retention, verification, and exporting to other systems. The information goes to Amazon S3 in Amazon Ion format.

At the time of writing, Amazon QLDB doesn't provide a backup and restore feature; the export functionality is mainly for additional data redundancy.

If you need to restore a QLDB database, it has to be done at the application level into a new ledger by using some kind of ingest mechanism.

Regarding durability, Amazon QLDB journal storage and indexes implement synchronous replication to multiple availability zones for every write. By doing so, AWS ensures that even in a full availability zone failure, the journal storage would not be compromised.

Additionally, the journal sends another asynchronous archive to a fault-tolerant storage. This feature supports disaster recovery in the highly unlikely event that several availability zones fail simultaneously.

Performance and Scalability

Amazon QLDB has a centralized design, so it won't wait for the consensus of the majority of members in the network to execute a transaction, like the common blockchain frameworks do. For the decentralizaed implementation, QLDB is capable of delivering from two to three times more performance than other ledgers.

Similar to Amazon DynamoDB on-demand capacity, you don't need to worry about provisioning capacity or configuring read and write limits in QLDB; it will automatically scale to support the demands of the application.

To keep the performance stable and be able to scale as demand grows, QLDB enforces throttling on a per-region and per-account basis using a token throttling algorithm. QLDB does this to ensure fair usage for all QLDB customers. For example, trying to acquire many concurrent sessions using the StartSessionRequest API operation might lead to throttling.

In addition to the token throttling algorithm, QLDB enforces an internal scaling limit per ledger to maintain the health and performance of the service as well. This limit changes depending on the workload size of each individual request. For example, a request can have an increased workload if it performs inefficient data transactions, such as table scans that result from a nonindex attribute query predicate.

The throttling and limit mechanisms help to mitigate potential scaling issues, but the real thing behind QLDB is the concurrency model implementation.

Amazon QLDB operates with optimistic concurrency control (OCC). OCC works on the principle that multiple transactions can frequently be completed without interfering with each other. Transactions in QLDB do not lock database resources and run with full serializable isolation. QLDB executes concurrent transactions in a series, so it has the same effect as if those transactions were started sequentially.

What if the result of one transaction affects the condition of the following one?

QLDB will reject a transaction if another one interferes with a read condition of the transaction itself before the actual commit. For example, if there is a wire transfer waiting to be executed in the sequence and the source account had a withdrawal in between, the wire transfer transaction commit will fail due to an OCC conflict (OccConflictException). You can retry the transaction and re-check if the source account still has enough balance. In other words, QLDB will keep track of any transaction in the sequence that could potentially tamper with the outcome of a read condition of the following transaction in the order.

Security

Amazon QLDB shares the same level as security as the rest of the managed AWS services; that's why it also complies with some of the most important compliance programs such as SOC, PCI, ISO, and HIPAA. Besides the standard security level provided by AWS, there are several ways you can secure the data on Amazon QLDB. Let's go through the features available for data protection and access management.

Access Management

Every time you read about security for an AWS service, you will see Identity and Access Management (IAM) as the main component. This happens because a good security posture begins with good access management control. IAM lets you control who can be authenticated and authorized to use each one of the Amazon QLDB resources.

There are two kinds of QLDB users:

- **Service users:** A simple user who is authorized to perform certain tasks on QLDB. A service user, in turn, can be one of the following principals:
  - IAM user or group using their username and password
  - IAM role with temporary credentials like an Amazon EC2 instance
  - Federated user from an external identity provider like Active Directory
  - Cross-account user from a different AWS account with a trust relationship
  - Service-linked role assumed by another AWS service, like an AWS Lambda function
- **Service administrator:** The one with full access to Amazon QLDB and with the responsibility of creating and assigning the right permissions over a QLDB resource to each service user. The resources that support the IAM policies are the following:
  - Ledger
  - Table
  - Catalog
  - Stream

The service administration has the following IAM features at their disposal to grant fine-grain access to the service users and, in that way, apply the least privilege principle:

- Identity-based policies
- Policy actions
- Policy resources
- Policy condition keys
- Attributes-based access control with TAGs
- Temporary credentials
- Service roles

Data Protection

Another key factor in security is the data protection itself. As explained earlier in this book, and probably in all other AWS certification preparation guides out there, data protection is a responsibility shared between AWS and the customers. The well-known AWS shared responsibility model also applies to Amazon QLDB. AWS is responsible for protecting the infrastructure while customers are responsible for maintaining control over the QLDB content that is running on that infrastructure.

AWS provides several tools and features to help customers fulfill their roles in the previously mentioned model. The following are the main ones for Amazon QLDB:

- All data stored in QLDB is encrypted at rest by default using AWS KMS. It can be with AWS owned keys at no additional cost. Or you can use your keys to have full control over the encryption keys, but KMS charges will apply.

- Amazon QLDB also ensures the encryption in transit by only accepting HTTPS connections using SSL/Transport Layer Security (TLS). Clients must support TLS 1.0 or later, though it is recommended to use TLS 1.2 or above.

- You can enforce the usage of MFA for Amazon QLDB administrator users or console service users.

- Amazon QLDB is compatible with VPC endpoints, so your application running in an Amazon VPC can communicate with the ledger in QLBD using AWS private networks instead of the public Internet.

- All nontransactional operations of QLDB are recorded on Amazon CloudTrail for audit or compliance reasons.

Monitoring

Monitoring is a key part of keeping the reliability and performance of all applications; Amazon QLDB is no exception. There are three main elements to watch for in QLDB: storage I/O, operation latency, and exception count. We will cover next how to monitor each one.

Like the other AWS services, Amazon CloudWatch will integrate natively with QLDB. You can build a CloudWatch Dashboard, aggregating the metrics available on a single pane of glass. You can also set up alarms to trigger; if some metric changes, it states for a given period of time. You can use CloudWatch Events to match a QLDB event and route them to a target function, stream, or queue to take further actions. You can also send QLDB CloudTrail logs to CloudWatch Logs to store, filter, or analyze them.

By default, CloudWatch provides the following metrics for QLDB:

- JournalStorage
- IndexedStorage
- ReadIOs
- WriteIOs

- CommandLatency
- IsImpaired
- Exceptions

Best Practices

The following are the best practices to consider when using Amazon QLDB:

- Amazon QLDB PartiQL operations are subject to transaction limits for a size of 4 MB and timeout of 30 seconds. You should design your applications considering these quotas.

- For data protection purposes, we recommend that you protect AWS account credentials and set up individual user accounts with AWS Identity and Access Management (IAM). That way, each user has only the necessary permissions to fulfill their job duties.

- The number of QLDB concurrent sessions is 1,500; when that limit is reached, any session that tries to start a transaction will result in a LimitExceededException error. The best practice is to use the session pool in your application by using the QLDB driver.

- For better performance, ensure that only one global instance of the driver exists on each application instance. This can be done by using dependency injection design patterns.

- PartiQL is SQL compatible. However, avoid table scans for production use cases in QLDB, as they can cause performance problems on large tables, including concurrency conflicts and transaction timeouts.

- Make your write transactions idempotent to avoid any unexpected side effects in the case of retries. A transaction is idempotent if it can run multiple times and produce identical results each time.

- Run multiple statements per transaction to optimize the performance of your application.

- You should run statements with a WHERE predicate clause that filters on an indexed field or a document ID. QLDB requires an equality operator on an indexed field to efficiently look up a document, for example, WHERE IndexKey = 9887.

Summary

This chapter explained the main concepts of a ledger database based on blockchain technology. We also covered Amazon QLDB features and components, as well as some details about the internal service mechanism that makes QLDB an excellent option to run a ledger database at any scale. There is a wide range of industries and use cases for QLDB. Banking and finance have various use cases for it involving the tracking of transactional history.

Ecommerce, and retail more generally, uses it to maintain inventory or track supplies. The automotive industry uses QLBD to aid in the driver and vehicle documentation registration process. Finally, the transportation industry uses QLBD to track goods.

Exam Essentials

Know the centralized blockchain use cases.   Some workloads require database versioning or high-standard audit capabilities. Audit capabilities provide proof of integrity not only to internal teams but also to external auditors or business stakeholders. The previous use cases along with a centralized approach, is the perfect match for Amazon QLDB.

Understand Amazon QLDB main features.   Every AWS service has specific availability, scalability, durability, performance, integration, and application-related features. The exam might include questions about how Amazon QLDB implements these features.

Know the available monitoring and troubleshooting tools.   Once you have the application running, you need to keep it in that state. Amazon QLDB provides the necessary traceability and monitoring features to do so. Amazon QLDB integrates with AWS observability services like Amazon CloudWatch metrics and Amazon CloudTrail for nontransactional operations.

Understand how to strengthen the security for Amazon QLDB.   Security is AWS's top priority, so every AWS service has strong security features built in. Amazon QLDB includes data access features with fine-grained authentication and authorization features via AWS IAM, data protection in transit and at rest, and private networking capabilities with VPC endpoints.

Exercises

For assistance in completing the following exercises, refer to the Amazon QLDB developer guide at docs.aws.amazon.com/qldb/latest/developerguide/accessing.html.

EXERCISE 10.1

Create a New Amazon QLDB Ledger Database

In this exercise, you will create a new QLDB database.

1. Sign in to the AWS Management Console as a user with the right QLDBB permissions.

2. Navigate to Amazon QLDB by finding it in the list of services under Database, go to the Getting Started page, and then click Create Ledger.

3. Enter a name for the ledger, leave the permission mode and encryption options at the defaults, and click the Create Ledger button. The creation process takes from 3 to 5 minutes, and you can continue once the status is Active.

EXERCISE 10.2

Load the Sample Data

In this exercise, you will load the Amazon QLDB database with sample data.

1. In the QLDB console, go back to the Getting Started page and proceed to the Sample Application Data section.

2. On the automatic session, choose the ledger you created in the previous task and click Load Sample Data.

EXERCISE 10.3

Query the Data

In this exercise, you will query the data you loaded in Exercise 10.2.

1. In the QLDB console, navigate to the Query Editor and select your ledger in the ledger panel.

2. Execute the following query to get a sample vehicle by the VIN number:

```
SELECT * FROM Vehicle AS v WHERE v.VIN = '1N4AL11D75C109151'
```

3. Execute this other query to join the Vehicle table and the VehicleRegistration table.

```
SELECT v.VIN, r.LicensePlateNumber, r.State, r.City, r.Owners FROM Vehicle
AS v, VehicleRegistration AS r WHERE v.VIN = '1N4AL11D75C109151' AND
v.VIN = r.VIN
```

As you can see, the PartiQL query language is similar to traditional ANSI SQL.

Request a Digest and Perform a Document Revision

In this exercise, you will request a digest from your ledger's journal.

1. Go to the Ledgers page of the QLDB console and select your ledger by clicking the radio button next to its name. Then click the Get Digest button and save it to your computer.

2. Execute the following query to get the metadata ID and block address of the sample Vehicle:

   SELECT r.metadata.id, r.blockAddress FROM _ql_committed_VehicleRegistration AS r WHERE r.data.VIN = '1N4AL11D75C109151'

3. Save the ID and block address to do the verification.

4. In the navigation pane, choose Verification.

5. Enter the metadata ID and block address you saved before, upload the digest file you downloaded in the previous task, and click the Verify button.

6. Check the Verification Results output session to view the proof of hashes and the entire block information in the Block panel.

7. Proceed with the deletion of all the resources created in the previous exercises. Notice that the ledger was probably created with the delete protection enabled, so you need to deselect it first.

Review Questions

1. A company is defining the backup policy for a vehicle registration application that leverages Amazon EC2, Amazon EFS, and Amazon QLDB. What is the best approach?

    A. Use AWS Backup to have a centralized management console to back up all the application components.

    B. Leverage the native Amazon QLDB point-in-time recovery or on-demand backup features along with AWS Backup to support Amazon EFS filesystems and Amazon EBS volumes.

    C. Amazon QLDB doesn't support any backups, so you will be able to back up only the EC2 instances and EFS filesystem. Use AWS Backup for those.

    D. Use AWS Backup for Amazon EC2 and Amazon EFS and implement a custom backup solution with an Amazon QLDB driver at the application level.

2. What is the appropriate type of data to store on Amazon QLDB?

    A. Time-series data with verification capabilities

    B. System-of-record applications, those for which data integrity, completeness, and verifiability are critical

    C. Structured data in rows and columns with multiple relationships among entities

    D. JSON documents to be used in a mobile app

3. An audit process is coming to a financial service company that uses Amazon QLDB to store their customer transactions history. What security mechanisms are already in place as part of the managed service? (Choose three.)

    A. Data encryption at rest using Amazon managed keys or customer managed keys.

    B. In-transit data encryption for Amazon QLDB API using TLS 1.0 or above.

    C. All management and data operations are automatically stored in Amazon CloudTrail for auditing purposes.

    D. Integration with Amazon IAM to write fine-grain security policies and conditions to grant access to Amazon QLDB resources.

4. Amazon QLDB is a distributed ledger or blockchain technology.

    A. True

    B. False

5. A solutions architect needs to propose the right AWS database service for an application project that needs an auditable database. The database schema may change over time, and there is no information about the potential traffic the app may have.

    A. Since there is not a fixed schema, the best solution is to use a NoSQL database like Amazon DynamoDB with the on-demand provisioned mode. To guarantee the audit part, all the logs from CloudTrail can be sent to Amazon S3 and Object Lock can be enabled in that bucket.

B. To provide full ACID properties for the audit, the only option is to use a relational database. Since there is no information about the scale, the best choice is Amazon Aurora Serverless. To keep track of the audit, the development team can enable an audit plugin like MariaDB Audit Plugin for MySQL. Then store the logs on S3 with an Object Lock in place.

C. Use the Amazon Managed Blockchain Service for Hyperledger Fabric. Leverage the native audit features of the blockchain technology.

D. Use Amazon QLDB as the database service. With QLDB you can have full ACID transactions, serverless provisioning, and built-in immutable and auditable features.

6. What are the authentication methods available for Amazon QLDB?

   A. A request signature to be attached to the HTTP requests

   B. Database user and password

   C. Anonymous authentication

   D. Federated authentication via Microsoft AD

7. Amazon QLDB provides private VPC integration. True or false?

   A. True

   B. False

8. How can you configure the scalability of Amazon QLDB?

   A. You need to set up minimum and maximum capacity units, and the service will add or remove nodes on demand.

   B. You need to configure an autoscaling group with the right metric to observe.

   C. There is no need to configure scalability because Amazon QLDB is serverless.

   D. The service currently does not offer scalability features.

9. How can you interact with the data stored in Amazon QLDB? (Choose all that apply.)

   A. Since Amazon QLDB uses JSON documents, you can use the same driver used for MongoDB.

   B. You must include the AWS-provided QLDB driver.

   C. Amazon QLDB supports access only through API calls, similar to Amazon DynamoDB.

   D. Amazon QLDB allows you to query your data using a subset of PartiQL.

10. Amazon QLDB supports ACID transactions. True or false?

    A. True

    B. False

Chapter

11

Caching Data with In-Memory Databases

THE AWS CERTIFIED DATABASE - SPECIALTY EXAM OBJECTIVES COVERED IN THIS CHAPTER MAY INCLUDE, BUT ARE NOT LIMITED TO, THE FOLLOWING:

✓ **Domain 1: Workload-Specific Database Design**

- 1.2 Select appropriate database services for specific types of data and workloads.

- 1.3 Design database solutions for performance, compliance, and scalability.

✓ **Domain 4: Monitoring and Troubleshooting**

- 4.3 Optimize database performance.

Modern applications tend to be faster than old ones, and to keep user engagement, it is important to respond quickly. One way to provide data with extremely low latency is to have it in a memory structure. This process is known as caching data.

Caching data is the action of putting data in a memory structure and accessing it when it is needed, as memory response times are faster than disk response times. By an order of magnitude, memory responds in nanoseconds, and an Amazon EBS volume disk usually responds in a few milliseconds. This means memory is thousands of times faster. According to the Amazon EBS documentation, the average response time from an EBS volume to an EC2 instance is 1 millisecond, but for the specific io2 Block Express disk type, you can expect submillisecond latency.

Of course, if the caching layer is not local, you must consider the network latency between the data and the application. The closer the cache structure is to the running application in terms of the network, the better.

In this chapter, you will learn about in-memory databases, how they are used for different use cases, and the options you can use in AWS. In-memory databases are volatile, so for persistent and durable data requirements, you need to consider other database services in conjunction with in-memory in your architecture.

Built-in Database Cache

A *built-in database cache* is a memory structure in a database instance where the engine caches frequently used data and object definitions to improve performance. From a database engine perspective such as Amazon Aurora, by default the engine uses built-in memory structures in each database instance for caching.

Database engines manage those memory structures automatically, with little interaction from the database administrator (DBA), but DBAs can still check their efficiency and tune them. Amazon Relational Database Service (Amazon RDS) automatically sets up memory parameters for each database engine according to the amount of memory the RDS instance has, but it also allows them to be tuned through database parameters.

For transactional workloads with repeated queries, memory usually improves performance. Working with memory-optimized instance families, such as R and X, can be beneficial to a majority of workloads. The instance size determines the amount of memory available to be used by database cache structures.

Cache invalidation is an important concept of a built-in cache, where the engine controls data changes and has mechanisms to invalidate old data versions from the cache.

The problem with those built-in memory structures is that the amount of memory available depends on the database instance size. A shutdown is required to increase the database server's memory. Also, to access this structure, you need to use compute resources from the database instance, increasing concurrency if this happens frequently.

Local Application Cache

In a *local cache*, a running application can use local memory to load and access frequently used data. This is the fastest way to use data, but it is restricted to the data that was previously loaded into the local device.

There are limitations of usage, as the device memory available is in general competing with other applications.

After some time, the local cache may not have the most recent version of data if this is a distributed application, so it needs to frequently look for newer data versions in the application database.

In-Memory Databases

In-memory databases are remote cache structures relying on machines with large memory. They are accessed by different remote applications, share content among themselves, and can integrate with other database engines that support remote cache integration.

In most architectures of distributed systems, this structure sits between the local applications and the database engine, but it can also be a stand-alone structure with dedicated data sharing accessed by the applications.

Amazon ElastiCache is the AWS service that provides an in-memory, fully managed caching service with options that are compatible with Redis and Memcached.

Caching Use Cases

Caching data can improve response time for lots of use cases. Database specialists usually know how the database engines use the instance memory layer in a database architecture, which is as a cache. Most database engines provide parameters to adjust memory utilization to have the best configuration for a given workload and database machine. Large database machines with hundreds of gigabytes to a few terabytes of memory and tens to hundreds of vCPUS usually use a high number of blocks from this memory layer, but the number is limited by the size of the database machines.

To speed up online applications' response time, frequently used data such as user sessions, preferences, progress, or choices, as these session attributes can be used several times, we can cache data. The cached data can be used to improve response times and to perform fewer calls to the back-end infrastructure for client reconnection and to make the user experience smooth.

An online game leaderboard is a classic use case for remote caching, as the latest status can be updated and viewed with no latency for a large number of users.

Most of the modern applications we use in our mobile phones take advantage of caching structure, local and/or remote.

It's important that you know what *cache hit* and *cache miss* are. Every time your application looks for a key in the cache and the key is there, you have a *cache hit*; every time the key is not there and has to be read from the disk on another database layer, you have a *cache miss*. You will find metrics for cache hit or cache miss percentage. Cache hit percentage is for all the times the application tries to find a key, and cache miss percentage is the percentage of not finding it.

To check the efficiency of your cache strategy, monitor the cache hit and cache miss metrics and try to keep the cache hit as high as needed by your application.

Remote Cache Strategies

Remote caching can be used with different strategies, considering the application functionality, freshness of data required in the cache, available memory for caching, and objectives for caching in the application architecture.

Two caching strategies are commonly used.

- *Lazy loading* is a cache strategy when you cache the data only when the application tries to read it for the first time.

- *Write-through* is a cache strategy when you cache all the data at the moment it is generated or whenever it has been updated in the database.

The lazy loading strategy is cheaper, as it uses the cache only for the data that it is required to, and it can handle node failure, as it will continue to cache data when needed after failure. However, it increases the time to retrieve data when a cache miss happens, and it can have stale data if the data is updated in the database because it loads new data only when there is a cache miss.

The write-through strategy will always have the most recent version of data in the cache, but it will potentially require more memory to store some data that may never be read, and there is also operation overhead to write all the data that has changed.

Time to live (TTL) Is an attribute used by some caching engines to expire old data from the cache after a configured amount of time to avoid keeping stale data in the cache.

To avoid keeping data that is never used with the write-through strategy or to avoid having stale data with a lazy loading strategy, it is useful to create a time to live (TTL) for cached data so that data will be expired from the cache after a defined amount of time; in other words, data is removed from the cache after the TTL time.

Lazy Loading

1. The application requests the data from the remote cache.

2. If it's there, it reads it.

3. If it's not there (a cache miss), it then reads from the database and writes the data to the cache for further usage.

Write-Through

1. The data is updated or created in the database.

2. The remote cache is updated with a new version or new data for every piece of data written to the database layer.

Time to Live

1. You can set up a maximum time a record will be in the cache after being added—for example, 600 seconds.

2. When a record reaches a TTL of 600 seconds in the cache, it is expired.

3. After it is expired by the TTL, the next time the record is needed, it will be read from the database and then populated again in the cache.

Caching Data in AWS

AWS provides several services that can be used for caching data. Let's take a broader look at them before we dive deep into Amazon ElastiCache.

As shown in Figure 11.1, application performance can be increased using different types of caching strategies.

- Amazon CloudFront for delivering static and some dynamic content, usually pictures and large objects

- Dedicated specialized structures using Amazon ElastiCache

- The database instance memory portion natively dedicated for caching in Amazon RDS and Amazon DocumentDB

- Amazon DynamoDB Accelerator (DAX)

- A mix of scenarios of Amazon ElastiCache between other databases and the applications

FIGURE 11.1 Caching option for applications

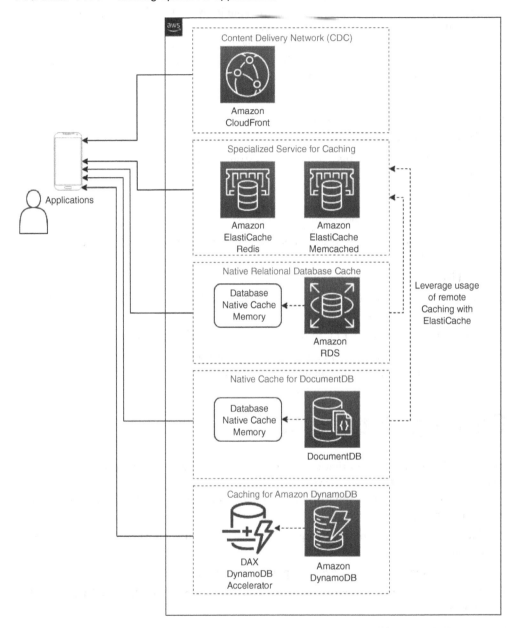

Caching Data with ElastiCache

AWS has a specialized service for caching, Amazon ElastiCache, which is compatible with two popular data caching software applications, Redis and Memcached, as a fully managed service.

Memcached or Redis?

To start with the ElastiCache service, we first need to determine which software is the best for the use case, Memcached or Redis. Both products can deliver the following:

- Extremely low latency, in the submillisecond range
- Easy API interaction for developers
- Data distribution within the nodes with partitioning
- Support for many programming languages, including Python, JavaScript, C, C++, Java, PHP, Node.js, Go, and Ruby
- In-transit data encryption
- String data type, the only data type supported by Memcached

As you can tell by the common features, for simple caching use cases, both Memcached and Redis can be used.

Memcached has multithreaded architecture, allowing multiple core utilization and making good use of compute resources. Redis, on the other hand, has the following set of enterprise-level features that can be used to improve resilience, integration, and application flexibility:

- Snapshots allow Redis to keep the data safe on disk for point-in-time recovery or archiving.
- Replication, with the capability of multiple replicas, enables database reads on Redis to scale and provides high availability.
- The use of transactions with Redis allows the control of commands as a whole group, for dependency checks.
- Pub/Sub messaging is a good built-in feature for application integration and streaming.
- Geospatial support can be a decision point to use Redis, as it has specific commands to interact with geospatial data in real time.
- It offers the ability to improve performance and reduce complexity using server-side Lua scripts.
- It offers the ability to add and remove shards dynamically (cluster mode).

- It offers encryption at rest.

- It offers compliance with the following certifications—FedRamp, HIPAA, and PCI DSS.

- It supports complex data types such as bitmaps, sorted sets, sets, hashes, and lists, not just strings.

  New features of the latest versions of Redis include the following:

- Data tiering, using memory and solid-state drives (SSDs) (version 6.2)

- Role-based access control with authentication (version 6.0)

After looking at the differences, if you have a simple caching scenario that can scale up and down with nodes being added and removed, that can use large nodes with multiple threads, and that has low security compliance regulations, you could choose Memcached.

Your choice should be Redis if you need more resilience or any of the Redis unique features mentioned: snapshots, replication, transactions, real-time Pub/Sub, geospatial support, compliance certification, data tiering, and role-based access.

Memcached Architecture on Amazon ElastiCache Service

Amazon ElastiCache for Memcached can be deployed in a single availability zone (AZ) or in a multi-AZ scenario, where you can specify the availability zones for the nodes or let the ElastiCache service choose the AZs.

An *ElastiCache for Memcached cluster* is a logical group of ElastiCache nodes, which are units of RAM memory securely attached to a cluster, with each node running an instance of Memcached. The cluster can be set up with up to 40 nodes in a region, spread among the AZs, and for each AWS region, you can have up to a total of 300 nodes.

The ElastiCache cluster can also be launched in an AWS local zone, which is an extension of an AWS region but physically closer to your users.

It also supports deployment on AWS Outposts, a service that extends the AWS infrastructure and functionality of several services, including Amazon ElastiCache, to your on-premises environment.

It's important know that, as Memcached does not support replication, the distribution across AZs is to avoid losing all the nodes in the case of an AZ failure, but this does not prevent losing the data that resides in the failing nodes. The application will need to reload data according to the caching strategy.

Although the failed nodes are detected and replaced automatically by the service, the failure can impact the data availability for the applications. So, using smaller nodes is a good strategy to reduce the impact of single node failures.

The Memcached option distributes the data across the cluster nodes and makes good use of distributed resources. The cache nodes can vary, from standard cache nodes (families *t* and *m*) to memory-optimized cache nodes (family *r*). Your cluster's total capacity will depend on the memory available per node, discounting system overhead, multiplied by the number of nodes, so using *memory-optimized cache nodes*, from the *r* family, will increase your cluster capacity.

You control how data is distributed across the nodes using a *hash* algorithm, and there are libraries that can perform a consistent hash, which minimizes the number of keys that need to be migrated in the case of adding or removing a node.

Using memory-optimized nodes will also save you money, compared to using standard cache nodes, as the price per memory unit is lower on memory-optimized nodes. This is also true for the Redis version.

AWS lets you horizontally scale *out* (adding nodes) and *in* (removing nodes) an ElastiCache for Memcached cluster, from 1 to 40 nodes, and the engine allows you to use a data partition strategy so that your application uses multiple nodes, spreading the data among them.

It is useful to use *autodiscovery* in your Memcached cluster so that you don't need to manually update your client application when you add or remove nodes.

You can also take advantage of scaling vertically with the Memcached option, using large instances, but every time you change the instance type you need to create a new cluster, and your application will need to populate the data to the new cluster.

ElastiCache for Memcached clusters are deployed in a VPC by default and rely on *VPC security groups* as firewalls to control and grant access to source security groups, source subnets, or IP addresses as usual. When you plan to scale, it is important to consider the number of free IP addresses in the subnets you will use for the service.

When you create a cluster, you will be able to configure it for TLS in-transit encryption. You will not be able to modify this cluster configuration after creation.

Redis Architecture on the Amazon ElastiCache Service

The Redis engine improves resilience because you can deploy it in a multi-AZ environment, which will create a secondary node, called *standby*, in a different AZ that receives data replication asynchronously from the primary node, enabling a failover scenario.

With multi-AZs enabled for Redis, the cluster availability for writing is fast and the loss of data is minimized, but due to the replication lag between the *primary* and the *read* nodes in different availability zones, it can still have minimal data loss in the case of a *primary node* failure.

Figure 11.2 shows the two different architectures of the Redis engine on AWS: with cluster mode enabled and with cluster mode disabled. Redis with cluster mode enabled can have several shards, each a node group with a primary node and up to five replica nodes. Redis with cluster mode disabled can have only one shard, comprised of a node group with a primary node and up to five replica nodes.

When choosing the Redis engine of Amazon ElastiCache, you need to determine whether you are going to use cluster mode enabled or cluster mode disabled. Table 11.1 illustrates some differences between the two.

FIGURE 11.2 Redis architectures

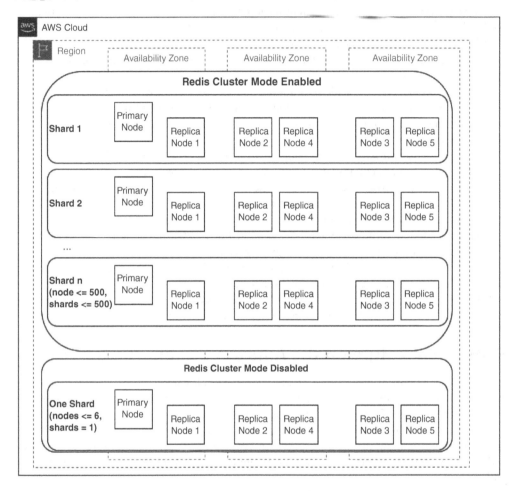

TABLE 11.1 Main differences between the Redis cluster modes

Feature	Cluster Mode Disabled	Cluster Mode Enabled
Multi-AZ deployment (optional, enabled by default)	Yes (requires at least one replica)	Yes
Node group/shard	One node group (a single shard)	Up to 500 node groups (one per shard)
Data partition	Not available; a single node must accommodate all the cached data	Yes, using shards

Feature	Cluster Mode Disabled	Cluster Mode Enabled
Read replicas	Zero to five per cluster	Zero to five per shard
Horizontal scale	Limited horizontal scale, up to five read replicas	Large scalability, adding/removing node groups (shards), with online resharding
Vertical scale	Node type change, affecting a maximum of six nodes	Node type change, affecting potentially hundreds of nodes
Write-intensive operations	Limited to one node	Spread by the shards

Working with cluster mode enabled is key for large scalability, mainly because you can work with multiple shards.

For scenarios with controlled cache size without much variation, where a single node can handle all the data, the cluster mode disabled option is the simplest to manage and work with.

Besides the replication in the same region, the Redis engine for Amazon ElastiCache has a replication feature to another region, named the Global Datastore for Redis. For this feature, you set up a secondary Redis cluster in another region as a passive cluster, and your primary cluster in the first region will be the active cluster.

All the replication between the two clusters is asynchronous and managed by the Elasti-Cache service. The secondary cluster in the secondary region is a read-only cluster, until you decide to fail over and promote it to your primary cluster. Cross-region communication is protected using VPC peering.

The Global Datastore for Redis supports encryption at rest and in transit, via Redis Auth and AWS KMS. Parameter updates from one local cluster are applied to all the clusters in the global datastore. It also has limitations: the version needs to be 5.0.6 or higher, old instance types are not supported, and the primary data store number should be the same in each cluster, but the replica numbers can be different.

Another feature available for the Redis engine for a limited set of instance-type R6gd nodes (graviton2-based) is *data tiering*, which allows the cluster to use SSDs and automatically move the least recently used data to the disk.

The shards for the Redis engine are also referred to as *replication node groups*, as the API and CLI commands work with `replication-group` commands, such as `create-replication-group` and `delete-replication-group`. The default limit for the number of shards or total nodes in a cluster is 90, but it can be increased to 500 per cluster.

Backup and Restore

The Amazon ElastiCache for Redis cluster provides the ability to back up the data and metadata of a cluster and, of course, the ability to restore a cluster from a backup, using the AWS console, the AWS CLI, or the ElastiCache APIs.

Running the Redis engine enables you to set up backups, which are .rdb files written to Amazon S3, along with the cluster metadata. You should schedule backups if you need to restore data after a failure. This is done by creating a new cluster and using the backup to populate it.

The backups for the Redis engine can be taken manually where you fully control the time they happen and the retention, or they can be automatically scheduled with the ElastiCache service and retained for 1 to 35 days. Note that setting the retention to zero will disable automatic backups.

The restoration process can also be used to change a cluster from cluster mode disabled to enabled, to change note types or shard numbers, or even to migrate data from a self-managed installation of Redis to ElastiCache, where you need to provide the .rdb file in an S3 bucket.

Redis Append Only Files (AOF) can be enabled in ElastiCache for Redis, and when enabled, ElastiCache creates a file to append all the transaction records written in the cluster to this file. This AOF file can be run against a cluster to repopulate data to it. AOF has some drawbacks, such as its size on disk and the time consumed when creating or provisioning a cluster.

There is no backup option for the Memcached engine on ElastiCache, so the strategy is to minimize data loss in the case of failure by spreading the data among many small nodes. You can always build your own scripts or applications to write data to the cache after a failure, but this will not be managed by AWS.

Security

The Amazon ElastiCache can be secured by creating the cluster in Amazon VPC and configuring limited access in the *security group* for only the applications interacting with the cache.

For Memcached, you should consider enabling in-transit encryption, and for the Redis engine, you should consider enabling at-rest encryption along with the in-transit encryption.

The in-transit option can be enabled by replication groups, with the option TransitEncryptionEnabled = True at the replication group creation time for the Redis engine. You can also improve security using an authentication called Redis AUTH, which requires a token or password for your client to communicate with the service and can be enabled only when in-transit encryption is enabled. You can later rotate or set new passwords to improve security.

Another option for user authentication over TLS is to use *role-based access control (RBAC)* with Redis 6.0 and later, where you grant user groups and roles access to specific replication groups and not to all the clusters as happens in AUTH; this allows a granular access control.

For Redis 7.0 or higher, it is also possible to use AWS IAM authentication, providing a relationship between IAM users and Redis users and user groups with fine-grained access.

Encryption at rest, available for the Redis engine, encrypts the disk sync data, backup data, swap operations, and Amazon S3 backups. Data stored in SSDs when data tiering is enabled is encrypted by default.

To interact with the Amazon ElastiCache service infrastructure, clients need Transparent Layer Security (TLS) support; AWS recommends TLS version 1.2 or later. The client application also will need to be authenticated with the AWS IAM access key and secret key or with AWS Security Token Service (STS).

Monitoring

Besides the default metrics that are sent to Amazon CloudWatch when using Amazon ElastiCache, like CacheHitRate or the number of bytes written or read, there is an integration between ElastiCache events and Amazon Simple Notification Service (SNS) that can trigger actions with other AWS components.

A cache miss is when the application looks for some record in the cache data and the item is not there. The metric that covers this is *CacheMisses*.

A cache hit is when the application looks for some record in the cache data and the item is there, so it is successfully read. The metric that covers this is *CacheHits*.

Cache hit rate is the rate of successful cache hits among all the queries for items in the cache. The metric that covers this is *CacheHitRate*, and it is calculated by dividing the cache hits by the sum of cache misses and cache hits. A CacheHitRate of 0.8 means that 80 percent of the time your application looked for an item in the cache and found the item there. For most applications, you would like this value to be as high as possible.

Specific to the Redis engine, there is a log delivery option to send the commands and metadata to Amazon Kinesis Data Firehose or Amazon CloudWatch Logs to be stored or consumed by other applications.

There are useful metrics related to ElastiCache infrastructure utilization and capacity planning like *CPUUtilization* and *EngineCPUUtilization*.

The *Memory*, *SwapUsage*, and *FreeableMemory* metrics can give you an idea about the amount of memory you have in the cluster for new data and how swap is being used. You should keep the value of *FreeableMemory* higher than your *SwapUsage* value to have a good cluster performance.

For network communication, the *Latency*, *ReplicationBytes*, and *ReplicationLag* metrics can help you to understand the usage, where bottlenecks are in the replication processes, and response time.

Amazon MemoryDB for Redis

Amazon MemoryDB for Redis is an AWS resilient database service, compatible with Redis. It was launched in 2021. It is a durable, in-memory database service that delivers extreme low latency, microsecond reads, single-digit millisecond writes, and scalability to hundreds of terabytes, and more than 100 million TPS per cluster.

Amazon MemoryDB for Redis is a good choice when resilience and durability are important but you don't have a durable database as another layer. All the resilience options we explored in this chapter for the Redis engine are available in MemoryDB by default, with the addition that transactions are durable, consistent, and recoverable automatically.

So, there is no need to have two separate layers, one for cache and another for persistence. With a managed database, you can still deliver an extremely low-latency response time for reads in the scale of microseconds.

The same option for the Redis engine on ElastiCache cluster enabled in terms of sharding and replication is available in MemoryDB: 1 to 500 shards and 0 to 5 replicas for each shard, limited to 500 nodes in total.

MemoryDB for Redis is deployed in Amazon VPC and so has all the security components such as security groups, subnets, network access control lists (ACLs), and route tables to control access to the service from other resources.

When you set up MemoryDB, you can also use an additional layer of security, based on the ACL, for authenticated users. You create an ACL, assign users and their permissions to it, and then create or assign clusters to the ACL you created. If you don't create ACLs, there is a default *open-access* ACL available with a user named *default*.

This ACL option for MemoryDB for Redis works similarly to *role-based access control* (RBAC) with Redis in Amazon ElastiCache but provides an easy way to set up and maintain ACLs and users.

The data at rest is encrypted by default for the service, and you can select to be an AWS-managed key or a customer-managed key (CMK); both use AWS Key Management Services (AWS KMS).

As with Amazon ElastiCache, MemoryDB allows you to use TLS encryption for in-transit encryption.

Summary

This chapter discussed caching strategies using lazy loading and write-through and how to use TTL to reduce the overall size of your clusters and avoid stale data.

The chapter also discussed the differences between the Redis and Memcached versions of Amazon ElastiCache so that you can decide what is best for extremely low-latency queries.

The chapter also explored Amazon MemoryDB for Redis and how you can achieve persistency for use cases that need data durability with caching.

Exam Essentials

Understand caching strategies.   Scenarios where latency is critical, such as mobile applications, require a cache structure (local or remote) that sits between the application and the persistent database. For remote caching, Amazon ElastiCache supports two engine options, Redis and Memcached.

Choose between Redis and Memcached.   Memcached is a simple option for use cases that need to scale to several nodes, spread the data around, and use multithread processing capabilities. Redis is more robust and resilient when data failover needs to be minimized, when you want to scale reads with data replication and read replicas, or when you have high security and compliance requirements.

Understand the difference between Redis cluster mode enabled and Redis cluster mode disabled.   Cluster mode disabled doesn't have a mechanism to partition data with shards, as it has a single shard and depends on the cached data to fit in one node and then replicate to up to five read replica nodes per cluster. In contrast, cluster mode enabled can have data distributed up to 500 nodes, with up to five read replicas per shard and a maximum of 500 shards.

Understand Amazon MemoryDB for Redis.   Amazon MemoryDB is an innovation on cache service, as you can rely on one structure for extremely low-latency caching; it also has transaction persistence, consistency, and recoverability, and you can interact with data using the same Redis APIs.

Exercises

For assistance in completing the following exercises, refer to the following developer guides:
docs.aws.amazon.com/elasticache/index.html
docs.aws.amazon.com/memorydb

EXERCISE 11.1

Create an Amazon Linux EC2 Machine to Be Your Bastion Host

1. Create a VPC security group in a VPC that you can access from your machine to assign to the cluster.

   a. In the AWS VPC console, go to Security Groups under Security.

   b. Click Create Security Group.

   c. Type a security group name: **for-cache**.

   d. Type a description: **Security group for caching data exercises**.

2. Add an inbound rule to allow port 22 to your IP address.

   - Type: Custom TCP

   - Port range: 22

   - Source: choose My IP

(Continues)

3. Add an inbound rule to allow ports 11211 and 6379 to your IP address.

   a. For Memcached:

   - Type: Custom TCP

   - Port: 11211

   - Source: your VPC IP range—for example, 172.31.0.0/16

   b. For Redis:

   - Type: Custom TCP

   - Port: 6379

   - Source: your VPC cidr—for example, 172.31.0.0/16

4. Click Create Security Group.

5. Create an Amazon Linux EC2 instance:

   a. From the EC2 Console, click Launch Instances.

   b. Type an instance name: **for-cache**.

   c. Select Amazon Linux AMI Instance.

   d. Select the t2.micro or other small instance.

   e. At Network Settings, click Edit.

   f. Select your VPC and settings and use public access to remotely access your instance if you don't have a VPN connection to your VPC.

   g. At Firewall (Security Groups), select the one you created in the previous step.

6. Launch the instance.

Create a Memcached Cluster

1. In the AWS console, open the Amazon ElastiCache service page.

2. In the left menu, click Memcached.

3. Click Create.

4. Select Memcached as the cluster engine.

5. Choose AWS Cloud as the location.

6. Enter **MyMemcached** as the name.

7. Choose 1.6.6 as the engine version compatibility.

8. Select 11211 as the port.

9. Select default.memcached1.6 as the parameter group.

10. Select cache.r6g.large (or another small node) as the node type.

11. Choose 2 as the number of nodes.

12. Click Advanced Memcached settings.

13. Click Create New To Create A Subnet Group.

14. Enter **my-cache-subnetgroup** as the name.

15. Choose your VPC as the VPC ID.

16. Check three subnets.

17. Choose No Preferences for availability zones placement.

18. Choose your for-cache security group.

19. Select No Preferences for the maintenance window.

20. Choose Disable Notifications for SNS.

21. Leave Tags blank.

22. Click Create.

23. After the cluster is created, click the created cluster and open the Nodes tab.

24. Take note of each of the two endpoints created, which should look as follows:

    - Node Name: 001

    - Port: 11211

    - Endpoint: `mymemcached.fjby0c.0001.use1.cache.amazonaws.com`

    - Node Name: 002

    - Port: 11211

    - Endpoint: `mymemcached.fjby0c.0002.use1.cache.amazonaws.com`

Cache Data with the pymemcache Python Library

1. Go to your AWS EC2 console, select your for-cache instance, and click Connect to connect to it using SSH.

2. Install the library for your Linux environment.

   ```
   $ pip3 install pymemcache
   ```

3. Substitute in the following Python code, <Endpoint 001> and <Endpoint 002>, with the endpoints you created in Exercise 14.2. You can either run it in the Python 3 console or save it as a file and run it.

   ```python
   $ python3
   from pymemcache.client.hash import HashClient

   client = HashClient([
       '<Endpoint 001>:11211',
       '<Endpoint 002>:11211'
   ])

   def put_value(key,value):
       print('put {} - {}'.format(key,value))
       client.set(key, value)
   def print_value(key):
       print('key:',key,' value:',client.get(key).decode('utf-8'))

   put_value('0001', 'my first key-value')
   put_value('0002', 'second value here')
   put_value('a', 'relational databases')
   put_value('b', 'nosql databases')
   put_value('c', 'in-memory databases')

   print_value('0001')
   print_value('0002')
   print_value('a')
   print_value('b')
   print_value('c')
   ```

EXERCISE 11.4

Create a Redis Cluster

1. In the AWS console, open the Amazon ElastiCache service page.

2. In the left menu, click Redis Clusters.

3. Click Create Redis Cluster.

4. Choose cluster mode Disabled.

5. For the cluster info, type a name: **MyRedis**.

6. Choose AWSCloud for the location.

7. Select Checked for Multi-AZ.

8. Set the engine version compatibility to 7.0.

9. Set the port to 6379.

10. Choose a parameter group: default.redis.7.cluster.on.

11. Select a node type: cache.r6g.large (or another small node).

12. Select the number of replicas: 2.

13. Go to the Connectivity Redis settings:

    a. Select IPV4 for the network type.

    b. Select my-cache-subnetgroup for the subnet group.

14. Choose No Preferences for Availability Zones Placement.

15. Click Next.

16. Go to the Security options:

    a. Leave encryption as the default.

    b. Click Manage For Security Groups and choose your for-cache security group.

17. Leave the backup options as the default.

18. Go to Maintenance:

    a. Choose No Preference for the maintenance window.

    b. Choose Enable for Auto Upgrade Minor Versions.

    c. Choose Disable Notifications for SNS Notification.

(Continues)

EXERCISE 11.4 *(continued)*

19. Go to Logs.

    a. Do not change Slow Logs.

    b. Leave Engine Logs unchecked.

20. Leave Tags blank.

21. Click Next.

22. Click Create.

23. After the cluster is created, click it and open the Nodes tab.

24. Take note of each of the primary endpoints created:

    Node Name: myredis-001

    Current role: Primary

    Port: 6379

    Endpoint: `myredis-001.m76vzo.0001.use1.cache.amazonaws.com`

EXERCISE 11.5

Cache Data with the Redis Library for the Python Library

1. Go to your AWS EC2 console, select your for-cache instance, and click Connect to connect to it using SSH.

2. Install the library for your Linux environment.

3. Install Redis.

   ```
   $ pip3 install redis
   ```

4. Substitute in the following Python code, <Endpoint 001>, with the endpoints you created in Exercise 14.4:

   ```
   $ python3
   import redis

   r = redis.Redis(host='<YOU REDIS PRIMARY ENDPOINT>', port=6379, db=0)

   def put_value(key,value):
       print('put {} - {}'.format(key,value))
       r.set(key, value)
   ```

```
def print_value(key):
    print('key:',key,' value:',r.get(key).decode('utf-8'))

put_value('0001', 'my first key-value')
put_value('0002', 'second value here')
put_value('a', 'relational databases')
put_value('b', 'nosql databases')
put_value('c', 'in-memory databases')

print_value('0001')
print_value('0002')
print_value('a')
print_value('b')
```

EXERCISE 11.6

Delete the Resources to Avoid Unnecessary Costs

1. Go to the AWS console on the ElastiCache dashboard.

2. Find your Memcached cluster, and delete the nodes and cluster.

3. Find your Redis cluster, and delete the nodes and cluster.

4. Go to your AWS EC2 console, and terminate your instance.

Review Questions

1. Your team is developing an application, and you need to provide a structure to store user preferences data to be retrieved by a mobile app and web version very quickly (consistently a submillisecond response time) for thousands of users. How can you achieve this while minimizing your team's overhead for managing the infrastructure?

   A. Set up an Amazon EC2 in a VPC, install your caching software, use a security group to allow access from your application, and include an application library in your application to interact with your caching service to store and retrieve values from the cache.

   B. Create an Amazon Aurora cluster in a VPC, use a security group to allow access from your application, and include a JDBC driver in your application to interact with your caching service to store and retrieve values from the cache.

   C. Set up an Amazon ElastiCache cluster for Redis or Memcached in a VPC, use a security group to allow access from your application, and include an application library in your application to interact with your caching service to store and retrieve values from the cache.

   D. Create an Amazon DocumentDB cluster in a VPC, use a security group to allow access from your application, and include a MongoDB library in your application to interact with your caching service to store and retrieve values from the cache.

2. A customer asks you to help him with an application that needs to store and update thousands of records in parallel. He estimates that he will require a large number of vCPUs (at least six) to write data and the same number to read data, and will need 40 GB to store the data. This data needs to be accessible for querying with a very low latency (submillisecond) response time. The customer doesn't want to use sharding. If the cache is lost, it will be repopulated by the applications, as data is frequently updated.

   A. Create an Amazon ElastiCache for Memcached, with an instance size of at least 12 vCPUs and 40 GB of memory to perform the reads and writes, using multithread writes.

   B. Create an Amazon RDS for PostgreSQL with a read replica option.

   C. Create an Amazon RDS for Oracle with a DataGuard option.

   D. Create an Amazon ElastiCache for Redis cluster with at least six vCPUs to perform the writes, using multithreaded processing, and perform reads on read replicas.

3. The application team wants to implement a low-latency data store cache layer to provide end users with faster response times to their last viewed products, recommendations, and profile. The current response time is about 20 milliseconds, and they would like to provide a no more than 2-millisecond response time. The information can be updated by application in the case of failure, and they expect to increase updates to this data store from hundreds per second to thousands per second. Which suggestion would you give them for faster implementation, low cost, and an easy setup and scale process?

   A. Use Amazon OpenSearch Service.

   B. Use the Amazon ElastiCache service and choose Redis.

   C. Use Amazon MemoryDB for Redis.

   D. Use the Amazon ElastiCache service and choose Memcached.

4. Your company is using a relational database and wants to improve cache capabilities, as they need to improve response times. Which AWS service would you advise them to start evaluating?

    A. Evaluate the AWS Lambda layer.

    B. Evaluate Amazon ElastiCache.

    C. Evaluate Amazon Managed Streaming for Apache Kafka (MSK).

    D. Evaluate Amazon DynamoDB DAX.

5. Your company application has a high response time for critical information to mobile applications running on AWS. It currently has a 40-millisecond response time, and the marketing team found out that this is one of the reasons for users abandoning the platform. The application should respond in less than 1 millisecond with the latest data version to keep users engaged. What do you suggest for them?

    A. Amazon ElastiCache, with a write-through strategy

    B. Amazon RDS, with a write-through strategy

    C. Amazon RDS, with a lazy loading strategy

    D. Amazon ElastiCache, with a lazy loading strategy

6. What is Amazon ElastiCache useful for?

    A. Creating a streaming layer

    B. Offloading database reads for frequently read data

    C. Improving database consistency

    D. Creating a cache layer for low-latency response time queries

7. You need to provide a data layer for an application that is persistent on disk and has a microsecond latency response time for read operations. Which AWS service is the best fit?

    A. Amazon MemoryDB for Redis

    B. Amazon ElastiCache for Memcached

    C. Amazon ElastiCache for Redis

    D. Amazon Aurora MySQL

8. Your team is required to provide a game leaderboard for thousands of simultaneous read access and single-thread updates, the application usage is extremely sensitive to latency, and there is already a persistent layer. What service would you consider for caching that is low cost, low effort to set up, and easy to maintain?

    A. Amazon RDS

    B. Amazon ElastiCache for Redis

    C. Redis on an Amazon EC2 instance

    D. Amazon MemoryDB for Redis

9. What is true about Amazon ElastiCache?

    A. You can choose between Redis and Memcached.

    B. You can choose between MemoryOnly and DiskMemory.

    C. You can choose between Redis cluster mode enabled or disabled.

    D. You can choose between cache mode enabled or disabled.

10. Your company is considering using Amazon ElastiCache. They would like an option to cache some JSON data to be read by a large number of users and rarely updated. They are not willing to deal with sharding. What would be a good option for this use case?

    A. Amazon ElastiCache for Redis with cluster mode disabled

    B. Amazon ElastiCache for Memcached with cluster mode disabled

    C. Amazon ElastiCache for Redis with cluster mode enabled

    D. Amazon ElastiCache for Memcached with cluster mode disabled

Deployment and Migration

Chapter

12

Migrating Your Data to AWS

THE AWS CERTIFIED DATABASE – SPECIALTY EXAM OBJECTIVES COVERED IN THIS CHAPTER MAY INCLUDE, BUT ARE NOT LIMITED TO, THE FOLLOWING:

✓ **Domain 2.0: Deployment and Migration**

- 2.2 Determine data preparation and migration strategies.
- 2.3 Execute and validate data migration.

When you are migrating existing databases to AWS, after you choose your target database environment, you need to decide on how you want to migrate your data.

Some important considerations include the amount of data, the conversion that may be needed, the time window to complete the migration, the network bandwidth, and, if any downtime is acceptable, how long it could be. You also have to consider how and when the dependent applications will be migrated.

There are several ways to migrate data to AWS. This chapter describes the options to migrate database workloads to AWS.

Network Communication and Data Migration

Network communication is key for data migration, not only for data transfer throughput but also for the security requirements you may have. AWS database services will be in a virtual private cloud (VPC) most of the time or have a VPC endpoint (for example, in the case of Amazon DynamoDB). Therefore, you can establish a connection with your current datacenters using an AWS Site-to-Site virtual private network (VPN) or using an AWS Direct Connect connection and then use security groups to allow traffic only from specific IP address ranges in a VPC, from application security groups in AWS, or from on-premises IP address ranges.

Even if you are not going to transfer data directly to a database service but instead use Amazon S3 as a staging area, you can use Amazon S3 interface endpoints with AWS Private-Link to allow on-premises communication with Amazon S3 over your secure AWS Site-to-Site VPN or AWS Direct Connect connections.

It's possible to send data directly to Amazon S3 over the Internet using the Transport Layer Security (TLS) encryption, but this is not the most secure. The most secure option is to use TLS over AWS Site-to-Site VPN or AWS Direct Connect.

Database migration is the relocation of the table definition and related objects, such as indexes, functions, procedures, views, and of course the data, from a source database to a target database.

When planning a database migration, note that one of the most limiting resources for data migration is network bandwidth. So, after gathering your database size, you can use Table 12.1 to help you figure out how long, in hours or days, a data transfer through the network will take according to your database size and the available network bandwidth.

TABLE 12.1 Estimated Time to Migrate Data

Database Size	Network Bandwidth	Data Migration	
(GB)	(Mbps)	(In Hours)	(In Days)
100	10	22h, 13 min	<1
100	100	2h, 3 min	<1
100	500	0h, 26 min	<1
100	1,000	0h, 13 min	<1
100	2,000	0h, 7 min	<1
512	10	114h	5
512	100	11h, 22 min	<1
512	500	2h, 16 min	<1
512	1,000	1h, 8 min	<1
512	2,000	0h, 34 min	<1
1,024	10	228h	10
1,024	100	22h, 45 min	1
1,024	500	4h, 34 min	<1
1,024	1,000	2h, 16 min	<1
1,024	2,000	1h, 8 min	<1
2,048	10	456h	19
2,048	100	46h	2
2,048	500	9h, 6 min	<1
2,048	1,000	4h, 33 min	<1
2,048	2,000	2h, 16 min	<1
10,240	10	2,276h	97

(*continues*)

TABLE 12.1   Estimated Time to Migrate Data *(continued)*

Database Size	Network Bandwidth	Data Migration	
(GB)	(Mbps)	(In Hours)	(In Days)
10,240	100	228h	10
10,240	500	46h	2
10,240	1,000	22h, 45 min	1
10,240	2,000	11h, 22 min	<1
51,200	10	11,378h	485
51,200	100	1,138h	49
51,200	500	228h	10
51,200	1,000	114h	5
51,200	2,000	56h	2

Several times you will not have a dedicated network tunnel for the database migration, so be aware that this bandwidth is considering only database traffic. If the network connection is shared with other applications or users, you may have traffic concurrency, which will increase the time to migrate. Work with your company's network team.

If your database to be migrated is 512 GB or less, you will probably finish your data migration in less than a week, if your network bandwidth available for this migration is at least 10 Mbps.

AWS Site-to-Site VPN throughput can be limited by the bandwidth you have contracted from an Internet provider in your site and by the network interface from your source database and target database. AWS provides two tunnels for AWS Site-to-Site VPN and limits each tunnel to 1.25 Gbps. If you have up to 1.25 Gbps Internet bandwidth in your site, you will be able to use all its capacity to transfer data, but if you have more bandwidth available from your site, your transfer rate will be capped at 1.25 Gbps per tunnel by AWS.

If you need a higher bandwidth or want to have a dedicated physical connection, you can use an AWS Direct Connect connection, which is available in speeds starting at 50 Mbps and scaling up to 100 Gbps. You will need to have a physical connection from your datacenters to at least one of the AWS connection locations. Check the available locations on the AWS Direct Connect Locations page.

Database downtime for migration is the time it takes to switch over the applications from the source database to the target database in a consistent manner, including the portion of time required to apply the latest changes from the source to the target, before allowing the application to connect to the target.

Change data capture (CDC) is the process that captures the changes in the source, while the data files are being copied, to update the target database with the transactions that happened during the copy time.

To plan for a minimal downtime migration, you need to add bandwidth for CDC updates to be sent over the network, while static data is also being migrated at the same time. Estimate the generation rate of your database changes to be captured such as Oracle archived logs, PostgreSQL write-ahead logs (WAL), MySQL bin logs, and Microsoft SQL Server transactions logs (usually measured as bytes per second, so convert it to Mbps and add this to your bandwidth requirements).

Also check if your source database hardware resources such as network speed, CPU, and disk read throughput are not being capped by your current infrastructure and have capacity to accommodate the migration process to provide fast read and data transfer rates.

Optimizing Bandwidth Usage

Compressing data when performing data migration over the network is a best practice. Database tools can deliver backup files in a compressed format for most database engines. When this option is not available or you have access only to the uncompressed backup files, you can use compress tools such as Gzip, Lzop, Bzip2, Zip, and others before sending them through the network. As the compression process takes time, perform some sample tests to estimate how long it will take so you can include the amount of time required in your planning.

Database Migration to AWS

Heterogeneous database migration is a database migration where the source and target database are different engines. You can use some native tools from the source to extract the data, but you need to convert the objects and then use a different tool to load the data to the target.

AWS has created two services that facilitate the process for heterogeneous database migration: AWS Schema Conversion Tool and AWS Data Migration Service.

Homogenous database migration is a database migration where the source and target are the same engine. The native tools for each engine are usually enough to perform the entire migration for the schema objects and the data.

AWS DMS can be useful for homogenous database migration, especially when minimal downtime is required, because of its CDC capability.

AWS Schema Conversion Tool

AWS Schema Conversion Tool (AWS SCT) is an AWS tool to convert a source database schema from one engine to another engine as the target; it works for several commercial and open-source database engines.

The main purpose of AWS SCT is to convert schemas from a source database engine to a target database engine. This is key, because the data types, Structured Query Language (SQL), and Procedural Language/Structured Query Language (PL/SQL) code may have different supported syntaxes, function names, and features such as partitioning and would require many hours for database specialists to manually convert them.

AWS SCT is a client graphical tool, as represented in Figure 12.1, that you install on a Windows or Linux machine. To convert a schema, perform the following steps:

1. Install AWS SCT on your Linux or Windows machine; you can use an Amazon EC2 instance as well.

2. Download the JDBC drivers for the source and target engines.

3. Connect to the source database.

4. Connect to the target database, or use a virtual target for planning.

5. Select the appropriate schemas and objects to migrate.

6. Create a conversion and migration assessment report.

7. Generate the SQL statements to create a target schema that has a classification for each object as an action item, enabling a comparison between the source and target codes.

8. Download the conversion scripts as a SQL file.

9. Apply the changes to the target database, creating a target converted schema.

10. Optionally, generate AWS Glue jobs for data warehouses from the SQL transformation.

11. Optionally, use the SCT extraction agents to migrate the data to Amazon Redshift from commercial data warehouses.

12. Optionally, integrate with AWS DMS to create the data migration tasks.

FIGURE 12.1 AWS SCT client tool

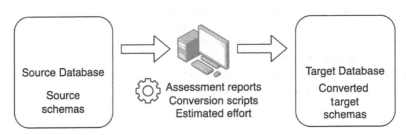

AWS SCT - Client Tool

When migrating from one database engine to another (for example, from a commercial database to Amazon Aurora), the AWS SCT migration assessment reports are useful, because they are easy to create and they display valuable information. You should always consider using AWS SCT to evaluate the level of automation for a schema conversion and the manual tasks you will need to perform for objects not converted automatically.

The report summary displays the schemas, tables, columns, and constraints. The schema migration is categorized as follows:

- **Simple:** Actions that can be completed in less than one hour
- **Medium:** Actions that are more complex and can be completed in one to four hours
- **Significant:** Actions that are very complex and take more than four hours to complete

After creating a report, you can navigate through the Action Items tab, which not only shows the issues for unsupported data types and object conversion, but also tells you how you should manually handle them. The action items are categorized as follows:

- Automatically handled by AWS SCT (in gray)
- Converted with a small automatic transformation that the database specialist may want to validate (in yellow)
- Could not be automatically converted, with recommendations for how to manually convert the schema items (in red)

Sometimes it will be easier to convert objects in the source, refresh the schema, and run the report again, but many times database specialists can adjust the SQL statement by rewriting it from the suggestion and either apply it to the target database or save it as SQL.

AWS SCT Extension Pack is an add-on module that emulates functions present in the source database that are required when converting objects to the target database. This is useful to reduce the number of manual changes to convert code from one database to another. For example, it creates a Sysdate function in the target to work as Oracle sysdate when converting from Oracle to PostgreSQL.

AWS SCT supports the following source databases. They don't need to be on premises, although that is the most common scenario.

- Oracle
- Microsoft SQL Server
- MySQL
- PostgreSQL
- SAP ASE (Sybase ASE)
- IBM Db2 LUW
- Apache Cassandra
- Azure SQL Database
- IBM Db2 for z/OS

The supported target database will depend on the source, but here are the available targets for AWS SCT:

- Amazon RDS for MySQL

- Amazon Aurora (MySQL)

- Amazon RDS for MariaDB

- Amazon RDS for PostgreSQL

- Amazon Aurora (PostgreSQL)

- Amazon RDS for Oracle

- Amazon RDS for SQL Server

- Amazon DynamoDB

The following are the supported data warehouse sources for AWS SCT:

- Oracle Data Warehouse

- Teradata

- Netezza

- Greenplum

- Vertica

- SQL Server Data Warehouse

- Azure SQL Data Warehouse (Azure Synapse)

- Snowflake

For a data warehouse's source, the target will be Amazon Redshift. For this type of migration, you can also use AWS SCT data extractor agents, which support most of these sources at the moment. AWS SCT extractors are agents that extract your data and upload the data to either Amazon S3 or an AWS Snowball Edge device. You then use another step in AWS SCT to copy the data to Amazon Redshift.

Extractors work in a parallelized way. You define tasks and subtasks as groups of tables, and each subtask runs in an autonomous way of extracting, uploading, and copying the data to Amazon Redshift.

You can use three levels of filter when creating a task.

- **Schema name filter,** for all schema names that contain the filter text

- **Table name filter,** for all table names that contain the filter text

- **Where clause filter,** to actually filter data based on a condition

Extraction agents are currently supported on the following operating systems: macOS, Microsoft Windows, Red Hat Enterprise Linux (RHEL) 6.0, and Ubuntu Linux (version 14.04 and later).

AWS SCT data extractor agents can also be used to extract data from Apache Cassandra to Amazon DynamoDB.

AWS Data Migration Service

AWS Database Migration Service (AWS DMS) can be used to migrate the databases to the same database engine as a homogenous migration, or to another database engine as a heterogeneous migration, making it possible to migrate from Oracle to PostgreSQL or Microsoft SQL Server to MySQL. AWS DMS also supports NoSQL databases as sources and targets.

The main purpose of AWS DMS is to perform database migration to AWS, but you can also use AWS DMS to migrate databases from AWS to somewhere else.

AWS DMS covers two main types of migration: full load mode, to copy the data from source tables to target tables, and CDC mode, where AWS DMS captures the ongoing changes and applies them to the target to synchronize the target database with the most recent version of the source. You can use a task with the Migrating Existing Data and Capturing Changes During Migration options to perform the full load from the existing data and automatically start the CDC applying process when the full load is finished. This allows you to decide when to stop the CDC applying process to switch over applications to the new target database or even when you want to create a point-in-time copy from the source database for test, development, or reporting purposes.

As mentioned previously, if you are changing engines, you will need to run AWS SCT or another tool to convert the schema, as AWS DMS will be limited to creating the target tables and primary keys and migrating the data; it doesn't create other indexes, procedures, functions, grants, and table references.

The following are the supported source databases, known as *source endpoints*, for AWS DMS:

- Oracle database 10.2 and later, 10g, 11g, and up to 12.2, 18c, and 19c
- Microsoft SQL Server database versions 2005, 2008, 2008R2, 2012, 2014, 2016, 2017, and 2019
- Microsoft Azure SQL database
- PostgreSQL database: version 9.4 and later, 9.x, 10.x, 11.x, and 12.x
- MySQL database versions 5.5, 5.6, 5.7, and 8.0
- MariaDB database versions 10.0.24 to 10.0.28, 10.1, 10.2, and 10.3, 10.3.13, 10.4, 10.5
- SAP ASE database versions 12.5, 15, 15.5, 15.7, 16, and later
- MongoDB database versions 3.x and 4.0
- Amazon DocumentDB (with MongoDB compatibility)
- Amazon S3, in comma-separated value (CSV) format files
- IBM Db2 for Linux, Unix, and Windows database (Db2 LUW) versions 9.7, 10.1, 10.5, 11.1, and 11.5

The *AWS DMS replication instance* is an instance that connects to the *source endpoint*, reads the data, converts the data into the target format, and writes the data to the *target endpoint*, which is a connection to the target database instance.

The *AWS DMS source endpoint* is a database connection configuration, such as hostname, port, username, or secret, to the source database, which is the one that has the data to migrate from.

The *AWS DMS target endpoint* is a database connection configuration, such as hostname, port, username, secret, to the target database, which is the one that will receive the data during migration.

The following are the supported target databases, known as *target endpoints*, for AWS DMS:

- Oracle database 10.2 and later, 10g, 11g and up to 12.2, 18c, and 19c

- Microsoft SQL Server database versions 2005, 2008, 2008R2, 2012, 2014, 2016, 2017, and 2019

- PostgreSQL database version 9.4 and later, 9.x, 10.x, 11.x, and 12.x

- MySQL database versions 5.5, 5.6, 5.7, and 8.0

- MariaDB database versions 10.0.24 to 10.0.28, 10.1, 10.2, and 10.3, and 10.4

- SAP ASE database versions 12.5, 15, 15.5, 15.7, 16, and later

- Redis version 6.x

- Amazon RDS instance databases for Oracle, Microsoft SQL Server, MySQL, or PostgreSQL

- Amazon Aurora MySQL-Compatible Edition

- Amazon Aurora PostgreSQL-Compatible Edition

- Amazon Redshift

- Amazon S3

- Amazon DynamoDB

- Amazon OpenSearch Service

- Amazon ElastiCache for Redis

- Amazon Kinesis Data Streams

- Amazon DocumentDB (with MongoDB compatibility)

- Amazon Neptune

- Apache Kafka—self-managed or Amazon Managed Streaming for Apache Kafka (Amazon MSK)

Figure 12.2 shows the following components of AWS DMS:

- **Source endpoint:** Connection details to the source database or files in S3 you want to migrate

- **Target endpoint:** Connection details to the target database, streaming service, or storage where you are migrating to

- **Replication task:** A definition of a set of tables or schemas to be migrated in a group

- **Replication instance:** A service instance that connects to both source and target, and executes the tasks for migration

FIGURE 12.2   AWS Data Migration Service components

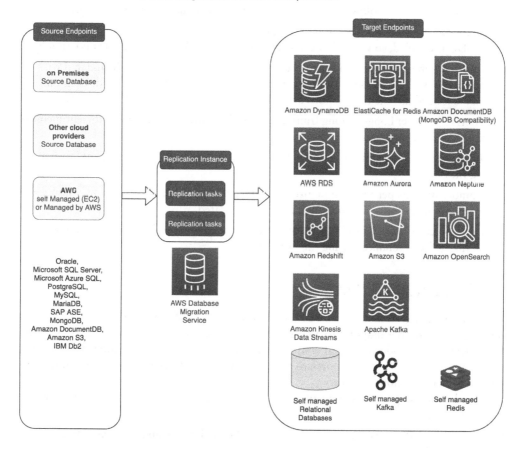

You will need to choose a replication instance type and size, according to the tables you are going to migrate and if you are performing full load, CDC, or both processes. Each replication instance can handle multiple tasks, and migration will consume vCPU, memory, and disk storage. The AWS DMS replication instance can be of the following types:

- Burstable general-purpose (T type) provides a baseline level of CPU performance with the ability to burst CPU usage; this is useful for generic, not intensive, replication tasks.

- Compute-intensive (C type) delivers cost-effective high performance for compute-intensive workloads; this is useful for heterogeneous migration, where a replication instance needs to translate and convert data types and transactions.

- Memory-optimized (R type) is useful for ongoing replications from high-throughput transaction databases.

The default disk size of replication instance is usually enough for the majority of tasks. Because log files are the great consumers of disk space in the replication instance, however, you should consider the following regarding replication instances and disk storage:

- **Table size:** Large tables take longer to migrate, and transactions need to be held in disk if CDC is enabled, so you will need to set up enough disk space for the transaction logs.

- **Source database change activity:** If the source database has been highly updated with transactions, these transactions must be cached until the tables are loaded. Each table that is loaded has the transactions applied at the end of the full loading process.

- **Transaction size:** Long-running transactions in the source will require sufficient memory to stream all changes in the transaction.

- **Total size:** Large migrations take longer, and they usually generate a large number of log files.

- **Number of tasks per replication instance:** More tasks in a single replication instance will require more caching, and more log files are generated.

- **Large objects:** Tables with large objects (LOBs) take longer to load, increasing the number of logs retained during the process.

Setting Up AWS DMS

The *AWS DMS migration task* is the configuration of the set of tables you would like to migrate, from a source endpoint to a target endpoint. You state the details of the transformation as well as the mode, namely, if it will be existing data only or a continuous replication.

To replicate tables from the source to the target, you need to create a migration task that will run on a replication instance.

The following steps are a sample of creating an AWS DMS migration task to migrate data from a source database to a target database:

1. In the AWS VPC console, create or choose a VPC with the proper subnets, and then create a security group in the VPC for your replication instance.

2. In the AWS DMS console, create a subnet group for your replication instance.

3. Create a replication instance in the subnet group, using the security group created.

4. On your source database, open a firewall rule to allow traffic from your replication instance to your source database at the correct port.

5. Create a user in your source database with the minimal privileges required according to the DMS documentation for your source database engine. Each engine has its own requirement. For ongoing replication, additional privileges will be required to read the logs on the source.

6. Create a source endpoint using the replication instance and the user you created. Test the connectivity and refresh the schemas.

7. On your target database, create a rule in the security group to allow traffic from your replication instance security group to the correct port.

8. Create a target endpoint using the replication instance and a user with privileges to create objects, check the DMS documentation for each database engine as a target, and test the connectivity.

9. Create a database migration task using the replication instance, the source endpoint, and the target endpoint.

10. Choose the migration type.

- Migrate existing data.

- Migrate existing data and replicate ongoing changes.

- Replicate data changes only.

11. Set up the task settings, as follows:

a. Select if you want to drop, truncate, or do nothing with the target tables before migrating.

b. Select whether LOB columns should be replicated and their maximum size.

c. Select whether to enable or disable the validation check, which is a comparison between the source and target tables after full load. Validation being enabled requires additional time to complete.

d. Enable CloudWatch logs and select the level—from default to detailed debug—for each log type. If you don't enable CloudWatch logs, you will not be able to troubleshoot failed migration tasks.

e. Choose the maximum number of tables to load in parallel, transaction consistency timeout, commit rate, and DMS control tables in the target in the advanced settings options.

12. Enable the pre-migration assessment to preview warnings on potential issues that DMS can detect before migrating, such as unsupported data types, tables with LOB objects but without a primary or unique key, tables for CDC without a primary key, or the presence of a composite primary key when the target is the OpenSearch service.

13. Set up the task to start automatically or manually after creation.

14. Assign the proper tags for your control.

As DMS can load tables in parallel, without control of the order, the referential integrity between tables may be broken until the end of the data load process, so you will need to disable referential constraint during full load. Also, database triggers should be disabled in the target to avoid creating records or actions that have already been done in the source database.

Groups of tables that have a relationship with or dependency on each other should be put in a single replication task, but you should not include tables with no relationship in the same tasks. Isolating groups of tables that have relationships with each other in tasks enables you to restart a task with a smaller group of tables in the case of failure, instead of restarting the whole migration.

Imagine that you are at the end of a migration with 200 tables that have been running for hours, and a single table fails. You have two potential solutions based on how you set up your tasks.

- **One big single task with 200 tables:** You will need to fix the cause of the failure and restart the task, potentially losing everything you have migrated until the failure.

- **Tables split into many tasks, and this failed table is in a task with 15 other tables:** You can restart the failed task without impacting the other 185 tables that have been migrated in other tasks.

Another benefit of splitting tables across tasks is that you have control of the parallelism for each task, as well as the commit rate and transaction timeout, which could address a fine-tuning for each group of tables more precisely.

After the full load of a task, you can enable constraints for that group of tables you have isolated in a replication task and re-create or rebuild indexes and recompile database objects in phases.

AWS DMS Continuous Replication

The most common migration types for AWS DMS are migrating existing data and migrating existing data and replicating ongoing changes, which handles all the consistency of change logs being applied to the target, but AWS DMS allows you to create a task to replicate data changes only.

Migrate existing data is an AWS DMS migration type that migrates only the data that is already in the tables at the moment the task reads it, and it doesn't handle any changes after this time.

Migrate existing data and replicate ongoing changes is an AWS DMS migration type that migrates the data that is already in the tables and after this continues to apply any changes that are occurring in the source database with a CDC mechanism.

Replicate data changes only is an AWS DMS migration type that applies the changes that occur only after the task starts or at a particular point in time, and it imposes some tracking activities for the database administrator who handles the migration, because it assumes you have already migrated the data with a full load, with AWS DMS full load, with AWS Snowball, or with another copy of the data.

To maintain the consistency between the source and the target, you need to know the exact time you took the copy from your source environment so you can apply the changes that happened after that exact moment. This is hard to track in terms of exact microseconds.

To facilitate this tracking, databases have a sequence number to track the changes, such as the following:

- Log sequence number (LSN), for SQL Server

- System change number (SCN), for Oracle

- Checkpoint replication slots, for PostgreSQL

- LSN, for MySQL

The use of LSN, SCN, or checkpoint replication slots facilitates the task of performing the synchronization with a full load copy and the changes that happened afterward. When you take a consistent, point-in-time copy from your source to perform the full load, you query and take note of the consistent number (LSN, SCN, or checkpoint). Then you use this number to apply every change that happened after the copy to your target database.

> Take care of your log (bin log, archived log, write-ahead log [WAL], or transaction log) area in the source database machine when performing continuous replication. You cannot delete the logs generated after the full load copy has been generated, until the replication instance is able to read them; otherwise, you will not be able to synchronize the target with the source database. So, many times you may need to disable the delete routines that happen after the backup of these log areas temporarily, and you may also need to increase this area to handle those files for more time.

AWS DMS Best Practices

AWS DMS has launched several features and options since its first release in January 2016 that help you configure and optimize a database migration. Here are some best practices regarding some of those features and options:

- Do not underestimate the effort of a database migration. Perform a proof of concept of database migration to know in advance your data profile and how large your database is. This will give you space to tune your replication instance size, distribute tables properly among the tasks, and evaluate the number of replication instances needed.

   With the tests, you will also know the bottlenecks of data migration by evaluating the performance in terms of vCPU, memory, network, and disk metrics, and by considering the source instance resources, replication instance size and storage, network communication, and target database instance resources. In the real world, for large databases, you will see 80 percent to 90 percent of your tables being migrated fast and without any issues, which means you will need to fine-tune 10 percent to 20 percent of them. Those are usually the very large tables, which tests will identify.

- Tune parallelism for tasks. By default it's set to eight tables in parallel per task. Separating large tables into specific tasks can help you to isolate them from other table errors, whereas for small tables, which are easy to migrate, you can increase parallelism. Try not to increase the workload in source databases too much, especially production ones. The workers will use disk reads and vCPU from your source database machine for each table being loaded in parallel at the same time. For engines like Oracle, Microsoft SQL Server, MySQL, Sybase, and IBM Db2 LUW, it's possible to parallelize loading large tables using *partition-load* task configuration, where data will be parallelized based on a list, a set of ranges, or automatically.

- LOB columns take longer to migrate compared to columns with regular data types of the same size. Do not migrate LOBs if you have a better strategy to store them in Amazon S3, for example. AWS has created a specific setup in the migration task to address this, so you can exclude LOB columns from the migration and, instead of migrating them, rethink where to store the objects. If you decide to migrate the LOB columns, you can set it to three different modes, depending on the size of source LOBs and behavior during migration, as follows:

  - **Limited LOB mode,** where DMS will truncate the objects that exceed the size limit. This is the AWS recommended mode, and the maximum LOB size should be set to up to 100 MB for optimal performance.

  - **Full LOB mode,** which can be very slow. This is a piece-by-piece migration of the objects and will take longer. It is split into chunk sizes that default to 64 KB.

  - **Inline LOB mode,** so small objects limited by size will migrate as an inline migration, and what exceeds the limit will be migrated using the Full LOB mode, piece by piece.

- Import other schema objects with AWS SCT or native tools. Keep in mind that AWS DMS only creates tables and primary keys; it does not migrate dependent objects and grants, so you may want to use a dump file from a native tool with metadata to import objects such as procedures and functions in your target database. For heterogeneous migration, you can use AWS SCT, which handles the schema conversion required from one engine to another. For homogenous migration, you can use native database tools such as Oracle SQL Developer, MySQL Workbench, or pgAdmin4 to move the complete schema with dependencies and use AWS DMS to migrate the data.

- Indexes, triggers, and referential integrity constraints can increase load time and may cause task failure. During the full load, you should drop or disable the indexes, referential integrity constraints, and triggers, and then re-create, rebuild, or enable them before the CDC phase.

- For an Amazon RDS target, disable Multi-AZ and turn off backups until the databases are synchronized.

- Enable CloudWatch logs, which are not enabled by default. You will not be able to troubleshoot failing tasks to determine the root cause and correct them.

- Monitor CloudWatch metrics for the migration tasks and set event alarms for high latency for long-running migrations.

- Enable validation for database targets so you can use the validation help in your final database migration validation.

- You can use JSON task definitions that are easy to maintain, duplicate, or update, with minimal effort. The following JSON example selects every schema and table from the source database and uses a parallel load for table SH.SALES:

```json
{
    "rules": [{
            "rule-type": "selection",
            "rule-id": "1",
            "rule-name": "1",
            "object-locator": {
                "schema-name": "%",
                "table-name": "%"
            },
            "rule-action": "include"
        },
        {

            "rule-type": "table-settings",
            "rule-id": "2",
            "rule-name": "2",
            "object-locator": {
                "schema-name": "SH",
                "table-name": "SALES"
            },
            "parallel-load": {
                "type": "partitions-auto"
            }
        }
    ]
}
```

- Use filters to migrate only a subset of the data if you don't need some tables to be migrated. For example, to pick only sales values greater than 1000, use the following filter:

```json
{
    "rules": [{
        "rule-type": "selection",
        "rule-id": "1",
        "rule-name": "1",
        "object-locator": {
```

```
            "schema-name": "SH",
            "table-name": "SALES"
        },
        "rule-action": "include",
        "filters": [{
            "filter-type": "source",
            "column-name": "SALES_VALUE",
            "filter-conditions": [{
                "filter-operator": "gte",
                "value": "1000"
            }]
        }]
    }]
}
```

- For a migration that takes too long over the network and puts the migration window at risk, consider using AWS Snowball or another hard-copy system for the full load.

AWS DMS Security

As a best practice, an AWS DMS replication instance should be set up in a private subnet in your VPC network. You will need to allow traffic from this replication instance to your source database instance and to your target database instance using an AWS Site-to-Site VPN or AWS Direct Connect connection.

For security purposes, AWS DMS encrypts the storage and endpoints connection information with an AWS Key Management Service (AWS KMS) key, with the default (aws/dms) or an AWS KMS that you can create.

AWS DMS also supports Secure Sockets Layer (SSL) to encrypt the connection for the source and target endpoints.

AWS DMS Resilience

The replication instance for AWS DMS is where all the processes of migration tasks are tracked and logged. To improve resilience, you should deploy a Multi-AZ replication instance so the service will automatically provision and maintain a synchronous copy of the replication instance in a different availability zone (AZ).

So in the case of instance failure or AZ failure, AWS DMS can continue to work with an automatic failover to the secondary AZ with the standby instance.

Other AWS Services for Data Migration

When performing a homogenous migration where the source and target are the same engine, you can use AWS DMS, but you also can use the native database tools. Some of them are supported only for self-managed databases on EC2; some native tools and third parties are supported for managed services. Here are some examples of native tools available for relational databases on EC2 and on RDS:

- **Oracle on EC2:** Oracle Data Pump, GoldenGate, Data Guard, and RMAN
- **RDS for Oracle:** Oracle Data Pump and GoldenGate
- **PostgreSQL on EC2:** Master-slave replication, pg_dump, pg_restore, and psql
- **RDS for PostgreSQL:** pg_dump, pg_restore, and psql
- **MySQL on EC2:** mysqldbcopy, mysqldump, Percona XtraBackup, and MySQL read replica
- **RDS for MySQL:** mysqldbcopy, Percona XtraBackup, and mysqldump
- **Microsoft SQL Server on EC2 or RDS for SQL Server:** Backup and Restore, Copy Database Wizard, and copy and attach database

In this section, you will learn about services that help data movement from on-premises to AWS as dump files.

AWS DataSync

AWS DataSync service is a service that can copy files from a specific filesystem on premises and transfer it to an AWS service such as Amazon S3, Amazon EFS, or FSx.

If you have a database-native backup tool and copies of data files or dump files on premises and want to transfer them over the network, you can use AWS DataSync. This tool is used to move datasets over the network into Amazon S3, Amazon EFS, or FSx for Windows File Server, using compression algorithms, and it also includes data integrity validation and encryption.

To speed up migrations, AWS DataSync uses a purpose-built network protocol and a parallel, multithreaded architecture.

AWS Snow Family

When the volume of data is high and the bandwidth is not fast enough to allow a reasonable window time for migration, you can use the AWS Snow family of physical devices. These are storage devices that AWS sends you. You connect them in your data center to copy data, and you send them back to AWS when the copy is finished.

AWS offers three main types of Snow devices for data transfer.

- *AWS Snowcone* is the entry-level member of the AWS Snow family of data transfer devices, with a capacity of up to 8 TB of storage. It also provides edge computing capabilities to run code inside them.

- *AWS Snowball Edge Storage Optimized* are devices provided with 40 vCPUs of compute capacity coupled with 80 TB of usable block or Amazon S3–compatible object storage.

- *AWS Snowmobile* is a 45-foot-long ruggedized shipping container that can move up to 100 PB of data; it should be considered for multipetabyte migrations.

Consider the AWS Snow family when you want to physically copy data and send it to AWS. If you need a CDC process for minimal downtime, it's possible to synchronize both processes and use time-based or database log–based controls along with AWS Data Migration Services (AWS DMS).

AWS Storage Gateway

AWS Storage Gateway is a way to move on-premises files, data files, backup files, or dump files over the network to AWS. It offers four different types of gateways: *Amazon S3 File Gateway*, *Amazon FSx File Gateway*, *Tape Gateway*, and *Volume Gateway*. The on-premises machines connect to the service through a virtual machine or gateway hardware appliance using standard storage protocols, such as Network Filesystem (NFS), Server Message Block (SMB), and Internet Small Computer System Interface (iSCSI).

The virtual storage is then mounted into on-premises machines, but the files you create there are actually stored in AWS storage services, such as Amazon S3, Amazon S3 Glacier, Amazon S3 Glacier Deep Archive, Amazon FSx for Windows File Server, Amazon EBS, and AWS Backup. It's possible to use local on-premises disks as cache areas to improve performance while the data is saved in AWS storage services.

The AWS transfer family can be another option used to transfer data securely from on-premises to AWS, with the Secure File Transfer Protocol (SFTP) or File Transfer Protocol over SSL (FTPS) protocols. The SFTP and FTPS services will store the received files to Amazon Simple Storage Service (S3) or Amazon Elastic File System (EFS) as configured as a totally managed service.

Choosing the Migration Path

The path to migrate the data will depend on the transformation you will perform, what your source and target database engines are, and if you are going to use managed services or self-management for a target.

One or Many Target Databases

The first thing to decide is whether you are going to migrate to a self-managed database on Amazon Elastic Compute Cloud (Amazon EC2) or an AWS managed service, like Amazon RDS.

Choose a database in EC2 when the source engine is not supported by AWS managed services and the application cannot be changed to use another database, such as a legacy application that uses IBM Db2 where you can't change application code.

A single source database instance may be split into multiple target database engines, because you are using the purpose-built database concept and choosing the appropriate database for each database workload that was previously running on the same database instance. For example, you are moving a product catalog search service to a NoSQL database, the orders service to an Aurora PostgreSQL, and historical records to Amazon Redshift. The application code and database schema will need to change, and you will use AWS SCT to convert the schema and AWS DMS to migrate the data.

Small, Noncritical Databases

For small databases being migrated with homogenous migration that can afford some downtime, consider using database-native tools, such as Oracle SQL Developer, MySQL Workbench, SQL Server backup, and pgAdmin4; or you can use third-party tools. Amazon S3 can be an intermediate storage for dump or backup files.

For MySQL there is a pattern using Percona XtraBackup and Amazon EFS for a migration to Aurora MySQL database that accelerates migration to AWS.

For Oracle, you can also use the Oracle Data Pump network link from RDS to load the data using a database link and a filesystem area for the logs.

For near-zero downtime, with full loads that can be done in a reasonable time window over AWS Direct Connect or AWS Site-to-Site VPN connection, you can use AWS DMS full load plus ongoing replication, or another tool with CDC capability that is able to synchronize the source and target with the transaction changes after full load.

Using AWS DMS for the continuous replication only is also possible, since you can perform a consistent copy and take note of the exact point in time of that copy to apply the change logs after the copy.

Consider also working with a DNS resolver to be able to point applications to the new database service with minimal reconfiguration time and create application copies in AWS before migrating the database.

Very Large Databases

For very large databases that don't fit in the time window for migration over the network, you may need to perform the full load using a storage device such as AWS Snowball. Or you can use *AWS DMS Agent*, which is a small software package that AWS provides to install in your on-premises environment, extract data in parallel with several worker threads, and then synchronize the source and target with continuous replication.

AWS Snowball and AWS DMS Agent will use Amazon S3 as a staging area before loading the data to the target, and then another DMS task loads from Amazon S3 to the target database.

Summary

This chapter explored the main AWS services for database migration, as well as services that can be used to accelerate migration using database-native tools.

When performing heterogeneous migration, you can use AWS SCT and AWS DMS. AWS SCT will perform schema conversion and also detect any manual changes needed, while AWS DMS will be in charge of the data migration.

When performing homogenous migration, you should consider using AWS DMS for minimal downtime or using database-native tools when downtime is acceptable. Then you can use AWS DataSync, AWS Storage Gateway, and the AWS Snow family to transfer the data files, backup files, or dump files to AWS. It is also possible to perform a continuous replication to synchronize the source and target using AWS DMS ongoing replication after the full load, even if the full load has been done by database-native tools.

Exam Essentials

Know how to migrate databases to AWS.   You have seen that AWS provides a set of services that can help with database migration, from the database-specific tools, such as AWS DMS and AWS SCT, to file movement tools such as AWS DataSync, AWS Transfer Family, and AWS Storage Gateway. You can move data over the network using AWS Direct Connect or AWS Site-to-Site VPN, or you can use an AWS storage device via AWS Snowball to copy the data and send it back to AWS.

Be able to use AWS SCT and AWS DMS.   AWS Schema Conversion Tool facilitates heterogeneous database migration, and it's aligned with a purpose-built database strategy. One source database can be migrated to more than one target engine, separating workload-specific tables for the appropriate service. AWS DMS then migrates the table data to each target database.

Understand AWS DMS best practices.   Enable AWS DMS validation for data migration to the target database, and enable logging activities for tasks for troubleshooting. Parallelize table migration at three levels: use the parallel partition-load to parallelize large table loads in several partitions, use the tables in parallel per task setting that defaults to eight, and create different tasks for groups of tables to run parallel.

Implement a database migration strategy.   Your migration strategy can vary according to the database size, the requirements for minimum or zero downtime, and the target database engine. For homogenous migration, you can use AWS DataSync, AWS Transfer Family, or AWS Storage Gateway along with database-native tools.

Know how to minimize downtime.   For minimum or zero downtime, AWS DMS ongoing replication can synchronize the source and the target, even if the full load has been done with another tool.

Exercises

For assistance in completing the following exercises, refer to the User Guides here:
docs.aws.amazon.com/SchemaConversionTool/latest/userguide/
CHAP_Welcome.html
  docs.aws.amazon.com/dms/latest/userguide/Welcome.html

EXERCISE 12.1

Create a MariaDB RDS

In this exercise, you will create a simple MariaDB engine RDS to be your source database for migration.

1. Open the Amazon RDS service page in the AWS Console.

2. Click Create Database.

3. For the engine options, choose MariaDB or another engine you would like to convert to PostgreSQL.

4. Perform a standard setup with no public access, for test purposes only.

5. Choose a VPC that you can set up as a public EC2 instance to install the SCT later.

EXERCISE 12.2

Create an Aurora PostgreSQL Target Database

In this exercise, you will create a simple Aurora PostgreSQL database to be your target database for migration.

1. In the AWS console, open the Amazon RDS service page.

2. Click Create Database.

3. For the Engine option, choose Amazon Aurora.

4. For the edition, choose Amazon Aurora with PostgreSQL compatibility.

5. For the capacity type, choose Provisioned.

6. For the version, choose Aurora PostgreSQL (compatible with PostgreSQL 12.7).

7. Set up a test instance with basic settings; use the same VPC as the previous step.

EXERCISE 12.3

Create an EC2 Bastion Host to Install the AWS SCT

In this exercise, you will create an EC2 Windows instance to install and use the AWS SCT for schema conversion.

1. In the AWS console, open the Amazon EC2 service page.

2. Click Launch Instances.

3. Choose an Amazon Machine Image (AMI) and select Microsoft Windows Server 2019 Base.

4. Choose t3.medium as the instance type.

5. Configure the Instance Details options by selecting Auto-assign Public IP: (Enable).

6. Set up security to allow you to connect to RDP and launch the instance in the same VPC from your RDS instances.

7. Update the RDS's security groups to allow your EC2 security group to access the database port.

8. Go to the AWS SCT installation page at docs.aws.amazon.com/SchemaConversion Tool/latest/userguide/CHAP_Installing.html.

EXERCISE 12.4

Set Up JDBC Drivers and Schema in EC2

In this exercise, you will download JDBC drivers and create a database/schema in a MariaDB instance.

1. On your EC2 instance machine, download the JDBC drivers and install them—in this case, for MariaDB and PostgreSQL.

2. Download a SQL editor of your preference in the remote instance. (You can use www.sql-workbench.eu/downloads.html.)

3. Using SQL Workbench, create a sample schema in the MariaDB database as follows:

```
CREATE DATABASE db1;
use db1;
CREATE TABLE teste_tbl(
student_id INT NOT NULL AUTO_INCREMENT,
student_name VARCHAR(120) NOT NULL,
entry_date DATE,
```

```
    PRIMARY KEY (student_id));
    INSERT INTO teste_tbl (student_name, entry_date) VALUES ("Cristiano Ronaldo","
2022-01-12");
    INSERT INTO teste_tbl (student_name, entry_date) VALUES ("Maria Hernandes","
2022-01-13");
    INSERT INTO teste_tbl (student_name, entry_date) VALUES ("Neymar Junior","
2022-01-14");
    Commit;
```

EXERCISE 12.5

Convert the Schema

In this exercise, you will use the AWS SCT application to convert the schema from MariaDB to PostgreSQL.

1. Within the SCT application, in your EC2 instance, make a source connection to your MariaDB database and a target to your Aurora PostgreSOL.

2. Right-click the sample schema db1 you created, and click Convert Schema.

3. Confirm to continue with the migration.

    You should see in the right window the objects to be created in Aurora PostgreSQL.

4. Click any table inside the tables on the Aurora PostgreSQL connection.

    This will open two sections in the center, one with the source DDL from MariaDB and another with the target DDL on the PostgreSQL database.

5. The table is not created in PostgreSQL yet; you need to right-click the PostgreSQL schema and click Apply To Database.

6. Confirm that it created the table and constraint.

EXERCISE 12.6

Migrate the Data

In this exercise, you will use AWS DMS to migrate the data you created.

1. Go to the AWS DMS console.

2. Create a replication instance in the same VPC.

3. Create a source endpoint that points to MariaDB.

(continues)

EXERCISE 12.6 *(continued)*

4. Create a target endpoint that points to Aurora PostgreSQL.

5. Test the endpoint connectivity for both.

6. Go to the Database Migration Tasks menu and create a task.

7. Choose the schema db1 you would like to migrate.

8. Choose Migrate Existing Data Only.

9. Start the task and perform the migration.

EXERCISE 12.7

Delete the AWS Resources

In this exercise, you will delete the resources you created to avoid extra costs.

1. In the AWS DMS Console, stop the task you created.

2. Delete the task.

3. Delete the source and target endpoints created.

4. In the EC2 Console, terminate your instance.

5. In the RDS Console, delete both the MariaDB instance and the Aurora PostgreSQL cluster.

Review Questions

1. A customer wants to migrate an Oracle on-premises database to Amazon Aurora PostgreSQL. What would be the best option to perform this migration with minimal downtime and minimal effort?

   A. Use ora2pg to convert the schema from Oracle to Aurora PostgreSQL, then develop a Java program that reads the data from Oracle and writes to PostgreSQL, and at the end of the copy, perform the switchover to Aurora PostgreSQL.

   B. Use the AWS SCT to convert the schemas from Oracle to PostgreSQL. Use AWS DMS to create a task to migrate the data from Oracle to PostgreSQL with full load and continuous replication enabled. After the full load of all the tables, wait for the replication lag to be minimal, stop the application at the source, stop the migration task, and perform a switchover to Aurora PostgreSQL.

   C. Use AWS DMS to create a task to migrate the data from Oracle to PostgreSQL with the full load and continuous replication enabled. After the full load of all the tables, wait for the replication lag to be minimal, stop the source, stop the migration task, and perform a switchover to Aurora PostgreSQL.

   D. Use Amazon RDS to create a task to migrate the data from Oracle to PostgreSQL with full load and continuous replication enabled. After the full load of all the tables, wait for the replication lag to be minimal, stop the source, stop the migration task, and perform a failover to Aurora PostgreSQL.

2. A customer has a large, multiterabyte SQL Server database to migrate to Amazon Aurora MySQL. Their database team estimated it would take three months to migrate the data over the current network link and would not fit the time window they have for migration. They also need minimal downtime on this migration. What is the fastest option to accelerate the migration while meeting minimal downtime for the migration?

   A. Request an Amazon Storage Gateway. Create a project in AWS SCT, configure it to use Storage Gateway, register an AWS DMS agent, create a local task to extract the data to the Snowball device, and perform the load to the device. Ship Snowball back to AWS, wait for the data to be loaded in Amazon S3, and use a DMS remote task to load the data to the target database. CDC apply will start after loading the table to the target by AWS DMS.

   B. Perform a consistent copy of the source database, take note of the database change number (SQL Server LSN), compress the files using popular compression tools, and send the files to Amazon S3 using multipart upload. After the copy, load the data with AWS SCT and synchronize the databases, informing the SQL Server LSN to start the continuous replication.

   C. Request an AWS Snowball edge storage-optimized device. Use the AWS SCT to extract data on premises and move it to the device connected to your infrastructure. Ship the edge device back to AWS. Wait for AWS to automatically load the data to Amazon S3. Use AWS DMS to migrate the data to the target store. Finally, let AWS DMS apply the CDC updates to the target store.

   D. Create an AWS DMS task with the compression-optimized option and put the source SQL Server in read-only mode. Set up all tables to be migrated in parallel at once using multiple AWS DMS tasks, and at the finish, start the failover to Amazon RDS.

3. You are assigned to design a solution for a customer that already has some applications in AWS in a VPC connected to their on-premises environment. The customer has an Oracle database on premises and wants to have a copy of some table data in a cheaper storage solution to create ad hoc analytics reports with a delay maximum of five minutes since the data is updated in the database. What would be the easiest way to set up a solution in AWS?

   A. Create a Kubernetes application that connects to Oracle and tracks changes from the database, launches an Amazon EKS, and deploys your application. Add a routine to save the extracted changes to Amazon S3 in a different path for each table aggregating data in a maximum window of five minutes.

   B. Create an AWS DMS replication instance, create an endpoint for source Oracle database on premises, create a target endpoint to Amazon S3, and create a task for continuous replication to capture changes on the database. Set up a task for continuous replication including the tables needed to be replicated. Create a table definition on AWS Glue and use Amazon Athena to query the data and generate the reports.

   C. Use Oracle Data Pump, including the tables to replicated, and configure it to generate files on premises; then transfer the data to AWS using AWS DataSync every five minutes.

   D. Create an AWS SCT replication instance, create an endpoint for source Oracle database on premises, create a target endpoint to Amazon S3, create a task for continuous replication to capture changes on the database. Set up a task for continuous replication including the tables needed to be replicated. Create a table definition on AWS Glue and use Amazon EMR to query the data to generate the reports.

4. Your company has a Microsoft SQL Server database server and is considering migrating to an Amazon RDS for the MySQL database. How can you estimate the impact of such a migration in terms of database objects?

   A. You can install AWS SCT on a machine that has access to your MS SQL Server database server and also to a possible target Amazon RDS MySQL test instance. Generate a Schema Conversion Assessment Report to check what objects will need help on the migration, what type of changes will be needed, and what will be converted automatically.

   B. You will need to perform a manual migration using a SQL Server tool to extract the table and other object definitions as CSVs and then convert them to a MySQL syntax.

   C. You can install AWS DMS in your laptop, load a table definition file to it, and run a Schema Conversion Assessment Report to check what objects will need help on the migration, what type of change will be needed, and what will be converted automatically.

   D. You can install AWS SQL Migration Studio and run a Schema Conversion Assessment Report that will clarify all the manual changes needed to perform the migration.

5. The company you are working for requires a migration path for a MySQL database from their on premises environment to an AWS managed service. They require that the migration have minimal downtime. What are the steps to perform the data migration?

   A. Set up an Amazon RDS for MySQL database instance. Create an Amazon EC2 Linux temporary instance. In the EC2, generate a mysqldump extraction connecting to your source database. After the extraction is completed, load the data to your Amazon RDS for MySQL and redirect the application traffic to your RDS instance.

   B. Set up an Amazon RDS for a MySQL database instance. Configure an AWS Lambda function to generate a mysqldump extraction connecting to your source database. After the extraction is completed, load the data to your RDS for MySQL database and redirect the application traffic to your RDS instance.

   C. Set up an Amazon RDS for MySQL database instance. Create an AWS DMS replication instance and create a source endpoint and a target endpoint using your source and target database connection attributes. Create one or more replication tasks, grouping tables that are related to each other and using full load and continuous replication. After the full load is completed and continuous replication is on, determine the time to stop writing to your source database and redirect the application traffic to your RDS instance.

   D. Set up an Amazon RDS for MySQL database instance. Configure an AWS Glue continuous replication. Create one or more replication jobs, grouping tables that are related to each other and using full load and continuous replication. After the full load is completed and continuous replication is on, determine the time to stop writing to your source database and redirect the application traffic to your RDS instance.

6. What service can you use together with AWS SCT and AWS DMS to move large volumes of data when you don't have enough network throughput bandwidth to move the data in a reasonable time window?

   A. Amazon EBS Attachable device is a physical device that can be used to send large volumes of data to AWS.

   B. Use the AWS Snow family of devices. AWS Snowcone and AWS Snowball are physical devices that can be used to send large volumes of data to AWS.

   C. You can buy any attachable storage device, save your data, and send to AWS with instructions to upload the data to your AWS account using Amazon S3 Upload Manager.

   D. AWS Storage Gateway can be used to store and upload data to AWS asynchronously.

7. What service can you use to optimize your network bandwidth using compression when moving data from on-premises to AWS?

   A. AWS Data Transfer Optimized.

   B. AWS DataSync.

   C. The only way is to use a third-party software to optimize bandwidth.

   D. Amazon S3 multipart upload.

8. Which of the following AWS services can help you to perform a heterogeneous database migration from on-premises to AWS? (Choose two.)

    A. AWS SCT

    B. AWS Step Functions

    C. Amazon EKS

    D. AWS DMS

    E. AWS DTS

9. Which component is responsible for keeping track of continuous replication using AWS DMS?

    A. The source endpoint

    B. The replication instance

    C. The target endpoint

    D. The replication manager

10. How do you migrate a small MySQL database from on-premises to Amazon Aurora MySQL?

    A. Use Amazon EFS to mount a filesystem in your on-premises server, the same one you mount on an EC2 instance. Use Percona XtraBackup to create a backup on the EFS area, then use EC2 to upload it to Amazon S3, and finally restore the backup from S3 to your Aurora cluster.

    B. Use the copy from the MySQL option in the Amazon Aurora cluster to point to MySQL and migrate the data.

    C. Use Amazon EFS to mount a filesystem in your on-premises server, which is the same one you mount on an EC2 instance. Use Percona XtraBackup to create a backup on the EFS area, and restore the backup from EFS to your Aurora cluster.

    D. Use Amazon EBS to mount a filesystem in your on-premises server, which is the same one you mount on an EC2 instance. Use Percona XtraBackup to create a backup on the EFS area, use EC2 to move it to Amazon S3, and then restore the backup to your Aurora cluster.

Chapter

13

Disaster Recovery

THE AWS CERTIFIED DATABASE - SPECIALTY EXAM OBJECTIVES COVERED IN THIS CHAPTER MAY INCLUDE, BUT ARE NOT LIMITED TO, THE FOLLOWING:

✓ **Domain 1: Workload-Specific Database Design**

  ▪ 1.1 Select appropriate database services for specific types of data and workloads.

  ▪ 1.2 Determine strategies for disaster recovery and high availability.

  ▪ 1.3 Design database solutions for performance, compliance, and scalability.

✓ **Domain 3: Management and Operations**

  ▪ 3.2 Determine backup and restore strategies.

  ▪ 3.3 Manage the operational environment of a database solution.

Building resilient workloads is critical to keep the business up and running, to avoid losing credibility, and, in several situations, to be compliant with regulations.

Databases are an important area of infrastructure resilience due to the volume, integrity, and technologies available to provide the required resilience.

Understanding and Planning Disaster Recovery Requirements

To build resilient workloads, it is critical to understand the impact of each specific service if it becomes unavailable for the business line.

Different areas inside the company might have different acceptable downtimes if something goes wrong with its provisioned hardware, software, or network infrastructure. All of those requirements and acceptable downtimes must be identified for the applications used by each business area to better design the business continuity plan.

The next step is evaluating the appropriate architecture for disaster recovery. Some businesses might require a strategy replicating the applications and respective databases across different availability zones and inside the same region. For other businesses, replicating to another region will better support their operations.

Defining the requirements and disaster recovery strategies might seem to be at a very high level, but they're critical for the business continuity plan. And they have an important impact on cost, for sure, and also on implementing a strategy that will be most appropriate to support their operations and business. Choosing them inappropriately may lead to making it impossible to implement the disaster recovery strategy.

Developing a disaster recovery plan in the cloud brings unprecedented possibilities, which this chapter discusses in detail.

Recovery Point Objective and Recovery Time Objective

Let's review some important definitions: RPO and RTO.

- *Recovery point objective (RPO)* is the maximum acceptable period of information loss in a failure situation. How much information may be lost in a failure situation from the database perspective? Is it acceptable to lose the information generated in the last five minutes, or must all the committed information inside the database be available?

- *Recovery time objective (RTO)* is the maximum acceptable time between the failure and the service time restoration. In a few words, it's the maximum acceptable downtime. From the database perspective, what's the maximum acceptable time for your database to be unavailable in a service failure situation?

After identifying the business areas and respective applications that must be addressed in the business continuity plan, the next step is understanding the RPO and RTO required by each application. Figure 13.1 shows how to measure and position the RPO and RTO in a disaster event.

FIGURE 13.1 Measuring and positioning the RPO and RTO in a disaster event

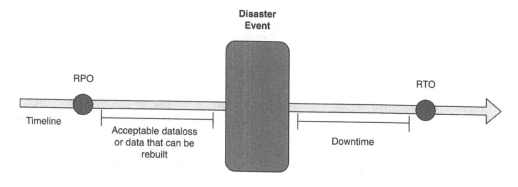

Challenges in Disaster Recovery

Defining the business areas and related applications that require a disaster recovery strategy is a process that requires integration from the technical IT team and business areas, and in general it takes a long time to complete.

Once the applications, as well as their respective RPOs and RTOs, are identified, you should identify the appropriate method to make your environment resilient. The upcoming section "Database Replication Methods: Multi-AZ and Cross-Region Replication" discusses the methods available for databases deployed in the AWS cloud.

The chosen method must also consider the cost perspective (see Table 13.1).

TABLE 13.1   Comparing the costs considering the different RPO and RTO requirements

Strategy & criteria	Backup & restore in the same region	Backup & restore in another region	Multi-AZ strategy self-managed	Multi-AZ strategy managed service	Multiregion strategy self-managed	Multiregion strategy managed service
Cost	$	$$	$$	$$$	$$$$	$$$$$
RPO	Usually minutes	Usually minutes	Usually minutes	Usually 0*	Usually minutes depending on the volume data changes	Usually minutes depending on the volume data changes
RTO	Might take hours depending on the database size	Might take hours depending on the database size	Usually minutes	Usually 1-2 minutes	Usually minutes	Usually less than 5 minutes

AWS Well Architected Framework - Disaster Recovery of Workloads on AWS: Recovery in the Cloud

*In Multi-AZ, if the primary instance fails, RDS will fail over to the secondary with no data loss. There are rare scenarios where re-creating from backup would be needed; for example, if corruption occurs on the primary's volume, it may replicate in the secondary's volume. But in the most common scenarios, the RPO is 0. Amazon Aurora automatically maintains six copies hosted in three AZs; if some corruption occurs, the corrupted protection group will automatically recover from one of the other five protection groups. Almost no scenarios require the restoration from a backup for recovering from a disaster in Amazon Aurora. The RPO is 0.

Choose the appropriate method according to the business requirements; otherwise, the replicated environment might not support your actual needs or might even make the strategy impossible to implement.

The systems must be prepared if components go down, as hardware and software are subject to failure. Even human errors and malicious and insider threats may occur beyond site outages.

An on-premises disaster recovery strategy requires a high up-front investment. As the volume of data grows, we face even higher hardware and operational costs. It's quite complex to test all the disaster recovery scenarios due to their complexity and dependencies.

In the cloud, there are no up-front infrastructure requirements. You can scale and update your environment if required and perform tests more frequently. It's also easier to orchestrate, automate, and test your strategy.

Managing Disaster Recovery Strategies

The AWS cloud enables you to deploy disaster recovery using different strategies, such as a backup and recovery approach, a Multi-AZ, or a cross-region strategy.

- **Backup and recovery strategy:** A backup and recovery strategy is a cost-effective alternative for less aggressive RTO and RPO metrics. It works for recovering from disaster scenarios in the same region and when replicating to a remote region is required.
- **Multi-AZ strategy:** Each availability zone in an AWS region consists of one or more data centers located in separate and distinct geographic locations, close to each other to minimize network latency and distant from each other to survive events such as earthquakes, floods, hurricanes, and power outages. This distribution reduces the risk of a single event impacting more than one AZ.
- **Multiregion strategy:** The AWS regions are distributed across the globe, and there are multiple resources to enable multiregion replication. This strategy enables an even higher protection level compared to the Multi-AZ, but it's important to keep in mind the RPO and RTO when replicating the environment over longer distances.

Backup and Recovery Strategy

For self-managed database resources, you can adopt the backup and restore strategy. Remember that you keep all the scripts and maintenance tools to manage the backup operation.

All managed services allow you to configure the backup retention from 1 to 35 days supporting point-in-time recovery, and you can use the automatic backup to recover from a disaster scenario.

Amazon RDS also allows taking snapshots for longer retention than the automatic backup definition. Remember that manual snapshots don't allow point-in-time recovery.

Amazon RDS allows replicating the automatic backups and transaction logs to another AWS region according to the business requirements. When enabled, it will replicate all snapshots and transaction logs as shortly as they are ready in the current DB instance.

You can automate and centralize data protection across AWS services using AWS Backup. You can create a backup plan, define frequency and retention, and copy it to another region.

Database Replication Methods: Multi-AZ and Cross-Region Replication

According to the database implemented in your environment, you can choose different replication methods. Let's explore how to deploy replication when you have a database deployed on EC2, Amazon RDS, Amazon Aurora, Amazon DocumentDB, or Amazon Neptune.

Keep in mind that on every database engine, you can always restore the database from your daily backup, if the RTO allows the downtime until the new database instance becomes available from the backup restore process.

Databases Deployed on EC2

Every database enables its own log shipping native replication: Oracle, PostgreSQL, MySQL, Db2, Microsoft SQL Server, and others. You can use native log shipping to replicate the database engine to another EC2 instance deployed in a secondary availability zone or even a secondary region. Table 13.2 describes the database engines and their respective log shipping replication methods.

TABLE 13.2   Database Engine Replication Methods

Database Engine	Log Shipping Replication
Oracle	Redo logs, Data Guard
PostgreSQL	Transferring WAL records
MySQL	Binlog
Microsoft SQL Server	Always On availability group
Db2	High availability through log shipping

Figure 13.2 demonstrates the replication at a high level using the Multi-AZ strategy.

FIGURE 13.2   Replication using native log shipping in Multi-AZ deployment

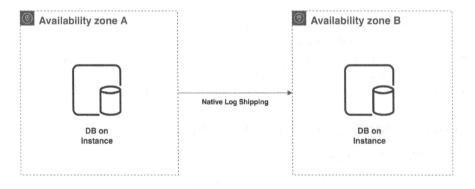

Figure 13.3 demonstrates the replication at a high level using the multiregion strategy.

FIGURE 13.3   Replication using native log shipping in multiregion deployment

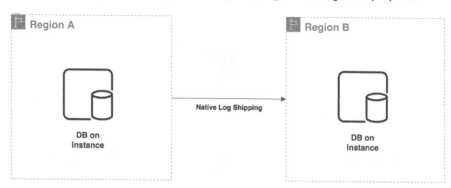

You can see that both strategies are implemented with the same method. The only difference is placing the database in a second availability zone or a second AWS region.

Whenever you decide on cross-region replication, keep in mind that the replication lag will be higher than replicating in a Multi-AZ strategy according to the log rate generated at the source database, and there are data transfer costs replicating data between regions.

All the replication configuration and automation for databases hosted on EC2 must be maintained and monitored by your operational team and must be configured according to the respective manual's provider and recommendations.

Amazon RDS

Amazon RDS allows you to choose backup and restore, a Multi-AZ, and/or a multiregion strategy.

Multi-AZ Strategy on Amazon RDS

Amazon RDS provides high availability and failover support for DB instances using Multi-AZ deployments, as described in Chapter 4, "Transaction Databases on AWS." Figure 13.4 represents the RDS Multi-AZ deployment.

Multi-AZ is a deployment method that writes synchronously to the secondary instance, so every committed piece of data on the primary instance is replicated to the secondary instance. It takes from 60 to 120 seconds to fail over in failure situations.

For disaster recovery in the same region, you can also use a read replica created in another availability zone. The read replica is based on asynchronous replication, which means it is subject to delay. However, it has the advantage of being open for read-only operation and can be promoted in the event of primary failure.

FIGURE 13.4   Amazon RDS Multi-AZ

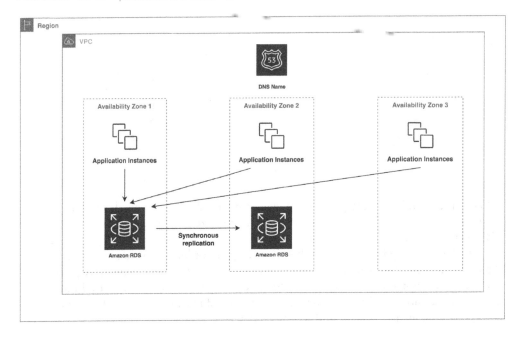

Figure 13.5 represents the Amazon RDS read replica.

FIGURE 13.5   Amazon RDS read replica asynchronous replication

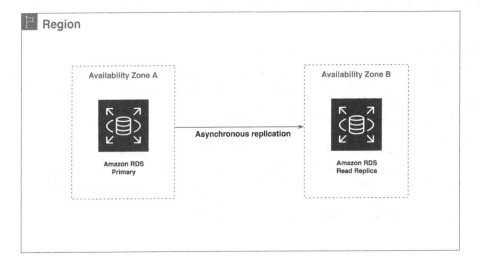

RDS will automatically fail over when Multi-AZ is enabled in the case of failure in the following situations:

- The operating system is being patched.

- The primary host instance is unhealthy.

- The primary host is unreachable due to a network connection failure.

- The RDS instance was modified by the customer.

- The primary instance is busy and unresponsive.

- The storage volume experienced a failure.

- The user requested the failover.

Multiregion Strategy on Amazon RDS

In a multiregion strategy, according to your RTO and RPO, you can choose between replicating automated backups to another AWS region or enabling cross-region read replicas.

Amazon RDS allows you to configure the RDS instances to replicate snapshots and transaction logs to a destination AWS region of your choice. Once this option is chosen, RDS starts a cross-region copy of all snapshots and transaction logs as soon as they are ready on the database instance.

You will be charged for the data transfer and the storage costs in the destination region.

The backup replication is supported by the engine's Oracle Database 12.1.0.2.v10 and higher, PostgreSQL 9.6 and higher, and Microsoft SQL Server version 2012 and higher.

Backup replication isn't supported for encrypted SQL Server DB instances.

To fail over, you should restore the backup that was replicated in the remote region.

> Always validate the available source and destination regions available in the AWS documentation.

Amazon RDS MariaDB, MySQL, Oracle, and PostgreSQL enable creating read replicas in different AWS regions from the source DB instance. Cross-region read replicas aren't supported for RDS SQL Server. Figure 13.6 represents a cross-region read replica deployment.

The cross-region read replicas for Amazon RDS are based on asynchronous replication, and the data in transit may be lost if the replication fails. The RPO will depend on the replication lag.

To fail over, you should promote the read replica in the remote region and configure the application to connect to the newly promoted instance.

The read replica promotion in the secondary region takes less than five minutes to accomplish.

FIGURE 13.6 Cross-region read replica deployment

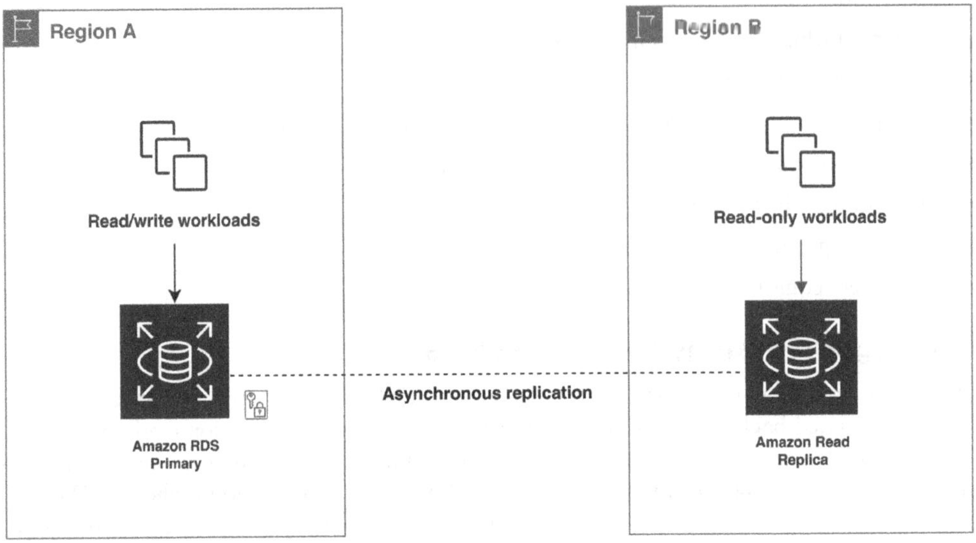

Amazon Aurora

Chapter 4 discussed the Amazon Aurora architecture. Because of the cloud-native architecture, we can explore it to build a resilient database environment. Let's better understand the Multi-AZ and multiregion alternatives to high availability.

High Availability Strategy for Amazon Aurora

The Amazon Aurora storage architecture is distributed across three availability zones, with two protection groups (PGs) in each availability zone (see Figure 13.7). In total, there are six copies of each PG.

Whenever you deploy a new Amazon Aurora read replica instance, it will be launched and share the same storage layer (see Figure 13.8).

Amazon Aurora automatically fails over to a read replica if the primary DB instance fails. You can also choose to fail over the primary instance; as described in Chapter 4, you can define the failover priority in the read replica configuration. Values vary from 0 for the highest priority to 15 for the last priority. If no failover priority is defined, the Amazon Aurora cluster will choose the largest read replica instance to become the new writer. If the read replica instances have the same failover priority and the same instance size, Amazon Aurora will arbitrarily pick up one read replica.

Multiregion Strategy on Amazon Aurora

Amazon Aurora enables two alternatives for cross-region replication and also enhances data locality in remote regions: cross-region read replicas and Aurora global databases.

FIGURE 13.7   Amazon Aurora storage architecture

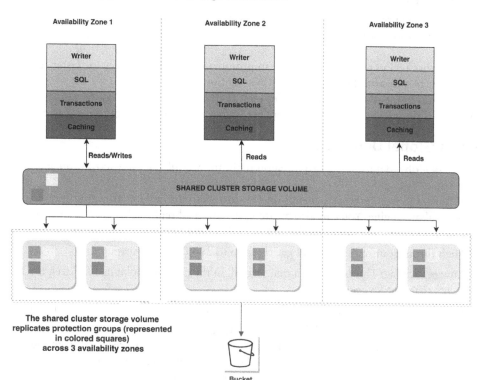

The shared cluster storage volume replicates protection groups (represented in colored squares) across 3 availability zones

FIGURE 13.8   Amazon Aurora read replica instances and the storage layer

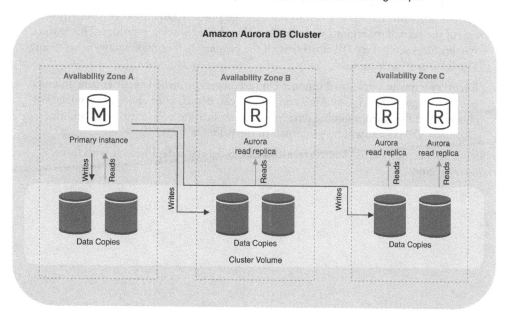

Cross-Region Read Replicas

Cross-region read replicas are available only for the MySQL engine, and they replicate by using binary logs. You can create up to five read replica clusters from your Aurora DB cluster.

Using cross-region read replicas, you can promote readers to a master for faster recovery in the event of a disaster (low RTO/low RPO solution).

The writer in the replica cluster applies logical changes. Depending on the volume of data generated at the source cluster, the remote read replica cluster is subject to replication lag.

Aurora Global Database

An Aurora global database is a cross-region replication available on Amazon Aurora clusters.

An Aurora global database depends on the cluster storage volume for replication and not on the database engine. You can also create up to five read replica clusters from the source.

An Aurora global database has the following features:

- **High throughput rates:** You will get rates up to 200,000 writes/sec.

- **Low replica lag:** This is less than one second. In the case of unplanned failover, the RPO is less than one second.

- **Fast recovery:** This is less than one minute of downtime after a region's unavailability.

- **Write forwarding:** MySQL 5.7 supports write forwarding. Using this feature, Amazon Aurora forwards SQL statements that perform write operations received from the secondary region to the primary cluster. Then the primary cluster will propagate the write operations to the secondary clusters in remote regions.

- **Managed planned failover:** This feature is used in controlled environments such as disaster recovery testing scenarios, operational maintenance, and other planned operational procedures. It allows you to relocate the primary DB cluster of your Aurora to one of the secondary regions without changing the replication topology. This feature synchronizes secondary DB clusters with the primary before making any other changes. The RPO is 0 (no data loss).

- **Recovery from an unplanned outage:** On rare occasions, when experiencing an unexpected outage in its primary AWS region, you can detach your chosen secondary DB cluster from the Aurora Global database. The replication will be stopped, and this secondary DB cluster will be promoted to the primary.

Figure 13.9 represents an Amazon Aurora global database deployment with three secondary regions.

FIGURE 13.9   Aurora global database with three secondary regions

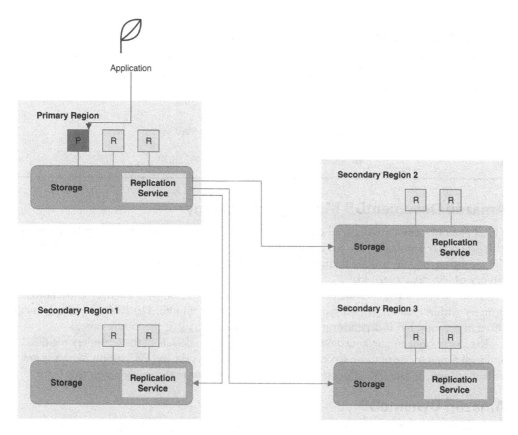

Amazon DocumentDB

Using Amazon DocumentDB, you can deploy a Multi-AZ or multiregion strategy according to your business requirements. Amazon DocumentDB consists of a cluster volume for storage service, one mandatory writer instance, and up to 15 read replicas in the same region, as described in Chapter 6, "Document Databases in the Cloud." You can enable global clusters and deploy up to five remote regions for global requirements.

Amazon DocumentDB Multi-AZ Strategy

The Amazon DocumentDB cluster requires one writer instance and allows scaling up to 15 replica instances across the three availability zones, sharing the same storage layer. Once a failure occurs on the writer instance, any read replica instance may be promoted to a writer instance. You can configure the failover tier number on the read replicas to define a priority order for a read replica instance to be promoted. The lowest numbers have higher priority when choosing a promotion.

To increase the availability level of your DocumentDB cluster, you can use the read replicas shown in Table 13.3.

TABLE 13.3   Availability Goal vs. Number of Instances

Instances	Environment	Availability Goal
1	dev/test	99%
2	production	99.9%
3	production	99.99%

Amazon DocumentDB Multiregion Strategy

The Amazon DocumentDB global cluster consists of one primary region and up to five read-only secondary regions. Every write operation issued on the primary region is replicated to the secondary regions using a dedicated infrastructure. This topology typically is subject to latency of less than a second.

In the event of a region-wide outage, you can promote one of the secondary clusters to a primary within minutes, with a typical RTO of less than a minute. The RPO is typically measured in seconds, but it depends on the lag across the network at the failure time.

To recover from an unplanned outage, make sure that you detach all the secondary regions and then promote one of those secondary regions to the new primary AWS region. With the new primary region, update the endpoint used by your applications to the newly promoted cluster.

Amazon DynamoDB

Amazon DynamoDB is a cloud-native NoSQL database, as described in Chapter 5, "Low Latency Response Time for Your Apps and APIs." It is a database engine that automatically replicates across three availability zones and allows cross-region replication using global tables.

Multi-AZ Strategy on Amazon DynamoDB

Amazon DynamoDB stores all data on solid-state disks (SSDs) and is automatically replicated across multiple availability zones in an AWS region, which offers data durability and integrated availability.

Because of the serverless nature, no action is required to be taken if one of the availability zones is experiencing unavailability issues. Amazon DynamoDB will natively redirect the reads and writes to the available storage nodes.

Multiregion Strategy on Amazon DynamoDB

Amazon DynamoDB global tables provide a fully managed solution for deploying a multi-region, multi-active database. DynamoDB global tables allow you to specify the AWS region where you require the table to be available.

When the data inside an Amazon DynamoDB global table is updated, all changes are replicated to the remote AWS regions, and typically, replication takes only a few seconds.

Allowing writing in multiple regions is subject to conflict. In conflict situations for Amazon DynamoDB global tables, the last writer wins.

In the same way as working in a single region, because of the serverless nature, there's no action required to be taken if one of the availability zones experiences unavailability issues.

Amazon Neptune

Amazon Neptune is a cloud-native database based on a shared storage purpose-built engine as described in Chapter 9, "Discover Relationships Between Objects or People Faster Than a Traditional RDBMS." It allows you to deploy a Multi-AZ and multiregion strategy.

Multi-AZ Amazon Neptune Strategy

An Amazon Neptune cluster must have one writer node and might have up to 15 read replicas. The read replicas access the storage layer, natively replicated across three availability zones. Figure 13.10 represents the Amazon Neptune Cluster architecture.

FIGURE 13.10   Amazon Neptune Cluster architecture

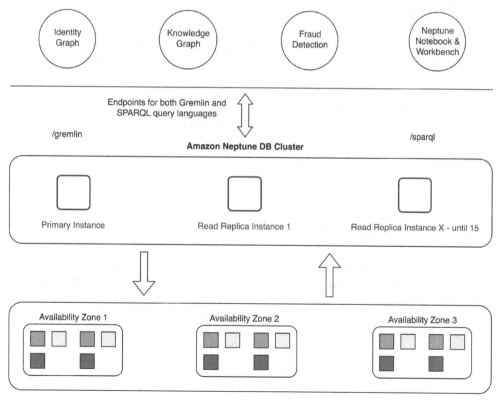

In the case of the failure of the primary node, Amazon Neptune promotes one of the read replicas to primary. You can also choose to fail over manually to a read-replica instance.

Multiregion Amazon Neptune Strategy

An Amazon Neptune global database replicates to multiple regions for low-latency global reads and fast recovery in disaster scenarios. With a global database, you can deploy up to five secondary regions, with latencies commonly less than one second.

You can perform write operations only in the writer node of the primary region, and the instances in the remote regions will be available only for read operations.

Amazon Neptune global database allows the following failover methods:

- Choose the manual unplanned detach-and-promote steps. This promotes a secondary region to recover from an outage in the primary region. Detach one of the secondary clusters; the secondary cluster will become stand-alone. Then promote it to turn it into a new primary master.

- Choose the managed planned failover for planned operational activities. You can relocate the primary cluster to one of the secondary regions with no data loss.

Summary

A disaster recovery plan and a business continuity plan are essential to support the business operation. In many industry sectors, it's also necessary to be compliant with regulation requirements.

Consider all aspects, including RPO, RTO, implementation and operational costs, and the orchestration. In the end, choose the appropriate method to best support your business.

Disaster recovery in the AWS cloud enables you to choose and implement the method according to your requirements, with the flexibility to choose the right service for each environment. Cloud-native databases enable flexible methods for replicating data, managing operations, and orchestrating them.

Exam Essentials

Understand the RPO and RTO required for support according to your business operation needs.   Database availability is essential to every business operation, and the different applications across a company have other availability and recoverability requirements. It is important to evaluate that very restrictive requirements will cost much more, and very loose requirements may not be able to attend to your business operations.

The first step is collecting precisely the time to be available again (RTO) and how much of the data you can afford to lose (RPO) in a failure scenario. You can choose the most appropriate database deployment method with this essential data.

Understand how to protect your database in RDS against disasters.   Determine the replication strategy (Multi-AZ or multiregion) and apply the replication method to enable it according to the database engine. Understand if replication lag is acceptable and its impact in a recovery scenario.

Understand the different replication methods and how long each takes to fail over.   It is essential to understand the differences between replicating self-managed solutions and managed services and the effort required for implementing and maintaining each replication method. The different replication methods in managed services will also allow faster or slower failover operations. For example, an Amazon Aurora global database allows faster failover and lower data loss compared to Amazon RDS cross-region read replicas.

Understand how to manage the different failover methods according to the database.   It is essential to clearly know how to handle a failure situation and which methods are available to fail over to another availability zone or even a secondary region. For example, when an Amazon RDS cross-region read replica is promoted in a remote region, the newly promoted RDS instance becomes a stand-alone database instance. An Amazon Aurora global database allows you to promote the secondary region and also allows you to manage the failover without breaking the replication topology.

Review Questions

1. A startup company uses Amazon Aurora to host their data and is planning to expand their market to other continents. The customer has a huge concern about latency reads and replication lag on the remote continents, so they plan to replicate their database to improve the data locality, using the remote region for disaster recovery purposes. What is the best solution to accommodate the customer requirements?

   A. Enable a cross-region read replica to improve the locality of the data. In disaster situations, they can promote the remote region to be used as a primary database.

   B. Enable backup replication to another AWS region.

   C. Enable the Aurora global database, with replicas in the remote region used to improve data locality. In disaster recovery situations, they can fail over to the secondary region.

   D. Configure the native binlog replication to replicate to a remote region.

2. Your customer has RDS for Oracle and has asked you to support him in choosing a disaster recovery alternative to host their environment if something goes wrong in the current region where they operate. They have a solid directive for avoiding high operational costs, the RTO is 10 hours, and the technical team already tested the restore operation, which was completed in less than five hours. Which is the best solution to host the environment?

   A. Enable cross-region read replicas at the RDS for Oracle, and promote the remote read replica in a disaster situation.

   B. Enable automated backup replication to another region, and restore the database in the remote region in a disaster recovery situation of the primary region.

   C. Establish DMS logical replication in the remote region.

   D. Set up native redo Data Guard replication in the remote region.

3. Company ABC hosts their data on Amazon Aurora. For regulatory reasons, they require replication of the database to a secondary region, and periodically they must test their disaster recovery strategy. However, they are really concerned about losing the database topology during failover tests. How can you support them?

   A. Enable an Amazon Aurora logical read replica, and promote the read replica just during the failover test.

   B. Enable an Amazon Aurora global database during the disaster recovery test, and use the feature Managed Planned Failover.

   C. Enable DMS replication to the secondary region, and stop the replication during the disaster recovery test.

   D. Enable native binlog replication to a primary Aurora DB cluster in the secondary region, and stop the replication during the disaster recovery test.

4. You received the request to build and deploy a resilient database within an AWS region, replicating the database between two availability zones. The acceptable downtime for the failover process is two minutes, and it isn't acceptable to lose committed transactions (RPO=0).

Which alternatives are able to meet these requirements with automated managed services? (Choose two.)

A. Amazon Aurora PostgreSQL with at least one read replica

B. Amazon RDS PostgreSQL with Multi-AZ enabled

C. Deploying PostgreSQL on EC2 with native replication enabled

D. Amazon Aurora global databases

5. You're developing an app that requires a relational database engine, and the app needs to read and write data on the same database in a secondary region. What database solution will better fulfill the application requirements?

A. Amazon RDS cross-region read replica

B. Amazon DynamoDB global tables

C. Amazon Aurora global database with write forwarding enabled

D. Amazon DocumentDB global cluster

6. Your company has asked you to create a database disaster recovery strategy to support the relational database replication and also to periodically test running the entire database and application in a secondary region without destroying the database replication topology and without losing any data. Which database solution will better meet those requirements?

A. Amazon DynamoDB global tables

B. Amazon Aurora global databases with managed failover

C. Amazon RDS cross-region read replicas

D. Amazon Neptune cluster using three availability zones

7. You are in charge of implementing a database deployment to allow replicating the relational database to a remote region, to allow read operations on the remote region, and in a disaster event to be able to promote the remote region to become the new primary database. Which deployment enables this solution with the lowest cost?

A. Launch Amazon DynamoDB global tables, allowing read and write operations on both regions.

B. Launch Amazon Aurora global databases with write forwarding enabled, and operate with two active regions.

C. Launch Amazon RDS cross-region read replicas, and promote them in a failure situation.

D. Launch Amazon DocumentDB and enable global cluster replication.

8. You've received the requirement to architect a highly available database environment across availability zones for supporting JSON documents, and each document size may reach up to 16 MB. For a production environment with 99.99% availability, it must be resilient to be available if an entire availability zone fails. Which architecture is the most appropriate?

A. Deploying an Amazon DocumentDB global cluster and enabling read operations on the remote region.

B. Deploying an Amazon DocumentDB cluster within a single region, with one primary node and two read replicas in different availability zones.

    C. Deploying Amazon DynamoDB will natively distribute the data across three availability zones.

    D. Deploying Amazon Aurora will natively distribute the data across three availability zones.

9. The company you work for is expanding operations onto new continents. You received the task to enable the current DocumentDB cluster data in another region, for better data locality and to promote this data in a disaster situation. How can you meet the business requirements with minimal application impact?

    A. Deploy a new Amazon DocumentDB cluster in the secondary region, establishing replication using DMS.

    B. Convert the Amazon DocumentDB to DynamoDB, and enable DynamoDB global tables.

    C. Deploying Amazon DynamoDB will natively distribute the data across three availability zones.

    D. Deploy an Amazon DocumentDB global cluster, enabling reading at the remote regions. If the primary region experiences a failure, you'll be able to promote the secondary region to be the primary.

10. You are the solution architect supporting a new app development. The app data must be available in three different regions, and the data must be available for read and write operations in the three regions simultaneously. The app has a defined key-value pattern to retrieve the information. Which database solution will be able to support the app requirements?

    A. An Amazon Aurora global database with write forwarding enabled.

    B. Amazon DynamoDB.

    C. Amazon DynamoDB global tables.

    D. Amazon RDS will be less expensive.

Chapter

14

Save Time and Reduce Errors Automating Your Infrastructure

THE AWS CERTIFIED DATABASE - SPECIALTY EXAM OBJECTIVES COVERED IN THIS CHAPTER MAY INCLUDE, BUT ARE NOT LIMITED TO, THE FOLLOWING:

✓ **Domain 2: Deployment and Migration**

- 2.1 Automate database solution deployments.

✓ **Domain 3: Management and Operations**

- 3.3 Manage the operational environment of a database solution.

✓ **Domain 4: Monitoring and troubleshooting**

- 4.2 Troubleshoot and resolve common database issues.

✓ **Domain 5: Database security**

- 5.1 Encrypt data at rest and in transit.

- 5.2 Evaluate auditing solutions.

- 5.3 Determine access control and authentication mechanisms.

- 5.4 Recognize potential security vulnerabilities within database solutions.

In this chapter, you will learn how to automate your infrastructure to save time and reduce error. AWS has services that can work together with database services to automate and build a whole environment with a few commands.

Automation is a key process that any company must have in its daily operations. *Infrastructure as a code (IaC)* is a process wherein you can write code to build resources, network, instances, and a whole infrastructure for your environment. You can use IaC as a template to help you maintain a consistent, secure, and agile development.

By using automation through IaC, you can easily reproduce your infrastructure in another region, in another AWS account, or within the same region as a disaster recovery plan, if everything has been deleted.

AWS CloudFormation

AWS CloudFormation is a service where you build your template and set up your AWS resources that you want to provision. There is no coding or manual operation through AWS Management Console; this all done via AWS APIs. AWS CloudFormation supports templates in YAML or JSON. All the examples in this chapter are in YAML format.

The following are the main benefits of building a template for AWS CloudFormation:

- **Simplify infrastructure management:** With AWS CloudFormation you can straightforwardly create, update, or delete some/several AWS resources; moreover, you can centralize your infrastructure management.

- **Quickly replicate your infrastructure:** You can easily create the same infrastructure in a disaster recovery (DR) target region and align with your recovery time objective and recovery point objective, especially during DR scenarios. AWS CloudFormation is supported in all AWS regions. Or you can have the same infrastructure for different purposes—for example, development, quality and assurance, and production. The *recovery time objective (RTO)* is the amount of time that a business process must be restored after a disaster to avoid unacceptable consequences associated with the disruption. The *recovery point objective (RPO)* is the amount of time that might pass during a disaster before the quantity of data lost is not tolerable by the business.

- **Easily control and track changes to your infrastructure:** Resources deployed through AWS CloudFormation can track and modify their changes. This could be helpful for maintaining compliance and following standards.

- **Increase productivity:** CloudFormation enables you to destroy and re-create any infrastructure on AWS. You can separate each template by layers, for example, network stacks, application stacks, and so on. This will help you to manage and update your environment.

When you use AWS CloudFormation, there are some concepts that you need to bear in mind.

- **Templates:** A CloudFormation template is a JSON or YAML text file. You can save these files with a `.json`, `.yaml`, `.template`, or `.txt` extension. The maximum size of the template body is 1 MB. The following is a YAML example:

```
AWSTemplateFormatVersion: 2010-09-09
Resources:
  MyDB:
    Type: 'AWS::RDS::DBInstance'
    Properties:
      DBInstanceClass: "db.t3.micro"
      AllocatedStorage: 20
      Engine: MySQL
      EngineVersion: 8.0.16
      MasterUsername: admin
      MasterUserPassword: secretpassword
      DeletionProtection: false
      DeleteAutomatedBackups: true
```

- **Stacks:** The CloudFormation template will create one or more stacks. Through stacks management you can create, update, and delete a group of resources defined by your template. To create any resource, you will create a stack by submitting the template that you created, and CloudFormation will provision all the resources for you. Stacks can be managed through CloudFormation's console, API, or AWS CLI.

- **Change sets:** When you need to change a resource deployed via CloudFormation, before making any changes to your resources, you can generate a change set, which is a summary of your planned changes. For example, if you rename an Amazon RDS database instance, CloudFormation will create a new database and delete the old one. If you did not back up your data, you will lose it. With change sets, you can see if your change will cause your database to be replaced, and you can plan accordingly before you update your stack to prevent any damage.

To use a larger template body, separate your template into multiple templates by using nested stacks.

AWS CloudTrail integrates with AWS CloudFormation, and it tracks anyone making AWS CloudFormation API calls in your account. Enable AWS CloudTrail and store the logs in an Amazon S3 bucket so that you can audit who made any operations with AWS CloudFormation.

AWS CloudFormation is a free service. You are charged only for the AWS resources you include in your stacks at current rates for each.

To create a stack in AWS CloudFormation, the template must be stored in an Amazon S3 bucket. Even if you upload a template file through the AWS Management Console, the file will be stored in an Amazon S3 bucket. You cannot edit the template once you upload it. Each stack must have a unique name.

When you delete a stack, every single artifact that was created by CloudFormation will be deleted.

CloudFormation is a declarative way of outlining the provision of your AWS resources (most AWS services are supported), and the template creates your resources in the right order with the exact configuration that you specify. There are two ways to create your template:

- **Manual:** By editing the template using CloudFormation Designer through the AWS console. *CloudFormation Designer* is a graphical tool for creating and modifying AWS CloudFormation templates. It allows users to create templates visually, using drag-and-drop components, and provides a preview of the template before it is deployed.

- **Automated:** By editing the template using any IDE of your preference that supports YAML or JSON formats. You also can use the AWS CLI to deploy the templates.

Figure 14.1 shows the first step to create a CloudFormation stack on AWS Console.

FIGURE 14.1   Creating a CloudFormation stack

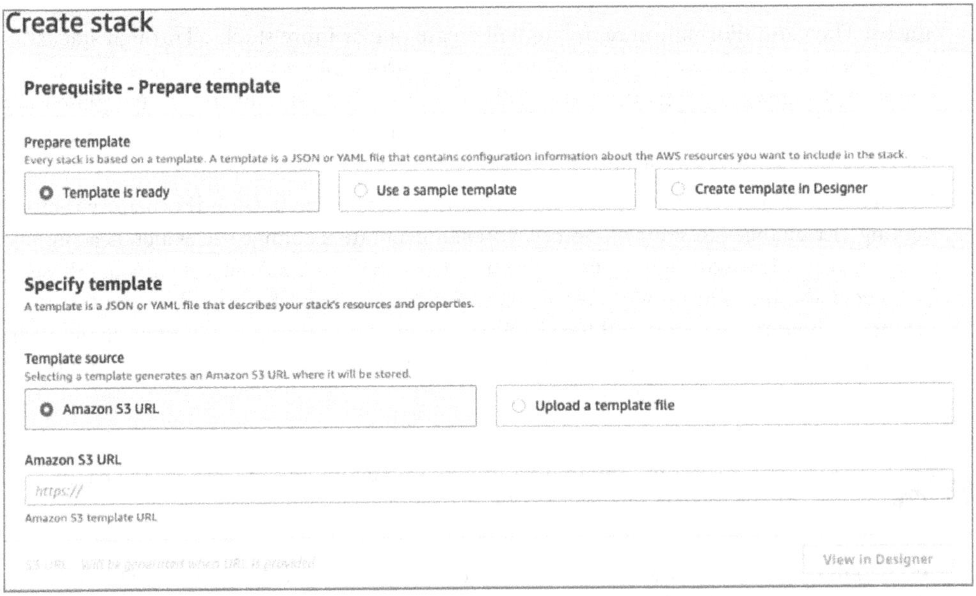

Components

There are several components in an AWS CloudFormation template. Only Resources are required.

- **AWSTemplateFormatVersion:** This is the CloudFormation template version that the template conforms to. The current version is 2010-09-09.

- **Description:** This is the text that describes the template.

- **Resources:** This includes your AWS resources declared in the template, such as Amazon EC2 or an Amazon Relational Database Service. That's the only section that is required in a CloudFormation template. Resource type identifiers have this form: `AWS::aws-product-name::data-type-name`.

- **Parameters:** These are dynamic inputs that you pass when creating or updating your template. These parameters can be referenced in the Resources and Outputs sections of the template. CloudFormation supports string, number, comma delimited list, list<number>, System Manager parameter types, and AWS parameters. Parameters have the following optional settings:

  - **Description(String):** An explanation that describes the parameter

  - **Type:** The data type for the parameter

  - **AllowedPattern:** The regular expression that represents the patterns to allow for String types

  - **AllowedValues:** An array containing the list of values allowed for the parameter

  - **ConstraintDescription(String):** Text that explains what's going on when a constraint is violated (i.e., a better error message)

  - **Mix/Max Length(Integer):** The minimum and maximum lengths for String types

  - **Mix/Max Value(Number):** The minimum and maximum numeric values for Number types

  - **Default:** An appropriate value for the template to use if no parameter value has been input

  - **NoEcho(boolean):** To mask the parameter value to avoid displaying it in the console
    There are two ways to pass parameters:

  - **Statically:** With AWS CLI or AWS Management Console or by using a flat file from the local filesystem or Amazon S3

  - **Dynamically:** With AWS Secrets Manager or Amazon System Manager Parameter Store

- **Rules:** Validate a parameter or a combination of parameters passed during a stack creation or update.

- **Mappings:** These are static variables for your template. They are useful resources for different environments, such as development and production and different AWS regions. The values are hard-coded within the template. They can be used by the `Fn::FindInMap` intrinsic function in the Resources and Outputs sections.

- **Outputs:** These are one or more values to return from resources' properties created or updated in your template. This value can be exported and used in different CloudFormation templates using `Fn:ImportValue`.

- **Conditions:** These manage some resources to be created. For example, if a parameter has an input, then create an IAM policy referencing it. A condition is used to define whether a specific set of resources will be created depending on environment—for example, if the parameter asks for the dev or prod environment and the user set it to prod, then only resources with the condition prod will be created.

- **Metadata:** This provides additional information about the template.

There are others components, but they are not relevant for this book or the exam.

Regarding using parameters, you can use `AllowedPattern` with regular expressions to restrict the string values that will be accepted. You can also use `ConstraintDescription`, which is a string that explains a constraint when the constraint is violated. In addition, the `Description` property is a string that you can use to describe the parameter. `MaxLength`/`MinLength` receives an integer value that determines the minimum and maximum numbers of characters you want to allow for String types. The following template describes Amazon RDS using MySQL as the engine:

```
AWSTemplateFormatVersion: 2010-09-09
Parameters:
DBUsername:
          Description: Username for MySQL database access
          Type: String
          MinLength: '1'
          MaxLength: '16'
          AllowedPattern: '[a-zA-Z][a-zA-Z0-9]*'
ConstraintDescription: must begin with a letter and contain only alphanumeric
characters.
      DBPassword:
Description: Password MySQL database access
Type: String
MinLength: '8'
MaxLength: '41'
AllowedPattern: '[a-zA-Z0-9]*'
ConstraintDescription: must contain only alphanumeric characters.
Resources:
          MyDB:
          Type: 'AWS::RDS::DBInstance'
```

```
        Properties:
        DBInstanceClass: "db.t3.micro"
AllocatedStorage: 20
Engine: MySQL
EngineVersion: 8.0.16
MasterUsername: !Ref DBUsername
MasterUserPassword: !Ref DBPassword
DeletionProtection: false
DeleteAutomatedBackups: true
```

The exam does not expect you to write a CloudFormation template, but you should be able to understand and read it, as well as be able to use it in automation and disaster recovery best-practices scenarios.

Intrinsic functions are built-in functions that help you assign values to properties that are not available until runtime. The following are some important intrinsic functions:

- **Fn::FindInMap:** Returns the value corresponding to the key in a two-level map that is declared in the Mappings section. In the following example, the intrinsic function used is FindInMap, and it will use MySQL5.7 if the engine chosen is Aurora:

```
Mappings:
    EngineMap:
        aurora:
        Engine: aurora
          EngineVersion: '5.7.12'
          ClusterParameterGroupFamily: 'aurora5.7'
          ParameterGroupFamily: 'aurora5.7'
Resources:
    DBInstance:
        Type: 'AWS::RDS::DBInstance'
         Properties:
        Engine: !FindInMap [EngineMap, !Ref aurora, Engine]
```

- **Fn::GetAtt:** Returns a specific attribute value from a resource created. In the following example, it will show on the Output tab the Amazon RDS endpoint created from the template. It can be used to reference attribute values between resources in the same template:

```
Outputs:
    DatabaseEndpoint:
        Description: 'The connection endpoint for the database'
        Value: !GetAtt 'DBInstance.Endpoint.Address'
```

- **Ref:** Returns the value of the specified parameter or resource.

Reference Parameter

```
Parameters:
  SecurityGroupDescription:
      Description: Security Group Description
      Type: String


Resources:
  DBSecurityGroup:
      Type: 'AWS::EC2::SecurityGroup'
      Properties:
            GroupDescription: !Ref SecuirtyGroupDescription
            ...
```

Reference Resource

```
Resources:

  MyVPC:
      Type: 'AWS::EC2::VPC'
      Properties:
            CidrBlock: ''10.0.0.0/16''
            EnableDnsSupport: 'true'
            EnableDnsHostnames: 'true'
  DBSubnet:
      Type: 'AWS::EC2::Subnet'
      Properties:
          VpcId: !Ref MyVPC

      ...
```

- **Fn::Join:** Appends a set of values into a single value, separated by the specified delimiter.

```
!Join
  - ''
  - - 'arn:'
    - !Ref AWS::Partition
    - ':s3:::elasticbeanstalk-*-'
    - !Ref AWS::AccountId
```

- **Fn::ImportValue:** Returns a value that was exported from an Output section in a template by another stack. You cannot delete a CloudFormation stack if its outputs are being referenced by another CloudFormation stack.

```
Resources:
  WebServer:
    Type: 'AWS::EC2::Instance'
    Properties:
      InstanceType: t3.micro
      ImageId: ami-a1b23456
      NetworkInterfaces:
        - GroupSet:
          - Fn::ImportValue
            'Fn::Sub': '${NetworkStackNameParameter}-SecurityGroupID'
          AssociatePublicIpAddress: 'true'
          DeviceIndex: '0'
          DeleteOnTermination: 'true'
          SubnetId: Fn::ImportValue
            'Fn::Sub': '${NetworkStackNameParameter}-SubnetID'
```

- **Fn::Sub:** Substitutes variables in an input string with values that you specify. Could use pseudoparameters or resources' names within the template:

```
Fn:ImportValue:
  !Sub '${AWS::StackName}-SecurityGroupID'
```

You can use pseudoparameters in your template. Pseudoparameters are predefined by AWS CloudFormation and include AWS::Region, AWS::StackId, AWS::StackName, and AWS::AccountId.

A deployment of an AWS CloudFormation stack can fail when you are creating, updating, or deleting it. You can access and view logs and messages to help troubleshoot the issue. If a failure occurs, one of three statuses will appear: CREATE_FAILED, UPDATE_FAILED, or DELETE_FAILED. There are several reasons for a failure. Here are the most common:

- Your IAM user or role doesn't have appropriate permission to execute the action.

- There is a dependency error between resources. You can solve it by including a DependsOn property and the resource's name with the dependency.

- There is an invalid value input in the Parameter section at stack creation.

- At CloudFormation Stack deletion, some resources need to be empty—for example, an Amazon S3 bucket.

- There are no updates to perform. You need to change the template in order to update your stack.

When a stack fails, you can specify one of the following actions:

- **Roll back all stack resources:** Roll back the stack to the last known state. You can define alarms and monitoring time when creating or updating the stack.

- **Preserve successfully provisioned resources:** Resources without a last known stable state will be deleted upon the next stack operation.

AWS CloudFormation supports nested stacks, which are stacks created as part of other stacks. You can isolate repeated patterns or common components of your architecture in separate stacks and call them from other stacks. To create a nested stack within another stack, use the AWS::CloudFormation::Stack resource in the Resources section.

For example, in a scenario of three-tier web application, you can use AWS CloudFormation to automate your infrastructure and separate each tier as a stack; thus, it may help with code maintainability and reuse components. This is different from cross stacks, which are helpful when stacks have different life cycles and use Outputs export and Fn::ImportValue to pass export values to several stacks.

Figure 14.2 illustrates nested stacks.

FIGURE 14.2   Nested stacks

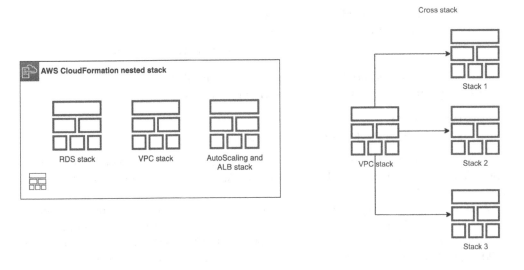

   Nested stacks are considered a best practice.

AWS CloudFormation supports cross-account and cross-region deployments using a feature called StackSets. StackSets can extend the functionality of stacks by enabling you to create, update, or delete a stack across multiple accounts and regions with a single operation. Figure 14.3 illustrates CloudFormation deployed from Northern Virginia using StackSets features to other accounts in different regions such as São Paulo and Oregon.

FIGURE 14.3   AWS CloudFormation StackSets

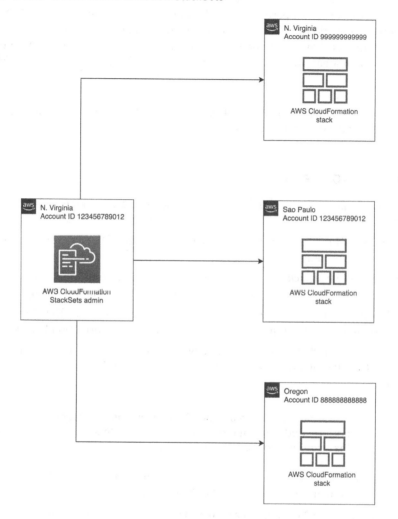

An administrator account manages the CloudFormation template creation and uses the template as the basis for provisioning stacks into selected target accounts and AWS regions. StackSets can be deployed using the AWS Management Console or the AWS CLI. A stack instance is a reference to a stack in a destination account within a region. It is created with or without a stack, and in case the stack could not be created for some reason, the stack instance shows the reason for the stack creation failure.

StackSets deploy resources across regions and accounts, so ensure that global resources such as IAM roles and S3 buckets do not have conflicting names.

To allow StackSets to be created, you must create permissions, which could be self-managed or service-managed permissions. Self-managed permissions create the IAM role and establish a trusted relationship between the admin account and the target account. Service-managed permissions allow you to deploy instances to accounts managed by AWS organizations, and you do not have to create an IAM role, because StackSets creates the IAM roles on your behalf.

You must enable trusted access with AWS organizations to use service-managed permissions.

Important Concepts

There are some important concepts for the exam when you are working with the CloudFormation template.

- **AWS::RDS::DBInstance:** This resource creates an Amazon DB instance and has the following key properties:

  - **DeleteAutomatedBackups:** This removes automated backups immediately after the DB instance is deleted. The default value removes all automated backups.

  - **DeletionProtection:** The database cannot be deleted while it has DeletionProtection on. For more information, see the "Deleting AWS CloudFormation Stacks" section.

  - **DBInstanceIdentifier:** This is the name of the DB instance. If you don't specify a name, CloudFormation will generate a unique physical ID and use that ID for the DB instance.

If you specify a name on the DBInstanceIdentifier property, you cannot perform updates that require replacement of this resource, only updates that require no or some interruption.

  - **DBSnapshotIdentifier:** This is the name of the Amazon Resource Name (ARN) of the DB snapshot that's used to restore the DB instance.

  - **MasterUsername/MasterUserPassword:** This is the master username and password for the instance. These are conditional properties; some engines do not require these attributes. Refer to the documentation based on the engine used. For more information to protect the password securely, see the "AWS Secrets Manager" section.

If you specify SourceDBInstanceIdentifier or DBSnapshotIdentifier, you don't need to specify MasterUsername. The value is inherited from the source DB instance or snapshot.

- **EnableIAMDatabaseAuthentication:** This is disabled by default and it can be enabled to map to AWS IAM, but does not replace the master username and password. It supports only RDS for MariaDB, MySQL, and PostgreSQL.
- **AWS::RDS::DBCluster:** This resource creates an Amazon Aurora DB cluster or Multi-AZ DB cluster. The instances will inherit configurations from the cluster.
  - **DBClusterIdentifier:** This is the identifier of the DB cluster that the instance will belong to.
  - **DeletionPolicy:** The default policy is Snapshot. You can preserve this attribute, in some cases, and back up a resource when its stack is deleted. There are three behaviors: Delete, Retain, and Snapshot. For more information, see the "Deleting AWS CloudFormation Stacks" section.

The following is an example of an AWS CloudFormation template for Amazon RDS for MySQL instance version 8.0.16 using "admin" as the master username and "secretpassword" as the password, with deletion protection enabled and the deletion policy set to Retain.

```
AWSTemplateFormatVersion: 2010-09-09
Resources:
  MyDB:
    Type: 'AWS::RDS::DBInstance'
    Properties:
      DBInstanceClass: "db.t3.micro"
      AllocatedStorage: 20
      Engine: MySQL
      EngineVersion: 8.0.16
      MasterUsername: admin
      MasterUserPassword: secretpassword
      DeletionProtection: true
      DeleteAutomatedBackups: false
    DeletionPolicy: Retain
```

The following CloudFormation template will deploy an Amazon Aurora cluster. You must have an Amazon VPC and subnets deployed in order to deploy this template and reference them in the Parameters section.

```
AWSTemplateFormatVersion: 2010-09-09
Parameters:
  Subnet1:
    Description: Subnet 1 ID
    Type: 'AWS::EC2::Subnet::Id'
  Subnet1AZ:
    Type: 'AWS::EC2::AvailabilityZone::Name'
```

```yaml
  Subnet2:
    Description: Subnet 1 ID
    Type: 'AWS::EC2::Subnet::Id'
  Subnet2AZ:
    Type: 'AWS::EC2::AvailabilityZone::Name'

Resources:
  DBSubnetGroup:
    Type: 'AWS::RDS::DBSubnetGroup'
    Properties:
      DBSubnetGroupDescription: !Ref 'AWS::StackName'
      SubnetIds:
        - !Ref Subnet1
        - !Ref Subnet2

  RDSDBClusterParameterGroup:
    Type: 'AWS::RDS::DBClusterParameterGroup'
    Properties:
      Description: "CloudFormation Sample Aurora Cluster Parameter Group"
      Family: aurora5.6
      Parameters:
        time_zone: US/Eastern

  RDSCluster:
    Type: 'AWS::RDS::DBCluster'
    Properties:
      DBClusterParameterGroupName: !Ref RDSDBClusterParameterGroup
      DBSubnetGroupName: !Ref DBSubnetGroup
      Engine: aurora
      MasterUserPassword: secretpassword
      MasterUsername: mysuperuser

  RDSDBParameterGroup:
    Type: 'AWS::RDS::DBParameterGroup'
    Properties:
      Description: "CloudFormation Sample Aurora Parameter Group"
      Family: aurora5.6
      Parameters:
        sql_mode: IGNORE_SPACE
```

```
RDSDBInstance1:
  Type: 'AWS::RDS::DBInstance'
  Properties:
    AvailabilityZone: !Ref Subnet1AZ
    DBClusterIdentifier: !Ref RDSCluster
    DBInstanceClass: db.t3.small
    DBParameterGroupName: !Ref RDSDBParameterGroup
    DBSubnetGroupName: !Ref DBSubnetGroup
    Engine: aurora

RDSDBInstance2:
  Type: 'AWS::RDS::DBInstance'
  Properties:
    AvailabilityZone: !Ref Subnet2AZ
    DBClusterIdentifier: !Ref RDSCluster
    DBInstanceClass: db.t3.small
    DBParameterGroupName: !Ref RDSDBParameterGroup
    DBSubnetGroupName: !Ref DBSubnetGroup
    Engine: aurora
```

See the complete list of Amazon RDS properties at docs.aws.amazon.com/AWS-CloudFormation/latest/UserGuide/aws-resource-rds-dbinstance.html and the Amazon Aurora properties at docs.aws.amazon.com/pt_br/AWSCloudFormation/latest/UserGuide/aws-resource-rds-dbcluster.html.

Updating AWS CloudFormation Stacks

When you need to make an update of an AWS CloudFormation stack, you might interrupt resources and/or replace updated resources, depending on which template properties you change. Behaviors on Amazon RDS that require some interruptions include DBParameterGroupName, Engine, and DBInstanceClass. Others require a complete replacement of the resource like DBInstanceIdentifier or Port.

AWS CloudFormation updates can require no or some interruptions, or even a replacement of a resource. Be aware that this could impact your environment.

There are two methods for updating stacks: direct update or creating and executing change sets. Figure 14.4 shows the first option. You can submit changes directly by uploading the template through the AWS console, by changing the parameters using the current template, by replacing the current template, or by editing the template in designer. When you submit changes, CloudFormation immediately deploys them. Use this option when you need to quickly deploy updates in your environment.

FIGURE 14.4   AWS CloudFormation direct update stack

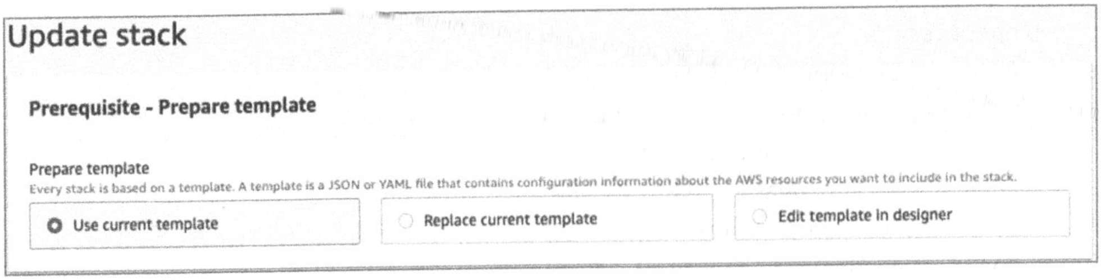

Update stack

Prerequisite - Prepare template

Prepare template
Every stack is based on a template. A template is a JSON or YAML file that contains configuration information about the AWS resources you want to include in the stack.

| ● Use current template | ○ Replace current template | ○ Edit template in designer |

> If you need to update a nested stack, always update the parent
> (root stack).

Using change sets, you can preview the changes that AWS CloudFormation will make to your stack, and then you can decide whether to apply those changes. This option will ensure that you do not make any unintentional changes or consider other possibilities.

You can create a change set of your stack through the AWS Management Console, as shown in Figure 14.5, or the AWS CLI. For creation you need to update the template using a current template (changing parameters directly on the console), using a template designer, or uploading an updated template through the AWS console or Amazon S3.

FIGURE 14.5   AWS CloudFormation update using change sets

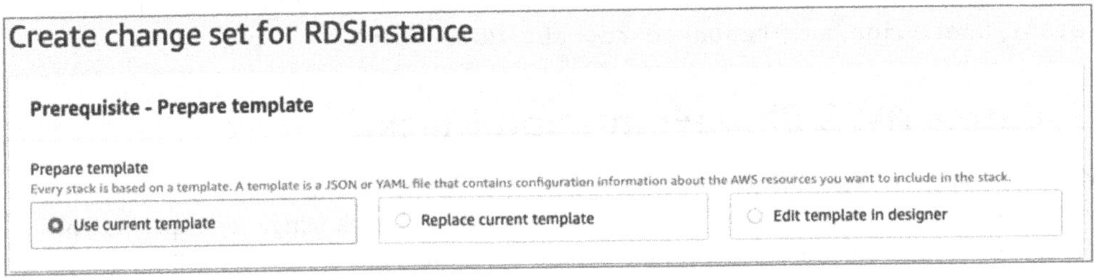

Create change set for RDSInstance

Prerequisite - Prepare template

Prepare template
Every stack is based on a template. A template is a JSON or YAML file that contains configuration information about the AWS resources you want to include in the stack.

| ● Use current template | ○ Replace current template | ○ Edit template in designer |

After you change a parameter or part of the template, a change set will be created. As Figure 14.6 shows, the change set will show the changes that will be made; in this example, you can see that no replacement is needed, since Replacement is False. You can review the changes and decide if you still want to deploy them.

FIGURE 14.6   AWS CloudFormation change sets

CloudFormation > Stacks > RDSInstance > Change sets: RDSInstanc		

RDSInstanc- ▮▮▮▮▮▮▮   Delete   Execute

Overview   ↻

Change set ID	Status
arn:aws:cloudformation:us-east-1:▮▮▮▮▮changeSet/RDSInstanc-▮▮▮▮▮▮▮	⊘ CREATE_COMPLETE

Description	Status reason
-	-

Created time	Execution status
▮▮▮▮▮▮▮	⊘ AVAILABLE

Changes | Input | Template | JSON changes

Changes (1)

🔍 Search changes   ‹ 1 › ⚙

Action	Logical ID	Physical ID	Resource type	Replacement	Module
Modify	MyDB	mydbinstance ↗	AWS::RDS::DBInstance	False	-

If you perform an update in Amazon RDS and it requires a replacement, a new database will be created, and your old database will be deleted. AWS CloudFormation deletes all automated snapshots but retains manual snapshots. For more information, see the "Important Concepts" section.

Take a snapshot before making an update. If do not, you lose the data when CloudFormation replaces your database instance.

Change sets do not indicate whether CloudFormation will successfully update a stack. If an update fails, CloudFormation attempts to roll back your resources to their original state.

Figure 14.7 shows the flow of an update using the change set. First, you create a change set from your original stack by submitting a modified stack template or input parameter values, and then you can view the change set. At this point, the change does not make any changes to your stack. After this, you can, optionally, create additional changes to your stack and do more changes at once and then execute the change set that includes the changes that you made to your stack.

FIGURE 14.7   CloudFormation change sets flow

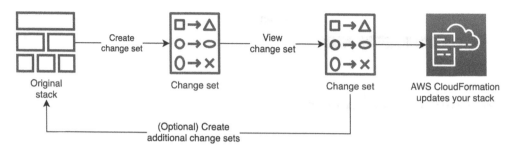

After you execute the change sets, CloudFormation sets the status of the specified resources to UPDATE_COMPLETE. As shown in Figure 14.8, note that the change set for nested stacks is enabled by default in the AWS console, but you can disable it.

 Delete the change sets to prevent executing a change set that should not be applied.

FIGURE 14.8   Change sets for nested stacks

When you update stacks in StackSets, by default it will update all stack instances, which means that updating a stack set with a large number of stacks can take significant time, and this could block you from performing other operations on the stack set, so plan accordingly. This is a standard behavior to have granular control over updating individual stacks and creating multiple stack sets.

When you create a stack, all updates' actions are allowed on all resources, which means that anyone with stack update permissions can update all of the resources in the stack. To avoid that, in your AWS CloudFormation stack you can put a stack policy, which is a JSON document that defines the update actions that can be performed on designed resources. A stack policy applies only during stack updates to prevent accidental updates to specific resources; if you want more granular control, use AWS Identity and Access Management. As Figure 14.9 shows, you can update your stack with no stack policy, enter a stack policy on the AWS console, or upload a JSON file.

FIGURE 14.9   Stack policy during update

Advanced options

You can set additional options for your stack, like notification options and a stack policy. Learn more ☑

▼ **Stack policy during update**
Defines the resources that you want to protect from unintentional updates during a stack update.

Stack policy - optional
A stack policy is a JSON document that defines the update actions that can be performed on designated resources

| ⦿ No stack policy | ○ Enter stack policy | ○ Upload a file |

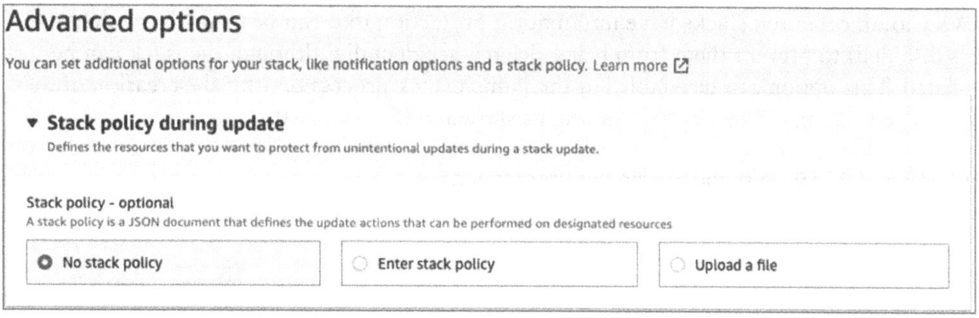

The following example shows a stack policy that prevents updates to all instances of Amazon RDS:

```
{
  "Statement" : [
    {
      "Effect" : "Deny",
      "Action" : "Update:*",
      "Principal": "*",
      "Resource" : "*",
      "Condition" : {
        "StringEquals" : {
          "ResourceType" : ["AWS::RDS::DBInstance"]
        }
      }
    },
    {
      "Effect" : "Allow",
      "Action" : "Update:*",
      "Principal": "*",
      "Resource" : "*"
    }
  ]
}
```

AWS CloudFormation has a mechanism to give you visibility into whether a specific resource and its configuration are different from what was configured by the original template. This feature is called *drift detection*. You can perform drift detection from the AWS Management Console or AWS CLI, and you can detect drift on an entire stack or on individual resources within the stack. Any property or resource that has been deleted is considered a drift. If any resource is detected as drifted, then the stack is considered drifted.

Deleting AWS CloudFormation Stacks

AWS CloudFormation stacks have termination protection that can be enabled (by default, it is disabled) to prevent them from being deleted accidentally, although the stack can be updated. This option can be enabled at the launch stack process or after the creation of the stack by editing the stack's configuration, as shown in Figure 14.10.

FIGURE 14.10   Editing termination protection

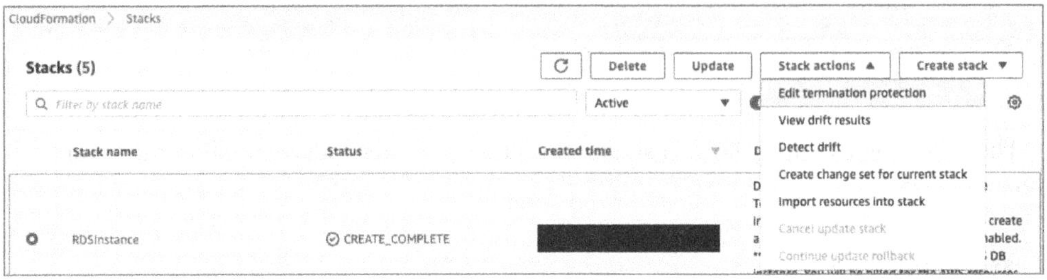

You can set a DeletionPolicy configuration to preserve or back up some resource when its corresponding stack is deleted. By default, if a resource does not have a DeletionPolicy attribute, then AWS CloudFormation deletes the resource. There are three DeletionPolicy options:

- **Delete:** When a CloudFormation stack is deleted, the resource and all its contents will be deleted. This is default behavior if you don't specify this attribute.

  ```
  AWSTemplateFormationVersion: '2010-09-09'
  Resources:
      myEC2Instance:
          Type: AWS::EC2::Instance
          DeletionPolicy: Delete
  ```

- **Retain:** CloudFormation keeps the resource and its contents when the stack is deleted.

  ```
  AWSTemplateFormationVersion: '2010-09-09'
  Resources:
      myS3Bucket:
          Type: AWS::S3::Bucket
          DeletionPolicy: Retain
  ```

- **Snapshot:** CloudFormation creates a snapshot for the resource before deleting it. This is the default behavior for AWS::RDS::DBCluster. The following resources are supported: AWS::EC2::Volume, AWS::RDS::DBCluster, AWS::RDS::DBInstance, AWS::Neptune::DBCluster, AWS::ElastiCache::CacheCluster, AWS::Elasti-Cache::ReplicatonGroup, and AWS::Redshift::Cluster.

Once CloudFormation completes the stack deletion, the snapshots that are created with this policy continue to exist and continue to incur charges until you delete those snapshots.

```
AWSTemplateFormationVersion: '2010-09-09'
Resources:
    myDBInstance:
        Type: AWS::RDS::DBInstance
        DeletionPolicy: Snapshot
```

The default policy is Snapshot for `AWS::RDS::DBCluster` resources and for `AWS::DBInstance` resources for which you don't specify the `DBClusterIdentifier` property.

AWS Systems Manager Parameter Store

AWS Systems Manager (SSM) Parameter Store is a feature within the AWS Systems Manager that provides secure, hierarchical storage for configuration data management and secrets management such as strings, database strings, Amazon Machine Image (AMI) IDs, and license code as parameter values.

You can store data as plaintext or `AWS::EC2::Image` with the type as a String, String-List, or SecureString. The SecureString parameter value is the only encrypted value. Sensitive data should use this parameter type. It encrypts using AWS Key Management Service (AWS KMS) keys from your account or another account.

AWS CloudFormation fetches the last values in SSM Parameter Store and supports plaintext and SecureString stored parameters. SecureString uses AWS KMS to encrypt and decrypt stored parameters. Plaintext and SecureString use `ssm` and `ssm-secure` as aliases, respectively. When you use a dynamic reference, you can reference SSM Parameter Store in your template, and during the stack's deployment or change set, CloudFormation will retrieve the specific value referenced.

The following example uses SSM Parameter Store as a dynamic parameter in plaintext as in `{{resolve:ssm:parameter-name:version}}` or as a SecureString as in '`{{resolve:ssm-secure:parameter-name:version}}`'. This template uses `ssm-secure` as a dynamic reference to the SSM Parameter Store named MyRDSUserName and named MyRDSUserPassword in version 2 in the proprieties `MasterUserName` and `MasterUserPassword`, respectively.

```
MyRDSInstance:
  Type: 'AWS::RDS::DBInstance'
  Properties:
    DBName: MyRDSInstance
    AllocatedStorage: '20'
```

```
      DBInstanceClass: db.t3.small
      Engine: mysql
      MasterUsername: '{{resolve:ssm-secure:MyRDSUserName:2}}'
      MasterUserPassword: '{{ resolve:ssm-secure:MyRDSUserPassword:2}}'
```

For dynamic reference using SecureString (ssm-secure), only AWS::RDS::DBCluster, AWS::RDS::DBInstance, and AWS::Redshift::Cluster resources are supported.

SSM Parameter Store integrates with AWS Secrets Manager, and you can retrieve Secrets Manager secrets. However, SSM Parameter Store does not support password rotation life cycles. If this is a requirement, use AWS Secrets Manager.

SSM Parameter Store offers two pricing tiers:

- **Standard:** The standard tier is free. You can have up to 10,000 parameters with a value size up to 4 KB each.

- **Advanced:** The advanced tier is for more than 10,000 parameters with a value size up to 8 KB each. Using this tier, you can apply parameter policies such as notification policies, which send notifications from Amazon EventBridge based on when this parameter expires or if the parameter has not changed for a given period of time. Additionally, you have parameter expiration, which deletes the parameter when a specific date and time are reached. Note that Advanced tier has charges involving storage and API interaction monthly. *Amazon Event-Bridge* is a service that provides real-time access to changes in data in AWS services, your own applications, and software-as-a-service (SaaS) applications without writing code.

You can use SSM Parameter Store as a dynamic parameter pattern in your AWS Cloud-Formation template, using {{resolve:ssm:parameter-name:version}} as your SSM Parameter Store parameter that could carry an AMI ID or password, etc., for plain-text information. For a secure string encrypted by AWS KMS, use {{resolve:ssm-secure:parameter-name:version}}. For both options you should specify the version of the parameter store, since the SSM Parameter Store organizes the parameters using version-ing. See the following examples.

Using ssm (plaintext):

```
   myDBInstance:
      Type:  'AWS::RDS::DBInstance
      Properties:
         MasterUserPassword:  '{{resolve:ssm:MasterPassword:2}}'
```

Using ssm-secure encrypted with AWS KMS:

```
myDBCluster:
   Type:  'AWS::RDS::DBCluster
      Properties:
         MasterUserPassword:  '{{resolve:ssm-secure:MasterClusterPassword:2}}'
```

AWS CloudFormation never stores the actual parameter value. The following resources support using dynamic parameters for secure strings (ssm-secure) in an AWS CloudForma-tion template regarding AWS databases services: AWS::ElastiCache::Replication Group, AWS::RDS::DBCluster, AWS::RDS::DBInstance, and AWS::Redshift::Cluster.

The following is a full AWS CloudFormation template with an Amazon RDS in MySQL 8.0.16 instance using AWS SSM Parameter Store to retrieve sensitive information using dynamic references for the master username and password:

```
Parameters:
  InstanceClass:
    Type: AWS::SSM::Parameter::Value<String>
    Default: /MyDB/InstanceClass
Resources:
  MyDB:
    Type: 'AWS::RDS::DBInstance'
    Properties:
      DBInstanceClass: !Ref InstanceClass
      AllocatedStorage: 20
      Engine: MySQL
      EngineVersion: 8.0.16
      MasterUsername: '{{resolve:ssm:/MyDB/RDSUser:1}}'
      MasterUserPassword: '{{resolve:ssm-secure:/MyDB/RDSUserPassword:1}}'
      DeletionProtection: false
      DeleteAutomatedBackups: true
    DeletionPolicy: Delete
```

AWS Secrets Manager

AWS Secrets Manager is a service that you can use to store, encrypt, and rotate credentials and secrets. With AWS Secrets Manager, you do not need to embed any credentials for accessing the database directly in the application code; you can use an API call to Secrets Manager to retrieve the secret programmatically. This gives you the direct benefit of ensuring that no sensitive information is stored in plaintext files and reduces the risk of compromising any credentials.

AWS Secrets Manager has a free trial of 30 days, after which you pay monthly, $0.40 per secret and $0.05 per 10,000 API calls.

The key point for AWS Secrets Manager, compared with AWS SSM Parameter Store, is the rotation of the secret. AWS Secrets Manager can schedule the secret rotation between 1 and 365 days, and the secret is encrypted by default using the default AWS KMS key or a custom key.

Use AWS Secrets Manager whenever the exam asks about the rotation of credentials.

You can use AWS Secrets Manager as a dynamic parameter pattern with
'{{resolve:secretsmanager:secret-id:secret-string:json-key:version-stage:version-id}}'. Dynamic parameter patterns for secure strings are the same as
those supported by AWS Systems Manager Parameter Store. AWS CloudFormation does not
persist any resolved secret value. Note that updating a secret in Secrets Manager does not
automatically update the secret in CloudFormation. To update the secret in your template,
consider using version-id to specify the version of your secret.

In the following example, an Amazon RDS MySQL is used as a CloudFormation resource
to retrieve the master username and password from AWS Secrets Manager, which are then
passed as a dynamic reference:

```
MyRDSInstance
  Type: 'AWS::RDS::DBInstance'
  Properties:
    DBName: MyRDSInstance
    AllocatedStorage: '20'
    DBInstanceClass: db.t2.micro
    Engine: mysql
    MasterUsername: '{{resolve:secretsmanager:MyRDSSecret:SecretString:username}}'
    MasterUserPassword: '{{resolve:secretsmanager:MyRDSSecret:SecretString:password}}'
```

AWS Secrets Manager integrates natively with Amazon RDS and Aurora, Amazon DocumentDB, Amazon Redshift, and databases (MariaDB, MySQL, PostgreSQL, Oracle, and
SQL Server) installed in Amazon EC2 or on-premises machines. Also, AWS Secrets Manager
can be used to store secret key-value and plaintext keys in JSON.

Figure 14.11 shows the workflow of the CloudFormation template perspective generating
a random secret using AWS Secrets Manager and then attaching it to an Amazon RDS.

FIGURE 14.11   AWS Secrets Manager with Amazon RDS

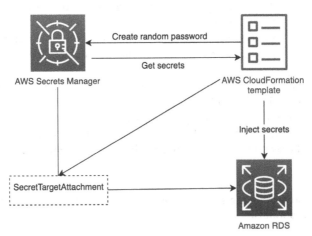

This is how it is works:

1. Create an `AWS::SecretsManager::Secret` resource in the template, and specify a `GenerateSecretString` property to randomly generate a secret.

2. Create an `AWS::RDS::DBInstance` that references that secret, using dynamic references.

3. Create an `AWS::SecretManager::SecretTargetAttachment` property that links to the Secrets Manager secret as `SecretId`, and the RDS database as `TargetId`.

The AWS CloudFormation template will look like this:

```
AWSTemplateVersion: 2010-09-09
Description: "This is an example template to demonstrate CloudFormation
resources for Secrets Manager"
Resources:
  MyRDSSecret:
    Type: "AWS::SecretsManager::Secret"
    Properties:
      Description: "This is a Secrets Manager secret for an RDS DB instance"
      GenerateSecretString:
        SecretStringTemplate: '{"username": "admin"}'
        GenerateStringKey: "password"
        PasswordLength: 8
        ExcludeCharacters: '"@/\'


  MyRDSInstance:
    Type: AWS::RDS::DBInstance
    Properties:
      AllocatedStorage: 20
      DBInstanceClass: db.t3.micro
      Engine: mysql
      MasterUsername: !Join ['', ['{{resolve:secretsmanager:', !Ref MyRDSSecret,
':SecretString:username}}' ]]
      MasterUserPassword: !Join ['', ['{{resolve:secretsmanager:', !Ref
MyRDSSecret, ':SecretString:password}}' ]]
      BackupRetentionPeriod: 0
      DBInstanceIdentifier: 'rotation-instance'


  SecretRDSInstanceAttachment:
    Type: "AWS::SecretsManager::SecretTargetAttachment"
    Properties:
      SecretId: !Ref MyRDSSecret
      TargetId: !Ref MyRDSInstance
      TargetType: AWS::RDS::DBInstance
```

In addition, you can have a rotation schedule of the secret, using `AWS::SecretsManager::RotationSchedule`. This property uses AWS Lambda to trigger the secret rotation. You can create a new Lambda or use an existing one by choosing `RotationLambdaARN`. For Amazon RDS, Amazon ElastiCache, Amazon Redshift, and Amazon DocumentDB, Secrets Manager offers two rotation strategies:

- **Single user:** This strategy is appropriate for most use cases. It is a simple rotation for one user in one secret.

- **Alternating user rotation strategy:** This strategy is appropriate for applications that require high availability, because Secrets Manager will clone the user and then alternate which user's credentials are updated. For example, if an application retrieves the secret during rotation, the application still gets a valid set of credentials. After the rotation, both users' credentials are valid.

During the rotation of your credential for a short time, there's a low risk of your database denying calls that use the rotated credentials, independently of the strategies you use. To mitigate that risk, you should consider implementing exponential backoff in your application. To learn more about rotation strategies, check the tutorial at docs.aws.amazon.com/secretsmanager/latest/userguide/rotating-secrets_strategies.html.

You can add a recurring schedule to rotate your credential. The following code adds a Lambda function, which is provided by the rotation functions templates and configures rotation, using a cron expression, between 8 a.m. and 10 a.m. UTC on the first day of every month. *Coordinated Universal Time (UTC)* is the primary time standard by which the world regulates clocks and time. A *cron expression* is a string of characters that represents a schedule for running a task.

```
MySecretRotationSchedule:
  Type: AWS::SecretsManager::RotationSchedule
  DependsOn: SecretRDSInstanceAttachment
  Properties:
    SecretId:
      Ref: MyRDSInstanceRotationSecret
    HostedRotationLambda:
      RotationType: MySQLSingleUser
      RotationLambdaName: SecretsManagerRotation
    RotationRules:
      Duration: 2h
      ScheduleExpression: 'cron(0 0 8-10 1 * ?)'
```

AWS provides Lambdas function rotations for the databases and resources supported. See more at docs.aws.amazon.com/secretsmanager/latest/userguide/reference_available-rotation-templates.html.

Summary

This chapter described using automation in AWS to save time and reduce errors. AWS CloudFormation is widely used to deploy applications, databases, networks, and other AWS resources. Together with AWS Systems Manager Parameter Store and AWS Secrets Manager, AWS CloudFormation can be a powerful tool to standardize the environment at scale across multiple teams and workloads by passing sensitive information for database resources using a template, avoiding hard-coding and plaintext values.

AWS CloudFormation is a free service that incurs charges only for underlying deployed services and integrates with a majority of AWS services.

Exam Essentials

Know the basics of AWS CloudFormation, AWS Systems Manager Parameter, and AWS Secrets Manager.   To be successful in the exam, it is important to understand the purpose of each service. AWS Systems Manager Parameter Store and AWS Secrets Manager are similar but have different features and fulfill different purposes. You should expect to interpret AWS CloudFormation template snippets and identify resources related to databases.

Know when to use advanced features such as StackSets, nested stacks, and change sets, as well as how to protect resources from deletion.   The exam will use CloudFormation features as part of an answer, especially regarding best practices, disaster recovery, and change scenarios. You should understand the main purpose of each CloudFormation feature.

Know how to use AWS CloudFormation with AWS Systems Manager Parameter Store.   AWS Systems Manager parameter storage is more cost-effective than AWS Secrets Manager, but the main difference is that it does not have a secret rotation feature. Use integration between AWS CloudFormation and SSM Parameter Store to work with dynamic references, especially with segmented environments and when you need to centralize several parameters in one place.

Know how to use AWS CloudFormation with AWS Secrets Manager.   AWS Secrets Manager integrates with some AWS database services natively and has a secret scheduled rotation feature. When the exam asks about the easiest way to do a rotation schedule for your secret, AWS Secrets Manager is the best answer.

Review Questions

1. A retail company wants to deploy a new application in multiple regions. The company plans to save local popular purchases in Amazon DynamoDB tables in each region. A database specialist needs to design a solution to automate the deployment of the database with identical configurations in additional regions, as needed. The solution should also automate configuration changes across all regions.

   A. Create an AWS CLI command to deploy the Amazon DynamoDB table to all regions and save it for other future deployments.

   B. Create an AWS CloudFormation template and deploy the template to all the regions.

   C. Create an AWS CloudFormation template and use a StackSet to deploy the template to all regions.

   D. Create DynamoDB tables using the AWS Management Console in all regions and document it for future use.

2. A three-tier web application was deployed using AWS CloudFormation. A database specialist needs to complete load testing, but the application team is changing the deployment by adding Amazon EC2 and AWS Lambda resources to increase the load testing capacity. The database specialist needs to guarantee that the changes made by the Application team will not change the Amazon RDS database resources already deployed. Which steps need to be taken to complete this? (Choose two.)

   A. Review the stack drift before modifying the template.

   B. Create and review a change set before applying it.

   C. Export the database resources as stack outputs.

   D. Define the database resources in a nested stack.

   E. Set a stack policy for the database resources.

3. A database specialist created an important AWS CloudFormation template that includes an Amazon RDS instance with sensitive data. What does the database specialist need to set on RDS settings to the CloudFormation template to avoid any potential data loss and accidental deletion? (Choose two.)

   A. Set Multi-AZ to true.

   B. Set TerminationProtection to True.

   C. Set DeleteAutomatedBackups to False.

   D. Set DeletionPolicy to Snapshot.

   E. Set DeletionPolicy to Retain.

4. An ecommerce website has a tiered web application hosted on AWS. The database tier is in Amazon. The application needs to be deployed to production and other nonproduction environments. A database specialist needs to specify different MasterUsername and MasterUser-Password properties in the AWS CloudFormation templates used for automated deployment.

The company also needs to meet compliance requirements by routinely rotating its database master password for production. What is the most secure solution to store the master password?

   A. Store the master password in a parameter file in each environment. Reference the environment-specific parameter file in the CloudFormation template.

   B. Encrypt the master password using an AWS KMS key. Store the encrypted password in the CloudFormation template.

   C. Use the `ssm` dynamic reference to retrieve the master password stored in AWS System Manager Parameter Store and enable automatic rotation.

   D. Use the secretsmanager dynamic reference to retrieve the master password stored in AWS Secrets Manager and enable automatic rotation.

5. How can a database specialist create standardized infrastructure for the core components such as Amazon RDS and the bastion host while handling environment-specific settings separately and minimize rework due to configuration errors? Which of these processes are the easiest way that the database specialist can meet these requirements?

   A. Organize common and environmental-specific parameters hierarchically in the AWS Systems Manager Parameter Store and then reference the parameters dynamically from an AWS CloudFormation template. Deploy the CloudFormation stack using the environment name as a parameter.

   B. Create a parameterized AWS CloudFormation template that builds the required objects. Keep separate environment parameter files in separate Amazon S3 buckets. Provide an AWS CLI command that deploys the CloudFormation stack directly referencing the appropriate parameter bucket.

   C. Create a parameterized AWS CloudFormation template that builds the required resources. Import the template into the CloudFormation console. Make the required changes to the parameters and deploy the CloudFormation stack.

   D. Create an AWS Lambda function that builds the required resources using an AWS SDK. Set the required parameter values in a test event in the Lambda console for each environment that the application team can modify, as needed. Deploy the infrastructure by triggering the test event in the console.

6. An enterprise wants to automate creating a secure test Amazon RDS with random credentials to be stored safely. The credentials should have sufficient information about each test database to initiate a connection and perform automated credential rotations. The credentials should not be logged or stored unencrypted. Which steps should a database specialist take to meet these requirements using an AWS CloudFormation template?

   A. Create the database with the MasterUserName and MasterUserPassword properties set to the default values. Then, create the secret with the username and password set to the same default values. Add a Secret Target attachment resource with the SecretId and TargetId properties set to the Amazon Resource Names (ARNs) of the secret and the database. Finally, update the secret's password value with a string set randomly generated by the GenerateSecretString property. Define your rotation schedule rule using a cron expression with the `AWS:SecretsManager::RotationSchedule` resource.

B. Add a Mapping property from the database Amazon Resource Name (ARN) to the secret ARN. Then, create the secret with a chosen username and a randomly generated password set by the GenerateSecretString property. Add the database with the Master-UserName and MasterUserPassword properties set to the user's name of the secret.

C. Add a resource of type AWS::SecretsManager::Secret and specify the GenerateSecret-String property. Then, define the database user name in the SecureStringTemplate template. Create a resource for the database and reference the secret string for the Mas-terUserName and MasterUserPassword properties. Then, add a resource of type `AWS::SecretsManagerSecretTargetAttachment` with the SecretId and TargetId properties set to the Amazon Resource Names (ARNs) of the secret and the database. Define your rotation schedule rule using a cron expression with an `AWS:SecretsManager::RotationSchedule` resource.

D. Create the secret with a chosen username and a randomly generated password set by the `GenerateSecretString` property. Add a `SecretTargetAttachment` resource with the `SecretId` property set to the Amazon Resource Name (ARN) of the secret and the `TargetId` property set to a parameter value matching the desired database ARN. Then, create a database with the `MasterUserName` and `MasterUserPass-word` properties set to the previously created values in the secret.

7. A company is using Amazon DynamoDB that is deployed by an AWS CloudFormation template. The template configures provisioned throughput capacity using hard-coded values. The company wants to change the template so that the tables it creates in the future have independently configurable read and write capacity units allocated. Which solution will enable this change?

A. Use Mappings and set values for the rcuCount and wcuCount parameters. Configure DynamoDB to provision throughput capacity using the stack's mappings.

B. Use Parameters; create two number parameters, rcuCount and wcuCount; and request input values from the user. Replace the hard-coded values with calls to the Ref intrinsic function, referencing the new parameters.

C. Use Outputs and add values for the rcuCount and wcuCount parameters as outputs of the template. Configure DynamoDB to provision throughput capacity using the stack outputs.

D. Use Mappings and set values for the rcuCount and wcuCount parameters. Replace the hard-coded values with calls to the Ref intrinsic function, referencing the new parameters.

8. Which of the options are *not* AWS CloudFormation best practices? (Choose two.)

A. Implementing StackSets

B. Embedding credentials into the template

C. Nesting stacks

D. Enabling termination protection

E. Creating a development and production environment in a single template

9. Which are the possible causes for an update rollback failure of an AWS CloudFormation stack? (Choose two.)

    A. Insufficient permissions.

    B. Termination Protection was enabled.

    C. Changes to a resource were made outside of AWS CloudFormation.

    D. The AWS CloudFormation template was invalid.

    E. The update was done via AWS Management Console.

10. What is the option to audit AWS CloudFormation operations on the AWS account?

    A. AWS CloudFormation console

    B. Amazon CloudWatch

    C. AWS CloudTrail

    D. Template designer

Appendix

Answers to Review Questions

Chapter 3: Purpose-Built Databases

1. D. Flexible data access patterns indicate a relational database reinforced by being fully ACID compliant. Scaling out and scaling in reads on demand with multiregion support are Amazon Aurora characteristics.

2. B. DynamoDB fits all the requirements except microsecond latency for reads. By leveraging Amazon DynamoDB Accelerator (DAX), the DBA could deliver all the application requirements.

3. C, D. Although we could use PartiQL to interact with DynamoDB with "SQL-like" commands, DynamoDB does not support 600 KB. Amazon Keyspaces fits the requirements and delivers the Cassandra CQL language, which is very familiar to SQL-proficient DBAs. Amazon Aurora fits the requirements as well, delivering the native SQL language.

4. C. Amazon QLDB is a ledger database that provides a transparent, immutable, and cryptographically verifiable transaction log.

5. C. Amazon DocumentDB has a maximum item size of 16 MB and has indexing in nested fields or arrays. Data remodeling techniques, such as unnesting, could be applied; however, in this particular scenario, the customer is not open to data remodeling.

6. B. Amazon DynamoDB offers high-scalability, single-digit millisecond latency even when scaling from hundreds to millions of requests.

7. D. Amazon Keyspaces delivers all the requirements, and CQL comes from Cassandra Query Language, supported in Amazon Keyspaces.

8. D. Amazon DocumentDB offers aggregation functions at the database level, including average, sum, and group by.

9. B. Amazon DynamoDB global tables enable regional write capabilities for global applications.

10. D. Deploying Amazon RDS and Amazon ElastiCache for Redis implies that we will have a cluster with multiple nodes, even if we don't have enough application traffic to be processed by the database. The most cost-effective solution is to leverage DynamoDB serverless capabilities with on-demand capacity.

Chapter 4: Relational Databases on AWS

1. A. To solve an RDS instance stuck in incompatible parameter status, the possible alternatives are to reset all parameters in the parameter group to default values or to reset the values of the parameters that are incompatible. You can't connect to or modify an instance in this state.

2. B. When you take a manual snapshot, you can configure the retention according to your business needs, and there's no maximum allowed time to retain it.

The automatic backup has a maximum of 35 retention days; although it supports point-in-time recovery, you cannot configure longer retention periods.

Cloning is allowed only for Amazon Aurora, and it isn't recommended for long-term backups.

Exporting to S3 is used when it's required to export to Parquet files so the data can be read by other services like Amazon Athena or Amazon Redshift Spectrum. Exporting to S3 is allowed only for RDS MariaDB, RDS MySQL, and RDS PostgreSQL.

3. A. The faster option is to check the top SQL sessions in Performance Insights. By default, Performance Insights is turned on in the console create wizard for all Amazon RDS engines.

You can use a native tool according to the database engine, but this option will take longer to configure the appropriate tool and also to search the appropriate view at the DB instance.

The execution plan will demonstrate which path the DB optimizer chooses to select the data, but it does not show if one SQL statement is consuming more resources than others.

Checking the slow query logs exported will tell you which SQL statement is taking more than the threshold seconds defined to run, but it won't identify which statement is consuming more than others.

4. D. The faster and cheaper alternative to make the database available without the restoring time is the Clone option, because Clone uses the same storage of the source database with the copy-on-write protocol.

All the other alternatives require restoring the database instance from a snapshot, which takes time to complete, and it will depend on the database size.

5. B. The SSL connection on RDS for PostgreSQL requires enabling the SSL on the database by modifying the parameter `rds.force_ssl` to 1, downloading the certificate, and defining `sslmode=verify-full` for the connection.

If you modify `rds.force_ssl` to 1 but don't use the certificate and `sslmode=verify-full`, you will get a connection error.

6. A. Using DAS, you'll enable a near real-time data stream of the database activity. Amazon Aurora pushes activities to an Amazon Kinesis data stream. From Kinesis you can configure AWS services such as Amazon Kinesis Firehose and AWS Lambda to consume and store the data. On S3 you can configure life-cycle policies to move your objects to different storage classes according to how frequently the data is accessed.

The MariaDB Audit plugin works for RDS for MySQL and RDS for MariaDB.

The `pgaudit` extension works for RDS for PostgreSQL and Amazon Aurora PostgreSQL, and the activity entries will be written on the `pgaudit.log` file.

The advanced parameters `server_audit_logging` and `server_audit_events` work for Amazon Aurora MySQL only, and the data activity will be stored on the database logs.

7. B. The best option for RDS for MySQL is enabling the MariaDB Audit plugin by the option group and publishing the logs to CloudWatch.

Only enabling the MariaDB Audit plugin at the option group, the activity will be stored only on the local log. You won't be able to access it at CloudWatch.

There's no need to configure logon trigger, because RDS for MySQL already has the capability to log database activity.

DAS is available only for Amazon Aurora.

8. B. The best alternative with lower downtime is creating an Amazon Aurora read replica and promoting the Read Replica to primary once it is synchronized.

The `pg_dump` and `pg_restore` options work, but they require more steps to be accomplished and also will result in longer downtime.

Using AWS DMS will also require more configuration steps. To create the schema first, check the objects, constraints, triggers, sequences, and so on.

It isn't possible to restore a backup generated from `pg_dump` directly at the creation step.

9. C. Amazon Aurora is able to restore backup files directly generated from the Percona Xtra-Backup tool and restore backups generated from `mysqldump`.

Although it's possible to use AWS DMS, it requires more steps to configure and to replicate the data.

Using `mysqldump` to generate and the MySQL client to restore won't keep the replication between the source on premises and Amazon Aurora.

You can't create an Amazon Aurora read replica from a MySQL on premises; this option is available only when the source database is an RDS for MySQL or RDS for PostgreSQL.

10. C. Since you can't directly modify an unencrypted database to be encrypted, and since a read replica will inherit the same encryption configuration from the source database, the only alternative available is to take a snapshot, copy the snapshot enabling the encryption option, and then restore the database from the encrypted snapshot.

Chapter 5: Low-Latency Response Time for Your Apps and APIs

1. C. Options B is invalid. Options A and D could do the job, but the optimal solution is to use the Time to Live (TTL) attribute for Amazon DynamoDB and enable Streams on the table. DynamoDB Streams events have a special flag you can use to archive the items expired by the TTL.

2. D. Options A, B, and C are invalid because the role is for AWS Lambda, not DynamoDB. User/password is not a valid authentication option for Dynamo, and using hard-coded access keys in AWS Lambda is a bad idea. The role then needs to be assigned to the Lambda function as the execution role to be able to inherit the DynamoDB permissions.

3. C. Options A and B don't support active-active mode; writing can be done only in the primary AWS region. Option D supports active-active but within a single region. The only option that fulfills the question's requirement is DynamoDB Global Database.

4. D. Option A requires a refactoring overhead, and it is false that the DynamoDB is the only serverless NoSQL database on AWS. Option B would work but won't fulfill the least amount of time requirement, since it is a single-threaded process. Option C in particular isn't cost-effective either because it proposes to use on-demand capacity. Option D is the best solution.

5. C. Options A and D are incorrect; dates are poor choices for partition keys because date is a low cardinality attribute. A similar thing would happen with option B with the Country of Origin. Option C is the best choice because a random prefix will be guaranteed to have high cardinality on the GSI and thus avoid the "hot partitions" issues.

6. A. Option C is invalid because LSI can be created only at table creation time and must share the same partition key with the main table. Options B and D are incorrect because the GSI index only supports eventual consistency, and the DAX cluster only allows queries on the same keys as the main table. The only feasible option is option A.

7. A, B, and C. Amazon Neptune is ACID compliant by default, so all operations provide strong consistency. DynamoDB has strong consistent read API operations. Keyspaces read operations with `LOCAL_QUORUM` will return strong, consistent results. DocumentDB, on the other hand, has the option to return the data from the primary node and will be strongly consistent in most cases; however, if the database is under a failover process, the read operation will be eventually consistent as long as the failover process lasts.

8. D. Options B and C are invalid because Performance Insights is an Amazon RDS feature and X-Ray is used to debug and trace request in microservice applications. Option A could work but is not the most cost effective. Option D is the right one because CloudWatch Contributor Insights can be used to determine frequently accessed attribute keys of DynamoDB tables.

9. D. One RCU represents one strongly consistent read for an item up to 4 KB in size. Since the application item size is 5 KB, you will need two times the number of required reads. Regarding the writes, one WCU is equivalent to one write operation for an item up to 1 KB in size. Since the question item size is 5 KB, you will need to provision five times the number of required write operations.

10. D. Options A and B are invalid since there isn't any `truncate` CLI command or API operation. Option C could do the job, but it would be costly, as it consumes both RCU and WCU proportionally to the size of the table.

Chapter 6: Document Databases in the Cloud

1. A. Amazon DocumentDB can export logs only to Amazon CloudWatch Logs. CloudTrail is an API tracking service. Amazon DocumentDB events cannot export logs to CloudWatch Logs, because events show recent events that occurred in your clusters. The cluster must enable the export of the logs to CloudWatch Logs and enable the `audit_logs` parameters in the cluster parameter group for CloudWatch Logs to receive such logs.

2. A. Amazon DocumentDB is a managed service. Since AWS DMS supports the service as a target, this is the only option. VM Import/Export is a legacy service for virtual machine migration. Cloud9 is an IDE in the cloud, and AWS SMS is an agentless AWS service for migration between virtual machines for supported hypervisors recommended for lift-and-shift approaches.

3. D. Amazon DocumentDB can support 15 instance replicas.

4. C. Amazon DocumentDB can support only one primary instance.

5. A. Amazon DocumentDB is not a software as a service of MongoDB. The integration with AWS services, backup, and replication features differs from an Amazon EC2 instance with MongoDB. Amazon DocumentDB does not follow the software life cycle of MongoDB. Amazon DocumentDB supports change streams.

6. A and B. Document databases are not a good fit for applications/workloads that need to do a lot of joins, because it tends to be expensive. Document databases usually are defined as a cluster, so it makes more sense to scale by adding instances horizontally.

7. A. DatabaseConnections shows how many open connections your cluster has. BufferCacheHitRatio is the percentage of requests that are served by the buffer cache. SwapUsage is the amount of swap space used on the instance.

8. B. `profiler` is the parameter that enables or disables query profiling. `audit_logs` defines whether AWS CloudTrail audit logs are enabled. `ttl_monitor` defines whether time-to-live monitoring is enabled for the cluster, and `profiler_threshold_ms` defines the threshold for the profiler.

9. B. This operation can be done by taking a snapshot of the unencrypted cluster and restoring it in a new cluster with encrypt enabled with AWS KMS. You cannot modify the cluster and enable encryption, since the encryption can be enabled only at the launch of the cluster. You can do it through AWS DMS, but this will add unnecessary operational challenges and tasks, which is the opposite of what the question asks.

10. D. Only the events that occurred in your cluster appear in AWS Management Console. Parameter groups are configurable parameters applied within your cluster. The change streams feature in Amazon DocumentDB provides a time-ordered sequence of change events that occur within your cluster's collections. Events subscription is the only way that you can be notified for something occurring in your cluster.

Chapter 7: Better Places Other Than Databases to Store Large Objects

1. C. As the question asks for the most cost-effective solution, we need to consider the feasible solutions that best address costs, and option C is cheaper than B, as you remove the LOB to S3. Option B is cheaper than option A if you consider only licensing. Option D is not actually complete, as you may need an EC2 instance to create and store the objects in an EBS volume, and it doesn't lower the cost, as EBS costs are 23x higher than S3.

2. C. There are no PCI compliance, Deep Storage, or Long-Term Archive classes for S3; the only available options are S3 Standard, S3 Standard-IA, S3 Glacier, and S3 Glacier Deep Archive.

3. B. Using versioning is an easy way to keep track of recoverability for objects in S3, and cross replication will add a new bucket in place and will not prevent objects from being lost in the case of being overwritten in the other region, and will add data transfer costs between the regions. Performing a check before writing objects to S3 will add a cost for DynamoDB reads for every operation.

4. E. All the options are valid for encryption for S3.

5. D. The object key is not a key to gain access; a key to gain access would be an IAM access key. An object key is required, and it's not a tag. When you create an object, you specify the key name, that is, the object key and its full name, inside the bucket, in the following S3 object, for example: `s3://123456789012-mypics/us/new-york/people/people0010.jpg`, where `123456789012-mypics` is the bucket name, and `us/new-york/people/people0010.jpg` is the object key.

6. C. You can have single objects from 0 bytes to 5 TB size in Amazon S3, so a 1 PB single file is out of the range. You can have multiple files that sum several perabytes, but you can't have a single file larger than 5 TB. For objects larger than 100 MB, you should use Multipart Upload. When you use the AWS CLI `aws s3 cp` command, it automatically chooses to use Multipart Upload for large files.

7. B. Option A is in reversed order from most expensive to cheapest. In option C, Glacier Deep Archive should be the first, and for options C and D, Infrequent Access appears with a lower cost than S3 Standard, which is not true.

8. A. Option A is correct. Option B is false because S3 replicates six copies of each object inside a region. Option C is false because cross-region replication is not automatically set up, and for option D S3 will keep six physical copies in each region if you set up cross-region replication.

9. B. Option A adds unnecessary PUT operations. Option C uses the wildcard * for users, which allows *any* user from AccountB, and option D uses a wildcard * for actions, which allows *any* operations, so A, C, and D are too permissive.

10. A. Amazon S3 API requires TLS, so using the AWS CLI or SDK will comply with the required TLS encryption. Options B to D are more complex and require more effort than option A.

Chapter 8: Deliver Valuable Information at the Speed Your Business Needs

1. C. Amazon Redshift is the first option when migrating data warehouses to AWS, and it supports star schema as well, so option C is correct. Option B is automatically invalid. Amazon Timestream is not the best solution for data warehouses and does not support star schema design, so option A is wrong. Option D is not true because Amazon Redshift supports a native star schema implementation.

2. C. The question asked for managed services, so option A is wrong, as it installs a time-series database over a container platform. Option B would work with some effort from the sensor side to send it to DynamoDB but would add a high cost for time-series queries over time. Option C will have a good cost efficiency for queries using Amazon Timestream and will use AWS IoT and Timestream, which are all managed services. Option D is not correct as it uses Amazon Neptune, a graph database that is good for finding relationships between data but not for performing statistics comparing time-series data.

3. B. As the question asked for a simple solution, that allows for scalability and reduces storage costs. There is no Dynamic Migration Services or AWS Object Conversion Tool (OCT) in AWS, and AWS Storage Gateway will require a complex setup to work with data. Option C suggested Amazon Aurora MySQL, which is not the best option for data warehouse workloads, and there is no COPY command for Aurora MySQL. Options C and D are similar, but there is no way to mix Redshift with SSD and HDD; also, elastic resize is used to add or remove nodes from the cluster to scale, while concurrency scale is used to handle workload peaks, so option B is the correct one.

4. C. Although options B and D can work, customers will need to code Lambda and create some logic to retry when it fails. Option D uses inserts instead of the COPY command, which is an anti-pattern for Redshift. Option A requires a lot of effort to set up and manage. Option C is straightforward, is easy to set up, and already has mechanisms for delivering retry and error messages to Redshift.

5. D. To optimize bandwidth to transfer the data, you should compress the data before sending it to Amazon S3. To parallelize work when using the COPY command, you should split the data in files in a multiple of your SLICE number, in this case 16. A single file as stated in options A and B will take longer to load as they will use only one SLICE to load all the data. Option C takes into consideration the memory size of the cluster, which doesn't help in the case of loading data. This will result in very small files. Option D is the correct one as it uses the number of SLICE to split the data and keep the files with a few gigabytes.

6. B. The Redshift COPY command enables us to load data using encrypted data from customer-managed symmetric keys (CSE-CMK). We can load compressed data with CSE-CMK directly from S3, using the ENCRYPTED parameter along with the compressed algorithm, as stated in option B. We don't need to uncompress the data using an Amazon EC2, so option A would add more effort. Option C would work but would also add unneeded effort using an Amazon EC2 instance. Option D is wrong because there is no Redshift Key Manager Service.

7. A. To load data into Redshift, the COPY command from Amazon S3 is the best way. Amazon Kinesis Data Firehose buffers streaming data and performs micro batches to load the data using the COPY command, so option A is the best option. Options B and C use INSERT and UPSERT, which are not optimized to load external data to Redshift. Option D is correct for data in files but uses the wrong component, Amazon Kinesis Data Analytics, instead of the appropriate Amazon Kinesis Data Firehose, so it is not the correct answer.

8. D. The best choice for cost efficiency is to use the proper engine for the workload, so Amazon Redshift for a data warehouse, Amazon Timestream for time-series data, and Amazon OpenSearch Service with Kibana for operational logs and dashboards are the natural choices. Amazon Aurora is not the best option for time-series data, so option A is not the best option. Amazon Aurora is not the best option for data warehouses nor DynamoDB for time-series, so option B is wrong. Option C is not correct, because it uses Neptune, a graph database, for the data warehouse.

9. D. Option A is wrong because it creates one single table; there is no customized data retention per payload in Amazon Timestream. You set one data retention period per table; also there is no autoscaling group for Amazon Timestream. Option B would have a higher cost for the queries and would not support SQL queries. Amazon DynamoDB will require a single attribute to perform the TTL and does not have a customized TTL per payload. Option C would not deliver the data with the data latency of milliseconds and would require extra routines to handle data purging. Option D is easy to set up, will scale per usage, and will deliver data with a latency of milliseconds.

10. A. Option A will handle the latest 24 hours in memory for the queries you need to improve and also set the overall retention on disk to one month, with low cost, so that is the correct one. Option D is the opposite, as it sets memory retention to one month, and it will cost 30 times more than option A, approximately. Option B is wrong, as you have the option to cache data in memory with Amazon Timestream to improve performance. Option C uses DAX, and DAX is available only for Amazon DynamoDB.

Chapter 9: Discovering Relationships Using Graph Databases

1. A. The query languages supported by Amazon Neptune are Gremlin, openCypher, and SPARQL. SQL is not a supported query language; you can use Python libs to use Gremlin, but not as a query language. Pyspark is an interface for Apache Spark in Python.

2. C. A graph database is the best solution to run recommendation engines, and Amazon Neptune is the graph database in AWS. Relational databases such as PostgreSQL don't scale appropriately to return billions of rows and complex joins. Amazon DynamoDB and Amazon Keyspaces aren't appropriate for exploring relationships.

3. D. The correct choice is to add a read replica and modify the application to connect the read-only operations to the read replica endpoint. If you only add the read replica, the application will not be automatically redirected to the read replica endpoint.

   There's no need to create a new cluster to receive replicated data because the Amazon Neptune database cluster accesses the same purpose-built storage, and the data will be available to the read replicas with minimal lag.

If you only modify the instance type to a bigger instance type, you will better accommodate the current workload, but you will not improve the cluster's high availability.

4. A. Amazon Neptune cluster allows the failover tier configuration in the read replica instance to define the priority to promote the instance. Instances with lower values in the failover tier are promoted.

Option B is not correct, because it mentions the highest value in the failover tier. Options C and D aren't correct, because you can manage it using the failover tier.

5. C. The Amazon Neptune cluster allows Global Database for cross-region replication; it enables fast recovery in a rare failure event of the current AWS region. Option A is not correct, because it is more complex to implement. Option B is not correct, because DMS does not support continuous replication for Amazon Neptune, only full load. Option D is not correct, because you can achieve cross-region replication using a global database.

6. D. Although you cannot modify the cluster encryption, to meet this requirement, you can do so by taking the snapshot and restoring the snapshot with the required encryption key.

Options A and B are not correct, because you can't modify the cluster encryption directly in the cluster configuration. Option C is not correct; although you cannot modify the instance encryption, snapshot and restore is an efficient method to meet this requirement.

7. A and B. Options A and B are correct, because the newer Amazon Neptune clusters only allow SSL, and for older versions you can do it by changing the parameter group to a newer version. Options C and D are not correct; you can meet this requirement even on newer or older cluster versions.

8. B. Option B is correct; the property graph data model is appropriate for representing the data in vertices and edges, and the programing language is familiar to SQL developers.

Option A is not correct; the relational database model is not efficient for querying highly connected data. Option C is not correct; RDF is most appropriate to represent in subject-predicate-object triples format. Option D is not correct; storing data in Parquet format is not efficient for querying highly connected data.

9. B. Option B is correct; the bulk loader command is faster and has less overhead for loading external files and supports Gremlin data. Option A is not correct; insert using addV and addE is better for small data sets. Option C is not correct; DMS is useful when migrating from another database. Option D is not correct; SPARQL INSERT does not work for the property graph data model.

10. C. Option C is correct; the instance endpoint purpose is to connect to a particular instance. Option A is not correct; the cluster endpoint purpose is to connect to the primary instance. Option B is not correct; the reader endpoint will load balance across the read replica instances. Option D is not correct. The custom endpoint is more appropriate when you need to configure a set of instances; for only one instance, it is easier and faster using the instance endpoint.

Chapter 10: Immutable Database and Traceable Transactions

1. D. Option A is invalid because AWS Backup doesn't support Amazon QLDB. Option B is also invalid because Amazon QLDB currently doesn't support PITR or on-demand backups. Option C isn't the right one because it is leaving the database without any backup strategy. Option D is right because AWS Backup supports both EC2 and EFS, and at the time of writing, there is no managed backup solution for QLDB; the customer needs to implement a custom solution.

2. B. Amazon Timestream is the better service to store time-series data. Relational data should be placed on Amazon RDS or Amazon Aurora. Although QLDB supports JSON documents, if there is no need to perform data integrity verification, then DocumentDB or DynamoDB would be the best choice.

3. A, B, D. Option C is incorrect because Amazon CloudTrail records only nontransactional API operations.

4. B. QLDB is a centralized ledger database built for customers who need to maintain a verifiable history of data changes within an application that they own.

5. D. Option A could do the job, but it will demand extra overhead to keep the logs auditable, and a bad actor could potentially tamper with the data by disabling CloudTrail for a given period of time. Option B won't work for the same reason as DynamoDB, and changing the database schema in the future won't be easy.

    Option C can work, but it doesn't have a serverless approach, and there is no mention that it needs to be a decentralized ledger.

    Option D is the right solution for the given use case.

6. A. Option A is the only available option for application access to an Amazon QLDB ledger database.

7. A. Amazon QLDB is integrated with AWS Private Link.

8. C. You create a ledger and define your tables, and QLDB automatically scales to support the demands of your application.

9. B and D. The MongoDB driver is just for MongoDB-compatible databases, and Amazon QLDB isn't one. You can use the API to access your QLDB ledger, but it is not the only choice; you can also use the driver or the SDK.

10. A. Amazon QLDB provides atomicity, consistency, isolation, and durability (ACID) properties.

Chapter 11: Caching Data with In-Memory Databases

1. C. Options B and C will not deliver submillisecond latency for queries consistently, so those options are wrong. Although option A is feasible, it doesn't minimize the team overhead, as they would have to manage the EC2 nodes and caching software.

2. A. Option A is the correct one, as Memcached will handle the writes with multithread processes. Options B and C are wrong, as they will not deliver data for submillisecond query latency. Option D is wrong, as Redis doesn't support multithreaded processing for applications.

3. D. Option A does not comply with the latency required of the service. Options B and C suggest Redis and MemoryDB for Redis, which is OK; however, providing scalability for writes will require advanced sharding techniques, as they are single thread for writing, so they would be good choices if the customer was looking for more resilience and fault tolerance. Option D is easy to set up and good to scale writes, as Memcached is multithreaded and is able to use more resources of the same hardware to write.

4. B. Option A does not implement a cache layer, so it's wrong. Option B is the correct one, where they can evaluate between Redis and Memcached. Option C is not a cache, but a data stream for Kafka application, so it's not correct. Option D is incorrect, as DAX is available only for Amazon DynamoDB, not relational databases.

5. A. Using a write-through strategy with Amazon ElastiCache will guarantee the cache layer always has the latest information, so option A is the best choice. Amazon RDS will not lower the response time to less than 1 millisecond, so options B and C are incorrect. The lazy loading strategy will not guarantee the latest information is already in the cache, so this could increase response time for cache misses, so option D is not the best choice.

6. B and D. Option A is not correct, as Amazon ElastiCache is not for streaming. Options B and D are correct because they implement a cache layer that can offload frequent queries from the database layer and improve response time. Option C doesn't improve consistency, so it is not correct.

7. A. Amazon MemoryDB for Redis provides a persistent layer with extremely low latency, so option A is correct. Options B and C are not persistent, as they use memory only, although Redis has good resilience. Option D is incorrect, as Amazon Aurora will not provide microsecond latency for reads; it will provide millisecond latency.

8. B. Option A is wrong, as it doesn't provide extreme low latency. Option B is correct, as it's a managed service for a cache option. Option C is not low effort and not easy to maintain. Option D exceeds the requirements, as the solution already has a persistent layer, so it will add unnecessary costs.

9.   A and C. Options A and C are correct. Option B is wrong because there are no such options for ElastiCache. Option D is wrong, as there is no cache mode option; in ElastiCache, you can choose cluster mode for Redis.

10.   A. Option A is correct, as you can work with a single shard and not deal with sharding data using cluster mode disabled for ElastiCache for Redis. There is no cluster mode for Elasti-Cache for Memcached, so options B and D are wrong. Option C will require sharding data, which is not what your company wants.

Chapter 12: Migrating Your Data to AWS

1.   B. Option A is wrong, as it doesn't apply the logs with a CDC or continuous replication to minimize downtime; ora2pg can convert a schema but will not be able to migrate with minimal downtime. Option B is the correct one, because it performs schema conversion with the SCT and then DMS data migration and continuous replication, minimizing downtime and effort. Option C is feasible, but it will require the conversion of Oracle objects not handled by DMS. Option D is wrong, as you don't create migration tasks in RDS; you create them in DMS instead.

2.   C. Option A is wrong, as Amazon Storage Gateway will not significantly reduce the time to transfer the data and doesn't have integration with AWS SCT. Option B will also not improve the time to load to S3 because it will still use the network connection. Option C is the correct one because it optimizes the transfer with an AWS Snowball edge storage-optimized device and also synchronizes the databases using AWS SCT with the AWS DMS agent. Option D is not addressing the connection bandwidth and is trying to force the load using all tables in parallel, so it will not help in this scenario.

3.   B. Option B is the correct one; by using DMS, you can create a continuous replication to the Amazon S3 target. Option A is feasible but is definitely not the easiest to set up, as it involves creating and maintaining a replication code. Option C is incorrect, as Oracle Data Pump generates snapshots of the table's data and does not offer continuous replication. Option D is incorrect, as AWS SCT is used to convert the schema and has extractors to load data from data warehouses at one time, with no continuous replication and no replication instances.

4.   A. Option A is correct, as the target and source are supported by the AWS Schema Conversion Tool (SCT). Option B is not correct, as it requires very intensive work to perform the assessment. Option C is also wrong, as AWS DMS is able to convert schemas when migrating data, but it's not able to generate an assessment report before the conversion. Option D is incorrect because AWS SQL Migration Studio doesn't exist.

5.   C. Options A and B are incorrect, as neither addresses the minimal downtime requirement. Option D is incorrect, as Glue doesn't have a continuous replication job by default; it does have incremental jobs based on a bookmark key. Option C is correct, as it will provide a minimal downtime scenario for the migration.

6. B. There is no such thing as an Amazon EBS Attachable device, so option A is wrong. Option D is the right choice; you can choose between AWS Snowcone or AWS Snowball according to the amount of data you need to send. There is no such service as Amazon S3 Upload Manager, so option C is not correct. Option D is not correct, as it uses your network connection to transfer data.

7. B. Option A does not exist as a service. Option B is correct; you can use AWS DataSync to compress data and use optimization algorithms to send data through a network connection. Option C is not correct because you can use AWS DataSync as well as third-party software, not only third-party software, for this purpose. Amazon S3 multipart upload optimizes throughput using parallelism but not compression algorithms, so option D is not the best answer.

8. A and D. You can use AWS SCT to convert the database schema and AWS DMS to migrate the data, so options A and D are correct. AWS Step Functions doesn't help on database migration, nor does Amazon EKS, so options B and C are not correct. Option E is not correct because AWS DTS does not exist.

9. B. The replication instance keeps track of each table replication, what changes have been applied, and what have already need to be applied, so option B is correct. Source endpoint and target endpoint map the connection string attributes for the source and the target. Option D is not correct because it does not exist.

10. A. Option A is a good path for small databases because it allows some downtime during migration. Option B does not exist. Option C is not correct, as you cannot restore directly from an EFS volume to the Aurora Cluster. Option D is not correct, as you cannot mount an Amazon EBS on premises.

Chapter 13: Disaster Recovery

1. C. The Aurora global database supports high write throughput with lower replication lag. That's the best alternative. Cross-region read replicas may face high replication lag depending on the data volume to be replicated, as well as native binlog replication. Automated backups will not improve data locality.

2. B. The customer has a huge concern about costs, and the RTO is 10 hours. This RTO time is enough to restore a backup that is already replicated to the remote region. Option A is valid, but cross-region read replicas are more expensive. DMS replication is difficult to manage in the event of a disaster, and native redo is more expensive. Data Guard isn't available to be implemented in RDS for Oracle; it must be implemented by a read replica.

3. B. The only alternative that will allow us to manage the failover operation without changing or rebuilding the topology is the Aurora global database with managed planned failover. All the other alternatives require rebuilding the topology after activation.

4. A, B. Amazon Aurora PostgreSQL with at least one read replica and Amazon RDS PostgreSQL with Multi-AZ enabled will fulfill the requirements.

PostgreSQL on EC2 is a self-managed deployment, and Amazon Aurora global databases are a multiregion strategy.

5. C. An Amazon Aurora global database with write forwarding enabled will support the relational model and allow it to accept the write operations on the remote region.

An Amazon RDS cross-region read replica allows only read operations on remote regions but not writing.

Amazon DynamoDB global tables allow read and write operations on remote regions but aren't compatible with a relational model.

An Amazon DocumentDB global cluster allows only reading on remote regions and isn't compatible with a relational model.

6. B. Amazon Aurora global databases allow managed failover to fail over to a secondary region without destroying the replication topology.

Amazon DynamoDB global tables allow replication, reading, and writing in remote regions. But they don't allow the relational model.

An RDS cross-region read replica allows the promotion of the remote read replica but doesn't allow you to revert to the primary master.

An Amazon Neptune cluster is not a relational database.

7. C. An Amazon RDS cross-region read replica allows read operations on remote regions, and in a failure situation the remote read replica can be promoted, with lower cost than Aurora global databases.

Amazon DocumentDB is not appropriate for relational models.

8. B. Amazon DocumentDB is able to support 16 MB document sizes, and to improve resilience across a single region, you can deploy read replicas across different availability zones.

This scenario doesn't require cross-region replication for choosing an Amazon DocumentDB global cluster.

Although DynamoDB also supports documents, the item limit size is 400 KB.

9. D. Amazon DocumentDB supports global clusters to replicate to a secondary region with minimal effort.

DMS does not support Amazon DocumentDB as a source.

Converting to Amazon DynamoDB will require an application code change.

10. C. Amazon DynamoDB global tables will enable DynamoDB tables on remote regions for read and write operations.

Amazon Aurora global databases with write forwarding enable write operations, but for an application with a defined known pattern to retrieve data, DynamoDB will be more efficient.

Deploying on DynamoDB will enable resilience only within a single region.

Amazon RDS does not allow write operations on remote regions.

Chapter 14: Save Time and Reduce Errors Automating Your Infrastructure

1. C. Although the AWS CLI is a doable option, it will create overhead regarding multiple regions. AWS CloudFormation supports using StackSet, which is a native feature. Using the AWS Management Console is out of the question, because it clearly asked about automation.

2. D and E. Options A and C will not guarantee that the RDS resources will not be affected by changes made by the application team. Option B could be right, but it is not guaranteed that future changes made by the application team will affect the RDS resources, and the question asks to avoid any harm to those resources. Option D is a best practice, and option E will effectively prevent any database resources from being changed.

3. C and E. Option B will not prevent accidental deletion. Option D is already the default behavior. Option D could be a good option, but it goes in a different direction from what the question is asking, which is to avoid any accidental deletion; option C will allow deletion but take a snapshot of the resources. Option B prevents accidental deletion in your CloudFormation stack. Option E will prevent data loss by retaining resources associated with this deletion policy.

4. D. The only option that meets the requirements is to use the AWS Secrets Manager, because it allows the stored secrets to be rotated and the question clearly asks for a routine master password rotation. SSM Parameter Store does not rotate the stored values.

5. A. The question clearly mentioned a separate environment, which means that AWS System Manager Parameter Store is a great option to fit for this feature, because the parameter can be used in the template dynamically. Using Amazon S3 and AWS Lambda would be more complex solutions.

6. C. The key point for this question is about the credential rotations. Option C is the only one that clearly mentioned AWS Secrets Manager, the AWS service that stores, encrypts, and rotates credentials. You must create as a resource an AWS Secret Manager, set the `GenerateSecretString` property, and then create a database that references that secret using dynamic references. Then create the resource `AWS::SecretManager::SecretTargetAttachment` linking the Secrets Manager secret as `SecretId` and the database as `TargetId`.

7. B. To provide more independently configurable read and write capacity, the template should allow the user to pass the values they will fit into Amazon DynamoDB. The only option that allows this is option B. Pass the values as parameters and then reference them using. The Ref intrinsic function in the model will give exactly the same number that was passed to the Parameters section. The use of Mappings and Outputs is out of the question because they are constructed for a purpose other than what the question is asking for.

8. B and E. StackSets is a great option for multiple accounts and region deployments. Nested stacks are a great option to modularize your environment and reuse your templates. Enabling termination protection could avoid accidental deletion of a stack. Option B is not a best practice; you should use AWS SSM Parameter Store or AWS Secrets Manager. Option E is not a best practice, since nested stacks or conditions are better choices. See more at `docs.aws` `.amazon.com/AWSCloudFormation/latest/UserGuide/best-practices.html`.

9. A and C. Option B does not cause rollback failure. If option D is true, you could not proceed with an update at all; every AWS CloudFormation template must be valid to move forward to deployment. Option E could not be a cause, because you can do updates through the AWS Management Console and AWS CLI. See more at `docs.aws` `.amazon.com/AWSCloudFormation/latest/UserGuide/troubleshooting` `.html#troubleshooting-errors-update-rollback-failed`.

10. C. AWS CloudTrail integrates with AWS CloudFormation, so you can see in AWS Cloud-Trail's dashboard all the API calls used by AWS CloudFormation. See more at `docs` `.aws.amazon.com/AWSCloudFormation/latest/UserGuide/security-best-` `practices.html#cloudtrail`.

Index